D1554588

PRAISE FOR *Dare to Un-Lead*

"I was designing a leadership program for Walmart. Céline Schillinger opened my eyes. I now see leadership as unleashing the power and potential of millions of people."

JAMES CAMERON CBE, Vice President of Global Leadership Development at Walmart

"Sweeping and intelligent, this book is an extraordinary contribution, deeply researched and penetratingly insightful. Céline Schillinger puts broad societal trends into historical perspective to explain the present moment. She explains what's at stake for the world and why it's urgent that we act now."

AMY EDMONDSON, Professor, Harvard Business School and bestselling author of *The Fearless Organization* and *Teaming*

"Céline Schillinger has written an insightful and timely synthesis of people-centered change principles, enabled by technology, powered by '*Un-Leadership*.' Impactful."

RICK WESTERN, CEO, Kotter

"Compelling and inspirational, Céline Schillinger's ideas on leadership show us that stepping back with humility so that our teams can freely ideate and innovate is the way to thrive in our rapidly emerging new world."

DAVID FORD, Chief Human Resources Officer at Intercept Pharmaceuticals

"It takes courage to un-lead, but it is absolutely worth it. The paths identified by Céline Schillinger are not just attractive ideas, they dramatically increase people's engagement at work and the velocity of change in our organizations. A highly valuable read."

DOROTHEA VON BOXBERG, CEO, Lufthansa Cargo

"Céline Schillinger takes aim at the flaws of traditional management and does not miss. With a depth of hard-won experience in creating change internationally, she reveals how to bring forth change, agency, and engagement by combining the power of networks and community with new models of leadership to foster liberty, equality, and fraternity at work."

SIMON TERRY, Chief Growth Officer, InLoop, and Change Agent at Change Agents Worldwide

"It was when I started to un-Lead that my team became motivated, engaged, and delivered beyond expectations. We can waste time pleasing the top management, or we can learn about authentic leadership instead: Céline Schillinger offers brilliant pathways in that regard. Realize the future of leadership now, from this smart and passionate book!"

ZSUZSANNA DEVECSERI, Vice President, Head of Global Oncology Medical Affairs at Sanofi Genzyme

"Brave and of breathtakingly vast scope, the emancipatory ideas offered in *Dare to Un-Lead* deserve to be read by all."

STOWE BOYD, Managing Director and Founder, Work Futures

"*Dare to Un-Lead* is an opus on the origins and possible solutions for the world's current issues through the lens of leadership. Bringing together wisdom from an amazing array of writers, Céline Schillinger crafts a clear message that without inclusivity, respect, and dignity, we will not succeed."

ANITA BURRELL, Chair, Global Committee Council at Healthcare Businesswomen's Association

Dare to Un-Lead

Schillinger, Céline,
Dare to un-lead : the art of
relational leadership in a fra
[2022]
33305253967545
ca   04/14/23

LINGER

FOREWORD BY MYRON ROGERS

DARE TO

The Art of Relational Leadership in a Fragmented World

UN-LEAD

Figure 1

Vancouver / Toronto / Berkeley

Copyright © 2022 by We Need Social
Foreword copyright © 2022 by Myron Rogers

22 23 24 25 26   5 4 3 2 1

All rights are reserved and no part of this publication may be reproduced, stored in a retrieval system, or transmitted in any form or by any means, electronic, mechanical, photocopying, scanning, recording or otherwise, except as authorized with written permission by the publisher. Excerpts from this publication may be reproduced under license from Access Copyright.

"A Means To An End," Words and Music by Ian Curtis, Stephen Morris, Peter Hook and Bernard Sumner. Copyright ©1980 Universal Music Publishing Ltd. All Rights Reserved. Used by permission. Reprinted by Permission of Hal Leonard Europe Ltd.

Cataloguing data is available from Library and Archives Canada
ISBN 978-1-77327-182-8 (hbk.)
ISBN 978-1-77327-183-5 (ebook)
ISBN 978-1-77327-184-2 (pdf)

Design by Naomi MacDougall
Author photograph by Marie-Thérèse Schillinger

Editing by Steve Cameron
Copy editing by Stephanie Fysh
Proofreading by Melanie Little
Indexing by Stephen Ullstrom

Printed and bound in Canada by Friesens
Distributed internationally by Publishers Group West

Figure 1 Publishing Inc.
Vancouver BC Canada
www.figure1publishing.com

Figure 1 Publishing works in the traditional, unceded territory of the Xʷməθkʷəy̓əm (Musqueam). Sḵwx̱wú7mesh (Squamish) and Səlílwətaʔɬ (Tsleil-Waututh) peoples.

Contents

Foreword

We are at the end of an era.
We are attending the emergence of the new.
Céline Schillinger is a midwife of what's next.
This book, *Dare to Un-Lead*, is a birth announcement.

HERE IS HOW I understand the painful unraveling of the dominant social organizing principles of the past that Céline powerfully portrays in this book. We have lived in a world ruled by a clockwork mechanism in which the best way to organize human endeavor was to organize it as a machine. This view can be seen most clearly in an organization chart. The philosophy of organizing dictates separating all work into a series of smaller and smaller boxes, then connecting them through a linear hierarchy of relationship and information that generates a whole that we can control, a whole that has predictable outcomes.

Does any of this echo our embodied experience of life? In a world lacking prediction, in a viral world of both virtual and actual space, in a world of pandemics evolving beyond our capacity to contain them, *what is going on?*

It's the end of our belief in the machine view of the world. The view once served us; as an organizing principle, for hundreds of years, the goodness it enabled—health, wealth, education, science, an extraordinary quality of life for some—was easily produced. But any organizing principle has both positive and negative elements, both light and shadow. We tend to reap the majority of the positive expressions of a dominant paradigm at the front end of its cycle in history. And then, the unintended consequences of that way of conceiving of the world take over. As our machine view of the world dies, there has been a fight to keep it alive, deepening the rift between what's possible (the quality of life we are trying to make for ourselves and each other) and what's actual—the growing inequity of the world.

My view is this. Organizations are living systems, not machines. They exhibit all the complex qualities of life—unpredictable creativity; self-organization; the endless generation of networks and structures; patterns of collective behavior that create the capacity to respond to a world of endless complexity; the emergence of new capacities and possibilities—all without imposition from a leader. The world is not about predictability and control, but about *reliability and order.* We can create systems that respond in ways we never imagined, ways that positively surprise us with their evolutionary congruence with what we want and need.

We have so much to unlearn. *Dare to Un-Lead: The Art of Relational Leadership in a Fragmented World* arrives as a teacher at just the right moment.

Céline Schillinger asks us to liberate ourselves from the false gods of the past. She challenges our notions of the leader as savior and asks us to contemplate a world where our best leaders are our peers in shared work. She invites us to migrate together from a narrow view of work as compliance with a hierarchical leader to work as a shared commitment to a view of our work at collectively creating a world that works for all of us. With the eternal qualities of liberty, equality, and fraternity as our companions on the journey, she guides us to a shared future that works *with* the dynamics of life, not against them.

My journey with Céline came some years ago when I was invited into her work while she was a corporate executive. I was blessed to stand beside her as she engaged a broad range of people, up and down the imposed hierarchy, as peers, around the question: *What are we trying to do together?* I listened as she took on the traditional hierarchy, as she confronted the powers that be, and as she spoke truth to power. Some of it worked, some of it didn't. Some of it required courage, and some actions had undesirable consequences. It was a real-life lesson in the very ideas Céline now generously shares with us in *Dare to Un-Lead.* These are not just ideas; they are lived ideals, born of hard-earned experience. Bringing the future to life now isn't a smooth or easy journey. But it is one worth taking together, and Céline Schillinger is a brilliant companion on the path.

I hope you find this book, its insight, ideas, and ideals to be powerful partners in your work and life. I do.

MYRON ROGERS
Consultant for large-scale change in complex systems
Coauthor with Margaret Wheatley of *A Simpler Way*
Leeds, United Kingdom

Preface

MY LATE MATERNAL grandmother, Lucienne, was born in Calais, France, in 1907. She was the daughter of a lighthouse keeper who was a father to twenty-one children—eleven with his first wife and, after she died, ten more with my great-grandmother. The children were so numerous and so spread out my grandmother told me she often forgot the names of her half-siblings.

Lucienne was seven years old when she started school, but soon stopped because of the First World War; by nine she was working to help the family make ends meet. Child labor in France was prohibited in 1874 but was still quite common in factories like the one that made lace where my grandmother worked. There she and the other children would do jobs that, because of their relatively small scale, were simpler for them. My grandmother's job was to crawl under the lace machinery to pick reels and thread that had fallen. I recall her telling me that the forewoman would lock her and the other child workers in the toilets on the days the labor inspector came to the factory.

By her early twenties, Lucienne was already a veteran wheeler at the factory. She kept on working hard and became a cleaner for well-off families after she and her husband moved to Bordeaux in the southwest of France.

Her experience of work and life couldn't be more dissimilar to mine. I was born and raised in a small town near Bordeaux, France, in a stable and loving family. My parents, both young art teachers, had met in art school a few years before. I'm the eldest of three daughters. My mother was the first of her extended family to attend graduate school. My father's family, with roots in Alsace near Germany, belonged to the lower middle class. Both my parents enjoyed a simple but joyful child-hood in a country recovering bit by bit from the Second World War. From an early age, my father enjoyed freedoms that would shock today—hitchhiking across Europe, for example, at the age of fifteen.

My parents were always curious, creative humanists. Together, they traveled the world, visiting close to a hundred countries in the sim-plest way possible, meeting and interacting with the locals. Since they retired, they have spent several months each year in remote locations around the globe, helping educational charities. My mother is a talented portrait photographer. Her hands are always at work; she cannot stop creating and never seems to tire. My father is also a maker, passionate about manual crafts that demand effort and precision, full of admiration for master artisans. He seems able to do anything.

This is the environment that I was lucky to grow up in: creative, stim-ulating, free-spirited, open to the world, not rich but financially secure. It was egalitarian, too. My parents shared the same profession, as well as the household chores. With no brother to compete with, we sisters grew up taking women's rights for granted. For quite some time, there was nothing in my personal experience to disprove this worldview. Oppor-tunities came my way and I grabbed them.

However, when thinking about leadership, societal change, and the contents of this book, my mind travels back to my grandmother's life. Being reminded of the hardships she endured as a natural course of the life she led at the time she led it compels me to not squander the oppor-tunities life has given me, and it keeps me connected to the hardship of labor still experienced today by many people across the world.

While child labor persists in some underdeveloped nations, in the West it is largely considered a tool of a bygone era; a tool which no longer serves us well. Across industrialized nations it was recognized that by educating children, we would, collectively, get further ahead. What got us through the beginning of the Industrial Revolution would not work to get us where we envisioned ourselves in the future, and so, we adapted.

Similarly, and much more recently, I've recognized a global need to adapt from traditional models of leadership to something that will pro-pel us forward with new collective work practices that respect people and drive economic growth.

Unfortunately, many dominant leadership and management prac-tices still in use around the world today are inherited from scientific management theory and its derivatives. These revolutionized manufacturing and enabled great business outcomes throughout the twentieth century and were gradually adopted by other fields, from education to sport. But the context in which we now live, trade, and work in the twenty-first century has little in common with that of Frederick Taylor or Henry Ford. The anachronism of their approach has fueled growing dissatisfaction about how decisions are made, how corporations are run, and how our societies function.

As globalization and technology accelerate, and as our values and social norms—especially those related to traditional hierarchies and authority—evolve, the business world needs to keep pace. Value creation has profoundly shifted in recent years, as have consumer expectations. All of this is pushing organizations to reinvent themselves. A new mode of leadership will need to be at the forefront of this change if it is to be sustainable and positively impactful on society.

And it is possible. A leadership model that is more respectful of people, while generating greater economic value, is within reach. There is no need for complicated methods; three universal values provide the pathways to reinventing leadership. They are Liberty, Equality, and Fraternity.

Liberty

Far from being an obstacle to the smooth running of an enterprise, Liberty is an accelerant. It allows people to exercise judgment, escape the pitfalls of arbitrariness, and develop their agency. Collective freedom begins with the emancipation of the individual, a transformational experience that is undergone by anyone who aspires to change agency. To extend freedom at scale, a different kind of leadership is required, putting new and sometimes counterintuitive principles at the heart of managerial practices.

Equality

Inequalities in status and access to information, domination relationships, and obedience have become obstacles to the performance of organizations. A semblance of equality cannot mask the difficulties organizations face when dealing with the diversity of people. Yet there is a phenomenal opportunity before us in the shape of networks, as well as the technology and human relationships that enable them. Networks, as organizational design principles, allow for new, highly effective collective work practices, replacing domination with peer leadership that has the capacity to inspire agility and innovation.

Fraternity

Fraternity is a challenge in a contemporary society marked by individualism, distrust, and competition. This is about so much more than teambuilding and efficiency. To focus on that alone will deliver no more than superficial results. True fraternity stems from a shared commitment to a common cause in an activist movement. Activism—its psychological drivers, its engagement mechanisms, its tools—offers organizations and leadership an immense opportunity to progress. Corporate activism enables the formation of communities based on intent and impact. These are two key drivers of human and economic performance that can activate the radical reinvention of leadership.

DARE TO UN-LEAD explores the opportunities we have to collectively transform leadership through the personal experiences I have had in working with others to plot and test people-focused, digitally enabled, collective work practices. All of them have been internationally recognized for their ability to engage people and transform business outcomes for broader social good. I wanted to understand why they worked and how they could be expanded to more organizations. This book is the result of a deep analysis of leadership, studied through multiple lenses, timely sources of knowledge, and a set of universal principles. The result is an offering of original insights and evidence-based pathways for reinventing collective performance in a post-pandemic world. This book will assist those looking to perform better individually and collectively and who desire to be agents of permanent change in leadership and governance.

From large corporations to small businesses, the lessons learned here, implemented individually and collectively over time, will make our workplaces more equal, our jobs more gratifying, and our economies more profitable. And that will make the world a better place.

Dare to Un-Lead

PART I

Leadership
Matters

The COVID-19 pandemic has forced the global population to navigate waters rarely traveled. Unlike with previous worldwide catastrophes in modern history such as World Wars I and II and the 1918 influenza pandemic, our new interconnected world—from global supply chains to expanded travel opportunities to our reliance on social media—has made this pandemic an unprecedented, shared experience. Across continents, borders closed and cities went silent. Citizens struggled with anxiety and grief. Many worked from home when it was possible. Many applauded the heroic healthcare workers. And across the globe as the virus spread, hordes of data were collected, analyzed, and shared. Yet the reaction to the pandemic was vastly different from country to country, from organization to organization. Some were seen as prompt, orderly, and quite successful in limiting the loss of life and the impact on human activity. Others were slow to respond and caused confusion with their messaging and actions, resulting in both chaos and rage. Why?

I believe the answer lies in leadership.

In *An Integrative Theory of Leadership*, Martin Chemers offers the following definition: "leadership is a process of social influence in which one person is able to enlist the aid and support of others in the accomplishment of a common task."[1] Leadership, then, has very real consequences. People's lives are shaped—in the worst cases, shortened—by the effects of leadership. Those endowed with leadership responsibilities, and their actions while occupying leadership positions, affect each and every one of us, for better and worse, in our everyday lives.

From the time I became interested in the outside world till now, I have observed patterns and trends that for the most part did not evolve as I had hoped. In my corporate life, for nearly thirty years, I have often struggled with traditional leadership. I call it "traditional" because I am convinced it reflects a bygone era and does not serve us well anymore. What got us here won't get us there: context and aspirations have changed vastly. Methods from the past no longer accommodate the evolution of our societies, of businesses, and of organizations. What is still revered as leadership is often a noxious set of obsolete behaviors that harm individuals and societies, and that must be reinvented.

1

What Got Us Here
Won't Get Us There

As we transition from an industrial society to a knowledge-based one, Canadian futurist Michel Cartier has identified five crises, one each relating to the economy, geopolitics, ecology, human generations, and energy, and all occurring simultaneously.[1] Since early 2020, the global pandemic has added a sixth. If there is a common denominator to all crises, I believe it is leadership. We have reached this multi-crisis state because we are stuck with a certain type of leadership that is profoundly detrimental to our world.

We need leaders who can gain a better understanding of the world around them, who can facilitate connections between different domains and areas of expertise, and who can enable us to change what doesn't work. If this can be achieved, then we might be able to take a systemic and multidisciplinary approach to resolving some of crises of the twenty-first century, making progress at greater speed and with more impact.

But how do we get there?

Societal Transformation

"Can we read together tonight?" In response to my daughter's increasingly rare request for a bedtime story, I selected a copy of *Grimms' Fairy Tales* from the shelf, lay down next to her, and started to read. It had been a long time since I had ventured into this world of wolves, witches, and princes, and this was the first time we had read these particular tales together. The first story gave me mixed feelings. The second story left me uneasy. I stopped in the middle of the third.

"Do you realize what the king is doing?" I asked. She did—far better than I had at her age. The king had claimed the poor peasant's daughter as a bride because she was *pretty*. The father had no choice but to give her to him. However, the king imagined three challenges for the young girl to complete, to make sure she was worth it. Should she fail at one, he would kill her. Only through magic was she able to complete the three challenges and become the king's wife. That's it. The story celebrated her ingenuity—and it chilled me to the bone. Thankfully, there was also a copy of Rebecca Solnit's *Cinderella Liberator* on the shelf, to which we quickly turned after setting aside the misogynist tales.

Our perceptions change. Our collective values and expectations evolve. Whether we like it or not, society transforms itself in many ways. It is a fact of life. But what precisely is it about these changes that is relevant to leadership today? What has caused the disconnect that exists between citizens, employees, and their leaders? What is it that makes traditional leadership feel obsolete?

Perhaps leadership hasn't kept pace with the dramatic changes we have experienced over the course of the past century. Those changes, from many perspectives, have been more rapid and more profound than anything our species has previously witnessed. They have transformed how we behave, as well as what we value.

Human Change

It is not just the world around us that changes ever more rapidly; we do, too. Collectively, we experience more friction and fragmentation than previous generations. Our lives have been transformed by the effects of technology and the anxieties created by contemporary uncertainties. These have all served to modify the context in which decision-making and leadership take place.

It has never been easy for humans to agree on anything. That's why rules, norms, and institutions have been created: by channeling dissent, by enabling consensus, they organize our coexistence. But it is a process that is becoming more and more arduous.

There are a number of reasons why, but one clearly relates to demographics. In 1907, when my grandmother was born, there were 1.75 billion people on the planet. Around a century later, when my daughter was born, there were 6.92 billion. By the time she turns fifty, it is predicted that there will be 10 billion. Thanks to sanitation, vaccines, and improved socioeconomic conditions, we now coexist for longer. In 1950, the average global life expectancy was 45.7 years, whereas by 2015 it had risen to 72.5 years.[2] What once were large cities are now mega-cities—huge metropolitan areas that are home to tens of thousands of people in each square kilometer.

Another reason we have difficulty coexisting relates to our increased mobility, with a large number of us moving away from our local communities because of work, study, poverty, war, or ecological and climatic disasters. Two hundred seventy-two million people, or 3.5 percent of the world's population, do not live in the country in which they were born. In France, close to 10 percent of the population was born in another country, and now find themselves blending beliefs and customs from different cultural traditions. The decline of religion in Europe and the Americas, moreover, means that there is a large proportion of young people who have drifted away from the normative practices that shaped their parents' and grandparents' lives.[3]

With the development of transportation and technology, global trade has boomed, expanding further with offshoring, outsourcing, and the development of complex supply chains. From the blue-collar worker in Pennsylvania to the farmer in Kenya, no one in the world is immune to the effects of globalization, experiencing the jolts of distant political upheavals, trade wars, and tensions regarding national borders and immigration. The rapid spread of COVID-19 from one part of the world to another illustrates this perfectly. Our interdependencies are very real and can create antagonism. When borders are suddenly closed, supply chains break down, food and key products like medicine and protective clothing become scarce, fingers are pointed, and scapegoats are sought out.

With even more people on the planet living increasingly fragmented lives that are shaped by cultural and economic frictions, it is next to impossible to achieve consensus on anything. This is a situation rendered even more complex by technological revolution.

Transformative Technology

In March 2020, Pascal Coppens reported on China's deployment of an impressive array of technologies as part of its response to the coronavirus outbreak and management of a lockdown situation:

> Drones are being deployed everywhere in the cities to see if people are wearing their masks, to disinfect areas, and to [check people's] temperature ... Everywhere on the streets you could see self-driving delivery cars hovering around to deliver groceries to people in lockdown ... Meanwhile, advanced AI has been used to help diagnose the corona virus and to find a vaccine.[4]

With the advent of the internet and of greater computing capabilities, tech revolutions keep coming at an ever-accelerating pace. In *Future Politics*, Jamie Susskind calls our future a "digital lifeworld": a system that links human beings, machines, and data. "Increasingly capable systems, increasingly integrated technology, increasingly quantified society" are its defining features. It is a world that produces and processes ever more information.[5]

We know that the way information is processed, tweaked, and presented affects how we behave, what we purchase, who we vote for. But Michel Cartier goes even further: each tech disruption actually changes the way our brains work. Their curves are exponential and interrelated. Cartier writes,

> In each new era (*Prehistory, Antiquity, Middle Ages, Renaissance, Industrial Era and post-industrial era*) there is a significant increase in population accompanied by an equally significant increase in the amount of information being put into circulation

and

> · With each major leap in population and information, society creates a new communication technology: printing, cinema, television and the Internet are all milestones in our history.
>
> · With each of these leaps, the human brain becomes more complex in order to adapt to the mutations of the new space-time.

- Our children will be different from us because their brains (in fact, their synaptic connections) will be configured differently.[6]

We are already very different from our parents, just as our children are different from us.

World-pain

In March 2020, the *Hamilton Spectator*, in Ontario, Canada, published a cartoon by Graeme MacKay that was frequently shared online as the scale of the COVID-19 pandemic became evident. It depicts a city in which the citizens are advised to wash their hands. On the horizon is the COVID-19 tsunami sweeping toward the city, behind which rises an even larger recession tsunami.[7] Later variants added two more gigantic waves, one relating to climate change and the other to biodiversity collapse.

From the start of the global lockdown, there was a historic rise in mental health problems, with the coronavirus pandemic adding to the anxiety induced by other major stressors, not least among them the climate catastrophe and its implications for life on the planet.[8] As I review these lines near Córdoba in Spain, the temperature has reached 49°C (120°F). This is unsustainable in the long term. Climate migrants are in the millions already around the globe. Economic turmoil, inequality, corruption, the decline of democracy in some countries, trade wars, and military conflicts are broadcast to billions of screens every minute of the day. The situation feels beyond anyone's control, creating a sense of helplessness. German Romantic author Jean Paul coined a term that succinctly sums up the feelings that are elicited by the MacKay cartoon, and that are felt by people across the globe daily—*Weltschmerz*, "a deep sadness about the inadequacy or imperfection of the world."[9] Or, in English, *world-pain*.

Fear is a political agenda in itself, fueled by those who reap its economical or electoral benefits. It is the source of conspiracy theories and of the rejection of science. Twenty-one percent of the French population believe in at least five conspiracy theories, the same proportion of Americans who believe that the Illuminati control the world.[10] Vaccine deniers dismiss scientific evidence that vaccines are safe and effective. Consequently, there has been a resurgence of diseases like measles and other avoidable illnesses, including for young children.

Uncertainty and fear also generate hate, found in abundance on social networks. The 2020 "Hate Panorama" conducted by online content moderation company Netino found that one Facebook comment out of eight was aggressive or hateful.

Some describe this distressed world in terms of VUCA, a U.S. Army War College acronym that means "*Volatile, Uncertain, Complex,* and *Ambiguous.*" Others, such as Jamais Cascio, find the term obsolete, referring instead to "an age of chaos" in which the world is BANI, or "*Brittle, Anxious, Nonlinear,* and *Incomprehensible.*"[11]

One thing is for sure: it is a world in which there are no "right" answers to problems. At best, we "manage polarities," making decisions that are not fully informed, and that impact people whose very values have changed dramatically over just a few decades.

Evolving Social Values

According to sociologists Michael Haralambos and Michael Holborn, social values represent our "belief that something is good and desirable."[12] Although deeply embedded in our collective behaviors, traditions, and institutions, they do evolve under the effect of changes in human interactions and relationships. Detailed data and fascinating culture maps have been produced by the World Values Survey (www.worldvaluessurvey.org), a global network of social scientists, over the last thirty years. As Ronald F. Inglehart says in the subtitle of *Cultural Evolution* (2018), "People's motivations are changing, and reshaping the world."

To illustrate my point, I will refer to the changes in Western societies that have come to challenge some of the beliefs on which traditional leadership used to flourish: social hierarchies, standardization, and authority.

THE CHALLENGE TO TRADITIONAL HIERARCHIES

At a conference for Innotribe at Sibos Boston in 2014, Jon Husband began his exploration of new modes of work with commentary on "the expanded understanding of family: blended, same-sex, interracial marriages and rights, singlehood."[13] His point was that the very basic social structures and preferences on which we have relied for so long are now being called into question, deconstructed, and reconstructed differently.

What used to be a powerful norm (such as the married, heterosexual, same-origin, nuclear family) is now one of many options people can choose from, at least in Western countries. The Church's influence over people's lives has receded sharply. In France, about 45 percent of marriages end in divorce, and 61 percent of children are born out of wedlock. More than one marriage in seven is mixed, involving a foreigner and a French national. In the United States, 67 percent of people supported same-sex marriage in 2020, as opposed to 11 percent in 1988. Seventeen percent of U.S. marriages now involve couples from different "races," which was illegal in some states until 1967. Twenty-three percent of U.S. children live with one parent only. The list of countries recognizing marriage equality continues to grow. Ireland, historically deeply rooted in the Catholic faith, voted in a monumental referendum held in 2018 to legalize women's control over their bodies and reproductive choices.[14]

Slowly but surely, economic hierarchies between genders are being challenged. On average, women still earn 15 percent less than men, and shoulder the responsibility and the mental load for most of the unpaid household chores—a situation, remarkably, made worse during the period of COVID-19 lockdown. However, an increasing proportion of women are now their families' main breadwinners: in 2019, about half of American women said they out earned or made the same amount as their spouse or partner, whereas among married women with children in 1960, only 3.8 percent earned more than their husband.[15]

Another example of social flipping has been evidenced by the number of pedophilia cases over the past decade involving celebrities and people in positions of authority, such as Larry Nasser in the U.S., Jimmy Saville in the UK, and Gabriel Matzneff in France, as well as other public figures, such as politicians and religious leaders. What was in the past quietly brushed under the carpet, despite broad awareness of criminal activity—or, in Matzneff's case, confessional literature—has now come fully into the public eye. Victims, such as Vanessa Springora, have found a voice and been given a platform.[16] Their own publications and media coverage have resulted in criminal prosecution and widespread public discourse. This has posed a challenge to at least three symbolic hierarchies: those of adult over child, man over woman, and perpetrator over victim.

Formerly oppressed or silenced groups now speak up, on the street and on social media, as exemplified by the #MeToo and Black Lives Matter movements. Their words and actions have triggered ongoing discussions about victimhood culture,[17] political correctness, and reversing the imbalance of power. Patriarchy and bigotry continue to resist as vigorously as they can. Nevertheless, today, their traditional power and hierarchy rest on very unstable foundations.

THE FRAGMENTATION OF EXPECTATIONS

What once was normalized has been disrupted profoundly: religious institutions, social class awareness, powerful work communities, the sedentary lifestyle, and other conditions that homogenize behaviors and expectations. Today, people are more disparate in the paths they follow, more diverse than their ancestors were. Capitalism exacerbates the need for individual recognition. As Francis Fukuyama observes in *Identity*, "Economic modernization and rapid social change undermine older forms of community and replace them with a confusing pluralism of alternative forms of association." Problems arise when seven billion individuals "demand public recognition of their worth."[18] Long-term work and strong affiliation to a single employer have given way to the gig economy and hourly contracts. Class or political affiliation reconfigure themselves constantly, as proven by the Brexit vote in 2016 and the election of Emmanuel Macron in France in 2017, both of which brought together people who would not have voted alike in the past.

The "common world" has fragmented. In *Une démocratie sans autorité?* (Authority-less democracy?), Alain Eraly attributes this fragmentation to three main factors:

- The segmentation of social groups—a vast movement of social differentiation that tends to multiply cultural and cognitive separation.

- Information bubbles—the diversification of information sources and the emergence of echo chambers.

- The market of opinions—the extreme difficulty of narrating society, of making sense of a continuous flow of disparate information.[19]

Fukuyama argues that another factor—"the triumph of the therapeutic"—is in play, too. In the past, a shared moral horizon was defined by religion. Then psychotherapy emerged as a new religion, establishing that an individual's happiness depended on their self-esteem, requiring them to liberate their inner selves, to become "authentic."[20] Modern liberal societies gradually took on the responsibility for raising the self-esteem of each and every one of their citizens, contributing, through "identity politics," to the fragmentation.

This fragmentation is paralleled by a polarization of society around competing identities. The ferocious culture war raging in the United States today between conservatives and progressives has even spilled beyond politics into public health. Whether you are a Democrat or a Republican, you perceive the COVID-19 pandemic as more or less threatening.[21] Even scientific messages are perceived through the filter of identity.

At a time when disagreements are so fierce and cancel culture is on the rise, does the common good mean anything anymore?[22] Eraly argues that "increasing inequalities, social exclusion, the cynicism of economic elites, the multiplicity of affiliations, geographical mobility and the omnipresent spectacle of identity conflicts all contribute to undermining the perception of a common fate."[23]

THE END OF AUTHORITY?

We now have a very different relationship to authority—political, scientific, intellectual, parental—from that experienced by previous generations. For my grandmother, the doctor was a godlike figure, whereas today many challenge doctors' advice, conducting searches for alternative points of view on the internet and placing trust in the opinions of celebrities instead. My parenting is probably quite different from my grandmother's, too—more permissive, more consensual. Disrespect for political or business figures doesn't surprise anyone anymore.

In 2005, the Edelman's Trust Barometer highlighted a shift in trust from "authorities" to peers. This "inversion of influence" was presented as a flipped pyramid.

[People] no longer rely on a few well-informed opinion shapers for news and information... Peer voices today are more powerful than the opinion of traditional authority figures. Respondents say that they find "a person like yourself" as credible as an academic expert (64 percent), and far more credible than CEOs (49 percent), NGO representatives

(48 percent), a Board of Directors (44 percent), let alone government officials (35 percent).

As a result, we have a new pyramid of influence, where the broader population has more influence than those with authority, creating a real challenge for those in positions of power and authority who need to find new ways of engaging and influencing opinions.[24]

Trust levels are significantly lower among the general, broader population than among the "informed public—those with higher income levels, higher education, and higher usage of traditional media," creating a gap that has reached its highest point in recent years.[25] Coronavirus, the great revealer of social failings, illustrates this gap. In the United States, for example, 25 percent of adults believe in a conspiracy theory that the COVID-19 pandemic was planned. This figure rises to 48 percent among those with a low level of educational attainment.[26]

Eraly defines *authority* as "the personal legitimacy that a person derives from occupying an exceptional position, playing a specific role, exercising power and assuming responsibility on behalf of an institution."[27] In theory, the holder of authority represents the community and exercises power in its name. However, those who have an aversion to centralized power, who fear oppression, and who resist demands for obedience often resist this model whenever they feel excluded by it. For them, authority confers a position of questionable superiority and unacceptable hierarchical distance, carrying with it the alarming possibility that decisions can be made without the consent of the very people who are being represented. Focus shifts, then, from the collective to the individual: the holder of authority. It highlights a crisis of legitimacy. Legitimacy can be restored only through equality and inclusion, through a horizontal democratic process. Legitimacy can no longer be derived from divine rights, social status, or economic privilege. Without the consent of the collective, authority has no foundation.

In this sense, empowered and connected citizens, consumers, and employees exercise new forms of power that counterbalance or even delegitimize the traditional ones. In *The End of Power*, Moisés Naím recounts how, having been appointed Minister of Development following his party's landslide victory in the 1989 elections in Venezuela, he became aware of "the enormous gap between the perception and the reality of my power."[28] Faced with riots as citizens protested against the new government's program, he discovered that despite having significant nominal power as an economic minister, in practice he had "only a limited ability to deploy resources, to mobilize individuals and organizations, and, more generally, to make things happen." This realization is shared by many people in positions of authority. When I worked for the pharmaceutical company Sanofi, I wrote an email directly to the CEO about the lack of diversity inclusion in the company. Slowly, my note, which I shared with three trusted colleagues, began a process of internal activism which grew to 2,500 women and men, in person and on digital channels, and even extended outside the company. When the CEO finally responded to my co-activists and me about workplace diversity, unlocking access to the company's Executive Committee, we thought we had reached *the* place where power resides. It was an incredible disappointment, therefore, to see so little change after the door had been opened. If the Committee couldn't transform the organization, then who could?

Business and Organization Transformation

There are other changes in addition to those relating to social values that influence how we lead, make decisions, and work together. Some of these relate to how, where, and with whom we work, how we organize ourselves, and how we have become outcomes-oriented. These all have had an impact on the business landscape, with leadership particularly affected by the shift in our understanding of value creation and by the evolution of customer expectations.

Value Creation

One of the most visible changes concerning value creation and its consequences for leadership has been the switch to a knowledge economy, although there are some, such as public policy specialist Nick O'Donovan, who question whether this itself is now moribund.[29] The knowledge economy is a system of consumption and production that is based on intellectual capital, taking root in the postindustrial period of the 1960s and accelerating through the 1990s with the exponential growth of information technology. Use of the hands, manual labor, was displaced by use of the head and digital literacy.

Prior to the COVID-19 pandemic, the global knowledge economy employed approximately one billion people, according to consulting firm Gartner.[30] In *Thinking for a Living*, Thomas Davenport argues that knowledge workers are "vastly different from other types of workers in their motivations, attitudes, and need for autonomy—and, so, they require different management techniques to improve their performance and productivity."[31] In one sense, all work is, of course, a form of knowledge work. However, those individuals identified as knowledge workers do present certain characteristics—often a high level of educational attainment, experience, and expertise—which they apply to jobs involving creativity and the application of specialist knowledge. Managers in the knowledge economy, then, are often placed in a position where they know less about the field than those they manage.

The expansion of the knowledge economy has also been accompanied by the disruption and adaptation of traditional business models. In recent years, we have witnessed a distributed approach to product development (with *Wikipedia* serving as an exemplar), the deployment of infrastructure as a service and software as a service offering, and the emergence of digital platforms and ecosystems (with Android and iOS initially leading the way). Today, as Jennifer Schenker reports in *The Innovator*, seven of the ten most valuable companies in the world are based on a platform business model.[32] This has a profound effect on our understanding of what constitutes a business, on the atomization of the workforce and the supply chain, on how people are contracted, on the role of the customer who may also be a partner or supplier, and on where power and authority lie.

As Simon Torrance of the World Economic Forum observes, "this model is not something that today's corporate leaders were taught at business school. Very few leaders at non-digital companies understand, to a profound degree, business models like [Apple's] and even when do they do it takes time to percolate through the strategy process."[33] The fluidity of relationships and interactions in the ecosystem overturn the traditional customer–supplier model, while there is a constant demand for adaptability and speed, seemingly making business more complicated than it once was. There is less clarity and certainty, little room for fixed mindsets and best practices. The COVID-19 pandemic has served to accelerate and broaden the reach of many of the emergent changes from these new working methods. Millions of people have now transitioned to distributed, digital work. Agility has become a condition for survival, which requires the capacity to reinvent oneself quickly and often.

Changing *how* we innovate is paramount too. Ever since Clayton Christensen's theory of disruptive innovation became popular in 1997, the profile of disrupters has changed dramatically. "They now enter the market with products and services that are every bit as good as those offered by legacy companies," Rita McGrath explains. Instead of investing time and money on the automation of old business models, established organizations need to work on their internal capabilities for discovery. Significant energy needs to be directed toward culture, attitudes, the circulation of information, and the development of a discovery mindset across the organization, not just in the R&D function. The aim, as McGrath suggests, is to "learn quickly, experiment, and then pivot to reflect the insights gleaned."[34]

In my time at Sanofi, the old world pushed back fiercely against new, innovative initiatives. With the strength of my 2,500 co-activists, eventually I was able to create a new function at the company—Stakeholder Engagement—to help bring the power of free will, purpose, co-creation, social media, and community engagement to product marketing and to have it support the launch of a new vaccine. I focused on the cause, fighting the disease, rather than on the product. I joined forces with different partners who shared the same purpose. From listening to activists, I created the conditions for global connections and action, so that more solutions against the disease could emerge, benefiting both the company and society. Viewed from the outside, the concept proved to be a triumph. Within a year, we had 250,000 worldwide members, and would go on to win multiple awards and secure the interest of the media and key stakeholders. However, internally, it seriously disrupted those with a vested interest in the traditional system of pushing communication toward passive audiences, of controlled messaging, and of siloed interactions.

Customer Expectations

The COVID crisis put a brutal stop to our economic systems. Only time will tell how temporary or long-lasting its effects will be. But the abrupt and dramatic disruption it has caused to our way of life has forced at least some level of reckoning. The pause enforced upon us by the pandemic threw into stark relief—as the roads and flightpaths emptied, supply chains broke down, and the smog lifted—the planetary cost of human activity and of globalization.

The extractive capitalism of the twentieth century helped lift hundreds of millions of people out of hunger and poverty, yet it was also an ecological and environmental disaster. Reliant on continuous growth, it has shaped human behaviors and expectations. Consumerism involves the consumption of objects, experiences, and natural resources. Consumers are maintained in a state of perpetual craving so that they purchase more. Status, identity, and pleasure are just some of the triggers that brands play on to encourage us to spend and accumulate.

For a long time, consumerism invited a general state of passivity and fake agency, with people considered the targets of, and skillfully maneuvered by, marketing and brand messaging. More recently, though, we have become demanding consumers. As Dave Gray and Thomas Vander Wal note in *The Connected Company*, the shift from the mass manufacture of homogenized goods to the development of services intended for diverse consumers has boosted the demand for flexibility and personalization.[35] One-size-fits-all doesn't work as much anymore. Organizations now have to be in tune with their customers, listening closely, responding, and co-creating with them where possible.

Market competition and the effects of decades of total quality management have created new expectations. Quality is a must-have, not a nice-to-have. We demand excellence of product, service, delivery, and customer support. While this is still to be achieved across many industries, some progress has been made. In 2005, Bain uncovered the "delivery gap," or customer experience perception gap: 80 percent of executives believed that they were delivering a superior customer experience, while only 8 percent of customers agreed.[36] Twelve years later, 75 percent of companies believed that they were customer-centric, while 30 percent of consumers agreed. It's a small step, but a start, nonetheless. We want excellence in a fast and reactive manner: our busy lives have rendered us impatient.

If unhappy about customer service or about companies' behaviors, we tell our friends and the whole world, because we can. Online shopping, price comparison apps, consumer forums, and social media offer new ways to challenge businesses, to the point that consumer activism has become a growing threat to corporate reputation. This is not a new phenomenon, but it has acquired unprecedented power with the development of new channels and technologies.[37] Empowered consumers expect freedom of choice, respect for who they are, and attention to their needs. Increasingly, they also expect the organizations to which they give their dollars to demonstrate social and environmental responsibility.

If consumers are making these kinds of demands of the brands they purchase from, it is reasonable to think they will make similar demands of employers and elected representatives in the near future, if they aren't already. The notion of what a consumer is, of how powerful they are, has been transformed.

Work structures are not spared from the effects of these changes, which should surprise no one. Workers are individuals whose life experiences are impacted by demographic evolutions and shifting values; they *are* those newly empowered consumers. As such, they feel the limits of traditional organizations.

We Are Not the Employees We Used to Be

Society's evolving values permeate the workplace. For example, the growing aversion to blatant manifestations of inequality has forced the removal of status markers in some workplaces. The reserved parking space has become the symbol of a leader's resistance to change.

From a simple demographic perspective, the workplace today is much different from that of thirty years ago. With looming retirements and an aging demographic, multiple generations now coexist in the same workforce. The Baby Boomers are still a visible presence, particularly at the top of hierarchies, in decision-making positions. Younger generations, though, bring different viewpoints and expectations to their work. They have different styles, different ways of learning and sharing knowledge. Intergenerational tension is a growing concern that can be detrimental to both engagement and productivity.

Women now account for 40 percent or more of the total labor force in many countries. Thirty-seven percent of the support and operations staff in the United States is non-white (however, only 15 percent of executives are non-white).[38] Technology and greater awareness of accessibility have made it possible for more people with disabilities to enter the workforce. The globalization of the workforce has brought people from different parts of the world to work together. In many countries, there are moves to embrace equality and diversity in the workplace, buttressed by legislative frameworks and social pressure.

What keeps the workforce busy has also greatly changed over the last few decades. Organizations require different skills as business and technology evolve. Artificial intelligence and automation will make redundant certain functions that were previously fulfilled by people. Of course, there is nothing new about this. All technological revolutions have generated changes in working practices, from the plow to the printing press, steam engine, and microprocessor. The COVID-19 pandemic, though, could accelerate the transition from human to machine labor in some fields. But it could also broaden the scope of what jobs will be affected as its economic effects bring into question the viability of some sectors. Company life cycles were already shrinking, with the average expected to be twelve years by 2027. COVID could shorten that even further.

People are going to have to become multidisciplinary and adaptive to retain relevance in the job market. Pre-COVID, it was expected that 17 percent of the occupations monitored by the United States Bureau of Labor Statistics would lose more workers than they added between 2016 and 2026, with some occupations losing more than a fifth of their workforce.[39] Mass layoffs accompanied the financial crisis of 2007 and 2008, and we are seeing large-scale redundancies again today. Many workers have experienced an emotional rollercoaster, protected for a time by government-funded furlough schemes then discarded like any other commodity from organizations they once thought of as family. Some sectors were already preparing for an uncertain future before the pandemic. Pharma sales representatives, for example, were being reskilled en masse. At the same time, though, there are professions such as cybersecurity and healthcare that are booming and experiencing a shortage of talent.[40]

Lack of job security, redundancies, automation, the erosion of loyalty to an employer, and uncertainty about the future are pushing a higher proportion of people into the gig economy. This accounted for 43 percent of the U.S. workforce prior to the COVID crisis, a figure likely to grow.[41] Work has become increasingly transactional in nature. Relationships between worker, colleagues, and organization are often ones of convenience rather than lifelong and deep-rooted. As one friend, who had witnessed multiple layoffs, told me, "I have learned not to love too hard."

The Limits of the Traditional Organization

To a much-changed workforce, the traditional organization can feel like a straitjacket. Its operating model was built on the principles of scientific management and has been only marginally adapted since then. The vast majority of large organizations, and many smaller ones too, still promote hierarchy, order, shareholder value, segmentation, individual merit, and bureaucracy.

In 2014, the *Washington Post* ran a story—"Sinkhole of Bureaucracy"—about an underground government facility located in a former mine in Pennsylvania where thousands of retirement papers are laboriously processed by hand in a totally inefficient process established forty years ago.[42] It is an extreme example but a good reflection of what happens in many places. Gary Hamel and Michele Zanini describe the issue according to a "bureaucratic mass index" (BMI). This refers to the layers of rules, processes, managers, and administrators that many organizations add, creating a "bureaucratic drag" and costing OECD countries around $9 trillion a year. Hamel and Zanini received seven thousand responses to their BMI survey, which illustrated how bureaucracy "produces parochialism, undermines empowerment, frustrates innovation, breeds inertia."[43]

Naturally, there have been many attempts to reinvent organizations and improve how work gets done. These efforts are not lost, and they made some progress possible. But there is nearly always a disjuncture between original ambition and achieved outcome. Consider the example of W. Edwards Deming, the "father of modern quality."[44] In Japan and in the United States, Deming oversaw new systems of organization that created much more space for people across the hierarchy to get involved. He developed a new philosophy focused on knowledge, ownership, and collaboration. His books are still taught, read, and commented on. Yet only about 20 percent of his teaching is properly implemented in organizations—the easiest part, related to statistical methods. The other 80 percent, the more challenging ideas about leadership behaviors, has been left aside. By focusing on processes, control, and exhortations, manufacturers have missed the essence of Deming's message.

Other attempts to modernize organizations have focused on reducing waste (of time, of resources) and simplifying work. This was and still is the promise of Lean manufacturing, which, unfortunately, has morphed in many organizations into an additional source of bureaucracy. Improving collaboration at work has been another avenue for reinvention. The "matrixed" organization, where people report to two lines of command (e.g., "Asia Pacific Business Unit" and "Marketing") was designed with this in mind. It is not a bad idea in theory but is crippled in practice by being a cause of confusion and a source of conflict. Project teams, Agile methodologies, enterprise social networks, holacracy, design thinking, process redesign, and self-management all have their advocates too and are still being trialed in some organizations. Each can have a positive effect where the whole company is mobilized and communication is effective. However, when good intent becomes a formula—a set of rules that people can apply—that's when its positive effect stops.

Behind the suffocating effects of bureaucracy and the failure of many change initiatives is a lack of effective leadership. We have fallen into the trap of mythologizing our leaders rather than challenging and questioning them. It is to the question of the fallacy of leadership that we now turn.

2

The Persistent Fallacy and Failure of Leadership

"I T HAS ALWAYS seemed strange to me," John Steinbeck wrote in *Cannery Row*. "The things we admire in men, kindness and generosity, openness, honesty, understanding and feeling are the concomitants of failure in our system. And those traits we detest, sharpness, greed, acquisitiveness, meanness, egotism and self-interest are the traits of success. And while men admire the quality of the first they love the produce of the second."[1]

What we understand by leadership today is revealed by who embodies it. Who does society refer to as "leaders"? It is incontestable that across the fields of politics, business, and science, among many others, there are leaders whose actions and behaviors cause significant harm, who are complicit in wrecking the world around them and negatively affecting our lives. Do they betray the notion of leadership or, on the contrary, do they conform to a model that has become obsolete? Furthermore, what lessons can be learned from, and in reaction to, these poor leaders—the *self*-mythologizers?

A Cross-Section of Bad Actors

Before we analyze what can be learned, I think it is important to see how invasive and damaging bad leadership is in our lives. While the topics of leadership, governance, and change management seem to be discussed, studied, dissected, and commented on now more than ever before, it is quite astonishing to find so many blatant counterexamples in our daily lives. What is outlined below is just the tip of the iceberg in the failure of leadership—an indication that leadership en masse is failing us.

Bad Pandemic Governance

If more examples of failed leadership were ever needed, the coronavirus pandemic has, unfortunately, provided numerous cases. Reasons cited for failure to lead include the denial of reality, obfuscation, lack of coordination, scapegoating, abdication of responsibility, contradictory communications, cronyism, delayed decision-making, and more. In a March 2020 *Politico* article titled "The Incompetence Pandemic," Matthew Karnitschnig asserted, "The first victim of the coronavirus? Leadership."[2]

The sinkhole of leadership in pandemic response in 2020 was found at the White House, where self-mythologization trumped all else. U.S. incompetence in responding to and controlling the pandemic certainly originates there. It was heart-wrenching to watch an unempathetic president make light of the pandemic, model disgraceful behavior, incite internal competition between states for medical supplies, spread conspiracy theories, and mock the efforts of other national leaders, who sought to mitigate the health, societal, and economic effects of the disease. One headline after another highlighted President Donald Trump's failure of leadership throughout the pandemic, as well as his administration's cynical exploitation of the crisis for its own political benefit in an election year.

Every country around the world has had to face the pandemic threat and design responses to it. Leadership is seen as a differentiating factor that affects the effectiveness of these responses.[3] Take the example of New Zealand Prime Minister Jacinda Ardern. Her leadership has been decisive throughout the coronavirus pandemic, with rapid introduction of restrictions, clear communication, and a very low national death rate. When New Zealand's health minister David Clark breached lockdown rules, he was quickly demoted, and he resigned not long after. Contrast that with the situation in the United Kingdom. Prime Minister Boris Johnson was indecisive and slow to introduce lockdown measures, causing thousands of avoidable deaths. When his own adviser Dominic Cummings was discovered to have breached lockdown restrictions, the issue was casually brushed aside, with the likely effect that some UK citizens then opted to disregard the rules themselves, resulting in more cases. The contrast between leadership founded on care and leadership founded on callousness is telling. Leaders have a responsibility that cannot be ducked. During the first wave of the pandemic, South Korea's and Germany's leaders, along with New Zealand's Ardern, all managed to limit the disease's impact on their population with a response based on science and technology. Donald Trump, Brazil's Jair Bolsonaro, Hungary's Viktor Orbán, and Nicaragua's Daniel Ortega, among others, created conditions for disaster instead.

Following the failure of the Trump administration to respond effectively to the COVID-19 crisis, Donna Ladkin, a professor of leadership and ethics, argues in a *Leadership* article that we should end our "romance with leaders." "Our collective focus on individual leaders such as Donald Trump," Ladkin writes, "distracts us from larger systemic dynamics which are contributing to the severity of the pandemic in the U.S. as well as obfuscating the influence of unelected parties whose interests are served by Trump's actions." Ladkin suggests that, instead, we should pay attention to the structural and societal forces that keep individuals in place as leaders and to the "irrational, primal dimensions" at play in the relationship with our leaders.[4]

Bad Business

Those unelected parties whose interests are served by world leaders tend to be wealthy and influential individuals from the world of business, media, and finance. Placed at the top of large organizations, these individuals act to protect their shareholders' assets—and their own. They are featured in yearly top CEO rankings and are asked to share insights about leadership on prestigious stages, explaining how they achieved career success, their personal purpose, and their leadership style. The internet is full of leadership quotes attributed to them, which can make amusing reading when they are subsequently convicted of wrongdoing. In fact, according to a 2019 PwC study, misconduct and "ethical lapses" feature among the top reasons for CEO departures at the largest companies.[5]

"Today, as CEO of Wells Fargo (WFC), I am proud to be the keeper of our company's culture," declared John Strumpf in 2015.[6] It subsequently was alleged that he had either covered up or organized massive fraud. Millions of phony accounts had been created by the bank. These boosted performance indicators, with a knock-on effect on the stock price value, which earned the CEO $200 million. Strumpf blamed low-level employees for the fraud, laid off 5,300 of them, and was then asked to step down himself.

"Leadership starts with transparency," stated Carlos Ghosn, chairman and CEO of Renault–Nissan.[7] He too was forced to step down in the face of allegations of underreporting his earnings and misusing company assets. Ghosn escaped Japan hidden in an audio equipment box. His flight was made "easy" by the extent of his power and his wealth, amassed from an annual salary of $17 million.[8]

Bob Iger, the Disney CEO, earns even more, with an annual salary of $65 million. The discrepancy in remuneration between senior executives and the many Disney employees who earn minimum wage and survive on food stamps has been heavily criticized and described as "insane" by Abigail Disney, grandniece of Walt.[9] Understandably, there is popular anger directed against corporate elitism and the ever-widening pay gap between the haves and the have-nots. According to the Economic Policy Institute, since 1978 CEO compensation at the top 350 U.S. firms has risen 1,007.5 percent, compared with 11.9 percent for the average worker. CEOs now make 320 times as much as the average worker, up from 20 times in 1965 and 58 times in 1989.[10]

Abigail Disney, Unilever's Paul Polman, and others who have formed the group Millionaires Against Pitchforks signed an open letter early in 2019 calling for tax reform and higher taxes for the rich to combat tax avoidance and evasion.[11] The fact that some of the signatories—Paul Polman himself, Innocent Drinks cofounder Richard Reed, and U.S. real-estate developer Jeff Gural—had been lobbying for years to reduce their organization's corporate tax bills was not lost on commentators. Their involvement, and the timing of the letter to coincide with the annual World Economic Forum gathering at Davos, prompted cynical responses. Were these people role models, opportunists, or, quite simply, hypocrites?[12]

Hypocrisy is certainly a trait that has been associated with Sir James Dyson, founder of the domestic appliance producer that bears his name. A fervent Brexit supporter, Dyson argued that leaving the European Union would bring more wealth and job opportunities to the UK, only to then announce the transfer of the Dyson company headquarters to Singapore. Most likely, Dyson's fellow Brexit backers who applied for

EU passports so as to keep enjoying freedom of movement around the continent—another form of moral elasticity—were not too shocked by his actions.[13]

In addition to fraud, lies, excessive remuneration, and insincerity, harm can arise from top executives simply leading people in the wrong direction. History is full of leaders who misled their organizations through major competitive or technological disruptions. In 2018, the *Wall Street Journal* ran a fascinating story that read like a thriller, "GE Powered the American Century—Then It Burned Out," about the rise and fall of General Electric across the tenures of several CEOs.[14] There are other leaders who experience success with consequences: Facebook CEO Mark Zuckerberg and Twitter CEO Jack Dorsey bear enormous responsibility regarding what worldwide public discourse has become. Questioned at TED 2019 in Vancouver about harassment, manipulation, and violence on Twitter, Dorsey admitted, "We made wrong choices at the beginning, and if it were to be done again, I wouldn't create a 'Like' function because this creates unhealthy conversations."[15] Too late, too bad. At least he expresses remorse; not everyone does. Some, like Robert Mercer, Rupert Murdoch, and Donald Trump, shamelessly and actively contribute to the world's chaos in order to serve their own interests.

Bad Science

Politics and business are not the only fields where leadership shows its dark side. To lead is human; to err is human. In science, for example, it is not uncommon to see people putting their leadership to nefarious use. French Nobel laureate Luc Montagnier, co-discoverer of HIV, has sadly become an advocate promoting anti-vaccine rhetoric.[16] French physician Didier Raoult, a leading voice for hydroxychloroquine as a treatment for coronavirus, has rallied populists behind his criticism of "the System," despite receiving significant financial and media support himself. With the development of the COVID crisis, Raoult has fallen on the side of the conspiracists, the anti-maskers, and the vaccine passport opponents. Adding his powerful voice to that of the far right, he has led his region in France to one of the lowest vaccination rates the country.[17]

Vaccination is an easy target for rogue scientists: since its inception more than two hundred years ago, it has constantly fueled fantasies and suspicions.[18] Fertile ground, then, for Andrew Wakefield. He managed to publish a fraudulent study in the highly regarded journal *The Lancet* in 1998 on the supposed negative effects of the MMR vaccine. The study was subsequently retracted, the journal apologized, and Wakefield was stripped of his medical credentials. But this did not prevent the disastrous consequences of his fraud, which persist more than twenty years later: dozens of deaths each year, throughout the world, that could have been avoided[19]—not to mention the millions spent to disprove Wakefield's myths, which would have been more useful elsewhere. Among the scientists who have damaged public health and our faith in scientific practice, Harvard scientist Mark Hegsted and his colleagues, too, must be given their due. Paid by the sugar industry in the 1960s to obscure the relationship between sugar and heart disease, the lies of Hegsted et al. might just prove the most difficult to overcome.[20] Unfortunately, the list goes on. And as it does, the collective mistrust of science and of the scientific approach increases.

Bad Actors

Authority and impact also come from fame and media exposure. The public gives celebrities leadership status simply because they are popular and beautiful. Actress Jenny McCarthy, the mother of an autistic child, attributed her son's condition to the vaccines he received and used her fame for virulent anti-vaccine activism. Women who followed actress Gwyneth Paltrow's care advice (vaginal steaming, insertion of a vaginal egg, and other oddities) put themselves at risk for serious burns, bacterial infection, and toxic shock.[21] Many influential celebrities have only made things worse by pushing their own agenda. Others do it gratuitously: iconic French actress Catherine Deneuve spoke against the #MeToo movement, undermining French feminist efforts to evolve the ambivalent national culture of seduction.[22] Popular public intellectuals whose views I used to enjoy greatly—including Alain Finkielkraut, Emmanuel Todd, and Raphaël Enthoven—today use most of their airtime to promote bitter and reactionary ideas, as well as outlandish conspiracy theories. Some celebrities pay the price for their misguided activism—French rap star Akhenaton was treated in hospital for COVID-related respiratory distress shortly after taking a public stand against vaccination—but this is not always the case. Attracting audiences, these celebrities and their nefarious beliefs continue to saturate the media space.[23]

Bad Bosses

People who experience workplace humiliation or harassment have stories to tell. I have heard too many of them throughout my career. Tales of sexual harassment clearly grab the headlines, but there are many other ways in which people are belittled, all of which chip away at their confidence in a vicious hierarchical game: they're left off organization charts, not invited to meetings, overlooked in reorganization announcements, assigned tasks that are impossible to accomplish. I recall one particular vice president who, thankfully, was not my manager. He was sexist and pretentious, and he reveled in the public humiliation of his subordinates. He considered anyone more than two levels down in the hierarchy a total idiot, unable to understand a concept. His rhetoric was a mixture of Latin quotes to look smart, corporate speak to look strategic, and macho obscenities to fit in with the other alpha males. To give such people positions of influence, social status, and elevated income is scandalous. A former colleague, after moving to a new organization, told me that she celebrated each day she interacted with her new manager. To her it was almost like she was slowly recovering from an abusive relationship in which everything was diminished, negated, undermined.

What Failed Leadership Says about Leadership

Do the poor behaviors of the numerous leaders above show a *failure* or a *lack* of leadership? My belief is that the behaviors are, in fact, an extension of classical leadership traits. They build on what our collective psyche considers to be *leadership*. They are not a perversion of this idea of leadership, but a logical consequence of it.

Humans will do everything we can to combat uncertainty. "Everything" in this regard includes trusting people who are not very trustworthy by forcing ourselves to be a little blind. For instance, the 53 percent of white American women who voted for Trump in 2016 chose to ignore his degrading treatment of women.[24] The British who gave Boris Johnson a majority in the 2019 general elections chose to ignore the lies and manipulations of the Leave campaign and the evidence that Brexit was detrimental to the United Kingdom. In these two situations, something felt appealing to those voters, despite the lies and outrage: a semblance of certainty and guidance, which elicits authority. Particularly when times are uncertain, we want to be reassured. "Trust me and everything will be fine" feels like a compelling message even if, as Donna Ladkin notes, "they lead us to our own destruction."[25]

If leadership provides a position from which an ideology can be promoted and even enforced, some, such as Peter Block, go as far as saying that leadership *itself* is an ideology, one that reinforces our habit of dependency and creates the possibility for those in power to expand their power. This is patriarchy in action: handing over our fate to a dominant personality, often a self-assured man, who takes charge—or pretends to. This trade is highly detrimental to our individual accountability, to our sense of community, and to collective action. As we crave leaders, we diminish our capacity to build a different future. In exchange, our own responsibilities and failures become less obvious, less unsettling. "The attention on the leader gives us someone to blame and thereby declare our innocence," Block writes.[26] We reduce the stress and anxiety created by our complex world. In fact, "leadership is construed as an explanatory concept used to understand organizations as causal systems," social scientists James Meindl, Sanford Ehrlich, and Janet Dukerich wrote thirty years ago.[27] In the complex adaptive systems we live in, there is no such thing as simple causes leading directly to simple effects. Yet our brains crave such reasoning. Despite our best intentions, we are wired to "focus on 'leaders' as figural while the other background interactions (which have a much more significant impact on outcomes) are perceived as 'ground,' and thus inconsequential," Ladkin writes about the findings of Meindl and colleagues. We have developed a leadership narrative to simplify the reality and to absolve ourselves from it.[28] This narrative presents key characteristics which explain the predominant practice of leadership in organizations.

An Individual Experience

A leader is singular person. She is alone. She also displays certain character traits that distinguish her from a manager, according to classical management theory. Questioning the conservatism and inertia of organizations, management scholar Abraham Zaleznik initiated the debate in 1977 with his *Harvard Business Review* article "Managers and Leaders: Are They Different?" He argues that there are differences of motivation, belief, thought, action, and personal history between leaders and managers. For Zaleznik, it is essential leadership characteristics such as "inspiration, vision, and human passion" that drive corporate success.[29]

Are inherent personality traits *really* what distinguish managers from leaders? John Kotter shifts the debate in a 1990 *Harvard Business Review* article, "What Leaders Really Do." He describes the different *purposes* served by leaders and managers, who may not be different people because leadership and management are distinctive yet "complementary systems of action." It should be possible for the same person to manage or to lead dependent on what the circumstances require: "Management is about coping with complexity. Leadership, by contrast, is about coping with change."[30] This new definition is an important inflection point in the history of the concept. In today's leadership textbooks, John Kotter is presented as someone who "opened the door for the 'democratization' of leadership." Donna Ladkin writes in *Leadership: Contemporary Critical Perspectives* that his work "could be seen as on the vanguard of theories suggesting leading could be accomplished by anyone, rather than a select and privileged few."[31] I have been lucky to work with John Kotter since 2014, and I have appreciated the very practical implications of his research.

However, if we are inclined to distinguish between leadership and management, it is clear that the emphasis placed in the popular imagination on the leader as an *individual* is loaded with all sorts of negative consequences. In particular, this concept impacts the dynamics between those in positions of responsibility and those who report to them. The latter can find themselves put in service of the achievements and aggrandizement of the former, feeding overblown egos and narcissism. The system itself tends to encourage individuals to self-identify as leaders, conflating and confusing "a position of authority" with "a leader," dwelling on the individual in performance management assessments, divorcing them from the wider context and the roles played by other people. Leadership then becomes a badge of honor, a status, rather than something fluid, contextual, enabling, and active.

Decisiveness and Confidence

The mythologized leader seems to know, before other people, what needs to be done, acting as a result decisively and confidently. It must be that their vision of the future is clear, that they're fearless in the face of the unknown and its potential dangers. Add a healthy dose of the alpha male fantasy—all virility, competitiveness, self-possession, and dominance—and here is the ideal specimen ready to be trusted and followed.[32]

Of course, this picture is likely to be far from the one many of us will have in mind concerning a leadership ideal. Nevertheless, for some of us, it resonates deeply with our primal instincts. In his 2013 *Harvard Business Review* article "Why Do So Many Incompetent Men Become Leaders?," Thomas Chamorro-Premuzic attributes the underrepresentation of women in management to an "inability to discern between confidence and competence."[33] It is common to mistake self-assurance for competence. But the connection between the two can be antipodal: the perception, rather than the fact, of mastery building confidence. The less we know, the more we believe we know. This is a cognitive bias known as the *Dunning-Kruger effect*. Self-assurance owes a lot to socialization factors, which affect men and women differently. Despite much progress since the 1970s regarding awareness of the social construction of genders, behavioral norms remain different between men and women. Some behaviors, such as hubris, are discouraged in women but viewed positively in men, for whom it is often described in terms of strength or charisma. Overconfidence in one's ability is more prevalent among men than it is among women, social sciences studies confirm.[34] This is unfortunate, because these very behaviors are commonly mistaken for leadership potential.[35] Leaderless groups tend to choose as leaders individuals who are narcissistic and believe they know better.[36]

What this leads to is, obviously, collective failure: epitomized by the inability to listen, to enable others, to integrate diverse perspectives, or to serve.

Above the Pack

There is a perception that a leader stands above everybody else. This is baked into the language we use, where we distinguish between leaders and their *followers*. It can be found, too, in the visual metaphors we rely upon: shoals of fish, flocks of birds, groups of humans depicted following a leader who is more colorful, brighter, shinier, bigger than the rest of them. The point is hammered home: the leader is better, stronger, and wiser than average people, who should resign themselves to their own mediocrity. In this sense, the leader is seen as a hero—and that creates all kinds of problems.

As essayist and cultural historian Rebecca Solnit comments in "When the Hero Is the Problem," a 2019 article for *Literary Hub*, "Lone hero narratives push one figure into the public eye, but they push everyone else back into private life, or at least passive life."[37] This is a view shared by French filmmaker Olivier Assayas, who has said of superhero movies that they "are based on the passivity of the spectator."[38] So much corporate, political, and cultural leadership today is depicted in terms of the hero's journey. They are narratives presented for our consumption rather than our active involvement.

Jacinda Ardern has had such a narrative thrust upon her unsolicited as her efforts to address the COVID-19 pandemic have been lionized by the global media. Her efforts have not been undertaken alone, but they have been depicted as those of an exceptional individual. It is as if the countless competent civil servants, doctors, and citizens don't matter, as if one person alone should stand in the foreground, blocking the light from everybody else. Naturally, storytelling gets easier this way. It simplifies—albeit dangerously. Earlier in this chapter I even used Ardern as a foil to Donald Trump and Boris Johnson. The way we view leaders as heroes makes this easy to do. Trump and Johnson are, without a doubt, leaders who made poor decisions. But so, too, did the people who reported to them—who enabled them.

When leaders are treated as heroes, as better than the rest of us, there is a sheeplike tendency to meekly follow their lead. In the worst cases, cults can form around them, in which they can do no wrong. Either way, there is a danger that we diminish our own capabilities and judgment and that we abdicate our responsibilities in deference to the mythical leader.

Senator Elizabeth Warren, during her campaign for the 2020 U.S. Democratic nomination, attempted to demystify and upend the hero narrative. As Rachel Happe explains in a blog post, Warren advocated "a collaborative and networked leadership approach, which is focused on bringing people along with her, developing a network of leaders, and eschewing the traditional power brokers (big funders and typical political strategists)."[39] Trying to get past the hero-driven approach, which is so predominant in politics, was brave but possibly still ahead of its time; it didn't work for Warren.

Beyond politics, the lone hero narrative is everywhere in our lives. It is in the books we read, the news we hear, and the movies we watch. It is woven through our history, which often appears to be composed of the tales of a succession of "great men"—*his story* indeed. The hero's journey is so embedded in our psyche, as an essential element of our human culture, that it serves as a filter through which we make sense of the world and of our own trajectory within it. This fiction is likely to be self-serving. It is entertained by "the people in charge of too many of our stories, who are themselves often elites who believe devoutly in elites, which is what heroes and stars are often presumed to be," Solnit warns. There is something very comfortable but also very disempowering in the idea that our fate is "handed down to us from above."

The Cost of Obsolete Leadership

The hero-driven approach to leadership carries a tremendous cost for society and for individuals (just look at the daily news and its succession of horrors), and two distinct problems arise from it: disengagement and populism. In many respects, they are two sides of the same coin. They may occur in the workplace or in the community, but in either, their effects are corrosive.

Disengagement and the Crisis of Work

Over the past decade or so, the measurement of employee engagement has become a widespread practice. Encouraged by vendors and consultants, organizations have started running large employee engagement surveys and smaller "pulse" surveys in between. The intention is to measure the degree to which employees feel engaged at work. But what does this mean?

WHAT EMPLOYEE ENGAGEMENT REALLY IS

A common misunderstanding equates engagement with satisfaction or happiness at work. Engagement is something quite different in nature. Gallup defines engaged employees as people who "are highly involved in and enthusiastic about their work and workplace. They are psychological 'owners,' drive performance and innovation, and move the organization forward."[40] Motion is an important element: not only do engaged employees move the organization forward, but they are in motion themselves, growing at a fast rate, in multiple directions, possibly even extending into territories outside their own remit. These are individuals who strive for impact, not just for action.

To analyze engagement from the perspective of those being engaged (as a status or outcome), employee engagement becomes the capacity for action and innovation created in the workplace by willing employees seeking to implement change and striving for impact. To analyze it from the perspective of those doing the engaging (as a process or discipline), employee engagement becomes the collective mobilization of willing employees in pursuit of a common purpose.

The latter raises a number of ethical questions. In the face of increased automation of work, what is the value of engaging employees? Can engagement be genuine where the relationship is contractual and imbalanced, creating dependency on the part of the employee for, say, healthcare coverage? Is employee engagement a manipulation of an employee's free will? Is it right to enable the extractive capitalist and neoliberal system to perpetuate itself through the mechanism of employee engagement? Is employee engagement a good thing for employees?

I will provide at least partial responses to these questions throughout the remainder of the book. However, I strongly believe that it is important for engagement practitioners to keep these questions in mind as open and unanswered rather than as closed. We should continually question our practice, challenging the ethics of what we do.

THE DEPTHS OF EMPLOYEE ENGAGEMENT

It is not easy to capture employee engagement information through surveys, especially if questions are confusing or if surveys take place in a culture of distrust, where people fear that their responses are not anonymized. Nevertheless, employee engagement surveys do produce data that can be analyzed by function or demographic or can be compared with industry averages, thereby informing strategy development. In my own experience as an employee, no significant change has ever come of these surveys, but they can be interesting all the same.

The global picture of engagement is thought-provoking. According to Gallup's 2019 *State of the Global Workplace* report, "Worldwide, the percentage of adults who work full time for an employer and are engaged at work—they are highly involved in and enthusiastic about their work and workplace—is just 15 percent."[41]

Gallup notes that "employee engagement levels tend to be lower in industries characterized by more routinized jobs, such as manufacturing and production." Regional (and possibly cultural) differences are noteworthy. In Western Europe, only 10 percent of employees claim to be engaged at work, whereas in the United States the figure rises to 33 percent. Although the 2019 global figure stands at 15 percent, it was 11 percent a decade before that, so it could be argued that there has been some improvement. Nevertheless, it is still strikingly low. Eighty-five percent of the global workforce is either not engaged or, and worse, 18 percent of all workers are actively disengaged. The latter are described in the following terms: "Employees aren't just unhappy at work—they are resentful that their needs aren't being met and are acting out their unhappiness. Every day, these workers potentially undermine what their engaged coworkers accomplish."[42] In other words, they sabotage the work.

Employee disengagement is not simply an abstract concept or an easily ignored statistic: it reflects very real behaviors in the workplace. Corporate inertia—or "the institutional imperative," as stated in Warren Buffett's 1989 letter to shareholders—is born of it. In large organizations in particular, workers are running around in a state of apparent busyness, but everything seems to take too long or is deemed impossible to accomplish. It is a situation well known to many employees, managers, and contractors. Quality issues result from it, relating to poor customer service, unethical behaviors, waste of resources, lack of innovation, and cybersecurity, among many others.[43]

According to Gallup, "that low percentage of engaged employees is a barrier to creating high-performing cultures. It implies a stunning amount of wasted potential." When we consider the energy invested by many organizations to increase their productivity ratios, such waste is appalling.

What is it, then, that makes the disengagement figures so high? Thirty years of workplace experience have taught me that the answer lies in obsolete leadership, which creates and maintains dysfunctional work environments. Jim Hartner, writing on the Gallup blog, concurs: "Dismal Employee Engagement Is a Sign of Global Mismanagement."[44] It is a theme picked up in the 2019 *State of the Global Workplace* report:

> Why is the global proportion of employees who are engaged in their work so low? There are many potential reasons—but resistance to change is a common underlying theme... In particular, organizations and institutions have often been slow to adapt to the rapid changes

produced by the spread of information technology, the globalization of markets for products and labor, the rise of the gig economy, and younger workers' unique expectations. Business and political leaders must recognize when traditional patterns in management practices, education or gender roles, for example, become roadblocks to workers' motivation and productivity, and when selectively disrupting tradition will help clear a path to greater prosperity and transformed company cultures.[45]

THE COST OF THE WORKPLACE CRISIS

No wonder untapped human capital is considered "the next great global resource."[46] The workplace crisis is incredibly costly to organizations. Lower sales, lower customer satisfaction metrics, lower productivity, lower profitability, lower quality, higher absenteeism, more safety incidents, and more shrinkage as a result of unsalable inventory are just some of the outcomes. The economic consequences of disengagement are estimated to be $7 trillion in lost productivity, according to Gallup. An actively disengaged employee costs their organization $3,400 for every $10,000 of salary.[47] According to Vitality's Britain's Healthiest Workplace study, ill health was tied to thirty-eight days per employee in lost productivity throughout 2019. Supported by RAND Europe, the University of Cambridge, and Mercer Marsh Benefits, the study estimates that these factors cost UK employers £91.9 billion per annum, almost 75 percent of which could be attributed to poor mental health and unhealthy lifestyles.[48]

The World Health Organization (WHO) calculates the cost of depression and anxiety to the global economy at $1 trillion a year in lost productivity.[49] Burnout, a syndrome understood to be a consequence of "chronic workplace stress that has not been successfully managed," was included by the WHO in the eleventh revision of the *International Classification of Diseases* as an occupational phenomenon: "It is characterized by three dimensions: feelings of energy depletion or exhaustion; increased mental distance from one's job, or feelings of negativism or cynicism related to one's job; and reduced professional efficacy."[50]

A former colleague whom I interviewed about this phenomenon observed that someone burning out had become a daily occurrence. In fact, it has become so common that at least a dozen people in my circle of personal and professional friends have suffered from the syndrome. Some of them have had to stay away from the workplace for up to two years; others have never returned.

Unfortunately, burnout is on the rise among younger workers too. Of 7,500 full-time employees surveyed by Gallup in 2018, 28 percent of Millennials claimed feeling frequent or constant burnout at work, compared with 21 percent among older generations. "Today's typical workplace is chronically grueling, especially for the millennial generation," the study summarizes.[51]

But burnout is just the tip of the iceberg.

In December 2019, after a highly publicized three-month trial, three former France Télécom executives and their employer (now known as Orange) were found guilty of "institutional moral harassment." This happened ten years after a wave of employee suicides, during which thirty-five people took their lives in a two-year period. Former chairman and CEO Didier Lombard, former head of operations Louis-Pierre Wenès, and former head of HR Olivier Barberot were all fined and given custodial sentences for having implemented an extreme policy of workforce downsizing between 2007 and 2008.[52]

With this ruling, the Paris Criminal Court brought into the jurisprudence the notion of institutional and systemic moral harassment, reflecting the impact of a company strategy "aimed at destabilizing employees, creating an anxiety-provoking climate, and having as its object and effect a deterioration in working conditions."[53] In addition to the intentional unsettling of employees and its tragic consequences, what shocked people was the cynicism and lack of empathy shown by the executives. Lombard even went so far as to dismiss the death of his colleagues as "a suicide fad."

Jeffrey Pfeffer's 2018 book *Dying for a Paycheck* studies the impact of organizational culture and workplace ideology on individual and organizational health. Pfeffer, Joel Goh, and Stefanos Zenios surveyed a broad range of employee health and wellness studies. From these, they identified ten workplace experiences, such as being laid off, having irregular work shifts, and worrying about health insurance, that contribute to 120,000 excess deaths in the United States every year.[54]

More than being an economic burden, the workplace crisis is actually killing people.

Populism and the Crisis of Democracy

The impact of obsolete leadership goes far beyond the workplace. It is felt in public life and in our social interactions; it attacks the very foundations of our democracy. Populism is a natural consequence of this leadership. It gives its proponents a kind of power against complexity and its constraints, which creates an illusory form of action.

DEMOCRACIES UNDER ATTACK

"Global democracy has another bad year," proclaimed *The Economist* in January 2020.[55] The Economist Intelligence Unit's annual Democracy Index, rating the state of democracy across 167 countries, recorded its lowest score (5.44 out of 10) since the index was first published in 2006. "Just 22 countries, home to 430 million people, were deemed 'full democracies' by the EIU. More than a third of the world's population, meanwhile, still live under authoritarian rule."[56]

Even in those countries where democracy remains strong, there are still concerns about the effectiveness of representation. How well do elected officials, senators, and parliamentarians represent the views and concerns of the people who vote for them? How much do they compromise once they are in office? To what extent can they be trusted? It is this disaffection that keeps people at home on Election Day (around 40 percent of those eligible chose not to vote in the 2016 U.S. election).[57] It is this disillusionment that prompts them to challenge—sometimes very shortly after electing them—those who fail to meet expectations or who fall short of their promises.

In a 2017 *Vox* article, Aziz Huq and Tom Ginsburg observed that while it used to be accepted that once a reasonably wealthy country implemented democratic rule it would not turn away from it again, this is no longer the case. Their argument is illustrated by the fact that during the era since the end of the Second World War, "one out of eight countries experienced measurable decay in the quality of their democratic institutions."[58] The global trend for democracies does not look positive.

The path from democracy to authoritarianism is described by Steven Levitsky and Daniel Ziblatt in their 2018 book *How Democracies Die*: a weakening of critical institutions, such as the judiciary and the press, while long-standing political norms gradually erode.[59] There is historical evidence of this pattern being followed by countries and territories as diverse as Peru, Egypt, the Philippines, Poland, Georgia, Sri Lanka, Ukraine, and, more recently, Hong Kong. The United States under the Trump administration seemed to be following suit: witness the federal government's response to civil unrest across the country in 2020, with the deployment of paramilitary federal agents in Portland, Oregon; the suggestion that the presidential election was rigged via mail fraud; and the disgraceful act of abdication of responsibility from the President himself (and the majority of the Republican Party leadership) during—and since—the January 6, 2021 Capitol riot.

Typically, during a process of democratic erosion, leaders target the "referees" of the state, including the judiciary, law enforcement agencies, taxation bodies, media regulators, and electoral monitoring institutions. They seek to ensure the loyalty of such institutions.[60] They target government opponents, in an attempt to weaken them and to discourage criticism. They also endeavor to entrench their political dominance, shifting the rules of governance by making changes to legislation, constitutions, and electoral systems, as well as through executive aggrandizement.

"Democratic backsliding," or de-democratization, is particularly vexing under its contemporary forms because it is "legitimated by the very institutions democracy promoters prioritize," Nancy Bermeo writes in *Journal of Democracy*.[61] Viktor Orbán in Hungary, Recep Tayyip Erdoğan in Turkey, Vladimir Putin in Russia, and many others have been democratically elected, confirmed in their authoritarian drift by voters. Ballot stuffing, the poisoning of opponents, and control of the media have helped ensure a lasting grip on power. The late Hugo Chávez of Venezuela was elected to the presidency on four occasions. Charismatic, corrupt, and a megalomaniac, he led what used to be the richest country in Latin America into chaos and ruin.

Sometimes, it doesn't even take autocrats to undermine democracy. Any society is informed by tensions and fears, prejudices and stereotypes, divergent opinions and interests. Social, economic, and moral crises can distort and destabilize. Groups form by seeking out scapegoats and spreading fear of the other—people who don't look or vote like them, who don't share the same faith or class as them. The Camp des Milles Foundation, located on the site of a French internment and deportation camp now open to the public, has developed an "analysis and alert" index to measure the erosion of republican and democratic values in France. The AARD index blends eight indicators: youth unemployment, beneficiaries of the minimum solidarity income, intolerance, right- and left-wing extremist votes, racist acts, personal attacks, crimes and offenses, identity, and security issues in parliamentary debates.[62] According to Alain Chouraqui, the Foundation's president, "The 2019 version of the AARD index reaches a level where the risk to democracy is more than four times higher than it was in 1990."[63]

New dimensions of conflict have emerged over the last few years concerning immigration, globalization, and civil rights. They have replaced the traditional divisions between the left and the right and between the classes regarding redistribution of wealth. In their 2019 article for CEPR (Centre for Economic Policy Research), "Identity, Beliefs, and Political Conflict," Nicola Gennaioli and Guido Tabellini studied how people affected by globalization became increasingly nationalist, prejudiced, and socially conservative, often voting against their own economic interests. The authors found that trade and technology shocks can cause the redefinition of social identity. Because of what happens to us, we identify with a certain group, pushing our beliefs toward stereotypes. This belief distortion increases polarization along new dimensions, while reducing it along others. Within this new space, the energy that builds around anger and resentment is exploited by political leaders and the media, further accelerating the polarization.[64]

In these conditions, the most vindictive invoke hatred and violence, taking advantage of the passivity of the majority. As the Camp des Milles Foundation describes it, there is a slippery path from racism to genocide. First, the rhetoric of the militants and racists becomes normalized, then this active minority takes power, either by force or through elections, gradually shifting from democracy to authoritarianism. Liberties are restricted, while racism, anti-Semitism, xenophobia, and violence are used as instruments of the state. Wider persecutions then follow, where anyone who does not conform can be viewed as an enemy of the state.[65]

Democracy is under attack, and populism is its main assailant.

THE POPULIST PANDEMIC

Populism, according to the political theorist Chantal Mouffe, "consists in opposing a 'pure people' to a 'corrupt elite' and conceiving of politics as an immediate expression of the 'general will' of the people."[66]

It is what the philosopher Peter Sloterdijk describes as an "aggressive form of simplification" in the face of a complex situation.[67] It offers a worldview that, for those who do not subscribe to it, can appear to be completely divorced from reality.

In France, there has been an inexorable rise over several decades of far-right populism among disfranchised workers, those with little education, and the young. The far-right Le Pen family progressed to the second round of the presidential elections in both 2002 (Jean-Marie) and 2017 (Marine) and may do so again in the future. The same forces have been at play in several other European countries, bringing far-right movements to power in Austria, Italy, Hungary, and Poland, as well as enabling populist right-leaning governments like those in the UK, Sweden, and Turkey. Far-left populism is also gaining support, securing 20 percent of first-round votes in the 2017 French presidential election. The extremes of the political spectrum are pulling people away from the middle ground in our modern age of uncertainty, the rhetoric and convictions (however unfounded they may prove to be) of their leaders serving as a magnetic draw.

Anti-populists breathed a sigh of relief in France when Emmanuel Macron was elected President. Blurring traditional electoral divides, Macron defeated his far-right opponent with 66.1 percent of the vote, albeit with record-low turnout. Young, brilliant, and favoring globalization, it was believed that here was a leader who would build on a diverse electoral base and enable the much-needed modernization of the country. But it didn't quite work out this way. Macron's exercise of power has been very traditional: top-down and driven by technocratic experts. Right-wing and left-wing populists soon coalesced into the Yellow Vest movement, which lasted several months and made some gains before the coronavirus pandemic diverted public attention.

To combat populism, rationality and shaming appear inefficient. Populist leaders lie over and over again. By early 2021, according to the *Washington Post*, President Trump had racked up an incredible 30,573 false or misleading statements while in office.[68] Yet he and others like him get away with it time and again. In her 2019 book *Populocracy*, political scientist Catherine Fieschi writes that lying serves several functions for politicians: it signals their ambitions and desires, defies the elites, and demonstrates "someone who is willing to take chances in order to get elected." Lying is also a demonstration of a leader's humanity and flaws, which makes that leader more "authentic" than those who are polished. What is conceived as authenticity serves an important social function: it helps us recognize others and validate knowledge. In this sense, *authentic* suggests an immediate, unspoken, mutual recognition of people as belonging to the same group because of their similar behaviors, aspirations, and references[69]—all things made more difficult with multiculturalism, because people lack common backgrounds.

Populism is a symptom of all the dysfunctions affecting contemporary society.[70] Right now, it is reshaping the way we conceive of and do twenty-first-century politics. Unless we tackle its root causes and address its legitimate challenges seriously, populism will be here to stay.

CLAIMING A VOICE

As our societies become more complex, the number of experts required to make them work keeps growing. But the reign of expertise is at odds with the logic of democracy. In theory, we all have an equal voice when the collective interest is at stake. Yet in practice, experts are removing people's free choice in relation to an increasing number of decisions that are considered too complex to be subject to democratic debate.

The problem is for some that when they feel their voice is not heard and doesn't matter, they lose interest in democracy. Some even favor a direct connection to a seeming "strong man" who, by brute strength and magical thinking, will solve their problems. Men like Trump and Bolsonaro grab the mike and make themselves heard. Populism, according to Fieschi, "is about triumphing over shame—by *speaking*. Conquering the perceived humiliation inflicted by the elite by being, literally, shameless." Speaking about cancel culture and online group shaming by mostly left-wing activists, historian Laure Murat explains that, while it is excessive in its takedown of people and ideas, "it is an expression of anger by a marginalized population with no voice other than the internet."[71]

What happens here is a clash between our democratic aspirations as a society and the reality of a locked power in thrall to expertise, interest groups, patriarchy, wealth, and the media. The clash is more visible in society than it is in the workplace, but it is happening there just as much, manifesting itself differently. Instead of populism and rage, there is burnout and disengagement. Voices remain unheard. In the workplace, which is rarely democratic, speaking up and speaking out are often close to impossible.

Can we have a voice in the corporate world? Corporate rules, workplace culture, and basic social norms restrain dissent for the sake of our collective efficiency.[72] Yet in recent years, to preempt the threat of disruption, organizations have introduced notions like "challenging the status quo," "acting for change," and rethinking performance evaluation systems. In reality, though, how well is challenging norms tolerated? With manager-driven evaluations serving as filters, corporate cultures usually reward sameness. How, then, can changemakers progress rapidly through the ranks of an organization? How much space for impact does the organization provide them with? From what I have experienced, the answer is not much. Raising your voice comes with risk, makes you an outsider, and slows down your career. Most workers understand this all too well and, as a result, keep their heads down and stay quiet. The prevailing image of organizations is an industrial one of well-oiled machines, where friction and risks must be reduced to a minimum. Unfettered, people's voices can interfere with a machine's orderly function.

It is not absurd to think that the populist sentiment we experience today has risen, at least in part, as a reaction against the workplace experience.

ON MY COMPUTER are two pictures I hold dear.

The first shows five female colleagues, smiling at the camera, having a great time at a farewell party—talented professionals, good friends, strong women, and amazing change agents in the enterprise. These women are the driving forces behind a diversity movement, an innovation movement, and a sustainable development movement. They are positive movers and shakers, the kind of talent any organization dreams of having more of.

Several years later, one of these women is on a long-term sick leave, hospitalized for eighteen months, and has sued the company for harassment. A second has suffered mental health issues, been on sick leave, and returned to the company a very different person: quiet and medicated. A third left the company simply because continuing no longer made sense to her. A fourth joined a sister organization, which was then divested; she struggled to find a way to remain in employment. A fifth was told she could not remain in the company and left to pursue an entrepreneurial project.

The second picture shows a tiny frog suspended in the claws of a huge crocodile—a perfect visual representation of risk and of the imbalance of power.

Those women were like five little frogs at the mercy of the system's powerful jaws. Some were bitten; some jumped away.

Leadership is broken. But it doesn't have to be that way. We can transform leadership through three core values: those of Liberty, Equality, and Fraternity.

PART II

Liberty

In 2019, I helped a major European airline deploy a new technology across its whole sales force. Rather than prescribing the use of the technology to the sales force and rolling it out with classical methods of adoption, I convinced the airline to opt for co-creation. We then invited employees of all ranks and nationalities to apply to join a volunteer group that would be given the task of leading the change. From the numerous applications, a group of thirty people was established. They were equipped with digital tools, and I supported them and their leaders as they started to develop and implement ideas on how to transform their ecosystem for the better thanks to the new technology. This volunteer engagement brought the sales force much beyond what they were used to doing in their regular day-to-day. It expanded *what* they did, and it expanded *how* they did it. Not one of them had been involved in digital transformation before, and they now found themselves working in a self-managed way, across hierarchical and functional lines, without the explicit or implicit regulations that normally framed their work. They had become change activists.

Six months into the project, we ran a pit-stop session to reflect on our progress and learning. "What stood out for you?" I asked. One of the volunteers stepped forward. "At first, we didn't know what to do with this freedom. Then, we realized we could use it to be more creative."

Liberty, an unprecedented experience in the workplace, initially had felt unsettling. But then it unleashed their creative potential. They surprised themselves with their imagination, resourcefulness, and audacity. Through the experience, people not only expanded their skill set but also enriched their perception of their work, of their interactions within the hierarchical system, and of their own ability to impact change. This new liberty made them exercise and develop personal and collective agency. For them, and for the organization, increased agency is a new asset that they've been able to carry forward beyond our project, creating more value along the way.

This is *engagement leadership*, and, unlike traditional modes of leadership, it seeks to enable more liberty at work. Liberty, in the sense of "free will," is a necessary condition of engagement. Liberty creates the conditions in which innovation, collaboration, and accountability flourish. Given the individual and collective changes we have experienced as a society, liberty is more effective and generates much more value than constraint.

But what is liberty in the context of work? It is hard to imagine a workplace without any constraint. So how does liberty manifest itself in the workplace? What follows is an examination of different aspects of the concept that characterizes liberty at work, and a reflection on how liberty starts within each individual. To create systems that make more space for freedom, we first have to self-emancipate. From there, collective liberty becomes a real possibility.

3

Can There Be Liberty at Work?

"LIBERTY IS THE power that we have over ourselves." So asserted the Dutch jurist Hugo Grotius at the turn of the seventeenth century. A more intricate reading of this would be to define liberty as the ability to exercise conscious choice, unlimited by necessity or by oppressive control or restraint.

Given that work establishes perimeters and defines modes of action which limit the liberty of the parties involved, it is generally understood that an individual cannot be as "free" at work as in their social life. However, liberty is at the very heart of the concept of work.

Occupational psychodynamics researchers Christophe Dejours and Pascale Molinier analyzed the relationship between prescription (objectives and means imposed on workers) and initiative (what depends on workers' judgment and choice).[1] They found that even in extremely prescribed, timed, and constrained work situations, there remained within the execution of the work an aspect that could not be designed in advance or prescribed in full. This is the irreducible human dimension of work, the space for liberty, negotiated among colleagues and resulting in work practices. It takes on the real world, which comes with all sorts of unexpected hurdles, glitches, bugs that must be overcome. The effort required is what transforms a task into an activity. It produces external change, but it also changes the worker from the inside, establishing ownership and modifying the person's relation to their work and to themselves.

According to Dejours and Molinier, "Work is the coordinated activity of men and women to cope with that which, in a task, cannot be achieved by the strict execution of the prescribed organization." Work mobilizes an intelligence that is "always subversive."[2] It happens in three spaces simultaneously, each with their own regulations, such that they therefore generate contradictions: the subjective, the social, and the objective. Work is a subjective mobilization experience, coordinated with that of others, in order to address the objective. If the experience is successful, work can become the source of individual and collective emancipation. If not, it can create alienation.

Before we delve any deeper, let's keep in mind that liberty at work is an idea that is understood differently from one culture to another. "I feel free at work" doesn't convey the same meaning on either side of the Atlantic, or even on either side of the Rhine. Anthropologist Philippe d'Iribarne sees subtle differences as he develops the debate about the compatibility of salaried work with citizenship, about whether a person can submit to a boss *and* simultaneously remain the free citizen of a democratic society. Anglo-American free workers are those who "have the ability to decide sovereignly on their own affairs." German culture, by contrast, favors community participation, where "to be free is to have a voice in the decisions made by the community." In France, a free worker is "not forced to stoop before anyone."[3] They are treated with all the respect due to the nobility of their trade. This may explain why we French pay so much attention to rank and status at work.

Culturally relative, the idea of liberty also differs from one individual to another. It may feel aspirational to some but like a burden to others—and this should be respected. Sociologist Frédéric Petitbon makes this useful reminder: "To consider that all employees seek responsibility and autonomy is a projection of the way of thinking of corporate executives, who themselves are very much a part of this culture."[4] Let's make sure we do not inflict violence on others by projecting our own sense of what's good or bad on the workplace.

There are varying degrees of liberty that are possible at work. One can feel totally constrained, very free, or anywhere in between. But what does "feeling free" really mean? I would like to offer my own definition of liberty at work, which is born of personal experience of workplace constraints and emancipation:

Liberty at work is the unconditional possibility given to workers to hold and express independent judgment on the matters of their organization, to avoid managerial arbitrariness, and to direct their work so that it not only produces value but contributes to their dignity as human beings.

Danger and Dissatisfaction in the Culture of Silence

The first, and most essential, liberty at work is that your employment (assuming it does not relate to military conflict) should not endanger your own or other human life. Indeed, by contrast with the threats to physical integrity that some employees experience, free speech can be seen as something of a first-world problem. Nevertheless, permitting workers to speak up about safety issues might have prevented over 250 of them from perishing in the fire that blazed at the Ali Enterprises textile factory in Pakistan in 2012.[5] Letting workers speak up about management policies might have prevented the thirty-five suicides at France Télécom.[6] It might help reduce worker fatalities, of which there were more than 2.3 million every year according to 2017 figures produced by the International Labour Organization, with more than one hundred per week in the United States alone.[7] These numbers are likely to have increased since 2020 in light of the coronavirus pandemic and the wider health effects of lockdowns.

A second fundamental condition for liberty at work is that it should be non-enslaving. How can we expect freedom of thought or speech when people feel alienated by their work conditions? Non-livable wages that leave workers unable to meet their basic needs and force them to rely on food banks are still common and legal in many places in the world, even in supposedly developed nations. In 2020, the U.S. media reported that "many restaurant employees continue to end up hungry due to a two-tiered wage system that allows tipped workers to be paid as little as $2.13 an hour."[8]

Laborers and domestic workers are so dependent on a single day's work that they stay in place when everyone else flees, such as when massive wildfires raged through California in 2019.[9] A review on Glassdoor about a job in the hospitality industry in the U.S. involving long hours and the expectation to achieve perfection states that "the wages wouldn't even cover daily parking." Ken Loach's 2019 film *Sorry We Missed You* exposes the harsh reality in the UK of zero-hours labor (contracts that keep employees tied to businesses but that guarantee zero work hours), which has been described as a modern form of slavery.[10] These contracts provide businesses with flexibility to the detriment of workers, offering low wages in addition to stressful uncertainty. In the gig economy, instead of freedom, the poorest are sold a lie that they somehow have choice. They are given the opportunity *in principle* to work when and for as long as they wish; but those workers soon realize that they must work at high cadences, according to plans established by an almighty algorithm, if they want to earn anything, all while providing the working tools themselves. Customers relish abundant choice, but workers—especially those who are undereducated or who did their schooling in a country different from the one they are seeking employment in—have little opportunity to enjoy it in the fulfillment of their own jobs.

In the United States, many people depend on expensive healthcare insurance paid for by their employer. This locks them into jobs that they may loathe, and it inhibits their ability to speak up for fear of losing not only their income but their health coverage. As with the welfare models adopted by other nations, there have been attempts to provide access to healthcare independent of employers in the U.S., most recently under the Obama administration. However, such initiatives have not fundamentally changed the dominant pattern where part of the glue that binds employee to employer is healthcare coverage. Is it possible that the mass unemployment that has resulted from the economic impact of the coronavirus pandemic will force wide change? Only the future will tell. For now, though, those who still have a job have every reason to keep quiet, even when unhappy about their workplace.

A likely result of employee silence is that employers mistake the absence of voices for unanimous agreement and high trust in management. Of course, discussion can impede action and trigger division. A job that is completed without debate is a job done faster (but not necessarily a job of higher quality or effectiveness). For managers who value efficiency, there tends to be a preference to cut down on the time for explanation, for exploring the whys and wherefores of each decision together. Managers value their own silence as much as that of their employees, opting to keep some matters confidential rather than sharing them. The workforce, then, is not only silent but is operating in the dark, without necessary information and context.

The fact is that when workers are discouraged from thinking differently from their employer, their manager, or their colleagues, when they are prevented from voicing new ideas and concerns or challenging decisions, tragedies happen.

The history of business is rich with disasters owing to the restriction of liberty at work. Dieselgate, the emissions fraud that was first uncovered at Volkswagen, caused thousands of deaths, health issues, and environmental damage. It cost the German car manufacturer billions of dollars, the loss of market share and reputation. How many employees knew about the misleading software designed to cheat on emissions tests? Possibly more than the handful of executives indicted. No one spoke out before the scandal erupted. In another example from the transport sector, a U.S. congressional committee found that the two fatal crashes in October 2018 and March 2019 of Boeing 737 Max aircraft that together claimed 346 lives occurred in part because of a "culture of concealment."[11] The few employees who tried to raise the alarm about safety and quality were ignored or punished. Concealment was perceived as necessary in order for these companies to speed up operations, catch up with the competition, and maximize profits.

These are very extreme examples of what silent cultures can lead to. More often, organizations suffer from less dramatic yet still very consequential issues. When employees fear or are apathetic about speaking up about concerns, quality problems arise. When it feels unsafe to share half-formed ideas, innovation stalls. When issues affecting the workforce are not discussed and solved, talent leaves. Sometimes senior executives are oblivious to the relationship between these problems and the organizational culture, to which their very own behaviors contribute.

Two former colleagues of mine once found a solution to a production issue that had been long troubling our employer. When they presented their idea to the head of manufacturing, he chewed them out, insisting they should have found a solution *earlier*. Instead of congratulating them on a job well done, the employees were scolded for not doing better, faster. It's likely a safe bet that the next time those two have an idea, they won't go to their boss. They have learned that it is safer to keep things to themselves and remain quiet.

It is often the case that leaders do not have access to all the information they require to make sound decisions, mitigate risks, and avert failures. Problematic information rarely makes its way to the top, because it is politically unsafe to convey it. This may contribute to the perception gap: studies repeatedly show that employees' and leaders' perceptions of their organizations differ, with management having a much rosier view of corporate culture.[12] Engagement surveys, diversity surveys, quality culture surveys, communication surveys—all the opinion audits that I can recall from my corporate life—demonstrated a disconnect between what was perceived at the top and what was perceived deeper inside the organization.

Leaders are often isolated at the top and unaware of the extent of the disconnect, despite efforts they may make at communication or ritualized employee engagement through open-door policies and monthly breakfasts. Their entourage generally does a great job at shielding them from reality by restricting access to people and filtering information. Megan Reitz and John Higgins of Hult Ashridge, in their research paper *Being Silenced and Silencing Others*, say that people notice when they are being silenced but often they don't notice when and how they themselves silence others.[13] Power differences, social norms, and cultural norms all contribute to a culture of silence.

However, for workers stuck in these toxic environments, staying silent is seen as a means of keeping their job. Voicing dissent, unfortunately, can be very risky, despite various attempts to protect whistleblowers. Colin Kaepernick, the football quarterback who knelt in 2016 during the national anthem in protest against police brutality and racial inequality in the United States, has been unable for years to secure a new contract with an NFL team since terminating his contract with the San Francisco 49ers early in 2017. Elsewhere, in 2017, interim truck driver Karim Ben Ali recorded videos of the industrial acid he was asked to dispose of in the countryside by his employer. For years he was been unable to find work, feeling so isolated that he has attempted suicide.[14] Li Wenliang, one of the first Chinese doctors to sound the alarm about the coronavirus outbreak in December 2019, was reprimanded by the authorities and exonerated only after he died of the disease a few weeks later.[15] Gaming company Ubisoft was in the headlines during 2020 for toxic culture problems that spanned more than a decade; employees who dared to complain of abuse to HR were dismissed, silenced, or blamed.[16] Who isn't afraid of blowing the whistle?

Work produces normative controls that shape identities and regulate behaviors. Cozy compromise is one such control; why antagonize colleagues or bosses when culture values consensus—consensus-building being another control? Bureaucratic consensus discussions water down innovation and favor agreement among all parties over speed and boldness. Even workspaces act as a control. The modern open-plan office creates a loss of acoustic, visual, and physical privacy, which takes a toll on worker morale. And yet another aspect of regulation is to channel speech, to reserve the right to speak to a limited number of people in the organization. Speaking up, as understood by many employees, is the prerogative of a small number of people who sit above them in the organizational hierarchy. Upper management may speak freely, while those below can only grumble by the water cooler or via its digital equivalent, the instant message. A large proportion of my professional experience has been in organizational cultures that discourage employees from holding independent opinions and expressing them. Distrust and control reign in these organizations. That is unfortunate, because it has been detrimental to engagement, to quality, and to innovation.

In *Humanocracy*, Gary Hamel and Michele Zanini report that only 20 percent of employees believe that their opinions matter at work, while only 10 percent feel free to experiment with new solutions. As they observe, this is "a waste of human capability."[17] Only one in eleven of the people surveyed claimed they could influence important decisions. Within their field of work, and by extension beyond it too, people are seldom asked for opinions and ideas. In fact, they are often actively discouraged from voicing any by managers, who identify strongly with and seek to maintain the status quo. Assigning workers to discrete tasks under hierarchical supervision in the hope that they will just do their job, and do it well, is an illusion. According to Gwynn Guilford, the long decline of General Motors can be attributed to such an approach and "its quest to turn people into machines."[18]

In fairness to managers, however, they are placed in "impossible situations" by their organizations. In "Why Managers Do Not Seek

Voice from Employees," a 2019 paper published by *Organization Science*, Elad Sherf, Subrahmaniam Tangirala, and Vijaya Venkataramani note that managers are caught between a lack of empowerment, which makes unwanted input from below burdensome, and a focus on short-term issues, which prevents any of the systemic changes that might be called out.[19]

The culture of silence prevails in relation to the external world too. Risk avoidance reigns supreme. Tight controls are put in place regarding who from an organization can speak about what, and are enforced through all sorts of procedures, prohibitions, authorization forms, and punishments. The result is a small army of professional communicators and media-trained executives who deliver all the communications on behalf of an organization, while everyone else is kept invisible and muted. In these conditions, there is rarely any original and authentic communication that would connect with people outside the organization. This is one of the reasons that the pharmaceutical industry has struggled to resolve its image problem for so many years.

Many in the corporate communications field tout ambassador programs to enable employees to communicate with the broader public. However, these programs still have control at their core; they instruct, prevent, and censor rather than liberate. That's why they seldom achieve their goals. A company that is serious about free speech and empowerment would be well advised to provide training to those employees who are willing to speak at public events. Fostering personal communication skills and supporting employees by engaging them with speakers' bureaus would instill confidence and allow them to speak with a passion about what they do. But organizational culture always seems to get in the way, with standardization and communication control valued above free speech and empowerment. Restrictions limit spontaneity and render the communication artificial. Above all, workers resent being instrumentalized. They'd rather stay silent.

Immunity from Managerial Arbitrariness

It is a severe restriction to your liberty if your fate depends on the judgment of another person.

I have worked at several organizations that have performance management processes. Generally, I found that I was evaluated more favorably by managers with whom I got along well than by those with whom the personal chemistry wasn't as good. Was my performance enhanced by good relationships? Maybe. Were relationships enhanced by a favorable evaluation? Perhaps. Another possibility, rarely acknowledged, is that the seemingly sacrosanct performance review process is purely a cultural artifact. It is a subjective, interpersonal encounter dressed up to appear rational, solid, and replicable. This is part of what business consultant Lee Bryant refers to as the "performative theater" of the workplace, which is full of such rituals, shaping behaviors and interactions in prescribed ways. Evaluation originally was intended to uphold the sacred managerial virtues of meritocracy, efficiency, and objectivity but, in effect, has become nothing more than a caricature of them. French philosopher Angélique del Rey criticizes "evaluation rationalism" as a tyranny of the visible and the explicit. Evaluation is part of a normative system of power in which everyone is led to identify with their evaluations as a "new voluntary servitude."[20]

It wouldn't matter so much if it didn't have such tangible consequences for people's lives. Career advancement, opportunities, current and future revenues (through compensation and pensions), reputation, morale, engagement, and hopes are being shaped by managers' evaluations. All resulting from a process that is rarely reciprocal, is difficult to dispute, and is highly dependent on both context and human subjectivity. The fact is that goals, metrics, key performance indicators, self-assessment, peer assessment, and development discussions do not account for the deeply relational and circumstantial nature of work. Objectivization is an illusion. Work cannot be compartmentalized. People do not fit neatly into the four- or nine-box matrixes favored by business consultants.

In *Out of the Crisis*, his book on quality, productivity, and competition, W. Edwards Deming called for the "abolishment of the annual or merit rating and of management by objective."[21] Deming argued that performance evaluation was among the "barriers that rob people in management of their right to pride of workmanship." It is counterproductive and wastes time because it focuses on individuals rather than on the system as a whole. Indeed, it is "the system that people work in and the interaction with people" that accounts for up to 95 percent of performance. Sadly, little attention has been paid by the corporate world to Deming on this topic. Professionals in production and quality have focused their attention on Deming's statistical tools rather than on his management philosophy, avoiding the profound mindset changes he proposed.[22]

I have always disliked the evaluation *experience*, but it was not until I participated in a course at the Deming Institute that I began to question the relevance of the *process* itself. What became evident is that it is completely possible to lead an organization without any individual performance evaluation. However, HR consultants and the performance management industry have been so skilled at selling the effectiveness of this approach that it has now become normalized. All the same, numerous studies, books, and articles have highlighted its inefficiencies over the last decade or so, triggering marginal improvements in the process, involving more interaction between people and the use of digital apps, as well as less emphasis on an annual salary negotiation. Ironically, General Electric, the company that in the 1980s played a prominent role in implementing toxic performance evaluation practices such as forced ranking, is now leading the way with new initiatives such as performance apps and talent marketplace platforms.[23] Regardless, the concept of performance evaluation remains arbitrary and flawed— founded on the logic that it is the right of one person to evaluate another, and subject to an array of cognitive biases.

Twenty years ago, Harvard University's Project Implicit provided startling evidence of our ingrained biases.[24] A wealth of subsequent studies have confirmed these findings, establishing the impossibility of providing truly objective judgment about another person's performance or potential. In the West, the effects of subjective opinion have contributed significantly to a culture in which good-looking, tall white men are clearly favored over other people. According to the findings of economist Daniel Hamermesh in *Beauty Pays*, there is a lifetime earnings gap of $250,000 between the best-looking third of the population and the least attractive.[25] In *The Tall Book*, Arianne Cohen reports that every inch of above-average height equates to an additional $789 in annual salary.[26] In the United States, only 14.5 percent of men are over 6 feet (1 meter 83 centimeters) tall, yet 60 percent of Fortune 500 company CEOs are. Even today, despite years of corporate-sponsored bias-awareness training, there remains clear evidence of gender and racial bias, with some people offered better opportunities than others on the basis of their name alone.[27] Given all this evidence, it seems ridiculous to expect a manager to be able to provide unbiased feedback to those reporting to them and inform them how they can improve.

Feedback tells us far more about the person who *gives* it than about the person who *receives* it. Each of us has a different understanding of what notions like "leadership" or "customer orientation" mean. This is shaped by our beliefs, our life experiences, what we value, and what we find distasteful. Because of this "idiosyncratic rater effect," feedback is not truth but *distortion*, which gets amplified the greater the number of people who provide feedback to the individual.[28] As Marcus Buckingham and Ashley Goodall explain in their 2019 *Harvard Business Review* article "The Feedback Fallacy," the only outcome of rating people is "bad data."[29]

When professionals believe, usually in good faith, that they have the capacity to make an objective judgment about and direct other people's actions, we find that liberty at work is severely eroded. But what happens when human evaluation is replaced by algorithms? The situation can be even worse. Your fate could be decided by an algorithm.

A former colleague of mine, one who had worked in communications for twenty years, was informed that she had been refused a higher-level position because her background was in psychology. If a human is so narrow-minded that they fail to see the relationship between psychology and communication, let alone the benefit of two decades of practical experience, what can we expect when these biases are then encoded into our algorithms? I am convinced that were I to apply for a job via one of the automated hiring systems that are commonly used today, I would never be selected. My professional path has been too circuitous and diverse to conform to programmatic expectations. Communication, business operations, people engagement? FM radio management in China, vaccine marketing in France, quality innovation in the U.S.? My profile rarely matches up with a job description and stands little chance of surviving automated processing.

It is claimed that current artificial intelligence can perform an in-depth analysis of an applicant's personality, values, cultural preferences, and skills based on their covering letter and résumé, drawing on standardized character profiling. But that makes little allowance for nonstandard, abnormal, and exceptional profiles to make it past the electronic gatekeepers. How many missed opportunities have there been because a candidate full of potential has not been able to interact with another human? In times of increased connection, hybridization, and relentless change, it is precisely those people who do not conform to the cookie-cutter profiles who are more necessary than ever to organizations that need to create, innovate, and evolve.

Algorithmic management first emerged in platform-based organizations but has now been adopted more widely. It is a system of control where decisions affecting workforces are delegated to self-learning algorithms. It relies on data collection and the surveillance of workers, limiting human oversight of the labor process. Algorithms are now inescapable in our professional lives. They schedule our tasks, measure our productivity, track our work, evaluate, reward and penalize us, recommend the termination of our contracts, and share our LinkedIn profiles with recruiters. Employee monitoring software, sometimes installed without our knowledge, can track our time use, keystrokes, location, apps used, and words typed, all while recording screenshots or even continuous video. Algorithms have become instrumental to corporate surveillance, further undermining trust between workers and management. With remote working on the rise in the wake of the coronavirus pandemic, the adoption of these practices is likely to escalate. It is necessary for us to challenge the assumption of neutrality in the algorithms deployed, especially when it is evident that they perpetuate and amplify rather than diminish the effects of bias.

This is a key point established by Data & Society researchers Alexandra Mateescu and Aiha Nguyen in their assessment of workers' rights issues relating to algorithmic management.[30] The authors raise three other concerns that are all additional limitations of liberty at work. First, the enhanced capability for control and oversight increases speed and efficiency pressure and reduces workers' ability to exercise free will and personal discretion. Second, power imbalances are reinforced by the opaque mathematical models on which algorithms are built. These are inaccessible to most users, who lack the deep expertise needed to understand how they work. Third, algorithms are a means to "distance companies from the effects of their business decisions," concealing managerial judgment and reducing accountability.

Long-established biases, such as gender stereotyping in hiring decisions, health diagnoses, and loan approvals, often resurface in automated or semi-automated decisions that are based on historical trends. Similarly, algorithms that draw on geographical data can reproduce social class or ethnic segregation, as happened in the examination results debacle in the UK in August 2020, where a grading algorithm was used to standardize A-level and General Certificate of Secondary Education results, disadvantaging pupils from poorer backgrounds.[31]

Even seemingly commonsense, innocuous moves like the decision to integrate customer ratings into a worker's performance review actually provide more weight to the customers' own biases. Analyses of consumer behavior on online marketplaces like Craigslist, eBay, and Airbnb have shown customers offer lower prices and respond less to those vendors perceived to be of a different ethnicity.[32] Joy Buolamwini's 2017 MIT master's thesis uncovered large racial and gender bias in AI services from companies like Microsoft, IBM, and Amazon, leading her to create the Algorithmic Justice League.[33] Learning algorithms reinforce our mistakes in systems that have a growing importance in people's work and lives. While the ongoing gender and ethnic imbalance in science, technology, engineering, and math professions does not leave much optimism for imminent remediation, at least there is growing awareness as a result of the efforts of multiple activists.

WORK IS A human reality and, as such, takes place in an evolving tangle of affects and interrelationships between people, contexts, trajectories, and interests. There is no feedback that can stand as the absolute truth, objective and impartial, even if given by an algorithm. To be able to exercise liberty at work, we must find ways to limit managerial arbitrariness, whether exercised in person or through software. Work lives should be directed by the work itself, not by systemic bias.

Is achieving this easier in small organizations rather than large ones? As Margaret Wheatley and Myron Rogers suggest in *A Simpler Way*, growing organizations mutate from passion and into "procedures..., rules and roles... Instead of being free to create, we impose constraints that squeeze the life out of us."[34] What gets eroded in this process is a fundamental aspect of liberty: our agency.

Capacity to Direct One's Work: Human Agency at Work

In 1911, Frederick W. Taylor summed up his work on labor efficiency in *The Principles of Scientific Management*—that efficiency could be improved by breaking work down into small and repeatable tasks, removing unnecessary motions by workers, and generalizing assembly line work.[35] Three years later, Louis D. Brandeis, not yet a U.S. Supreme Court Justice, praised scientific management in his own book, *Business— A Profession*, cautioning, however, that Taylor had disregarded the issue of assent.[36] "In a democratic community men who are to be affected by a proposed change of conditions should be consulted," he wrote. "The consent and the cooperation of the worker must be secured." A hundred years later, this message still needs to be heard.

Of course, not everything in the workplace is open for discussion. Safety, for example, is nonnegotiable. Construction workers are not invited to voice their opinion on whether or not they should wear a helmet. But, interestingly, safety is much better and more widely enforced when some dialogue takes place around it—when a space for consent exists. The same applies with quality, with ethical behaviors, with just about everything in the enterprise. We have more respect for the rules we help establish. As John Kotter has observed in his book *Accelerate*, change occurs more readily, completely, and lastingly when people *want to* make the change rather than *have to* make it.[37] "People own what they help create," Myron Rogers writes in one of the six maxims on change that bear his name.[38]

As an employer, a manager, or an owner, it is tempting to avoid the necessity of consent. Making space for dialogue takes time and slows down decisions that are needed in a heartbeat. Dialogue sometimes confuses issues instead of clarifying them. Why bother with consent when you are in a purely transactional or utilitarian relationship, as is increasingly the case with a fluid workforce comprising time-bound project teams, talent-on-demand, and gig workers? Why bother when the job to be done is encapsulated in a comprehensive set of workflows and processes? According to French philosopher Pierre-Olivier Monteil, in his book *Éthique et philosophie du management* (Ethics and Philosophy of Management), norm-based management serves to avoid conflict that can potentially arise from dialogue or the sense of subordination.[39] It replaces power relations among individuals with a seemingly neutral and objective description of the tasks to be accomplished.

There tends to be an assumption that people lower down the hierarchy have less opportunity for consent than people higher up. It is true, however, that the development of quality culture and innovations like the Andon cord, which enables any worker to stop a production line when they identify an issue, have advanced shop-floor empowerment. Nevertheless, the range of autonomy remains very limited. Shift work, job descriptions, pace and output objectives, standard operating procedures, and management oversight provide a rigid frame for what people do and how they do it. Choice occurs only in the micro gaps between prescribed and actual labor under the effect of the unexpected.

By contrast, managers may appear freer, not least because they enjoy a freedom of movement. They can go to the restroom anytime they want. They have more control over their calendar, and their participation in certain discussions, meetings, and projects involves a degree of consent. Yet many of them complain that they too are without choice— sometimes with justification. The introduction of standard calendars for manufacturing managers, for example, has seen their whole workweek prescribed and shaped by a common template, hour by hour.

Why do so many knowledge workers submit to constraint? Needing the money to live and support their family is an oft repeated and valid point. But it is also an easy excuse to avoid questioning one's own willingness to expand the space for consent. In their 2016 article "(Un) Conditional surrender?," Mats Alvesson and André Spicer analyze how professionals surrender their autonomy and willingly comply with managerialism.[40] To cope with paradoxes and all forms of power imposed on them, professionals combine overcompliance (or "functional stupidity") with distancing, whereby they see work as a "game," in order to maintain a flattering sense of self.[41]

There are limits, though, to what processes or coercive management can achieve. Without the possibility of choice, under the pure pressure of compulsion people are rarely at their best. When organizations do not actively seek consent from their workers, the result is infantilization, disengagement, and deviant behaviors. Mistakes are made and innovation opportunities lost. What emerges is a *compliance* culture rather than a *quality* culture—one where, for example, operators follow a prescribed internal process *while aware* that this process has become inappropriate because of a change in external conditions. I have witnessed this myself. The internal process, not the updated customer requirement, was king.

When I think about consent in the workplace, I recall Monteil's notion of "the effective and fair search for convergence, through discussion."[42] The search for consent recognizes the freedom of the other party, who has every right to say *no*. Exposing oneself to a negative response introduces personal vulnerability into the relationship, which contrasts with the asymmetry that is at the heart of managerial relations. This probably explains why managers are uneasy when it comes to creating space for consent.

Yet autonomy and choice relate to basic human needs. Self-determination, or a person's ability to make choices and manage their own life, has been proved to play a key role in their motivation and personal growth. Popularized by Daniel Pink in his 2009 book *Drive*, the work of experimental psychologists Edward Deci and Richard Ryan on human motivation is considered foundational in this regard.[43] In *Self-Determination and Intrinsic Motivation in Human Behavior*, published in 1985, Deci and Ryan establish that motivation grows from within us, grounded in our needs for competency, relatedness, and autonomy (which they define as the "desire to be causal agents of one's own life and act in harmony with one's integrated self").[44]

In addition to the exercise of choice, human agency at work is about the possibility of making an impact through one's craft. At the end of the working day, people want to feel a sense of pride and achievement in relation to their own mastery or to what they have helped produce and the wider effect that will have.

The reality of work, though, is so different for many people. "The activity of self-directed labor, conducted by the worker, is dissolved or abstracted into parts and then reconstituted as a process controlled by management—a labor sausage," Matthew Crawford writes in *Shop Class as Soulcraft*. Crawford laments the separation of *thinking* from *doing* that gradually took hold in the twentieth century.[45] This has resulted in the devaluation of manual work and the glorification of intellectual work.[46] Successive "improvements" in industrial management, economic theory, and technology have enabled the radical division of labor we experience today, separating knowledge workers from other roles and functions. Consumer society requires mass production, which was only made possible through the endless breakdown of tasks: intellectual activities parceled out from production; production divided into unexciting, repetitive tasks.

Intellectual activities is a more flattering term for what the late David Graeber referred to as "bullshit jobs."[47] Research by Graeber and others indicate that about 37 to 40 percent of workers claim that their jobs make no difference and add no value, with roles like workflow managers and process controllers, for example, supporting nothing but their own processes in a self-fulfilling, pointless loop. Some jobs serve no other purpose than to massage a supervisor's ego, a bitter irony in times of workforce optimization. According to Graeber, the money saved through downsizing and speed-ups on the shop floor enables executives "to fill their offices with feudal retinues of basically useless flunkies," who are often better remunerated than those with more impactful jobs.[48]

The development of information technologies confers growing autonomy onto workers, as demonstrated during the lockdowns of 2020, when millions of people shifted to working from home. But it also carries the risk of a further disconnection between work and reality, where impact can only be perceived as an abstraction.[49] Work becomes cut off from the experience of reality and, as such, is harmful to humans, leading to an explosion in workplace-related mental illnesses. The flurry of corporate communications around purpose and social impact is a pragmatic response to this. It aims at increasing employees' subjective mobilization through identification with a greater cause.

To support self-determination and ownership, work must offer more deliberation spaces, more opportunities to discuss, exchange, and debate. Usually, people in an organization spend most of their meetings or calls solving problems and negotiating outcomes. They are much less often invited to reflect on work, rules, procedures, and decisions. Speed and control are prioritized over sense-making and relational dynamics. A two-hour townhall in which senior leaders answer a few questions from the audience is the closest many organizations come to open discussion and debate.

In December 2010, disappointed with the amount of diversity among the decision-making bodies at the pharmaceutical company I worked for, I sent an unsolicited message to the CEO. In it I suggested relatively simple actions that would greatly increase diversity. The message circulated internally and triggered a coalition of volunteers to join forces to evolve the culture of the organization, to make it more modern and inclusive, to tune in with the diversity of its ecosystem. We discovered free speech, unprompted collective work, co-creation of value. We organized debates and lunch-and-learn sessions. We engaged our colleagues on the internal social network. We crowdsourced ideas, involving more people, creating awareness. We spared no effort and were oblivious to irony and cynicism, instead choosing to be elated by the change we created together. When I reflect back on this period, I retain a vivid memory of agency, deliberation, togetherness, sense-making, and impact—a thrilling and rare experience of liberty in the context of a large enterprise.

Such experiences, I've come to learn, always start with oneself.

4

It Starts with Oneself: On Becoming a Change Agent

I think that progress is not possible without deviation. And I think that it's important that people be aware of some of the creative ways in which some of their fellow men are deviating from the norm, because in some instances they may find these deviations inspiring and might suggest further deviations which might cause progress, you never know.

FRANK ZAPPA (1971)

A FEW YEARS AGO, I hosted an international delegation of around twenty senior executives from a leading material production company. My organization was one stop among many on their innovation discovery tour. They had been directed to my work because it exemplified human innovation. I explained some of the transformations I had been involved in—how they started, how they grew, what outcomes they achieved, what form of resistance they encountered, and how that was navigated with varying degrees of success. As I unfolded my stories and anecdotes, I watched the room. Some delegates were hooked, bending forward, taking notes and nodding. Some were uninterested, possibly impatient to return to "real" innovation of tools, apps, and technology. I was talking about people engagement and liberty instead. Then it was time for them to ask questions.

"How can you be so free?"

The question caught me by surprise. It was a good one, but not easy to answer.

I had been an advocate for liberty at work for quite some time, and yet I had never observed my practice from this particular angle. I knew with certainty *why* I supported emancipation: because it's a human need, and it makes organizations work more effectively, which contributes to making society healthier. But *how*? I knew my ideas about the workplace were not the ones favored by traditional leadership, including at the organization where I worked. The freedoms I was able to exercise at work, such as speaking up, being open, direct, and honest, were done within organizational constraints. Was I really as free as my questioner believed? Or was it an illusion of freedom?

That question has stayed with me, prompting constant reflection on my part. In fact, in some respects, this book represents my ongoing attempt to answer it. Of course, as with all good questions, it gives rise to further questions. It is not so much the answers that are of interest as the journey of exploration and inquiry itself. What was it about the account of my workplace experiences that would lead another person to view them as exemplifying liberty? What was it about my down-to-earth, no-nonsense stories that suggested the notion of freedom? We all filter stories through our own subjectivity and cognitive biases. Maybe it was the case that my questioner's personal experience—maybe *your* personal experience, too—contrasted so strongly with what I described that they could see only the positive in what I told them.

So, perhaps I should have responded to the question with one or two of my own: *How can you be so unfree? What makes you feel so devoid of liberty?*

Don't get me wrong. I empathize and I understand. I have not been a free agent all my professional life. I have definitely been a conformist on more than one occasion. To some extent, I probably still am, for I am neither an anarchist nor a libertarian. I feel comfortable with rules and restraint. My teenage children might even argue that I am *too* comfortable and familiar with them. Nevertheless, I have learned that there is something in my story of self-emancipation at work that can be helpful to other people, which is why I want to share it here. I believe that creating change starts with yourself and that stories are among the most powerful ways to inspire action. From one individual journey, I will outline the attributes and actions that define what it takes to become a change agent.

A Personal Journey from Employee to Change Agent

My Awakening to a Different Possibility

I had accumulated close to twenty years of professional work life by 2010. I had experienced small and large organizations, Asia and Europe, times of economic growth and crisis, exhilarating expansion and painful downsizing. I had worked in five different industries, with bosses both wonderful and nefarious, who either valued me as a high-potential talent or disregarded my contribution entirely. I was determined to fit in and to excel. In order to project an image of reliability, I dressed up in a skirt-suit and heels. I learned the acronyms, processes, organizational charts, and jokes. I worked hard. I referred to the company as "we" and to the competition as "them." I became friends with my colleagues. Often, though, I felt out of place and would try even harder to adapt and achieve.

On several occasions, things were not to my liking. Either the pace of business felt too slow or internal stakeholders acted contemptuously; the business environment became toxic or it was impossible to see eye to eye with the latest boss; the long-awaited reorganization was a mess or a new recruit ruined the team spirit. On almost every occasion, I managed to escape, transferring to another position, moving office, or finding a new role with another company. When I couldn't, I resigned myself to my fate and tried to make the most of the time spent in the corporate wilderness.

Eventually I found myself in the pharmaceutical industry, and though I was there ten years, it was apparent that my atypical career path—bouncing from industry to industry and continent to continent— had given me an external knowledge and experience that sharpened my eye, providing me the benefit of an outsider's perspective. Some of what I experienced at work felt amazing, some of it extremely unpleasant. I started to understand that this wasn't purely the outcome of *my* performance or *my* personality, just as it didn't purely result from *my* manager's actions or beliefs. There was something else at play that greatly influenced interaction, judgment, and work.

By 2010, I also had a five-year-old son and a newborn daughter. The arrival of my son increased what had been a loose interest in gender dynamics. How to raise a boy exempt, if at all possible, from the gendered biases that hold society back? Of the cultural norms I was about to transmit, which of them perpetuated oppression and injustice? What did I need to be aware of? I started to read more articles and books about women and gender equality. Simone de Beauvoir's *Deuxième sexe* (The second sex), of course, but also Marie-Joseph Bertini's *Femmes: Le pouvoir impossible* (Women: The impossible power), Sylvie Schweitzer's *Une histoire du travail des femmes aux XIXe et XXe siècles* (A history of women's work in the nineteenth and twentieth centuries), Françoise Héritier's *Hommes, femmes: La construction de la différence* (Men, women: The construction of difference), Margaret Maruani's *Femmes, genre et sociétés* (Women, gender, and society), and Avivah Wittenberg-Cox's *Why Women Mean Business*.

Stefan Bollmann's *Women Who Read Are Dangerous* was another book I enjoyed reading. To this bookworm, its title rang true. Equipped with more concepts, data, and perspectives than I had had before, I deciphered with increasing clarity the reality of my workplace. For the past eight years, my career had stalled. Progression from one job to another had been "lateral," in HR parlance. This contrasted starkly with the skyrocketing careers of several men who had been hired at the same time as me. Looking at the situation more closely, I realized that the careers of nearly all the women around me had stalled at some point. Hardly any of them had a role in their company's decision bodies or at the level of senior management. Just one of twelve Executive Committee members was a woman. The law requiring a minimum of 40 percent of women (or men) in French corporate boards was still under discussion and would not be voted in until early 2011, with sanctions set to be imposed six years later. Interestingly, I noticed that not all men were promoted equally, either. There were certain *types* of men who found that their careers soared. Men with a background in science or finance. Men with strong analytical skills. Men with a comfortable socioeconomic background. White, heterosexual men who had graduated from a small number of prestigious schools. Men with a competitive spirit. Men who took work very seriously. Men in whom senior executives saw echoes of their ambitious younger selves. Those who were funny, unique, creative, sensitive, or supportive were generally not among their number.

I was not sure if anyone else had noticed what I saw. The elimination of a large proportion of available talent was not necessarily intentional.

It was unfair for sure and, from a pragmatic standpoint, detrimental to the operation of the organization. Our field at Sanofi was healthcare, where women are known to make the vast majority of purchasing decisions, forming the public opinion that influences government choices. The market was no longer restricted to old, Western economies but was truly global, diverse, largely female, and often underprivileged. Nothing could be further from those who were making decisions on their behalf in the boardrooms of pharmaceutical organizations. How long would this system hold? We were heading for a fall.

This wasn't *my* problem, it was a much bigger, age-old, systemic problem. It far exceeded the boundaries of a particular organization. Instead, it was (and remains) a societal issue, with adverse consequences for the economy, innovation, relationships, and engagement. How can we seriously address the global challenges that face humanity with just a tiny fraction of its perspectives represented in the command post?

Exploring this new subject was exciting. I shared what I learned with a few colleagues, when we happened to sit down for lunch together. While some people always socialize with the same group of colleagues, I had maintained a habit from childhood of catching up with different people each day. Some of them were totally impervious to the topic of gender and diversity. They would laugh it off and label me a "feminist," a label they did not intend to serve as a compliment. Nevertheless, I had stimulating conversations with Corinne, Caroline, and Véronique, among others. Our interaction was informal, local, and small-scale— there was no hint of employee resource groups or enterprise social networks back then. We exchanged articles, facts, impressions. We recognized some of the cultural norms that had shaped our lives thus far. We shared the belief that some of that was wrong and needed to change.

The opportunity to act came unexpectedly but was instantly spotted. The new CEO asked for strategy input from his close team. I wasn't a member of that team, but I provided my suggestion anyway, and forwarded it to Corinne, Caroline, and Véronique. From there, it went viral and so began a movement. This was the first of several movements for workplace change that I contributed to.

Finding Inspiration and Support

Following an avalanche of supportive emails in response to my message to the CEO, a dozen of us gathered in person. Corinne asked the group,

"Why does gender balance matter to you?" Each of us spoke, and all of us listened. It was a deep and moving conversation. We realized how much we had in common, irrespective of our job titles, functions, or ages. From there, what could we do? One of us asked about gender quotas. The question was in the air, as the law was then being discussed in parliament. Did we support or reject female quotas in our organization? We decided to organize a public debate, a one-hour discussion hosted in a meeting room during the lunch period and open to anyone in the company. It started with a short presentation of arguments, figures, and examples, followed by a lively discussion, after which a collective position was decided: no support for quotas. This may seem trivial, but it was quite a revolution. A number of employees, from across the organization, had decided to take charge of a societal topic, had come together as a self-organized group for dialogue and consultation, and had made a decision. The passion and the energy were unprecedented. What was it that felt so new, so different, so empowering? Liberty.

Digital communication has been a huge asset for the movement, and a personal catalyst for change. From our first gathering, we wondered how to communicate among ourselves. Our email inboxes were already crammed. A colleague working in Communications suggested we take a look at Yammer, which at the time, in early 2011, was a nascent enterprise social network solution. It was being piloted by one of our business units, but not yet formally supported by the company. I knew nothing about digital communications, but I did take a look that same day, and it was so intuitive that I understood how it worked within fifteen minutes. Ten minutes later, our online community was born. It was visual, engaging, and mobile—an amazing channel for communicating broadly in the absence of institutional resources.

In October 2011, I opened a Twitter account and found that great content was available there, *already curated*, and sometimes commented on or challenged by experts, authors, and thought leaders. It was even possible to contact and interact with them, to see what they read, and to find out who they learned from themselves. Twitter also enabled me to meet people who shared my interests.

The discovery was mind-blowing. I remained a lurker for a while, not daring do more than absorb content, then eventually I took the plunge and joined the social conversation. Nothing could have been more beneficial to my personal and professional growth. While much has changed in the social media landscape over past decade, some of my best friends today are people I met through Twitter. Many of the insights upon which I designed the last ten years of my professional life came via Twitter. Over time, I broadened my use of channels to LinkedIn, Facebook, and a few others that have now disappeared, but Twitter retains a special place. It is where I connected with the communities of changemakers who expanded my horizons and supported me in rough times, including the Enterprise 2.0 Summit community, Rebels at Work, Corporate Rebels United, and Change Agents Worldwide.

Back at work, our internal movement for diversity thrived in 2011–12. It reached 2,500 employees across more than 50 countries, expanding to sister organizations and to the holding group. To create greater awareness, we would have loved to be funded by the company, but an external consultant advised the HR leaders to keep our grassroots movement "pure," unspoiled by corporate money, which meant we had no access to additional resources. We were so determined, however, that occasionally we invested our own money. Mostly, though, we relied on the internal social network and on our sense of purpose, which gave us the courage to proceed. We were corporate rebels.

Collectively, there was a feeling among the group that echoed Peter Vander Auwera's *Corporate Rebels United Manifesto*:

> Our organizations no longer serve our needs. They cannot keep pace with a high-velocity, hyper-connected world. They no longer can do what we need them to do. Change is required.
>
> We love our organizations and want them to succeed. We want to reboot our corporate and organizational culture to install a 21st century, digitally native version, to accelerate positive viral change from deep within the fabric of our organizations, and to reclaim our passion for work.[1]

A few months after launching the movement at Sanofi, the company officially opened up to the topic of diversity. Our network began to work alongside the senior leadership, and some small changes started to happen. We felt particularly proud that we had managed to impact corporate policy for the greater good. We had expanded the network to an additional twenty organizations, connected through a nonprofit association set up and led by Corinne. We had won several national awards, shining a positive light on our own company. I could have stopped there, content that a mission had been accomplished, but this journey had opened my eyes to more change opportunities.

Creating More Change

I had experienced, firsthand, the kind of incredible energy generated from a collective when it is diverse, engaged around a common purpose, connected through digital networks, and given the liberty to collaborate and to create. I had learned through my colleagues, and through those people I met on Twitter, that business and work could be so different from, so much better than, what I had been accustomed to. Change could benefit the many, not just a select few, and we had both the technology and the management practices to enable it.

However, I also knew that for this kind of shift to take place it was necessary to demonstrate *business value*. Any success in having this approach taken seriously and embraced by the whole organization depended on it.

The upcoming launch and marketing of an important product at Sanofi represented an ideal opportunity to demonstrate the value of our approach. I read everything I could about stakeholder marketing—engaging communities to understand their needs, values, and interests so as to create mutually beneficial relationships that also minimize harm—interviewed colleagues to find out what kind of support they would require, developed a solid business case, defended it, showed patience and determination, and eventually was offered a role in Stakeholder Engagement in the second half of 2012.

Everything that we'd experimented with and learned in the diversity movement, I could now apply to a recognized business challenge: to support the successful launch of a new vaccine by engaging as many people as possible around the world. I also had access to resources. I teamed up with a colleague in IT to create a collaborative work platform for the four hundred colleagues working on this project, scattered over different functions and countries. There was a collaborative calendar, so that, regardless of function or level, people could be made aware of events related to the common work. There was also an automatic, collaborative monthly newsletter populated directly by employees, without any need for an editor. This ultra-simple system empowered people to share their work stories and achievements. It created accountability while bypassing the traditional communications gatekeepers and avoiding the costs traditionally associated with corporate newsletters. It took some effort on my part to resist the request that each article be submitted for approval by an editorial board. Trusting employees and keeping it simple are not the strengths of large organizations.

In order to engage externally, I suggested an approach that went completely against the grain of what pharma companies were used to at the time. Instead of focusing on the soon-to-be-launched vaccine, we would focus on the cause it served (fighting the disease dengue). Instead of believing we had the ultimate solution to people's problems, we would acknowledge that our vaccine would be most effective as part of an ecosystem of solutions that could benefit from our help. Instead of pushing messages to a passive audience, we would connect activists, interact with them, and enable them to co-create additional solutions. Instead of segmenting stakeholders, we would aim for a diverse community. Instead of limiting interactions to one channel, we would use all mainstream social media. Instead of doing this alone, we would form an alliance beyond the world of pharma. Instead of a pseudo-community instrumentalized for marketing purposes, an independent editorial board would be in charge of all the content that was shared.

We were able to hand over the digital platform at the core of the initiative to a Brussels-based organization, The Synergist. Business value would come not from control but from the *absence* of control. It was a hard sell internally, but it worked. Beginning in 2013, a quarter of a million people all over the world made use of our open platform Break Dengue (www.breakdengue.org), where activists had their work promoted and where people were connected, funded, informed, and given a voice. Key stakeholders in the world of healthcare recognized the importance of this unprecedented initiative. It won several awards, including for "best use of social media for healthcare," "most impactful emerging initiative," and "best alliance for corporate social responsibility." Most importantly, it advanced the fight against a disease that impacted so many people's lives.

Breaking Down Imposed Barriers

Our dengue work gained the attention of Anders Vinther, a senior executive who had joined the organization in mid-2014 as Chief Quality Officer. Because of quality issues, the company was unable to provide all the vaccines its customers needed. Former Quality executives had attempted to solve the problem through "push" approaches, failing to achieve consistent improvement. Vinther suggested we work together. I was a bit dubious at first. In the highly regulated, heavily processed pharmaceuticals industry, the role of Quality has been traditionally viewed as an enforcer of the rules rather than as a force for innovation. Despite my reluctance, a result in large part of the company's cultural conservatism and pushback, I agreed to work with Vinther, and it wound up that we would lead change in a radically different way, along the lines I'd experimented with twice already. In addition, we sought external assistance from John Kotter and his firm.

The stakes were high. The company was just recovering from its umpteenth warning letter from the U.S. Food and Drug Administration. Vaccine shortages in several countries put public health at risk. Ten thousand people worked in manufacturing operations worldwide. Failure to meet quality standards carried enormous financial and reputational costs. As with many similar organizations, the company relied on expensive external and internal experts who regularly reshuffled processes, imposing their favored methods on employees who were presumed incompetent, unaware, or lazy. "My job is to put these people back to work," a self-satisfied Lean consultant told me with contempt. The only people whose working practices were not challenged were those in upper management.

Our intuition told us that quality was undermined not only by dysfunctional equipment, processes, or people, but by the context in which they operated. The culture was hierarchical, top-down, averse to change, siloed, and bottlenecked. Frontline staff were expected to apply procedures, not to speak up or collaborate. Control was thought safer than trust. A compliance-driven quality culture had developed. My job, with the rest of the Quality leadership team, was to change that. I was appointed Head of Quality Innovation & Engagement at the end of 2014, moving to Boston, where I would be closer to the Kotter office. My mission was to transform quality from an imposed constraint to a shared passion. We would start a global movement to change and evolve the work culture of our organization.

We began with purpose—not another utopian corporate vision, but a collective response to the question "What is it we want to fight for, now, together?" Our "Big Opportunity" statement, which was co-created by a diverse group of people, proclaimed that we would change the way we work in order to make our vaccines available to all who wanted them. Its concluding challenge became our motto: "What will I do differently today, to save more people tomorrow?" This served as a catalyst for a dramatic transformation. Enabled by Yammer, supported by management, inspired by living systems approaches, a peer-to-peer conversation started to grow. Volunteers from across the organization, from different sites and from different hierarchical levels, became activists of change and engaged their peers. Within eighteen months, over four thousand people joined the movement. I set up and supported a volunteer team of around twenty people, the membership of which was renewed each year. This team was responsible for leading change globally. Working in various sites and functions across Europe, North America, and India, they did not report to me. Yet we worked together as a team, learning from each other, trying things out, igniting passion and intrapreneurship in our colleagues.

Not everything was a success. Some people were not convinced, while others actively sabotaged the change effort. However, after twelve months or so, there were clear signs that complacency was being supplanted by agency, collaboration, and mutual care. A culture founded upon control was opened up to trust, community, and talent development. Individuals and teams got together, unprompted, and made change happen. Leaders supported volunteers, instead of setting directions. People felt empowered and proud of their mastery. Solutions were co-created, revealing leadership in places where it hadn't been identified before. Silos fell as people collaborated across teams and departments. Health authorities were impressed. About ten international awards were won. More importantly, the quality indicators turned positive for the first time in ten years. This meant more vaccines for more people.

What It Takes to Be Free at Work

"Being a change maker at a hierarchical company in a highly regulated sector is not for the faint-hearted." So began a 2014 article that Jennifer Schenker wrote about me and my work, which ruffled a few feathers despite, or maybe because of, its accuracy.[2] I had gained independence by writing an unsolicited email in 2010 and had not ceased to extend my zone of autonomy since then. At the invitation of the organizer of the International Association of Business Communicators Europe, I began speaking at events in the spring of 2013, sharing what I did and what I was learning with an ever-growing network of connections. I didn't seek permission, received little organizational support, and occasionally encountered resistance regarding my participation at events. As such, I spoke for myself rather than the company, using these occasions to further my own professional development.

The fact was, had I asked for permission and received some official stamp of approval, this would have undermined the honesty and spontaneity I owed to the other change agents I interacted with. While it was not always appreciated, my freedom served my company's purpose just as well as it served my own. Nevertheless, I usually refrained from naming my employer when delivering talks or interacting with other attendees, drawing instead on my involvement in the group Change Agents Worldwide. To ensure both my attendance and my freedom from corporate restrictions, I would take leave from work and request that event organizers cover my travel expenses. Failing that, I paid them myself.

I also started a blog in the summer of 2013 and became very active on social media. More people interviewed me for articles, podcasts, and books. For the most part, however, my public activity flew under the radar. Few people in my business were on social media or demonstrated any interest in the future of work. The press reviews made available on the intranet included only those interviews in which authors had mentioned my company's name, rendering it visible to news aggregators. Sometimes there was a nice surprise, such as a congratulatory email from the CEO when one of these articles was published. On other occasions I had to duck my head and wait for the storm to blow over. Several years on this rollercoaster made me reflect on what choosing liberty at work implied.

Independent Thinking, Limiting Beliefs, and Semantic Straitjackets

It is surprisingly difficult to exercise independent thought in the workplace in relation to the work we do and within the organization we work for. Commenting on functional stupidity in *Qu'est-ce qu'un régime de travail réellement humain?* (What are truly humane conditions of labor?), economist Michel Volle observes that critical thinking is poorly received, as it challenges tacit conventions.[3] This perception forces professionals to operate in a degraded mode: "You have to be smart enough to be stupid!" But even when given the latitude to act differently, we tend to default to normative and obedient behaviors. Some of the biggest obstacles to change are not external circumstances or the lack of resources, but the beliefs we hold about what can or should be done, what must be avoided, and how to proceed.

As a consultant, I see people restrained by themselves. Some of them blame "the culture" or "the system" for preventing change without realizing *they* enforce the very same culture or system themselves. I've witnessed a corporate volunteer prohibit members of his team from volunteering because they needed to put their day jobs first. I've seen a change movement facilitator withhold volunteers' communications to the wider employee community in order to avoid upsetting senior leaders. I've observed a group that hoped to develop self-organizing teams kick off their initiative by writing a report to senior management, oblivious to the fact that asking for permission is the exact opposite of self-organizing. Hierarchy, control, the separation of thinking and doing, and the attribution of better judgment to senior leadership are among the behaviors and practices that have become normalized and ingrained to the point that we don't notice them anymore. They act as mental shackles, and they act fast, as evidenced by the speed with which newcomers conform to an organization's ways of doing.

We get constrained, too, by what Jon Husband refers to as "semantic straitjackets,"[4] that is, the language and models that have shaped corporate management and operations since the Industrial Revolution. Models generally arise when a good idea is expanded beyond its original context and transformed into prescriptive advice. An unintended consequence, Husband notes, is that models "create and maintain boundaries for action and interaction that present obstacles to adaptability, responsiveness and the co-creation of innovation." As we have developed management science, we have created powerful methodologies, each of which have tightened the straitjacket a little more. Organizational belief systems, performance pressures, and time constraints inhibit our critical thinking, limiting our ability to question and challenge. As Dave Gray explains in *Liminal Thinking*, we find ourselves sealed in a bubble, constructed from selected facts and experience.[5] Belief systems form the basis of our interactions with others, but they also create blind spots, narrowing down possibilities and encouraging us to protect our corporate identity as "a good manager" or "a dedicated professional."

Counselor and psychotherapist John Wenger has drawn parallels between this workplace situation and the condition known as Stockholm Syndrome, whereby hostages sympathize and empathize with their captors.[6] He draws on the work of Joseph Carver, who examined how this phenomenon develops in abusive relationships when victims find that establishing an emotional bond with those who abuse them serves as a strategy for survival.[7] According to Wenger, all four of the Stockholm Syndrome conditions identified by Carver—perceived threats, small kindnesses, isolation from any perspective but that of the captor, and an inability to escape—can be found in the modern workplace.

So how do we overcome these limiting beliefs? Gray argues that we need to pay attention to the edges, the boundaries, the doorsteps and thresholds. As Marshall McLuhan's writings show, "Once you see the boundaries of your environment, they are no longer the boundaries of your environment."[8] The challenge is to *see* them in the first place and examine context, our own actions, and the actions of others; importantly, we must look critically but with kindness. Personally, I enjoy the company of corporate cynics rather than corporate sheep because they have a sharp eye which helps me see things differently, even if I do not share their negativity and prefer to assess and critique more constructively than they tend to. But what has really helped me see and become more attuned to the corporate world around me can be narrowed down to three significant factors.

First is the practice of "radical diversity," which I learned while living as a foreigner in several different cultures. The experience helped me understand that my own perspective is just one among many and that I need to remain open to novelty and change. This has been a source of both personal joy and growth, and because of it I try hard to maintain a beginner's mindset. Second is the minority experience. Mine is definitely not of the radical and oppressive kind that LGBTQI+, disabled, or racialized individuals sadly sometimes encounter—an unbearable violence against them that must stop. As a white, able-bodied, cisgendered, educated woman, I am aware of my numerous privileges. Nevertheless, I am still a woman in a male-driven corporate environment, and as such I have frequently experienced what it feels like to be devalued, overlooked, unheard, and powerless. To be rejected by the dominant system has a way of opening up new perspectives about that very system, perspectives that are unlikely to occur to those comfortably occupying the unchallenged positions of power. Third is my interest in art that challenges aesthetic, social, and political norms. Artists change the world by challenging the status quo and offering different perspectives. In organizations, too, I believe we can take creative risks for the greater good. We can nurture corporate artistry.

Suspicions about self-serving intentions are often leveled at those campaigning for gender or racial equality in the workplace. I've encountered this skepticism myself and recognize it as one of the classic status quo mechanisms of defense. However, any aspiring changemaker should pause to reflect, questioning their own motives: Do you push for change in general, or do you push for the change *you* want instead? Do you challenge a system of domination so that more voices can be heard, or do you leverage opportunities to increase *your* power, hiding your true motives behind a collective agenda? Your willingness not only to change a situation but to change yourself, before becoming vulnerable to the scrutiny and challenge of others, will require the courage of conviction to proceed and to withstand the attacks that are likely to come your way.

Rocking the Boat

It was change agent Helen Bevan who inspired my early steps in this field. Since 2013, Bevan has been leading NHS Horizons, the UK National Health Service agency in charge of facilitating large-scale change throughout the British health system. I enjoyed the brilliance of Helen's input and her generous sharing of knowledge on many channels. In 2013, Bevan and her team launched an online School for Health and Care Radicals, later renamed School for Change Agents. Open to anyone, the school ran several editions of its change-agent course, attracting thousands of participants from all over the world thanks to highly relevant content, a bold combination of digital tools, and a remarkably interactive experience. The subtitle of the course was "Rocking the boat and staying in it."[9]

This reflects one of the main challenges faced by change agents. We are not trying to jeopardize, weaken, or overturn our organizations. We have seen possibilities outside the dominant belief bubble, and we have argued that another way is possible. We have exposed ourselves. From there, we must be tactical and careful, because any misstep may be held against us and, in the case of dismissal or transfer, may impact our ability to bring about any change. It is important to act as a "good rebel" rather than a "bad" one. The differences between the two have been illustrated by Lois Kelly and Carmen Medina on their website Rebels at Work and in their book of the same name.[10] Bad rebels tend to complain, break rules, and alienate, while good rebels are more likely to create, change rules, and attract. The former are often self-centered, pessimistic, and obsessive. By contrast, the latter are mission-focused, optimistic, and reluctant to impose their own solutions or leadership on others. Some fight *against* with anger; others fight *for* with passion. True, the line can be blurry at times. Behaviors can be interpreted in different ways, and something intended as good may be perceived as bad. It has been a long-established defense mechanism to label someone "angry," undermining their passion, activism, and credibility, when they propose something that challenges the status quo. We see it all the time in relation to equality arguments regarding gender and race. Whatever kind of rebel you are, one thing is certain: it is not enough to think differently. Thinking is easy. Most people I've met in my professional life have wanted "things to change," yet few have been active in doing something about it.

Taking Action through Agency

Agency can be defined as the "independent ability to act according to one's own will." Surprisingly, no French word is able to accurately express the concept of agency, and the same applies for *empowerment*. We French must use paraphrases, suboptimal substitutes, or English words to discuss these ideas. In a 2012 article about "agency as word and as engagement," historian, activist, and translator Caroline Mackenzie recognizes three essential elements in agency behavior: a person's *ability* to act (competencies, ideas), their *capacity* to act (resources, support network), and their *willingness* to act.[11] Mackenzie highlights that all three must be present together in any act of agency. You may have the skills and the desire to act but be incapacitated for some reason. You may have the resources and the ideas but feel reluctant to put yourself forward. You may want to act and have access to a support network but feel overwhelmed by the complexity of a situation.

Organizational culture, leadership style, and challenges can all either hamper or boost agency. Mackenzie relates the happy story of The Australian National University in the 1980s.[12] Ahead of a new workplace Equal Opportunity Act, the university offered its female employees an opportunity to become involved in assessing the organization's recruitment and human resource practices with respect to fairness and inclusion. Employees responded with enthusiasm, which led not only to a global reflection on the part of the university, but also to the implementation of profound changes at all levels. All the corporate changes I have been involved in for the last decade build on this very approach, which is to expand and leverage human agency.

If they understand the benefits of greater agency among their staff, organizations can support the development of all three aspects of agency. *Ability*, however, is probably the most straightforward. Skilled employees are needed to deliver well against customer demands and to keep up with technology and market changes. In large, resourceful organizations, some massive investments were made over the past decade in education, knowledge management, learning expertise, and learning technologies. The ongoing effects of the coronavirus pandemic permitting, the trend will continue. As of June 2020, market analysts predicted that the global learning management system market would grow from $13.4 billion in 2020 to $25.7 billion by 2025.[13] However, the abundance of technology and content is no silver bullet.

One of my former clients, a global construction company, became aware of the limits of its learning approach. It found that making lots of learning material available on a great platform actually perpetuated the corporate culture that it wanted to evolve. Its offer encouraged a "consumer mindset," where employees passively absorbed content that often was already obsolete. Such an approach can contribute to the limited development of skills—albeit divorced from contextual application—but it does not contribute toward agency. This particular organization understood that it was agency that was most required, so we worked together to devise an approach that encouraged and supported people in "learning to learn" rather than simply feeding them content.

We assembled a small volunteer team that included an array of employee perspectives from different parts of the organization. Together, we created a peer-to-peer engagement mechanism around the idea of curiosity. This combined physical and digital experiences, making people explore new territories, encouraging them to actively seek and share knowledge. The volunteers were brave, passionate, and motivated by a shared sense of purpose. They demonstrated to their colleagues their vulnerability and curiosity as learners, inviting them to join the exploration. Several months later, someone with no prior knowledge of my contribution spoke about a friend of hers who had participated in this project and had described it as the best corporate initiative she had ever been involved in.

In addition to *ability*, our project nurtured the other two aspects of human agency. The support network helped people understand that they were not alone, further developing their *capacity*. Meanwhile, all the participants demonstrated a *willingness* to act in service of the greater good rather than in pursuit of individual achievement.

THE PERSONAL TRAITS OF ACTION

There are many other ways to develop human agency at work. But I have noticed certain traits that are often present among people who frequently display this behavior. Foremost among these is what psychologist Carol Dweck describes as "a growth mindset" in her 2006 book *Mindset*. According to Dweck, people with a fixed mindset "spend their time documenting their intelligence or talent," while those with a growth mindset strive to develop their abilities, which are not felt as defining or set features. For these individuals, challenges are perceived as opportunities to grow, not as identity-crushing catastrophes. This view creates both a love of learning and resilience, underpinned by the self-compassion that can help us respond positively to the occasional failure.[14]

In fact, people who seem to be fearless about taking action may be more prone than others to "positive illusions," a set of three related beliefs described in a 1988 paper on mental health by Shelley Taylor and Jonathon Brown.[15] Under the effect of positive illusions, people tend to have unrealistically favorable attitudes toward themselves (*illusory superiority*), as well as about their ability to control environmental events (*illusion of control*) and about the future (*optimism bias*).[16] Positive illusions are not bad in themselves, and they can be a useful driver of action and psychological well-being. Nevertheless, there are pitfalls that have to be navigated. *Illusory superiority*, for example, can trigger the "savior syndrome" that affects some change agents, unhealthily positioning themselves as *rescuer* and their colleagues as *victims*. This dynamic is sometimes described in terms of the Karpman Drama Triangle, with those in positions of authority assigned the role of *persecutor*.[17] This is not what we should aim for. Someone with agency should strive to enable others. The *illusion of control*, by contrast, can undermine our evaluation of what is required (time, money, people, technology) to achieve certain targets. Finally, there is a tendency among the *optimists* to overlook difficulties and jump into action, when a more prudent approach can sometimes be the better option, especially if there is a need to win over the hearts and minds of others. But joyful rebellion, as Lois Kelly refers to it, is hard to resist.[18] Movers and shakers love the adrenaline and the joy that comes with making things happen.

IMPAIRED ACTION
Quite often, especially in large and established organizations, human agency remains an untapped potential. Emancipation and liberty can seem threatening, and, because we're tied into the semantic straitjacket of productivity, it becomes very difficult to act freely, sometimes even close to impossible. Paradoxically, employees tend to be trusted more when they behave *with little agency*. They are denied the personal and collective freedom to act, subject to the negative, controlling, oppressive behaviors that are the symptoms of bad systems rather than of bad people. How, then, in such an environment, does an independent thinker advance their ideas for change?

Sometimes, compromise is the only way. The good rebel can try their luck with the regular decision-making channels, allowing for the possibility that their ideas for change will have to be watered down in order to gain executive buy-in. I've experienced this myself when securing a slot to speak about a change initiative at an organization's Executive Committee meeting. Prior to the meeting, the gatekeepers stripped out all the color and images from my presentation, misunderstanding my intentions and perverting the underlying philosophy of our initiative. Rather than retaining the emphasis I wanted to convey on people, they instrumentalized and dehumanized, making it all about data. They left me with nothing to illuminate either the progress to date or the future vision I intended to relay to the senior leaders. I had to rely only on words and on my own enthusiasm. In this particular instance, I was listened to politely. However, soon after, I realized that being allowed access to the inner sanctum did little more than send a political message to other parts of the organization that our initiative was worthy of attention. I got invited to a couple more executive meetings, where I spoke, was thanked, and that was it. Everyone continued on their own course, unchanged.

Sometimes, however, an organization will pick up on a change agent's ideas and make them its own. I have seen this in action too. In one case, the company in question did not seek to leverage and expand upon the original initiative but instead launched its own program that in large part replicated it, using similar language and means of engagement, but exercising more top-down control, which had the adverse effect of creating yet another silo and displacing the catalytic effect of the original change agent. In "How the Organization Subverts Its Subversives," living systems consultant John Atkinson describes how an organization is able to undermine the work of change agents by providing superficial support, setting substance aside, and transforming the initiative so that the status quo is preserved.[19]

Inevitably, patience can run out, while the experience of being undermined, overshadowed, or sidelined can be demoralizing. An option then left to the change agent is outright rebellion, speaking up, mobilizing others, building a community around the vision of a different future. Such an approach, though, carries many risks, not least that of excommunication and exile.

Facing the Risks

Management consultant John Hagel has long maintained that we should never underestimate the organizational immune system, for it is "adept at recognizing foreign bodies as soon as they appear and very effective at protecting the institution from infection."[20] Change is perceived as foreign, threatening the integrity of the system. Add this defense mechanism to the natural competition that reigns at work, and you can see how challenging things can be for anyone seeking to put forward different ideas. If they wish to remain within the organization, despite the cost to their freedom, then they have to become both resilient and persistent.

When engaging in my first collective mobilization, I was too fired up by the purpose to think seriously about the consequences. For me, enabling diversity and fairness was too important. What was the harm, where was the difficulty, if we were acting *in* the interests of the organization, not against them? After all, there were many of us, and we were having a lot of fun while effecting change. Over the years, though, as I have been exposed to more change initiatives and witnessed the casualties along the way, I have been made more aware of the difficulties. Thinking freely in the workplace, challenging norms and identities, can have very serious consequences.

One that is often overlooked is self-sabotage. Lack of self-consciousness or psychological flexibility can lead straight to bad outcomes. I have seen people who have great potential to deliver lasting change frozen by frustration because they have encountered resistance. They become caught in a vicious cycle of anger and embitterment. The more their ideas are pushed back, the more mistakes they make, and ultimately, their self-esteem falls. Some in this position withdraw entirely from the change arena in order to protect their mental health. By contrast, I have seen very successful change agents commit self-sabotage too. Previous success has blinded them to the contextual aspects of their approach, leading them to try to impose the same types of solutions in entirely different scenarios, missing the nuances of a situation. Every new project is a nail to their hammer. They become increasingly conservative, stop learning and growing, contributing less and less to change. In some cases, sadly, their egos become inflated, and they attribute prior success to *themselves* alone, to *their* ideas, *their* heroic leadership. Hubris and complacency then get in the way of what had once been a positive energy for change but is no longer beneficial to others.

There are other consequences that arise from speaking up in an environment that is not particularly favorable to it. Tall poppy syndrome can invoke jealousy and denigration among colleagues, who expect you not to stand out but to keep your head down and the spotlight of managerial scrutiny away from them.[21] Neither do they wish to feel belittled by your sense of adventure or displays of greater knowledge than they possess. This attitude is often baked into the organizational culture. As such, compliant people tend to be entrusted with high-profile projects, prestigious roles, and international assignments, while the careers of the curious and the rebellious stall. I am amazed, considering their impact, at how these people are left to sit stagnant in the corporate hierarchy while senior colleagues who appear to add little value are consistently rewarded with promotion. Clearly, these change agents are considered too dangerous to be given free rein.

Another consequence takes the form of reprimands and punishment. They sting. The promotion and payraise you were promised fails to materialize. You are required to undergo coaching and behavioral correction. You get summoned for an interview by a vengeful HR bureaucrat. Your employee record becomes a narrative of poor discipline. Your previously supportive manager fails you. Doors close; emails are not responded to; allies fall silent.

Liberty can be terribly isolating.

How Change Agents Can Self-Protect

Change agents need courage, humility, and patience. But they also need to self-protect in order to negotiate the inevitable consequences of acting for change. In 2015, I published a blog post, "Regain Freedom at Work," about a twenty-four-hour follow-the-sun "Rebel Jam" organized by Corporate Rebels United, Rebels at Work, and Change Agents Worldwide. In it, I listed fifteen practical tips:

· Stop asking for permission.
· Realize you have more power than you think.
· Find the purpose no one can disagree with.
· Find friends, have fun.
· Map, identify, network, lobby.
· Shine outside.
· Involve external stakeholders.

- Search for impact.
- Claim big success, even if it's still a work in progress.
- Cultivate bravery.
- Empower others.
- Be faultless with ethics and compliance.
- Learn, learn, and learn.
- Deliver results.
- Out-love everyone else. [22]

In 2018, a reader posted this comment: "I love this article. So much so that I have a repeating task on my list to remind me to read it twice a year." He was serious and commented again two years later, after another prompt by his reminder. I should have added "show persistence" to my list.

Shining outside is a sensitive weapon because organizations often dislike employees' shining on their own, outside corporate reach and control. Yet it is an essential tool for securing and expanding liberty at work. Having a voice, one's *own* voice, can take many forms. Some people write blogs. Some speak at conferences. Some become involved in industry associations. Some express their own ideas on LinkedIn or Twitter. I can't recommend this enough. So much institutional effort is expended on clipping the wings of change agents that sometimes public exposure is the only way to counteract it. Having a voice is a form of personal branding as self-protection strategy. Running for awards is a useful tactic, because organizations love good news. When an edgy initiative that has been resisted internally is then rewarded externally, the organization is left with little choice but to speak about it in good terms, taking pride in the external recognition. Rewards come with a feel-good factor that can benefit a change project's implementation and reach in the long term.

For change agents who are at risk in their jobs, it is also a great idea to nurture external networks and develop portable skills. I was struck a few years ago by the results of a study conducted by Harvard Business School professor Boris Groysberg. Analyzing the performance of one thousand high performers in the finance industry during the early 2000s, Groysberg found out that when leaving their employer for another company, women fared much better than men. The reason was that male professionals tended to cultivate internal networks,

whereas their female counterparts had much stronger external relationships. Carol Muratore explained to Groysberg, "For a woman in
any business, it's easier to focus outward, where you can define and
deliver the services required to succeed, than to navigate the internal
affiliations and power structure within a male-dominant firm."[23] The
skills and the network acquired this way may prove vital when it's time
to leave the organization—which might very well happen. When change
becomes repetitive because it's not being given oxygen or more space
to flourish, the fun is lost. When the immune system coalesces against
the bearer of change, the battle is lost. Liberating oneself includes the
realization, ideally early on in the change process, that you are not tied
forever to your employer.

Leaving can be both difficult and a relief, and is made easier if those
external support networks are already in place, if you are willing to be
self-compassionate, and if you remain true to your values. Integrity
results from the alignment of values, ideas, and action. It creates a sense
of liberty that can never been taken away from you.

CHANGE BEGINS WITH oneself: by distancing oneself from dominant norms and ways of doing, and by critically observing the system
of which one is a part and the dynamics that govern its interactions. It
is an emancipation as well as a risk-taking process. Those who engage
in this course recognize themselves under the banner of rebels, disrup-
tors, outcasts, troublemakers, mavericks, change agents, rule breakers,
originals, renegades, mischiefs, contrarians, deviants, pirates, here-
tics, radicals, nonconformists... (did I miss any?)—so many flattering
labels found in management articles and books. They romanticize the
experience and flatter the ego. And why not? The day-to-day corporate
change experience tends to be one of struggle and obstacles, where the
changemakers are more likely to be described as "a pain in the neck"
or "difficult" by their managers and peers than to be lauded in playful
terms. But self-emancipation and a critical perspective are not enough,
far from it, to produce systemic change. We must also create the conditions for many more people to exercise greater freedom.

5

Creating Collective
Liberty at Work

AN EXCESS OF standardization and constraint in modern work is
being called out as a barrier to collective creativity, engagement, and innovation. However, liberty at scale raises doubts,
even prompts fear, among corporate decision-makers. It seems like
a risky venture for organizations. What would happen if people had
more freedom at work? Would production and services be delivered
with consistency? Would compliance and safety be ensured? Would
there be more chaos? More risk? These are legitimate concerns. The
very survival of organizations is tied to customer satisfaction, regulatory
compliance, profitability, and competitiveness. A workforce comprised
entirely of people who follow individual preference could be viewed
as disorderly both from the outside and from the top. Yet such freedom and agency are very much on the agenda. Rising societal trends
in liberty are shaping worker aspirations, particularly those of younger
generations. The Business shelves of bookstores are filled with treatises
on liberated companies and un-leaders, while there are some five thousand *Harvard Business Review* articles that explore the topic of freedom.

Change is already underway, from small-scale trials to radical overturn. Traditionally controlled structures are being opened up, enabling
a degree of liberty for people at work. Yet these are only the first steps,
leaving some distance to travel if we are to enjoy work conditions that
match the definition explored in Chapter 3:

Liberty at work is the unconditional possibility given to workers to hold and express independent judgement on the matters of their organization, to avoid managerial arbitrariness, and to direct their work so that it not only produces value but contributes to their dignity as human beings.

While some leaders who have embraced liberty have achieved their hopes, publishing books and articles about their experiences so that others can follow their lead, many others express frustration about the outcome. Employee apathy and an unwillingness to exercise autonomy or to become more involved in company matters seem to stand in the way. It is a similar story with change agents, community leaders, and network facilitators, who often find that no matter how much they try to enable and empower the people around them, they are still expected to make most of the decisions and take on much of the workload themselves. Why is that so?

Perhaps it can be attributed to the discrepancies between theory and practice. Freedom at work can look great on a slide deck but can feel burdensome to someone who simply wants to be told what to do, deliver their work, collect a paycheck, and get on with their lives. Then, as discussed in the previous chapter, there are self-preservation impulses that may make some wary about exploring liberty to its fullest. In the following pages, we will explore why some sincere and well-intentioned attempts to create freedom fail, then contemplate how much collective liberty can be achieved through intentional organizational design.

Liberty under Control

The notion of liberty at work was sidelined at the turn of the twentieth century by the scientific management pursuit of efficiency. But it resurfaced after the Second World War amid the general trend toward social democratization. Psychologists like Kurt Lewin, who pioneered organization development, as well as business theorists like W. Edwards Deming and Peter Drucker, influenced evolving practices whereby workers became more involved in decision making. Small and large companies began to make use of quality control circles, credited to the Japanese automobile industry for its spectacular postwar development. Scandinavian organizations initiated the movement toward participatory management in the 1960s and were soon followed by businesses in other European countries in the 1970s.

Experiments with participatory production structures, giving workers a voice in company decisions, took place in a favorable political context, reflected by the developing role of works councils, the 1976 Codetermination Act in West Germany, and the early 1980s Auroux Laws for collective bargaining in France. European systems have inspired progressive policy proposals in the U.S., where, despite a long history of labor's involvement in corporate governance—including the oldest law still in force today, from 1919 in Massachusetts—worker participation in the private sector remains very limited.[1]

The original spirit of these initiatives was lost over time as participatory structures morphed into rigidity and bureaucracy. Engineering-inspired management models that trended throughout the 1990s and 2000s tilted the balance back in favor of standardization and rationalization. However, societal, technological, and market changes during the 2010s have reinvigorated and broadened aspirations to reinvent organizations and liberate workers. In addition to the pioneer organizations that have reinvented their management models, there are a number of mainstream companies now taking baby steps toward the practice of collective freedom at work. All these organizations are learning that there are several pitfalls to negotiate.

Shallow Liberty

Systems intended to create more space for worker self-expression are largely designed with good intentions in mind by people sincerely convinced of their benefits. Unfortunately, they are often too tainted by the managerial desire for control to produce any significant outcome. So pervasive, in fact, is the corporate control habit that many well-meaning liberators do not appreciate that their new initiatives are adding to rather than alleviating a deep-rooted system of constraint.

In one of my previous roles, a colleague working at a foreign affiliate came up with an idea inspired by my work around people engagement. Her intention was to involve colleagues more effectively in innovation and continuous improvement, listening to and acting on what they had to say. With her manager, she had devised a highly organized and very complex system that would allow "the best" ideas to materialize. But who got to determine how "the best" should be defined? The flow chart separated ideas from people and put those ideas through an internal vetting system. The proposed system had lost the person who had the idea in the first place. As such, there was no accountability, participation, or engagement. To me, all it seemed to do was reinforce the gatekeepers in their roles and in their identities. There was nothing about it that was suggestive of collective freedom or of an evolving work culture, but much that was indicative of distrust, bureaucracy, and control.

Sadly, this not an uncommon scenario. In fact, even Agile is being implemented in many organizations as a set of rigid rules, processes, and vocabulary, which contradicts the very essence of agility. Systems in which collective liberty is shallow, limited, and controlled are generally designed by professionals who don't put skin in the game. They don't take risks. They want only the "good side" of employee engagement: the productive outputs. They want more ideas, more honesty, more commitment, all focused on the *execution* of work. But engagement is holistic; a person shouldn't be expected to give at prescribed times or for predetermined purposes. Engagement is an *engaging* proposition. Internal communication campaigns urging people to speak up, to make use of suggestion boxes, to participate in employee surveys, to join focus groups, and the like perpetuate the control of speech and creativity. They are informed by the illusion that action can be kept disconnected from thinking, that behavior change can be triggered by posters on the wall and video clips on the intranet, and that hierarchy is little more than a matter of organizational design. This is a shallow and inefficient form of protoliberation. It expresses fear of change, lack of imagination, and lazy thinking.

Collective dialogue, too, should not be mistaken for an emancipatory practice. In his article "Emancipatory Discourse and Liberation," Joseph Raelin reminds us that context, relationships, and rhetoric can all inhibit discourse, preventing people from truly expressing themselves.[2] What may appear an open and rational situation for one party may be perceived as the diametric opposite by another. This is particularly true when people from marginalized groups are invited to participate in "decontextualized and depoliticized" dialogue with colleagues of a higher socioprofessional status. They are given little chance to call out the systemic forces that keep power relations in place. According to Raelin, many see such offers as little more than "window-dressing" or, more problematically, as a means of "colonization." Whether we agree or not with this critique, it is important that changemakers keep this worldview in mind as they develop their work.

Granted Liberty

Liberty that is bestowed on or granted to recipients denies them the chance to actively participate in the process. "Not even the best-intentioned leadership can bestow independence as a gift. The liberation of the oppressed is a liberation of women and men, not things," warned educator and philosopher Paulo Freire in his 1968 book *Pedagogy of the Oppressed*.[3] Freire's thesis centers on liberation as a means of manipulation. This belittles or nullifies people's agency, failing to produce the expected outcomes. This is the main criticism usually made against the notion of empowerment.

The word *empowerment* was popularized in the early twentieth century by American feminists claiming rights for women and, from the 1930s, by sociologists who studied the struggles of oppressed groups. It was then used in the decolonialization movement, in the Black Power movement, and, naturally, in the modern feminist movement. From the 1970s, right-leaning commentators and neoconservatives used *empowerment* to refer to the liberation of the individual from choice-limiting government policies. In her article "Empowerment: The History of a Key Concept in Contemporary Development Discourse," sociology professor Anne Calvès regrets the loss of the word's collective value.[4] From its strong and meaningful beginnings, *empowerment* has become a "vague and falsely consensual term," serving an individualistic agenda and, ultimately, the status quo. It has lost its emancipatory potential. But it is still very popular and widely used. HR Zone, for example, defines it as "a management strategy that aims to give employees the tools and resources necessary to make confident decisions in the workplace without supervision."[5] In the field of social work and development, empowerment aims at increasing human agency so that people develop a greater capacity to act, serving their own development and the development of their community.

Researcher Catherine Neveu of the Interdisciplinary Institute of Anthropology of the Contemporary brings an insightful illustration of an empowerment project in "Un projet d'émancipation à l'épreuve de sa mise en pratiques" ("An emancipation project put to the test"), a 2016 paper published in *Revue du MAUSS*.[6] The setting was an ordinary social center in a French region. A diverse group of women from the neighborhood met there every Monday afternoon in a "convivial encounter," to chat over coffee and share a few other casual activities. Leaders of the social center network decided to launch an empowerment initiative and commissioned a consultant to visit the center. They hoped that guidance on topics such as relations with social-housing landlords could help emancipate the group and empower its participants to deal with neighborhood life. The consultant facilitated group-project work for a month until, on the fifth Monday, the participants demanded that the initiative be stopped and that they return to their former social afternoon routine. Neveu draws several lessons from this experience, some of which relate to the ambivalence of the social center employees toward the notion of empowerment. But clearly, the women's group hadn't been *asked* whether they wanted more agency. However generous the intention, it had been assumed that they could be empowered from above. Naturally, it didn't work. Had there been some energy to begin with, perhaps with an activist in the group asking for support to expand their potency and impact, things could have been very different.

The fact is that, as John Wenger observed in a 2014 article, you can never empower someone; you can only *enable* them.[7] If you consider that you have the right to give power or potency to someone, then it is possible that you will consider yourself equally entitled to take it away again at some point. In this sense, an agent of empowerment is, at the same time, a potential agent of disempowerment. The dynamic is founded on a relationship of dependency and inequality. That's why empowerment can never come from anyone but yourself.

That has certainly been my personal experience. My colleagues and I felt empowered by taking a stance on diversity together, and by educating ourselves. Sandrine, an introverted administrative assistant, reflected on her newfound agency in a message shared with 2,500 people a year after the start of our diversity movement:

> Thanks to our movement, I was led to read exciting articles that helped me develop new skills. I discovered videos that inspired me, and useful information for both my professional and personal life. I was introduced to great people from other parts of the company. I made new connections and learned from others. This helped me to overcome my fears and take action. The movement changed my life.[8]

The volunteers I have supported at work over the years empowered themselves too, by exploring new territories for collective action. Sometimes they had to do it *despite* their management. But it was when they were fully *enabled* by their management—actively supported, trusted, and resourced—that the biggest successes were achieved. This happened when empowerment was a mutual process, gaining agency and taking more ownership on one side while relinquishing control and removing barriers to action on the other.[9] It was a "reciprocal moral relationship," as Joanne Ciulla of Rutgers University's Institute for Ethical Leadership refers to it: one based on honesty, sincerity, and authenticity. Ciulla notes that many leaders "talk about empowerment and participation and even believe that they are participatory, but in practice they lead in autocratic ways." They urge employees to act freely while simultaneously demanding that they be kept informed of everything that is done, that no risks be taken, and that the end product be perfect. Ciulla called this "bogus empowerment."[10] Some managers, argues consultant Didier Marlier, are intellectually and emotionally unready to give away power.[11] He recalls his own discomfort when allowing all employees of an association he led, including apprentices, to sign documents on his behalf. However, he discovered that the gains in engagement and performance proved that it was a risk worth taking. Empowerment doesn't work in a culture of fear and blame, but it thrives in a culture of dialogue and respect.

What, then, can leaders do to increase collective freedom and avoid the traps of "shallow" or "granted" liberty? Consultant Francisco Miraval puts it bluntly: "To liberate people and organizations, first liberate them from *your* ideas."[12] But this requires the assent and active cooperation of leaders. In order to secure true emancipation, independent of managers, some have imagined and tested another way: liberty by design.

Liberty by Design?

The COVID-19 pandemic has accelerated the possibility of working from anywhere. Does that mean that work has become structurally freer? Your manager may not be breathing down your neck in person for the time being, but all other elements of the constraint framework—reporting and delegation, compensation, performance management—remain in place. Could this change?

Work could take place in organizations designed so that collective freedom is not only possible and effective, but also detached from the individual preferences of its leaders. Whether enlightened or not, comfortable with real empowerment or not, managers would have to respect and support their colleagues' liberty because it would be embedded in the organization's ways of working.

An abundant corpus of ideas, illustrated by some famous examples at pioneering organizations, has explored the structures and the practices of collective liberty by design. Many of them propose alternatives to command-and-control structures, creating more freedom in order to be more effective. I will refer to a few of them in the following pages, highlighting similarities and differences with my own experience. While I find these examples stimulating and useful, it is also worth noting that some of them generate unexpected and unwanted effects. Rather than an exclusive focus on the redesign of our organizations, we should pay attention to how our collective work experience can be liberated.

Good Riddance, Control Structures!

In 2001, after I returned to Europe from Asia, joining Sanofi, I entered the Human Resources department. Its priorities were naturally shaped by the company strategy, but it was also influenced by current trends. One of these was de-layering: the reduction in the number of hierarchical levels and, as a consequence, the increase in the number of people reporting to each manager to ten or more. A smaller number often resulted in micromanagement and unnecessary overhead costs. As Peter Block observed in 1993, if the aim is to effect changes to organizational architecture, supporting stewardship rather than traditional leadership, then a flattened and multifunctional structure is helpful.[13] This is a preferable approach to decentralization, which tends to only "push patriarchy down a level."

Other companies have gone much further in their attempts to emancipate workers and transform how they operate. Their names have become iconic: FAVI and Poult in France; Morning Star, Patagonia, and Zappos in the United States; Buurtzog in the Netherlands; Haier in China. Among them are the "liberated firms" celebrated by Brian Carney and Isaac Getz in *Freedom, Inc.*, the "teal organizations" praised by Frédéric Laloux in *Reinventing Organizations*, the "post-bureaucratic firms" hailed by Gary Hamel and Michele Zanini in *Humanocracy*, and the role models that have inspired countless corporate change agents but few corporate executives.

The organizations mentioned above have all implemented elements of the classic participatory model. In addition to reducing hierarchy, they opened up to negotiation topics that previously had been the exclusive preserve of senior leaders. They also handed over more responsibility to cross-functional work teams, they involved field workers more often in corporate decision making, and they mobilized employees around company projects and values. In a 2018 article, researchers Patrick Gilbert, Ann-Charlotte Teglborg, and Nathalie Raulet-Croset pose the question "The liberated firm, a radical innovation or a mere avatar of participatory management?"[14] They identify several ways in which truly liberated organizations move beyond this basic template. These include making participation "the default mode of operation," establishing the CEO's role as that of both liberator and enabler, encouraging innovation and an entrepreneurial mindset among all workers, and supporting big goals that have a societal benefit.

Some of them have created, adapted, or experimented with new and disruptive management practices. In 2013, for example, the U.S. online shoe and clothing retailer Zappos decided to get rid of jobs, managers, and hierarchy by implementing a decentralized method of organization and governance known as *holacracy*.[15] Inspired by sociocracy, holacracy was developed by Brian Robertson's company Ternary Software.[16] It comprises roles (rather than job descriptions) and self-organizing circles, each of which has a specific purpose, account-abilities, governance, and operational processes. Zappos has continued to experiment, eventually moving away from holacracy toward an internal marketplace where "employees earn their budgets by selling their skills and services to each other and directly to external customers."[17] This has similarities to the platform model known as RenDanHeYi, created by the Chinese home appliance company Haier.[18] The Chinese company was split into more than four thousand self-organizing microenterprises, collaborating or competing with each other, loosely connected via platforms and common norms, all entirely dependent on their performance with clients. One way or another, these companies are well on their way to what Margaret Wheatley and Myron Rogers once referred to as "the irresistible future of organizing."[19]

In my time working at command-and-control companies, I was

envious of these liberated organizations. At the same time, I became suspicious of the seemingly magical thinking that surrounded ideas about organizational structure. Most executives I've witnessed in a new role start by changing the structure of their organization. It is almost as if these executives believe that everything originates from and is conditioned by structure, and that to make structural changes will inevitably catalyze changes in culture and behavior too. This is not to belittle some of the positive effects that can arise from structural change, but to flag that we have to be very mindful of and alert to the negative ones.

The Unwanted Effects of Structural Change

Radical structural transformations come with obvious risks. Even apparently straightforward changes like de-layering are not always easy to implement and often do not deliver the expected benefits. In practice, when removing hierarchical layers, many companies fail to revisit their processes to expand workers' autonomy. They change the underlying architecture but leave the mindset untouched. I have witnessed de-layering result in bigger bottlenecks for more people and in increased bureaucratic work for managers.

Sometimes structural change is legitimized in an organization as a tool for productivity even though no serious critical assessment gets performed over its actual efficiency. Once, I asked one of our senior executives why the organization kept changing structures. He replied that it was "the best way to keep people agile," working on the assumption that if you regularly shake affiliations, break up ties, and prevent smaller group identities, then people will remain alert. However, what those changes really do is slow the work down, diminish trust, and drain the energy of the workforce. That employees maintain their resilience and organizations continue to function *despite these changes* is all the more remarkable.

Big changes like the ones inspired by pioneers are interesting until they morph into cults. This phenomenon is often found when charismatic leaders spearhead new organizational approaches with the support of internal disciples. The effect is not dissimilar to that of the heroic leader, which can generate blind followership but not always to positive effect. While enthusiastic support can help with the promotion and even the adoption of new models and practices, the overall impact can be harmful. These initiatives, rather than bringing people together and uniting them in common purpose, can fragment organizations, creating division between believers and nonbelievers. The sectarian nature of the organization NXIVM became apparent when it was revealed that its founder had organized the extortion and trafficking of many women, with the help of some of his followers. It was only after eighteen thousand people had taken his "Executive Success Programs," among other personal development courses, and after a series of trials against him and his cronies that the leader was sentenced to 120 years in prison.[20]

When liberating organizational architectures turn into mandates, they become instruments of oppression.[21] In an article for *Nonprofit Quarterly*, consultant Simon Mont performed the "Autopsy of a Failed Holacracy," analyzing what went wrong at an organization that tried to adopt this model.[22] He describes the conflicts that quickly arose between the enthusiasts and the skeptics; the nefarious power dynamics at play even though the circles had wiped away formal hierarchy; the gaslighting and the blame game. According to Mont, this happens when organizations "create a powerful narrative of equity or transformation while leaving the underlying undemocratic dynamics unaltered." Instead of the new world they promise, they are actually "repackaging old mistakes." Former CIA analyst and Rebel at Work cofounder Carmen Medina notes that some of these allegedly liberating methods actually stem from a "desire for control" and from the false assumption that people act rationally in the workplace.[23]

The development of ready-made models seems to come at the expense of critical thinking. We tend to forget that they were designed by human beings, influenced by their beliefs and singular perspectives.[24] They are an interpretation, a simplification, of reality. Many models do not necessarily work in another cultural setting. This is evidenced by the challenges of implementing the Buurtzorg healthcare model in the United Kingdom after it had enjoyed so much success in the Netherlands.[25] When existing schemes and models are "applied" in a new context, people are deprived of their agency, undermining collective sense-making and perpetuating a state of consumerism and dependency.

Can we do without structure at all? Wouldn't we be at our freest in a structureless organization, where people radically self-organize? In the 1970s, such was the ambition of several activist movements. Feminist and political scientist Jo Freeman wrote *The Tyranny of Structurelessness* after her own experience of the women's liberation movement.[26] Freeman highlights that the absence of a formal structure does not prevent informal ones from emerging: "A 'laissez faire' group is about as realistic as a 'laissez faire' society; the idea becomes a smokescreen for the strong or the lucky to establish unquestioned hegemony over others."

So, how should we get organized together, to increase the autonomy we crave and deliver the best possible collective performance? There is no single answer. Often what is presented as "the answer" proves to be useless. Existing models, research, and experiments are only interesting as stimuli for a collective reflection anchored in context. It is the thinking and the co-construction process that really matter. Overall, I believe that we spend way too much time and energy on grand structural design and not enough on the conditions for collective emancipation.

The Microstructures of Collective Liberty

I was working with a volunteer network at Sanofi when we requested support from living systems experts Myron Rogers and John Atkinson. It was Twitter that had first connected us and, following an in-person meeting in London in 2014, I was excited by the opportunity to work together two years later. Myron and John first helped a specific project on one of our production plants, then offered to support our upcoming quarterly volunteer meeting. As our diverse volunteer group laid down our plans for the meeting, Myron and John asked us about our design intentions. We didn't understand the question. There was no design. There were agenda items and topics that would be addressed during the meeting. We would have discussions. Simple! We didn't know any other way. We had no idea, before being trained by our consultants, that more intentional ways existed to run fruitful collective work.

Subject to the same lack of knowledge and imagination, leaders tend to trust structural design and ignore the rest. This can have a huge impact on how people work. As Henri Lipmanowicz and Keith McCandless argue in *The Surprising Power of Liberating Structures*, these leaders believe in "buildings, strategies, policies, organization structures, and core operating processes" (*macrostructures*), which are intended for the long term.[27] This is at the expense of "the small structures that we select routinely to help us interact or work with other people" (*microstructures*), and it affects how workspaces and meeting rooms are designed, how online meetings are held, and how discussions take place.

Microstructures include not only the physical spaces where work takes place but also the intangible elements that support our interactions, such as how we structure the transmission of knowledge, collective brainstorming, and decision-making discussions.

Most of the time, organizations default to the same few, antediluvian formats: the presentation, the open discussion, the managed discussion, and a couple more. These are *conventional* structures, the ones my colleagues and I were about to use for our volunteer gathering because they were all we knew. The problem with them is that they prevent the full engagement of all participants, by offering what Lipmanowicz and McCandless refer to as "too much control of content or too little structure." They perpetuate the tradition of putting a handful of people in charge of the next steps.

Instead, we can design empowering, collective experiences, in which every participant is a co-creator, with ownership and accountability. This can be achieved without massive, costly reorganizations. Through intentional layout for groupwork, it is possible to "liberate everybody's contribution to the group's success." Lipmanowicz and McCandless suggest several *liberating structures*, some of which were created by other practitioners.[28] They include the fishbowl conversation (where a subset of people have a conversation, while surrounded by a larger outside circle of participants), the open space (where people co-construct an agenda and convene or attend the sessions they want), Discovery & Action Dialogue (a guided conversation to find home-grown, small-scale solutions to chronic problems), and the world café format (a conversation structured in several rounds, where people participate in a café-like setting), which Myron Rogers helped develop.[29] Other methods, models, and approaches such as future searches and action learning, are curated by John Atkinson, Emma Loftus, and John Jarvis in *The Art of Change Making*.[30] Unconferences, BarCamps, and open spaces are increasingly familiar to conference goers, future-of-work and change practitioners, and people involved in nonprofit organizations. They are all engaging, participative, productive, and valuable methodologies that transform how people work and make decisions. So why are they not more widely used in the world of business?

In May 2020, I interviewed Myron Rogers about what he had learned from four decades in change consultancy.[31] One significant insight was that despite most corporate projects in which he was involved having a senior sponsor, with varying levels of investment and understanding, the people who immediately and deeply understood the benefits of liberating approaches were workers with "the smallest amount of agency, the smallest amount of power." Rogers explained, "You know, people want to be able to create their own lives. And that's what we bring. Now, we're suddenly opening the floodgates for that. For all that stifled creativity and commitment and desire to come forward."[32] In fact, people higher up the hierarchy *already* have a sense of agency and often do not feel any urgent need for emancipation. In the worst cases, they don't even appreciate or respect what is possible from the people they lead. Perhaps, in the future, they can be inspired by real-life examples of collective liberty that do not draw on perilous structural change but on the mobilization of people. Hopefully, they can take on the responsibility of emancipation leadership.

Emancipation Leadership

A healthy and strong collective performance, imbued with liberty, can be fostered by organizational structure and collaboration design. But it stems from human behaviors. Behaviors depend very much on how we perceive ourselves, others, the communities we form together, and the world we're in. Our actions are shaped by our individual and collective identity.

Margaret Wheatley argues that "we are all self-authoring."[33] We choose to notice or incorporate certain things rather than others, in order to be consistent with who we already are. This urge to protect our existing self is, paradoxically, the only way we change. As Wheatley observes, "Whenever a living system changes, it is attempting to save itself." Unlike a machine, a living system can never be directed. That's why initiatives aimed at "changing people" are flawed and useless. As change agents we should never delude ourselves that we can change our colleagues, our manager, or our CEO. That should never be the objective. A living system can only be disturbed in such a way that its identity generates change, through dialogue and co-creation, the result of which can never be assumed.

Because identity is the key to cognition and change, the experience of greater liberty at work may stem from how we define ourselves, as individuals and as collectives. From there, change *devices*—the various mechanisms supporting change—can work, if and only if they are congruent with this intentional perception. With the title of her 2017 book *Who Do We Choose to Be?*, Margaret Wheatley poses a challenging question rich in growth potential. Action arises from the ways in which we choose to respond to the question.[34] The way I want to see myself and others is as creative free agents, bound by purpose. This is my personal declaration of intent. From what I have observed, such an aspiration creates capacity for liberty in action.

We Are Free Agents

To make the claim for our free agency assumes the existence, or at least the possibility, of free will. According to Oxford's *Lexico*, *free will* should be understood as "the power of acting without the constraint of necessity or fate; the ability to act at one's own discretion." But does it exist at all? It has been a topic of philosophical inquiry for centuries, certainly since the time of Plato and Aristotle, if not longer. More recently, Yuval Noah Harari has seen in free will "a myth inherited from Christian theology" that serves to justify God's punishment of our poor choices.[35] How we lead our lives is largely determined by biology and by socialization. Behavioral economists have shown how easily we are fooled into making choices and how we can be nudged, or unknowingly influenced, to make different ones.[36] In his 1954 book *The Technological Society*, however, philosopher Jacques Ellul argued that the framing of "determined vs. free" is incorrect.[37] He observed that "man is indeed determined, but ... it is open to him to overcome necessity, and that this act is freedom. Freedom is not static but dynamic." Understanding all the limitations of free will doesn't make it less necessary; free will underpins moral responsibility and enables us to recognize each other as full human beings.

This mutual recognition shouldn't stop at the entrance to the workspace. Assumption of free will for self and others is an essential counterpoint to Taylorism, Fordism, automation, AI, and robotization. The free individual is the basic unit of change. No freedom will ever be granted that we don't initiate in the first place. We are free agents at work. We exercise our free will. We understand that powerlessness to act (or at least, to form independent judgment) is never absolute.

If we recognize the same capacity for free will in others as in ourselves, then we need to ensure the even distribution of this capacity, enabling those whom the system might otherwise hinder. Those working at the very bottom of the organizational hierarchy, as with those working at the top, can't be denied the possibility to make choices. The very moment we forget that and envision co-workers or subordinates as cogs in the machine, as abstractions, we become complicit in their dehumanization. In *Community*, Peter Block argues that the real task of leadership is to enable people to face up to and accept their freedom.[38] Leadership work should be a humane collaboration between those who enjoy agency and those who have, by the nature of their job or by social conditioning, less of it. This is what creates more accountability and more liberty for all in the system.

Once, I was asked to assign three hundred people to different workshops for an upcoming event. I suggested that we let them go where they wanted instead, but my boss feared "chaos" and preferred to restrain the participants' liberty, as well as waste my time. On other occasions, I have seen people being told by their boss to volunteer as leaders of initiatives they didn't believe in. That lack of belief showed. I have also witnessed uninterested "high-potential people" being invited to events rather than volunteers who would have benefited most from them and injected energy with their enthusiasm. Too often, where energy is required, it is lacking, whereas immense effort is wasted on new management fads and structural reorganizations that are imposed from above. For many in large corporations, this endless cycle of mandated change becomes normalized. But it does not have to be this way.

The quality improvement program I was involved in at Sanofi between 2014 and 2018 provides an illustration of what expanding free will at work can be like (please see Chapter 4, pages 72-75). Quality management has for many years and in most organizations made use of a rigid set of norms, rules, and constraints. For decades, the trend has been to restrict little by little the liberty granted to individuals involved in the manufacturing process, providing ever more standardized operating procedures, with the objective of saving resources and avoiding mistakes. Despite their good intentions and attempts at "engagement," quality departments have evolved their work into strict internal policing. Anders Vinther and I understood that the usual quality approach did not work. Instead, we tried something radically different—something that was counterintuitive in the world of quality. We created more freedom in the system by recognizing, respecting, and encouraging people to have free will. Instead of mandatory implementation, we offered choice, by creating an invitation to join the movement.[39] A volunteer governance group supported the movement, and this team of volunteers was renewed each year, selected by a peer jury from strictly anonymized applications that were submitted from all over the organization.

John Kotter makes the limitation of mandate an essential aspect of his approach to change. "Create an environment where people are given a choice and feel they truly have permission to step forward and act," he suggests.[40] The difficulty—and this why so few leaders do it properly or even try—is that it takes a lot of work, and it takes personal engagement and humility. What makes people want to change differs from person to person. A leader's approach to this may not work at all for all the people reporting to them. One size does not fit all. To nurture the desire to change, rolling up one's sleeves, being creative, and adopting enabling behaviors are essential. For the quality movement, we eschewed the tendency to throw posters up on the wall and make a big splash on the intranet. Instead, we had hundreds of conversations with people around the globe. We diversified the messengers and deliberately declined to leverage the power of authority, encouraging peer-to-peer conversations rather than a hierarchical cascade. We refrained from imposing time constraints, allowing people time to absorb our message and form their own opinion. We accepted that some people would join the movement later than others, while others would never join. Those who didn't feel like connecting, volunteering, or changing the way they worked would be progressively outnumbered by the others. The time we invested at the beginning was recovered at the end, as performance results improved. We took a risk, but we believed that injunction and mandates carried a far greater risk than invitation and liberty.

In *Éthique et philosophie du management* (Ethics and philosophy of management), Pierre-Olivier Monteil observes, with multiple references to philosopher Paul Ricœur, the conditions under which management can take place "by consent."[41] How can managerial practice be compatible with the consent of those subject to it? Because human action is unpredictable, it is tempting to try to "harden" or engineer it through norms and processes that standardize behaviors. Some of the negative consequences of this approach are the execution of ineffective routines, reduced possibility of consent by people who are "objectified," and the potential for poor quality of work. Consent supposes that people in management overcome the impatience of doing, the certainty of results, and the benefits of an unbalanced relationship in favor of "an effective and fair search for a convergence, through dialogue." This exposes each party to one another's perspective in an egalitarian relationship. Modern leaders need to shift from voluntarism to exchange, from professionally determined roles to those self-determined in relation to others, and from bringing certainties and a vision based on knowledge to offering an aspiration or a hope, where any arising vision is formed by the collective that is feeding off the aspirations and hopes of the group. These changes "lighten the burden of action" by making it stem from an agreement, liberating both parties from the pure rule of necessity. The transformation toward the "modesty" of the leadership role actually augments its impact and contributes to fulfilling the essential need for mutual recognition among human beings.

Not surprisingly, it takes efforts to be free at work. Constraint—the opposite of consent—is internalized from a young age, as part of home life and our school systems; it takes a lot of time, patience, and fortitude to unlearn before one can operate successfully in a self-organizing team. Initially, people struggle with making decisions without a higher authority to refer to, as well as with dealing with disagreement.

To unlearn is not to forget, but rather to know when a particular skill is useful or not, and to be able to operate with a very different skill set when needed. The toxic trio I have seen impede the action of volunteer teams are the urge for control, the push for perfectionism, and the

quest for territorialism.[42] Control can be helpful until it becomes counterproductive. We need to learn to let go and replace control with trust.
Perfection is rarely achieved, and its pursuit tends to take us down rabbit holes from which it is difficult to escape. Tinkering is often a better
option. We should be able to start with good enough and improve from
there. It is preferable to act, to get things in motion, rather than wait
for the ideal conditions and resources to materialize. Territorialism is
associated with the protection of what is (teams, functions, roles, rules,
responsibilities), the fear of intruding into another's domain, and the
anger that arises when this happens. It hampers collaboration and innovation. We need to focus less on territory and much more on connection.
Organizational life would be refreshingly different if we were willing to
regularly ask one another, "What can we create together?"

Creators Generate Ownership

"People own what they help create" is the first of six maxims in which
Myron Rogers encapsulates the essential characteristics of successful work within living systems.[43] It is not the first one by chance. In
order to deal with ever faster and more disruptive change, our complex organizations, which are themselves living systems, require every
constituent's active participation. They need all voices, brains, eyes,
hands, and hearts. If they rely on only a tiny proportion of their people
to make sense of their environment, to design strategies, and to for-
mulate implementation plans on behalf of everybody else, they do so
at great peril. Whenever possible, the whole system should be involved
in creating the change, not just in executing it. If the system is too large
or too widespread, then leaders need to develop the habit of including
people who are representative of its diversity—not just for one symbolic
culture-related topic, but on any matter pertinent to the organization's
ongoing existence and operation. They need to let go of old reflexes that
nudge them toward elitism and secrecy.

A much-repeated scenario sees the decision to reorganize a company,
department, or function made behind closed doors by a leadership team,
possibly with input from external consultants, and with the involvement
of HR. At some point, a change management team is set up. As the number of people in the know grows, it becomes increasingly challenging to
keep the matter secret from those who will be affected first. There is fear
that if they find out too soon, the situation could demotivate and anger

them, and possibly even lead to a strike. Instead, energy is invested in crafting a smooth change narrative that will "provide meaning" and appease anxiety when the news gets out.

This misguided approach has no chance of shrinking the grief curve.[44] It will not shorten the time employees spend mourning the past and anguishing about the future. It certainly will not build or maintain trust and engagement. People don't resist change per se. They resist *bad* change, and they resist *being* changed. Too often Elisabeth Kübler-Ross's stages of grief, which she formulated in 1969, are taken out of context and normalized, used by executives and change management professionals lacking in imagination and devoid of any sense of guilt to justify the imposition of endless and senseless cycles of change and explain away their ill effects on people.

However, collective intelligence can result in solutions that override or mitigate the possible negative perceptions associated with change. Ownership creates the possibility to grow, to learn new skills, to build partnerships, and to establish trust across functional and hierarchical barriers. This happens whenever people are no longer kept in the back seat but are invited to copilot. One senior executive of a manufacturing company that had to close several factories told me that they had adopted such a counterintuitive approach very successfully. They involved local teams of peer-elected volunteers in the closures. Not only were the factories closed on time and on budget, but there was no deterioration in production or quality, and the whole process generated high employee engagement. The trust placed in the factory employees, empowering them to oversee the closure process themselves, built a perception of fairness. But it also created self-confidence and resulted in those involved acquiring a new set of valuable skills. The possibility of ownership transformed bad news into an opportunity.

In their article "Un travail à soi" (A work of one's own), researchers Amaury Grimand, Johan Glaisner, and Anouk Grevin explain that ownership of work is first of all the mobilization of personal resources in order to overcome contingencies and obstacles.[45] It is also a meaning-making and mutual recognition process through which a worker's competency is recognized by their peers. "Working involves not only producing, it also involves one's own transformation," claims Christophe Dejours.[46] Ownership turns the experience of work and its difficulties into one of pleasure, subjective expansion, and freedom.

Dejours' 2013 book *Travail vivant* (Living work) explores how the affective, subjective, and embodied experience of *working* can contribute to self-actualization, and to the expansion of subjective powers. Leadership that creates the conditions for people to deploy ingenuity, an "intelligence that goes to explore the world in order to feel, transform, and expand itself," enables work as a path to emancipation and ethical living.

Ownership is not simply an individual process; it is a collective one too. It is "a social relationship, a way of defining 'togetherness.'"[47] Leadership can enable this understanding of ownership by creating or supporting spaces for blame-free discussion and genuine debate about the work. It is this collective deliberation that creates ownership around a common goal, while building mutual aid and solidarity among workers. These are the foundations for collective action.

A system that builds ownership instead of suppressing it increases its tolerance to variety and change. Its leadership does not lament that people are imperfect robots but celebrates their rich creative potential. In such organizations, employees, even those whose roles are repetitive or of low status, are never considered as interchangeable units.

The problem is that the world of business hates surprises. Performance is very much linked to matching forecasts—to the point that in some sectors, forecasting now seems to be even more important than the trade itself. Analysis of the analysis of business has become the real business. Standardization of everything is a common obsession. One executive I worked with even insisted that any document submitted to him had to make use of a specific typeface, font size, and vocabulary. Meanwhile, as far as talent is concerned, consistent mediocrity is preferable to unpredictable genius. The most creative businesspeople I know all end up wanting to leave the big organizations they work for. They find that their creativity is unwelcome and discouraged, and they are rarely given space to innovate. Yet organizations have so much to gain from welcoming variety. Increasing a system's tolerance of diversity can be done in many ways:

- Alleviating the pressure to achieve goals and leadership's control of implementation

- Forming partnerships at an early stage

- Inviting, supporting, and rewarding creativity

- Encouraging exchanges so that ideas form beyond people's usual scope of work
- Role-modeling creativity in the way regular work gets done

We did precisely this at Sanofi in the field of quality, which was notoriously averse to variations. Our approach was described by Anders Vinther and me in a 2017 article, "Deming, Finally!":

> Variation should be reduced for equipment, systems, and processes to ensure consistent output batch after batch. However, we can't apply the same approach to our employees. They are humans, not machines. Instead, variation of individuals should be leveraged to continuously co-create and improve quality. When people are involved in finding solutions and are not feeling "standardized" that is when quality will improve.[48]

With this approach, we extended an invitation to create across all manufacturing sites and job levels. We networked; we showed interest; we activated support for creators and innovators. We realized there were hundreds, possibly thousands, of people we had never heard of coming up with solutions to problems we didn't even know existed or creating fun and engaging videos and other communications to explain in easily accessible terms seemingly dull topics.

One innovator was a shop-floor technician trainer named Chuck who suggested a change in a machine connection. His simple idea generated substantial savings and better production outputs. When I congratulated him, he wrote back, "Thank you for getting this off the ground after nine years." During all that time, no one had shown any interest in Chuck's idea or given him the permission to pursue something outside his job description. No one had allowed for the possibility that ideas for improvement and innovative practices can come from *anywhere*. The company had denied itself nine years of cost savings, output improvement, and employee engagement. Energized by the sudden recognition of what he could add, Chuck turned his mind to more areas for potential innovation, triggering the creation of a specific role dedicated to the field.

Bound Together through Purpose

As Ayelet Baron says in *Our Journey to Corporate Sanity*,

> It is liberating when you realize that in a world of opportunities, there is no need to focus on pointless divisions and conflicts. Organizations benefit greatly when they tap into their people's talents and passions, and pursue with collective purpose the ideas that spurred the creation of their organizations in the first place. [49]

We are bound by purpose. Wherever we stand in an organization, whatever our origin, our age, our gender, we share the desire to contribute to something bigger than ourselves. People engage around a common purpose and identity, not around an organizational or company setup. It is the opportunity to contribute freely to a shared, purposeful vision that keeps people together and guarantees the quality of their work—as long as that vision is not contradicted by the behaviors of colleagues, in particular those at the top of the organization.

The source of organization is *identity*, Wheatley and Rogers write in *A Simpler Way*.[50] An organization "is an identity in motion." Because of that, any collective effort should begin with a common exploration of purpose: "We need to explore why we have come together." Nothing meaningful or sustainable can be produced if this collective engagement is bypassed. This is something that must be undertaken again and again, as the work, the group, and the world evolve.

Some organizations attempt shortcuts, creating a "vision" in a boardroom with the assistance of external advisers, then displaying it on the office walls, on the corporate website, in strategy documents, and in the annual report. This is no way to engage employees, and it is certainly no way to catalyze behavioral change. People are very much aware of the difference between a shared identity emerging from within a group and a marketing slogan that is pushed at them. They feel it viscerally.

"What are we trying to be? What's possible now? How can the world be different because of us?" Some of the questions suggested by Wheatley and Rogers are exactly those I and my fellow change agents asked ourselves when we joined forces for our diversity movement. These identity-forming questions also remain embedded in my consultancy work with clients today. They are absolutely critical, not only because the discussion process creates ownership, but because a collective identity enables us to connect narrower identities (tied to job, function, place of work, language, and hierarchical rank) and to overcome divisions.

The quality transformation effort I was involved in at Sanofi required the creation of a powerful sense of strategic urgency among ten thousand people across three continents. It was, as John Kotter suggests in *Accelerate*, "a force for change that aligns people's feelings, thoughts, and actions."[51] In October 2014, we started by gathering about forty people from different sites and various levels in the organization to define our purpose and establish what "Big Opportunity" we were addressing. They produced a half page of emotionally compelling, client-focused text that acknowledged that we had to improve, that we could and wanted to do things differently, and that each of us could play a role in this. Many wondered why we spent time on this at all, especially as the company already had a mission and vision statement. But our ultimate success owed much to this exercise and to encouraging peer-to-peer conversations around what was produced. The involvement of a variety of perspectives, as well as the rich conversations, established a sense of authenticity, helping build energy for change among those who participated and others they then spoke to.

The result of this effort was the creation of a powerful "compass," a collective manifesto through which people aligned actions and behaviors *by themselves*. This is what can replace command-and-control. It yields much better outcomes in an era when people hold their autonomy dear. From this collective purpose that connected everyone to the identity and true mission of the company, people were free to create solutions. Anything was welcome as long as it supported the purpose. This approach saved significant supervision time. Instead of being seen as the chief mechanic tasked with lubricating each cog in the machine, the leader became the head gardener who needed to ensure the soil was fertile. There was no need to form rules about the expected height and color of each plant. Anything could grow—but everything would contribute to a beautiful garden. Unsurprisingly, results significantly exceeded our expectations. Had we set objectives for everyone involved, we would have limited them with our own perspectives and knowledge. Instead, we created liberty in the system and kept it together through purpose. We invited people to be co-creators of a common future and did our best to enable them in this endeavor.

The one big obstacle to this approach, an obstacle that needs to be carefully managed, is incoherence. People are bound to the collective identity by mutual trust, but this trust can be fragile. People let purpose guide their actions and behaviors in the workplace as long as they understand this purpose to be authentic, shared, and free of manipulation. This type of approach is doomed to fail if leaders do not relentlessly role-model and if their behaviors do not show integrity and consistency. One CEO I knew of urged colleagues in his organization to dare to become more collaborative and more digital but refused to join the company's internal social network himself. He was incensed when someone highlighted the inconsistency. Throughout my work with corporate volunteers, I have seen numerous examples of managers paying lip service to empowerment. They say all the right words, but their actions say the opposite—and the hierarchy allows them to get away with it and continue in their inconsistency. This is the type of multiple personality disorder, as it were, that creates confusion and prevents the system from growing to its full capacity.

It is integrity, the coherence between our actions and who we are, that makes all this work. Without integrity, any engagement effort is useless. It takes individual coherence with respect to the collective identity, but also team and organizational integrity, to sustain an emancipatory system. As Wheatley and Rogers say in *A Simpler Way*,

> With coherence, comes the capacity to create organizations that are both free and effective. They are effective because they support people's abilities to self-organize. They are free because they know who they are.[52]

Liberty at work not only is possible but is a necessary condition for good work. It starts with self-emancipation and grows with emancipation leadership. If such leadership had a manifesto, it might look like this: "We are creators at work. We understand that separating the thinking and the doing undermines the essence of work, dehumanizes workers, and fuels disengagement and anger. We contribute to healing society by restoring confidence in the symbolic abilities of ourselves and others. We *own* the work, and we resist the false comfort of being led, chosen, decided for. We seek others' creative capacity just as much as we develop our own. In everything we do that has consequences for others, we invite them to think and create together with us. We create conditions that allow them to genuinely contribute, and we welcome the possibility to be changed as a result of this creative confrontation."

BUT LIBERTY IS not enough. Other principles are needed for organizations of today and tomorrow to thrive, drawing on all of their talents, not just a fraction. This means establishing new, less unequal patterns of relationship between their members. The good news is that it's not so hard to do.

PART III

Equality

Hear the tempo so compelling,
hear the blood throb in my veins.
Yes, my drums are beating nightly,
and the rhythms never change.
Equality, and I will be free.
Equality, and I will be free.

MAYA ANGELOU, "EQUALITY"

"How could we improve diversity in our company?" he asks. It's June 2011, and the CEO sits across from Corinne and me in the executive lunchroom, where we have been invited to discuss the topic with him. Six months earlier, the two of us started a movement with several of our colleagues, taking the initiative when he had ignored a letter recommending action. The situation feels different now. A growing number of employees have gathered to debate, brainstorm, and make suggestions for improvement. By taking a new perspective on our environment, by deciding to shape it rather than be shaped by it, we have exercised an unprecedented liberty within the power dynamic of the company. By connecting through a network, we have created a rich collective that is informed by our differences in position, specialism, seniority, background, location, and more. It feels like the distance in power that hid us from the organization's decision-making circles has shrunk just a little and, as a consequence, we are becoming increasingly visible.

Equality is deeply tied to liberty. That is why they often come together in declarations of independence. Liberty without equality is just a privilege that favors the powerful. It is equality that makes liberty effective, Billy Bragg writes in *The Three Dimensions of Freedom*.[1] It is "the responsibility to recip-rocate the liberties that we enjoy." But then, of course, this reciprocity limits individual freedom, so where is the balance to be found? Philosopher Isaiah Berlin called the collisions of fundamental values such as these an "intrinsic, irremovable element in human life."[2] Personal ethics and collective political choices inform negotiations and compromises between equality and liberty.

The articulation of "basic liberties for all" and "fair equality of opportuni-ties" is what enables social justice, which philosopher John Rawls envisioned in his theory of justice. Rawls laid out two foundational principles in his 1971 book *Justice as Fairness*.[3] The first states that each person has the same irrepressible claim to a fully adequate scheme of equal basic liberties, which is compatible with the notion of liberties for all. The second states that social and economic inequalities are acceptable only if they satisfy two condi-tions: first, they have to be attached to positions that are open to all under conditions of fair equality of opportunity; second, they have to be of greatest benefit to the least-advantaged members of society. If inequalities cannot be totally avoided, they must be reduced as much as possible and be "fair." Discrimination must be resisted. For Rawls, it is through this articulation of liberty and equality *together* that society must ensure fairness and continue functioning effectively.

In modern democracies, equality *in rights* is nowadays a widespread real-ity. Blatant legal discrimination between individuals has become rare. Early proclamations of equality between "men" by the end of the eighteenth cen-tury, leaving aside vast parts of the human population, were later extended to "all members of the human family" and enshrined in legislation.[4] Different thinkers warned against the dangers of pushing further toward egalitari-anism. Alexis de Tocqueville, for example, warned that we must beware an exaggerated "passion for equality" that could limit the freedom of the individual.[5] He saw in democracy a tendency toward uniformity and the tyranny of the majority, which could degenerate into mild despotism. Karl Marx himself was not an egalitarian, viewing equality and its relationship to freedom as a political concept, a value upheld by the bourgeoisie to promote its own interests.[6] Marx argued that instead we should rid ourselves of social classes. However, if equality in rights is supposedly guaranteed, there remains extensive inequality in the *conditions* experienced by different people. This inequality needs to be mitigated as much as possible, but it remains a fact of life: we don't all have the same abilities, the same aspirations, the same appetite for power, or the same skills in handling power.

Is there a problem, then, if inequality is evident in workplace interactions but doesn't infringe people's legally protected rights? What does equality add to the idea of liberty at work? Is it even realistic to think of equality as a principle to guide the work experience? In Chapter 6, I will share what has helped shape my response to these questions, including experiences of equality and what its absence produces. Equality, I believe, is very much tied to the possibility of different relationships that networking technologies enable. This will be the subject of Chapter 7, after which we will look at how equality is created among workplace collectives in Chapter 8.

6

Can There Be Equality at Work?

I AM OLD ENOUGH to remember the coveted corner office. Before the open-floor plan became the norm, most senior executives were allocated large, sunlit offices while their subordinates crammed into cubicles with artificial illumination. The status and wealth discrepancies were evident again in the early days of the coronavirus pandemic, when senior executives participated in Zoom calls against the backdrop of their second-home swimming pools before learning to make use of digital backgrounds for their calls.[1] At one company where I used to work, the CEO enjoyed a godlike status, with a private elevator that enabled him to move from his reserved parking space to his office without any encounters with other employees. Those of us of low rank were almost invisible, buried under the hierarchical layers, while senior personnel played the role of sycophantic courtier, deferential and subservient to the CEO. This engendered harmful, distrustful, and treacherous behaviors as colleagues who should have been collaborating instead competed for the limelight.

Such workplace realities bring people together through shared criticism and ridicule. However, as Alessia Contu argues in "Decaf Resistance," falling back on humor, parody, and cynicism is a smokescreen that shrouds the fact that those complaining carry with them no real intent to effect change.[2] Their cries of injustice are noise without any action, without any true disruption to the established order and their role within it, with all the subservience that that entails. That being said, what those cries attest to is the permanence of power imbalance, which is a basic form of inequality. Is this unavoidable? Is this imbalance a necessary feature of the orderly organization of people into productive work collectives? What would workplace equality look like? How would it be different?

I offer this working definition to inform the following exploration of the topic:

> Equality at work welcomes differences and recognizes the contribution of each individual, enabling opportunity for all. It is the foundation from which networks connect people in all their diversity, producing collective intelligence.

Equality, then, represents a huge economical advantage for organizations, in addition to being a powerful enabler of individual dignity and social cohesion. Yet some organizations don't pay enough attention to it, allowing hierarchy and power imbalance to pervade and skew relationships at work. Other organizations do pay attention, but they strive for equality in ways that have negative consequences.

Hierarchy and Power

Not so long ago, I attended a change conference that had enlisted among its speakers a retired industry executive. After a successful international career, having managed important manufacturing facilities and large numbers of people across the world, he now was a leadership consultant. "Care harder," he urged the audience. "You have to have tough love; you have to push the teams and drive them through the tough unpopular aspects of culture change." He continued, "Driving change, driving hard for the future, is an emotional journey, the leader must stand strong with unwavering commitment, leading from the front to take people where they may not want to go."[3] To which he added, "Expect casualties." If the entire team was still intact at the end of the change journey, he believed, the leader hadn't pushed hard enough. When I shared some of these comments on Twitter, change specialist Simon Terry observed, "This view is widespread. It refers to emotions only to discard them in the pursuit of a leader's vision. This isn't change. It is abuse. It fails."[4]

In *Hidden Connections*, Fritjof Capra notes that because people are able to affirm preferences and make choices accordingly, "conflicts of interest will appear in any human community, and power is the means by which these conflicts are resolved."[5] Hierarchy in an organization is always a hierarchy of power. Before elaborating on its adverse effects, Capra acknowledges in an interview with the *International Journal of Communication* that this structure "is an effective way of dividing tasks and labor, so that the company as a whole can act in an effective way."[6] However, we can't lose sight of the fact that hierarchy is not the natural human construction for organizing and coordinating large groups of people. In a 2020 article for *Management Learning*, Joseph Raelin cites numerous authors who have studied the ability of humans through the ages to self-organize without hierarchical structure.[7] Hierarchy, though, has become the dominant norm today, entailing unfortunate relationships of control and subordination.

The subordination of the employee to the employer is a fundamental legal feature of the labor contract. A subordinate relationship, according to the French Supreme Court, "is characterized by performance of duties under the authority of an employer who has the power to give orders, monitor execution of assigned duties and punish his subordinates' breaches of duties."[8] These general principles are shared in the labor contracts of most, if not all, modern democratic societies.

It is unfortunate that the legal relationship of subordination is characterized by a word that also means "submission," but, in effect, that is not incompatible with our workplaces.[9] A survey conducted in 2008 by the Workplace Democracy Association found that one in four working Americans likened the way their organization was controlled to a dictatorship.[10] In *Private Government*, philosopher Elizabeth Anderson equates workplaces to "small tyrannies" and top business managers to "the heads of little governments."[11] They have little accountability and are faced with hardly any counterpower, contrary to how democracy limits *public* government. Anderson's argument is reinforced by the many examples of how employers control their staff. This includes the prohibition of casual conversation and the denial of bathroom breaks while on duty, both of which are considered "time thefts."[12] Conversely, employers are happy to steal time themselves from their employees with lengthy, daily bag searches, suggestive of their lack of trust.[13] These abuses are frequent and persistent. Anderson suggests that "in many cases, people willingly support the regime and comply with its orders because they identify with and profit from it. Others support the regime because, although they are subordinate to some superior, they get to exercise dominion over inferiors."[14]

Hierarchy expresses not some kind of natural order, but an ideology. Consider, for example, the advantage of competition over collaboration. Shortsightedness and the misreading of Darwin's evolutionary theory of natural selection tend to present competition as the ultimate source of innovation and progress. In fact, as leadership theorist Esko Kilpi explained in a 2015 blog post, "competitive selection leads to exclusion."[15] This is always detrimental to the diversity and sustainability of an ecosystem, impacting its agility and capacity to solve complex problems. Worse, it creates an ever-widening gap between winners and losers. Kilpi elaborates:

> As losers are excluded from the game, they are not allowed to learn. The divide between winners and losers grows constantly. Losers multiply as winning behaviors are replicated in the smaller winners' circles and losing behaviors are replicated in the bigger losers' circles. This is why, in the end, the winners have to pay the price of winning in one way or another. The bigger the divide of inequality, the bigger the price that finally has to be paid. The winners end up having to take care of the losers.[16]

The economist Joseph Stiglitz refers to this situation as "the price of inequality."[17]

Another ideology relates to the superiority of cognitive work over manual and care work, which David Goodhart analyzes in his book *Head, Hand, Heart*.[18] It is possible, though, that the coronavirus pandemic may have shifted perceptions with the designation during lockdowns of certain roles that were previously looked down upon as "essential." It remains to be seen, however, whether the newfound respect for nurses, cashiers, garbage collectors, delivery people, and factory workers will translate into improved pay or higher status. Kilpi saw in the very classification of work as skilled, semi-skilled, and generic the source of some of our biggest problems today.[19] To reduce cost and enable competitive mass production, our systems rely on the generalization of low-paid, low-skilled jobs. The holders of these jobs are not given responsibilities and have fewer opportunities for learning, which leads to "a slow but certain deskilling."

Unequal social relations also enable people to inflict violence on one another. In French office-speak, a superior is referred to as an "N plus" followed by a number: N+1 is my manager, N+2 is my manager's manager, N+3 is the N+2's manager, and so on. When you report to someone, you are his or her "minus." An executive I had to deal with used to disregard anyone who was at the level of N–3 or below, lumping them together as an indistinguishable and unappealing mass of cognitively limited executants. The worth attached to your role is informed not only by the size of your salary but by how other people see you, and, ultimately, by how you see yourself. When someone is compelled to drop rank in the corporate hierarchy after a reorganization, it often comes as a blow to their pride.

Hierarchy, when not balanced by other forms of interaction, produces unfair advantages and entitlement. It perpetuates and reinforces what was started long before. In *Enfances de classe: De l'inégalité parmi les enfants* (Childhood class: Inequality among children), a collective of researchers led by sociologist Bernard Lahire demonstrate that, from the earliest age, "children live at the same time in the same society, but not in the same world."[20] Inequalities in housing, food, language, and leisure opportunities create a gap between "increased" and "decreased" lives, influencing individuals' social destinies. Somehow meritocracy, which lies beneath much corporate work and career progression, is supposed to address these shortcomings.

Meritocracy promises success proportionate to one's efforts and talent. In reality, though, as Daniel Markovits argues in *The Meritocracy Trap*, it is simply the new face of inequality.[21] Over the past fifty years, a vicious stranglehold has been exerted whereby elite workers secure the best jobs then use their income to ensure elite education for their children, who themselves further displace middle-class labor from the center of economic production. Not only does meritocracy prevent social mobility and collective progress, but it also makes the overworked people at the top miserable. For them, life turns into an endless and lifelong competition where they are expected to treat themselves as assets to be managed. This competition, Roge Karma explains, "consumes their life quantitatively but qualitatively as well, leaving no room for self-expression, actualization, or discovery—only self-exploitation, value extraction, and endless anxiety."[22] Our current system places too much weight on too few shoulders.

Nicolas, a former colleague, discussed his past experiences with me. "Weekly meetings with my manager always got canceled. She always had more important meetings to attend. I was treated as an adjustment variable." At best, Nicolas felt that his boss saw him as an abstraction; at worst, as a time-wasting nuisance. As a result, he adjusted his behavior toward work, with less emotional commitment to his tasks, less energy invested in improvement and innovation. He dedicated more time to activities outside work, in an effort to regain some positive energy and a sense of self-worth. The area Nicolas worked in should have been vibrant with ideas, but instead it had been maintained as a dull bureaucracy, from which he eventually managed to escape after years of frustration, moving on to another job.

I, too, managed to escape from a manager who acted as an exclusive gatekeeper between his team and the upper echelons of the corporate hierarchy. Insecure about his status and contribution, this manager—unlike his predecessor, who had facilitated contact and connection—opted to protect his main "asset": direct access to the CEO. Guided by the adage that information is power, he filtered and limited access to knowledge, using confidentiality as a pretext for hoarding information and limiting its cascade. Stimulated by workplace competition for attention and resources and by the rarefied opportunities at the top of a hierarchy, such behavior curbs the richness of context available to workers, limiting the potential for collaborative work and inhibiting the effectiveness of decision-making. It also favors what transactional analysts like Eric Berne refer to as *parent-child dynamics*, which often are a major source of organizational underperformance.[23] With this type of relationship in the workplace, thinking remains the prerogative of "parents," with "children" encouraged to execute. Ideas that come from the top are not challenged, while obedience trumps independent thinking. Conversely, the consultant David Pollard argues that the best ideas come from those elsewhere in the organization but, because they lack hierarchical status and are not listened to, they have to find inventive ways to work around blockages and limitations. In this sense, hierarchy becomes the enemy of learning.[24]

The fundamental problem with hierarchy, though, concerns not so much the layered structure itself as what it permits. Hierarchy gets in the way of business achievement by triggering disengagement, pushing for uniformity to the detriment of diversity, enabling inequality, and causing exhaustion.

Hierarchy as a means of codifying behaviors and solving conflicts is an example of collective efficiency that bears its own enemy: domination through inequality. Hierarchy enshrines social and status inequality. It even exacerbates it. This was acceptable in the past; it is much less so today. When society was more homogeneous and less educated than it is today, professional hierarchy felt like a reasonable deal. It was an exchange of obedience for protection, it provided the framework for rules-based jobs, and it offered the theoretical possibility of climbing the ladder through the acquisition of more knowledge. As expectations have become much more diverse and widespread societal challenges against authority and inequality have multiplied, hierarchical organization structures can seem like a relic of the past. Yet organizations, for the most part, continue to follow traditional operating models, even if there is greater effort today to erase the most visible manifestations of identity inequality. Hierarchy, in one form or another, may be here to stay, but it can become very different, more enabling and facilitative, if we can only let go of the past and the old ways.

Some have tried to invert the hierarchy, promoting servant leadership instead. "The servant-leader shares power, puts the needs of others first and helps people develop and perform as highly as possible," Robert K. Greenleaf wrote in *The Servant as Leader* in 1970.[25] In the 1980s, Jan Carlzon put these ideas into practice as president of Scandinavian Airlines. He opted for an "upside-down pyramid" approach, arguing that frontline employees, the ones dealing directly with customers, should be placed at the top rather than the bottom of the organizational structure. These frontline staff then had to be served and enabled by the rest of the company, with the flipped model enabling greater autonomy and decision-making where it mattered most: at the interface with the customer. Nevertheless, a generous flipped hierarchy is still a hierarchy, whichever way you look at it. It doesn't challenge the structural assumptions behind the layered segmentation of people and statuses. But it does make the experience of unbalanced social relationships a little less painful. Releasing hierarchical control can sometimes be of limited benefit anyway.

As Raelin notes, in organizations that are strongly hierarchical, any managers "espousing or actually engaging in democratic practices" are likely to be frowned upon.[26] If they permit their teams to experiment or to make decisions, it is likely that the managers themselves will "be viewed as indecisive and weak" by their peers and senior executives. For all the freedom granted to their teams, these managers are rendered "powerless to effect change." In the words of Bernard Bass, it is hard to operate as a *transformational* leader when the organization values or even permits *transactional* leadership alone.[27]

Reflection on subordination relationships at work evolves naturally with the transformations of the labor market. Lifelong affiliation to an organization is no longer the norm, and more workers are now more directly subject to market forces. Many, including social scientist Pierluigi Digennaro, propose the need to rethink or replace the traditional employer–employee relationship, extending the protections granted by labor law to new forms of work.[28] In "The Changing Concept of Subordination," Felicia Rosioru argues in favor of intermediate categories, ranging from full subordination to full autonomy, so as to recognize and protect a wider set of relationships.[29] These are "categorized by personal service and economic dependence on the part of those working." Sadly, early hopes that the digital economy would enable a rebalancing of relationships in favor of workers as independent entrepreneurs have turned to disappointment. Platformization, digital labor, and "taskification" have increased the exploitation of "underpaid, micro-paid, or unpaid" work, according to Antonio Casilli's assessment.[30]

A quarter of a century after the term was first coined in a report by the U.S. National Telecommunications and Information Administration, the "digital divide" keeps reinforcing legacy social inequalities and a new array of digital inequalities have emerged.[31] Landmark legal battles are now underway in a number of countries in an attempt to recognize the persistence of subordinate relationships, with employers ducking their obligations to provide social protection for their workers. This practice is well illustrated in the case of ride-hailing companies. Ride-hailing attracts drivers and consumers in search of flexibility, but also attracts controversy over the negative impact of the business model on the climate, on public transportation, and on drivers' working conditions and wages.[32] In France, Uber was recognized as an employer by the Supreme Court in March 2020. "When connecting to the Uber digital platform," the Court ruled, "a relationship of subordination is established between the driver and the company."[33] In California, on the other hand, as a consequence of intense corporate lobbying, drivers continue to be identified as "independent contractors," and, therefore, are denied the rights of an employee.[34]

Equality in Sameness

If conflicts of interest and power relationships are inherent to human collectives, then at least domination ought to feel bearable to those who are subject to it. This is how the system perpetuates itself. Economic power holders, in particular, have a strong interest in avoiding the resentment of workers. Yet there has been a great decoupling of productivity gains from pay over recent decades, along with the further enrichment of the wealthiest to the detriment of middle- and low-income workers.[35] Work, for large numbers of people, is now less the place where self-esteem and collective solidarity are forged, and more—as we saw in Chapter 2—a source of stress, economic anxiety, and ill health. For how long will the unlucky ones burn out in silence?

While *structural* equality seems unthinkable within our current structures of economic domination, increasing attention is being given to *symbolic* equality. In response to the growing democratic expectations of society and to the rejection of authority, some effort is made within organizations to affirm the equal recognition of people's dignity and worth. What I have seen happen most often as a way to achieve such symbolic equality among people is the pursuit of sameness. If we behave as equals, if we treat each other as such irrespective of our differences, then maybe domination, submission, and unproductive power relationships can become a thing of the past. Maybe we can finally clear the sand from the gears of the system.

In this endeavor, two main strategies are implemented, sometimes simultaneously: difference nullification and difference compartmentalization. Difference nullification turns a blind eye to disparities in social class, nationality, sexuality, gender, ethnicity, physicality, age,

education, and worldviews, among other things. Difference compartmentalization segments these differences in order to reduce friction.
Can we trust either of these shortcuts to equality?

Uniformity: The Nullification of Differences

Managing increasingly heterogeneous individual differences and preferences is hard work. They create tensions and frictions. People fear that
heterogeneity might slow down decision-making and hamper collective
performance. One way of dealing with the problem is simply to conceal
it—pretend differences don't exist or don't matter, and actively shape
a fiction of uniformity that alleviates perceptions of status inequalities.

Without it being necessarily a deliberate policy, many organizations encourage social and cultural uniformity because it feels easy
and is more comfortable than diversity. Their recruitment policy, performance management systems, work practices, and communications
foster a homogenizing cultural norm that aims at unifying the social
body. Employees are invited to conform to a singular archetype inherited from the past: what the artist Grayson Perry refers to as "Default
Man"—straight, white, middle-class, middle-aged.[36] Women who rise
to the top often display masculine behaviors. In fact, I was once encouraged by a female manager to "show my authority more," banging my fist
on the table, otherwise I would appear insufficiently leaderlike. A former colleague recalls her uneasiness when, in a flowery summer dress,
she joined a meeting full of colleagues all adorned in their gray suits.
The discomfort was mutual.

The companies I have worked for in Europe, perhaps through unconscious social screening, have tended to lack cultural diversity regardless
of the region in which they are based. I have worked with far more
diverse teams in North America. My experience there, however, is not
one shared by everyone. In *Disrupted*, science and technology journalist
Dan Lyons recalls the prevalent ageism and lack of diversity he encountered at a U.S. tech start-up.[37] Resembling a cult, the company seemed
to "recruit a certain kind of person: young and easily influenced, kids
who belonged to sororities and fraternities." These recruits were "not
just white but a certain kind of white: middle-class, suburban, mostly
from the Boston area. They look the same, dress the same. The uniformity is amazing." Such observations have filtered into *Silicon Valley*, a
television series that mocks the tech industry's monoculture.

The byproduct of exclusion may be serious strategic failure, with one blinkered, dominant perspective overshadowing and unwilling to understand all others. In France, President Macron was elected in 2017 by overturning the political status quo of both the right and the left, as well as by raising hopes of unlocking the nation's potential while reducing its inequalities. In fact, his policies have proved to be not much different from those of his predecessors. Marie Tanguy, a young woman with union work experience, joined the team tasked with writing Macron's political program ahead of the electoral campaign. She stayed for four months, suffered a mental breakdown, and left just before the election. Interviewed on the radio about the book she published four years later, Tanguy observed,

> We were asked to be disruptive, but it was very difficult to be so, because we were among people who were very much alike, who thought the same ... On this promise of disruption, we ended up being quite weak. This was a team of people who looked very much alike, mostly males, Parisians, with a high level of education. They were in a comfort zone. The pace was very intense, adrenaline ran high ... but they were among themselves and in a familiar environment, disconnected from the real world and ordinary lives. There was a great concentration of intelligence, some of the most capable and successful talents; but they lacked that experience, that human depth, that would have informed them more and made them more aware of the consequences that their decisions could have on people's lives.[38]

I could have repeated exactly the same words about the corporate environment. It is this very perception that triggered my own activism for diversity.

Most of the time, inequalities are invisible to those who benefit from them. Dominant groups are likely to entertain the fantasy that they are not biased in their judgments of others and that the system offers equal opportunities to all on the basis of talent alone. They experience "advantage blindness," or blind spots pertaining to social and economic advantages.[39] Megan Reitz and John Higgins show how even as leaders believe they've created favorable conditions for open dialogue, speaking truth to power is actually perilous, and sometimes materially impossible.[40] One of the leadership teams I worked for as a

consultant was literally shielded from the rest of the company employees. Picture their desks in a restricted, escort-only access area, behind
a badge-controlled entry lock at the top of a tower. My contact person
in this organization wasn't even allowed to join a meeting because he
was not an employee but a contractor. It wasn't like this company was
handling sensitive or top-secret information; there was no discernible
reason for the barriers these leaders had created around themselves.
Yet they were eager to develop a "speak-up culture" and wondered why
it didn't happen.

Making a show of horizontality while in effect silencing differences
prevents difficult, discomforting conversations. Some people are just
not *seen*; their voices are not heard because they are not invited to the
table. I've lost count of the number of times when important discussions happened about groups of people who were not invited to join
in. These groups found that decisions were made on their behalf, without their input, and they were then expected to be excited about the
last-minute project they were suddenly expected to deliver. Similarly,
some topics are ignored because they threaten to reveal the fiction of
equality for what it is. I know of one leadership team that committed to
reviewing gender diversity data at the start of each monthly meeting but
managed to do so only once, maintaining their pretense of ignorance.

Some conversations, especially when they concern recognition and
power, are unavoidably uncomfortable. In 2017, a Google employee
claimed that he felt discriminated against as a conservative white man,
triggering a controversy around his employer's "ideological echo chamber"—and his own dismissal.[41] Being made invisible in the workplace
fuels an "emotional plague of resentment," which philosopher Cynthia
Fleury analyses in her book *Ci-gît l'amer* (Here lies bitterness).[42] At the
junction of individual and democratic crises lie anger and hate. Both are
likely to be exacerbated by a poor work experience.

To combat this dangerous pattern, people among the socioeconomic
elite attempt to restore some level of equality. But, as Anand Giridharadas notes in *Winners Take All*, these are often pet projects conducted
on the side while the structure of inequality is left unchanged.[43] It is
usually the case, too, that the well-intentioned benefactors stop short
of making personal sacrifices. In a pointed example, the journalist Rut-
ger Bregman ruffled a few feathers at the 2019 World Economic Forum
event in Davos when he castigated the super-rich attendees, gathered to

discuss global opportunities and challenges, for avoiding paying taxes that could help address some of these issues. The paradox of so-called change agents enabling inequality is not lost on everyone.[44]

Separation: The Compartmentalization of Differences

To alleviate frictions stemming from diversity, another approach is to welcome the differences but compartmentalize them. This tactic, however, relies on underlying assumptions: "We are equals in our respective silos. We are different and we deserve equal respect, separately. We coexist in harmony." The situation can be likened to a mosaic, in which colored tiles are laid next to each other but don't mix. This is a low-risk, low-gain approach to diversity. It's lazy and it can seem complacent.

Social interest in questions of equality, identity, and diversity has inevitably permeated the workplace, focusing attention on the cultural homogeneity that exists in most organizations, especially among senior executives. My fellow workplace diversity activists and I had some mischievous fun one year contrasting the fantasy cover image on the company's latest annual report, which featured youthful men and women of all colors, with the stale organizational reality of a senior group of aging white men.

Human resources departments in many organizations have begun to catch up to the idea that the workforce they provide resources for is diverse, and many have created diversity and inclusion (D&I) roles and teams. They mean well, and the people hired in those teams are often skilled professionals genuinely motivated by the topic, striving for impact. Unfortunately, good intentions often crash against the wall of corporate and business reality. I have often seen these teams mostly limited to defining D&I indicators, capturing data, and completing reports. They will attempt to raise awareness through mandatory D&I training courses and support identity-based employee resource groups and marginal projects linked to communications and marketing. But there their ambitions stop or are curtailed from above. Moreover, these teams are often made up of visible-minority employees. This approach can simultaneously serve to raise awareness and send out an unintended negative message. For many, the topic of diversity is then associated with people who "look or sound different," rather than with *everyone*. D&I becomes viewed as a self-serving preoccupation rather than an initiative that adds value across the organization.

Diversity and inclusion initiatives may have granted more opportunities to a wider range of people, but genuine progress, reflected in executive diversity, has been limited.[45] It is also probably fair to say that there has not been structural progress toward equality in the workplace. One of the problems is that D&I is constrained as a channel distinct from how the organization as a whole operates. Diversity is *used* as a tool for marketing, employer branding, and employee satisfaction purposes, not for the improvement of the business itself. The way diversity is handled freezes perceptions and locks people into single stories instead of enabling co-creation, collaborative work, and collective enrichment. Diversity initiatives may even have contributed to an insidious backlash; white male colleagues, for example, might complain that they have been unable to gain promotion because of a given hiring imperative that seeks to identify talent from diverse groups, or that they have been reluctant to dismiss a poor performer because of their gender, ethnicity, or sexual orientation.

Journalist and filmmaker Caroline Fourest comments in *Génération offensée* (The offended generation) that claiming the right to be different doesn't erase stereotypes but reinforces them.[46] We must be wary of framing diversity across a single cultural perspective that strives for a "separatist vision of identity." The excessive denunciation of cultural appropriation at the expense of cultural mixing and the creation of safe spaces at the expense of dialogue both stem from generous intentions, Fourest argues, but teach people to flee from debate and otherness—contradicting the very essence of diversity. Instead of for identity-based antiracism, it is possible to strive for a universalist antiracism and for the right of anyone to enjoy *indifference*—that is, the right not to be placed in a box or blocked by a glass ceiling because of one's appearance, ethnicity, place of birth, class, sexuality, or gender. Writer Eddy L. Harris writes in *Paris en noir et black* (Paris in black and Black) about his relief, following his departure from the United States, to no longer be considered only as a Black person, but also and mostly as an American author.[47]

One of the main partitions in the corporate world happens between hierarchical layers, which sometimes reflect social stratification. Organizations solve problems layer by layer. They almost never enable cross-sectional work. Layered problem-solving is such an ingrained practice that it is hardly noticeable. Yet the persistence of strong horizontal silos, where people in one silo don't know what people in other silos feel, think, or see is problematic. After I helped an organization conduct an important cross-layered piece of work, which involved workers from all levels of the company, one frontline volunteer observed for the first time of the senior leaders he had worked with that "they were just humans, like us." Imagine if this were a generalized perception!

Any engagement activity that values identities in relation to a "territory," either symbolic or real, is by its very nature self-delimiting. Take the example of an internal communication campaign aimed at engaging an organization's Commercial Operations employees. "We Are ComOps!" the campaign claims. It may feel nice for these ComOps employees, yet no one else but them will take pride in this initiative or feel engaged by it. Anyone who is *not* a ComOps employee is excluded. They do not conform to the bounded and limited identities that are associated with the world of ComOps. For this reason, I find that encouraging territorial pride is both shortsighted and potentially dangerous. A better approach is to bring people together around what they collectively stand for.

Can equality be pursued by the elite? Do those who have the greater share of economic, social, and intellectual capital hold the solution to inequality? According to political philosopher Matthew Crawford, it is highly doubtful.[48] With reference to Christopher Lasch's *Revolt of the Elites* and to François Furet's writings on revolutions and democracy, Crawford asserts that in liberal economies and societies, the elite is consubstantial with inequality.[49] The elite may loathe the notion of inequality, but their own status as elites depends on it. In a radical shift from aristocratic regimes, the bourgeois society claimed equality but, in effect, was based on competition. This was its moral failure; it was founded on a lie. As the bourgeoisie developed, inequality grew, and its legitimacy was undermined. So, in order to hold on to power, the elite traded equality for identity.

The equality imperative is broken down into multiple, smaller struggles that sometimes compete against and neutralize each other. In Crawford's words, "a young liberal can now blame her father not for being a capitalist, but for being a racist." Class struggle disappears behind a cultural struggle, and somehow we give ourselves permission to withdraw from shared norms, highlighting their corruption and blaming society in general for its deep flaws. Such a stance on equality appears to authorize the personal quest for moral autonomy. It favors individualism, on which our capitalist system is based. Anti-maskers and anti-vaxxers epitomize this, as they dismiss solidarity and the common good in favor of their personal preferences. This trend toward individualism conveniently shields economic interests from the temptation of revolution. Antiracist and antisexist rhetoric, the propensity to judge and apportion blame, and the tendency to focus on victims—these are all methods that the governing class uses to relegitimize itself in the face of the populist threat. They enable a show of morale that distinguishes the elite from lower classes, a class-conscious marker that reflects economic interests.

I am suspicious, to say the least, of approaches to equality that emphasize identities and frame them as distinct badges of honor. The same is true of approaches that essentialize experience, that prevent evolution and exchange, that form new silos when we desperately need to open them up to each other. A better way to equality would be to organize a fairer share of power among the diversity of people. To ensure a greater diversity of people gather at the table and contribute to all steps of the common work, from sense-making to designing, implementing, and assessing the impact of collective action. Let diverse people influence outcomes together rather than simplistically celebrate who they are.

Gender Inequality in the Workplace

Making one's mark as a professional woman is a long and tortuous journey with painful setbacks, including exposure to predatory behavior. I admire and pay tribute to the courageous #MeToo women around the world who have exposed their harassers. As I watch my children grow, I hope that my daughter will be spared from such concerns and that my son will be spared from conforming to toxic masculinity. I can't be sure of either, though. In France and elsewhere, tacit social norms like seduction, the importance of looks, and the eroticization of domination remain anchored and detrimental to gender equality in the workplace.[50]

Being a woman in the workforce, even a socially privileged one, has provided me with plenty of examples relating to what I have described in this chapter: the burden of domination, the plague of invisibility, the pitfalls of identity. As with social interactions in general, I have learned that work is shaped by misogyny and pervasive inequality. I have personally endured numerous occasions on which my only perceived value to my bosses and colleagues was my femaleness. I've been hired because I was thought to be pretty instead of smart; at trade fairs I'm often confused for a hostess (though a noble job it is); I've had to leave business deals that were finished by the men in the presence of female escorts; I've had to endure female pornography on display in the workplace (in the office of the Human Resources Officer, no less!) and paternalistic behavior or outright harassment by some of my managers; once I was confused by an Asian businessman for a "gift" for when the deal was sealed. As soon as it was clear that I was not a gift but indeed the salesperson, I was nothing but a trivial nuisance to this man. I have witnessed women reproducing typical male behaviors as they attempted to conform to what they felt was expected of them. They became so busy undermining other women that the men had free rein to advance their careers. And many times, I have been brushed off condescendingly as a feminist.

Without saying more, of which there is much I could share, gender inequality has been my entry point into corporate culture, the future of work, digital networks, systems thinking, and leadership. I have explored many more fields, too, in my attempt to address some simple questions. What is it that justifies the fact that half of the human population are kept away from power by the other half? Why is gender inequality so deeply rooted in our society that it persists across time and geographies? Why does gender equality feel threatening to so many people, including to many women? Over the years, I have educated myself through countless personal experiences, books, articles, videos, conferences, podcasts, and conversations. I have come to understand that social expectations, more than biology, shape how we live our gender identity. I have learned that gender is not binary, and that feminism is divided on a number of topics. In short, it is complicated. One thing is very clear, though: the foundations for gender inequality are laid long before people enter the workforce.

The United Nations Development Programme (UNDP) exposed in its 2020 *Human Development Perspectives Report* the restricted choices and power imbalances experienced by women around the world.[51] The UNDP's comprehensive analysis and wealth of data are remarkable, but the life-cycle perspective on gender inequality is particularly resonant.

As a woman, daughter, mother, wife, and worker, there is much in the UNDP's findings that seems very familiar.

What is unfamiliar, though, is the revelation of parents' preference for boys, which is having a growing and disastrous effect outside the West. "In 1990," the report says, "when only few countries had access to technology to the determine a baby's gender, only 6 countries had imbalanced sex rations at birth—today it is 21 countries." Young children in these countries are then subject to gender-specific norms in how they are raised, socialized, dressed, and even fed.

I gave birth to our son, Gustave, in late 2005 and to our daughter, Violette, in early 2010. I have tried as much as I can to resist gendered clichés in toys, games, and clothes. But I have not always been successful. For example, raising a daughter means being exposed to a permanent tidal wave of princess pink. I made my preference clear thanks to a children's book titled *Marre du rose* (Fed up with pink).[52] I also made a conscious effort never to tell my daughter or any other girl that they were pretty without also telling them that they were clever or strong or generous too.

On school playgrounds and in cities, girls are given less space, as geographer Édith Maruéjouls reveals. In the classroom, they do not receive the same attention from teachers, and are subject to stereotyping that may affect, for example, their performance in mathematics. Studies like the one conducted by researchers Pascal Huguet and Isabelle Régner with middle-school students show that eleven-year-old girls perform better than boys at reproducing a complex figure when the exercise is announced as a drawing test but lag behind when made to believe it is a geometry test, even though it is the *very same* exercise.[53] At this young age, the girls have already internalized a social perception about their gender and math, as well as about women and certain types of job. Self-perception, performance, interests, and occupational choices have already been strongly influenced.

In adulthood, women tend to make lower-paid career choices, going into healthcare or teaching, for example; working part-time; and taking career breaks to raise children. Even when we attain the same grades and choose the same professions as men, we find that we are paid less. We *expect* less, from the very start. Throughout my career, I have had no idea how my own compensation packages compared with those of my male colleagues, because I never dared to raise the topic and was never asked to, either. As with many women, I feel very uncomfortable when it comes to negotiating a salary. I have often accepted what is on offer without bargaining because I wanted to come across as accommodating. Talking about money feels a bit dirty. A short conversation with a coach made me realize this was all social construction.

A 2018 Universum survey of 533,351 business and engineering students in twenty-nine countries demonstrated that wage inequalities between women and men arise *even before the first job*.[54] When asked what salary they expected to receive in their first job after graduation, regardless of the field of study or country, men's salary expectations were higher than women's. In France, female business-school students expected 10 percent less than their male counterparts. This is not through a lack of ambition. It is the consequence of disgraceful societal inequality.

In 2017, Camille Rainville wrote a blog post, "Be a Lady They Said," which Paul McLean adapted into a short video that went viral in 2020.[55] Rainville's text lists some of the impossible double standards women have to live by. Many of these surface in the professional arena too. Women and men are not evaluated in the same way for similar actions. Performance evaluations are known to reinforce gender stereotypes. Research finds that women are more likely than men to receive both subjective critical feedback and less constructive critical feedback. A woman's performance is more likely to be attributed to characteristics rather than skills or abilities. Women entrepreneurs are evaluated differently from their male counterparts by venture capitalists, limiting their access to funding.[56]

Are women thought to be lacking in leadership qualities *by nature*? In "The Tragedy of Hillary Clinton," a *Vox* article published in August 2020, Ezra Klein compares the hurdles faced by the presidential candidate throughout her 2016 campaign with those encountered by Joe Biden in 2020. "When she chose her words carefully," Jay Newton-Small adds, "it was considered calculating; when she emphasized her competence, she was dismissed as cold; when she tried to show her passion, she was told to stop shouting." Klein quotes linguist Deborah Tannen, who explained that "the requirements of a good leader and a good woman are mutually exclusive. A good leader must be tough, but a good woman must not be. A good woman must be self-deprecating, but a good leader must not be."[57]

Society has a problem with women's voices in general. Often higher-pitched and more variable than male voices, they affect reactions to both content and messenger. This is useful information for voice-assistant manufacturers. In 1997, a study by Stanford professor Clifford Nass showed that we react differently to a synthetic voice depending on its gender.[58] In Nass's experiment, male voices were perceived as inspiring more respect and competence, while female voices were received negatively when they were authoritative but positively when they were compassionate and sociable. A 2019 policy paper by the EQUALS Global Partnership for Gender Equality in the Digital Age dedicated a whole section to the rise of gendered AI and its troubling repercussions.[59] The report examines the proliferation of voice assistants gendered as female and details some of its most important adverse effects. These include the reflection, reinforcement, and spread of gender bias; the tolerance of sexual harassment and verbal abuse; the representation of servility and error; and the association of female voices with simplistic answers, referring complex questions to higher authorities.

In her 2017 book *The Mother of All Questions*, Rebecca Solnit notes that "violence against women is often against our voices and our stories."[60] Research conducted by Christopher F. Karpowitz and Tali Mendelberg on the role of gender in deliberative situations shows a substantial gap between women's voices and authority.[61] They speak less and, when they do, are perceived as less competent and influential. They are also interrupted more.[62] Our body language matters too.[63] Every head tilt, nod, or "girlish" gesture is noted. For women, as Brittany Karford Rogers argues, having a seat at the table does not mean having a voice.[64] Neither tokenism nor a lean-in mindset can change this dynamic.[65] Unless *deliberative design* intentionally addresses the gender gap (for example, by setting unanimity rules for decision-making when women are outnumbered in a group), women won't be able to contribute equally. Companies that turn to women for help are generally in a desperate situation. This is the glass-cliff phenomenon, placing women at a greater risk of failure and thereby reinforcing biases regarding gender performance.[66]

In addition to all the above, numerous other factors limit further gender equality in the workplace. The weight of family care, for example, is felt disproportionately by women and has become even harder to bear since the onset of the coronavirus pandemic.[67] Many women now care for two generations: children and aging parents. At the same time, they have paid jobs and perform the majority of unpaid household work. Among dual-career couples, women often have to navigate the challenges more than men, with the latter occasionally forgoing egalitarian ideals when offered professional opportunities. In the title of a 2017 article for *Harvard Business* Review, Avivah Wittenberg-Cox offers this advice to professional women: "If You Can't Find a Spouse Who Supports Your Career, Stay Single."[68]

Then, of course, there is domestic violence, the figures for which are depressing and have been on the rise since families were stuck in lockdown.[69] Add to this attacks against women by antifeminists, online harassment, and more. The UNDP finds that, after decades of progress in advancing basic women's rights, the world has reached "a plateau in gender inequality" and even "an increasing bias against gender equality" in some countries, with evidence of a *backlash* in attitudes among both men and women.[70] Surveys have shown that younger men may be even less committed to equality than their elders, and no country is on track to achieve gender equality by 2030, one of the UN's sustainable development goals.[71]

The situation might appear desperate, but it is not. True, hierarchy-induced power relationships still prevail in the workplace. True, attempts to "equalize" people through uniformity and segmentation have limited effects on systemic equality. True, social perceptions still prevent women from holding the space they should hold, denying society the benefit of their talent. However, one thing gives me hope: networks.

7

The Network Opportunity

Over a long period of time, the main force in favor of greater equality has been the diffusion of knowledge and skills.

THOMAS PIKETTY, *Capital in the Twenty-First Century*

LOCATED ON A terroir that also grows lavender and truffles, Bonetto Fabrol produces a range of French organic wines. It is a small estate established by the current owner's grandparents, located in the Drôme Provençale in the Rhône Valley, near La Garde–Adhémar and its thousand inhabitants. I stumbled upon it by chance toward the end of 2019, finding myself in a small, rural cottage that served as the vineyard's reception. As I tasted a few wines, Philippe, the winegrower, hinted at an end-of-summer party he and his wife, Magali, host every year.

Eight months later, the world had changed dramatically. The coronavirus had hit hard, and France had been through a two-month lockdown, with social fractures becoming evident in public expressions of fear, rage, blame, and despair. Summer was coming to an end, and I needed a break from the COVID routine. I decided to return to the winery and attend what I expected to be a small gathering. To my surprise, however, it was a big event, attended by three hundred people. Dozens of bar tables and stools were scattered around the cottage grounds. There was a fine catering service, complete with waitstaff, a jazz band, orderly parking, and, in a sign of the times, strict physical distancing.

How had Philippe and Magali managed to organize and stage the event given the upheaval and constraints we had all experienced? I discovered that, in addition to their excellent winemaking skills, they're also very good at using Facebook. Their activity on the network has enabled them to keep in touch with a growing number of customers and friends, to stay top of mind, and to draw crowds to their vineyard.

Philippe and Magali's example illustrates both the power and opportunity of networks, which resonates with my personal experience, especially in relation to social networks. Before the advent of social media, the concept of networking was anathema to me. It made me uncomfortable, and I was just bad at it. Networking seemed to me to be the commoditization of relationships, and I had no interest in attending cocktail parties in order to distribute business cards and "sell" myself or my organization to "interesting people." Keeping in touch with former colleagues or acquaintances for the sake of keeping in touch or, worse, to leverage the connection for a job or business opportunity was beyond me. This distaste remained with me until online social networks entered my life.

To connect with co-workers around the topic of diversity, I began to make use of Yammer in early 2011. To feed a growing internal network with ideas and expand my own knowledge, I then started to use Twitter and to become more active on Facebook. One of the reasons for this was that I discovered that many of the influencers I followed on Twitter were also posting useful content to Facebook. In 2013, I joined Change Agents Worldwide, a closed social community operating on the now defunct Socialcast platform.[1] And I set up a blog, adding longer and deeper content to what I shared on social media. I also began work on a major corporate project that made use of social media.

Social networks enabled me to reach people I would never have had access to through regular communication infrastructures; to learn from people I would never have heard from through my regular information channels; to deliver far greater business benefits than could have been achieved before the digital era. These networks have expanded my social, professional, and intellectual world. By facilitating knowledge-sharing, networks connect a wider diversity of perspectives, providing each with a level of influence that was not possible under traditional systems.

Networks, however, are more than simply a way of connecting with other people or channels through which knowledge and skills are exchanged. They constitute conceptual frameworks, helping us view and understand the world, our organizations, and their operation. Yet there is a caveat—there's *always* a caveat. Throughout the past decade, the evolution of digital networks has tainted the original optimism that accompanied their development. They retain a large part of what makes them powerful tools for thriving, healthy collectives, but we are also more aware now of how they can be used to influence, manipulate, deceive, and distort.

Our World Is Networked

From its early origins as a word related to the interlacing of threads to its broader use for the interlacing of city infrastructure, the application of the word *network* has continually expanded as we have needed new metaphors to organize and visualize reality and to describe the complexity and entanglement of our world. Today, networks have displaced the tree as the representation of living systems, human knowledge, and social structures, gaining currency in a variety of fields, including biology, cybernetics, neuroscience, history, mathematics, sociology, and management theory.

At some point in human history, networks became no longer a simple means to classify and represent knowledge, but objects of knowledge themselves. An increasingly sophisticated science of networks focuses on the study of relationships, links, and interconnections between things, not on things themselves. It is an interdisciplinary field of research that aims at discovering properties common to the behavior of these heterogeneous networks through the construction of algorithms and tools. Although network science is considered an emerging discipline—it was established in the United States as an autonomous discipline in 2007—it has roots in the eighteenth and early twentieth centuries: in graph theory, with mathematician Leonard Euler, and in social science, with psychiatrist Jacob Moreno.

The first time I made use of network science in my professional practice, I was astonished. The ability to visualize the existence or, in this case, the nonexistence of networks was a real eye-opener.[2] In 2012, as my employer prepared to launch a vaccine against dengue, I proposed that they adopt a stakeholder engagement approach to complement the traditional "push" messaging. I teamed up with Stéphane, a colleague from the IT department, to find out who was talking about dengue online and whom they were talking with. Twitter proved to be a particularly rich source of data. We collected all the tweets that contained the word *dengue* in a variety of languages over a three-month period. This gave us 250,000 tweets. We then generated a visualization of how the accounts were related. The map we came up with was striking in many respects. It showed the absence of traditional institutional health activists from this conversation; the volatility of loose, sporadic clusters of conversations formed around outbreaks; and, most interestingly, that most activity consisted of unconnected monologues. The map signaled that there was an enormous, untapped pool of ideas and engagement, one that could turn into a hugely valuable activist community against the disease, if only these voices could be connected to each other. This became the purpose of the Break Dengue project.

A Brief History of the Web

Through her Emergent Code project, exploring the transition to a world shaped by artificial intelligence and code, social and business culture practitioner Anne McCrossan chronicles the "History of Human Connectivity." This has taken us from cave paintings to the internet. The latter, according to data networks historian Valérie Schafer, is a "socio-technical" object, one that is shaped by both the technical and the social, a reflection *and* a consequence of a rich, complex human context in which it emerged.[3] It can be traced back to at least the mid-nineteenth century.

- **1843**: Ada Lovelace creates the first algorithm.

- **1945**: Vannevar Bush imagines a theoretical machine to enhance human memory through rapid access to information and association: the "memex."[4]

- **1960**: Ted Nelson initiates a "digital repository scheme for world-wide electronic publishing" and coins the term *hypertext*, "a non-linear form of reading and writing."[5]

- **1964**: Marshall McLuhan announces in *Understanding Media* the networking of society.[6]

- **1960s**: Research progresses into the sharing of computing resources, connecting computers, and grouping data into packets to transmit them. This is of interest to the U.S. Defense Advanced Research Projects Agency (DARPA), because a distributed network appears more resilient than a centralized one when under attack.

- **1966**: DARPA funds ARPANET, a packet-switching network through which, for the first time, in October 1969, two distant computers communicate.

- **1971**: Roy Tomlinson invents email. Project Gutenberg is launched; at the time of writing, it is one of the oldest online content providers still in operation.

- **1972**: Pamela Hardt-English creates the first public computerized bulletin board system (BBS). BBS prefigures the modern form of the web and social networks.

- **From 1973**: Building on global initiatives—such as France's CYCLADES network, led by Louis Pouzin—Vint Cerf and Bob Kahn develop the foundational TCP/IP internetworking protocols; these are standardized by the U.S. military in March 1982, and the migration from ARPANET is completed on January 1, 1983. Some consider this to be the official birth of the internet.

- **1985**: Stewart Brand and Larry Brilliant launch the WELL, one of the oldest virtual communities still in operation.

- **1990**: Tim Berners-Lee borrows from hypertext and internet protocols to create the World Wide Web, for which he designs and builds the first web browser.

- **1990**: In New York City, Stacy Horn starts and maintains EchoNYC, a widely popular BBS online community.[7]

- **1995**: Aliza Sherman founds Cybergrrl, the first online space created specifically for women.

- **1996**: The Internet Archive starts archiving web content.

- **1999**: *The Cluetrain Manifesto* is published.[8]

- **1999**: Darcy DiNucci envisions Web 2.0, which really takes off after the first dot.com bubble bursts in 2001. Users switch en masse from content-viewing to becoming active contributors on social networking services, blogs, and video-sharing sites. This influences businesses' interactions with consumers and employees.

- **2001**: *Wikipedia* is launched, followed by Myspace and LinkedIn (2003), Facebook (2004), Reddit and YouTube (2005), Twitter (2006), Pinterest and Instagram (2010), and TikTok (2016).

  As Schafer warns, however, "there is no such thing as an Internet history."[9] Rather than a single and linear progression, which might be inferred from this timeline, there are multiple narratives, initiatives, genealogies running in parallel, intersecting, hybridizing. We should, then, be wary of dominant founding myths, which tend to overshadow or sideline the contributions of many people, including numerous women.[10] This is a diverse and complex narrative involving numerous pioneers, some of whom, either by choice or through omission, have never stepped into the limelight.

Network science, along with research on complex systems, has gradually matured and grown in sophistication. Today, simple graphs appear insufficient for assessing the complex interdependencies in most systems. The links that form networks are often variable. As Mikko Kivelä, Alex Arenas, Marc Barthelemy, James Gleeson, Yamir Moreno, and Mason Porter indicate in the *Journal of Complex Networks*, "they can be directed, have different strengths, exist only between nodes that belong to different sets, or be active only at certain times."[11] The researchers suggest that there are no less than twenty-five different types of multilayer networks, including multiplex, multivariate, multirelational, multidimensional, multislice, interacting, coupled, multitype, networks of networks, and metanetworks. Many of these have internal variations, too. The tools and methods used to understand and model these networks have themselves become increasingly sophisticated.

Only a small fraction of this knowledge is understandable to us nonexperts, but what we do grasp is definitely thought-provoking. Are we really connected to many other people around the world by only six degrees of separation? Or, in this age of social media and digital interaction, is the number even less, as Facebook claims? Do smoking cessation or obesity spread through social ties?[12] Today, networks and the science of connectedness are popular themes for books and films, as well as a coveted topic of academic study and a research discipline. It's no surprise, given how pervasive networks are in our everyday lives.

No human being lives, thinks, or acts in a vacuum. We belong to multiple social networks, connecting people through family ties, neighborhoods, friendship relations, professional or political affiliations, language, and culture. In Pierre Bourdieu's words, the network constitutes a person's "social capital," a set of actual or potential resources linked to the connection with others through more or less institutionalized relationships. Human collectives of any type are networks of people and things; they produce links that connect and enable flows of people, information, objects, money, images, and risk.[13] The network pattern in a human community, Fritjof Capra explains, is a pattern of communications that "interconnects individual processes of communication that create ideas, information and meaning."[14]

Within these networks, the variable strength of connections (weak and strong ties) impacts the spread of information, as demonstrated by sociologist Mark Granovetter. In the economic domain, Granovetter argues, "market forces" pertain to a misleading abstraction since individuals and organizations are *embedded* in the social networks they belong to.[15] This embeddedness enables, constrains, and shapes our actions. Reflecting on the transformational impact of the digital age, Manuel Castells argues in *The Rise of the Network Society* that networks constitute "the new social morphology of our societies."[16] The basic unit is no longer the individual but the network. Found everywhere in the living realm, the network pattern has come to characterize ecosystems where interacting organisms are in high interdependence with their physical environment.[17] The 1997 cover of *Nature* introduced Suzanne Simard's research on resource-sharing connections among trees as "the wood-wide web."[18] In fact, all living organisms *are* so much networks (of cells, molecules...) that biology professor David George Haskell declares, "Life is the network, not the self."[19] For Capra, author of *The Web of Life* and coauthor with Pier Luigi Luisi of *The Systems View of Life*, the network is the "unifying set of patterns of organization that goes through all life."[20]

The Rhizome

In a 1976 article that became the introduction to their book *Mille plateaux* (A thousand plateaus), philosophers Gilles Deleuze and Félix Guattari developed the abstract concept of "rhizomes."[21] Their idea was inspired by plant stems that grow horizontally along or under the ground and generate roots and shoots from their nodes. *Rhizome*, for them, referred to a decentralized mode of interrelations, and subsequently has been co-opted to describe digital networks and the internet. Rhizomatic thinking is also proposed as a counter to hierarchical and binary thinking. Connection and heterogeneity are among the rhizome's basic principles: "any point of a rhizome can be connected to anything other, and must be." Deleuze and Guattari draw a distinction between the rhizome and the *tree* or *root*, which marks a spot and sets an order. *Tree* describes systems whose elements converge toward a principle of centralized authority, the structure of power. While trees are centered, the *rhizome* is similar to acentered systems. There, communication flows "from any neighbor to any other," and no central agency is required to coordinate local operations. Synchronization happens organically. The rhizome doesn't direct, impose a structure, or enclose. Instead, it *maps*. The map, itself a part of the rhizome, stimulates connections between fields.

As with the rhizome, a network does not develop linearly and can grow only from what is already present, from the current connections, practices, and identities that nurture it. With its innumerable links signposting and connecting to other articles, *Wikipedia* is said to be the largest rhizomic structure ever created by humankind. Unfortunately, neither Deleuze nor Guattari lived long enough to see it. However, they described such a system's development pattern. The rhizome, with its multiple entryways, is always accessible to the many, operating by variation, expansion, acquisition, and assimilation rather than replication. As complexity theorist Dave Snowden argues, complex systems scale not through imitation but as a result of "decomposition and recombination."[22] Nonlinearity is characteristic of complexity.

Our Work Is Relations

For many years, whenever a newly hired employee or a candidate asked me for information about the work, my first reflex was to grab a pen and draw on a piece of paper the organizational chart. It felt like the most straightforward way to describe what we did and did not do, the perimeter for which we were responsible, and our distance from supreme authority. It was a time when I still believed that authority was concentrated at the top of an organization. My perspective changed, however, as I gained more experience studying networks and practicing in them. As I built support for an idea via digital social networks, formed ties beyond my regular scope of interactions, connected with more people through external social channels, created business value by connecting internal and external stakeholders, and developed a professional practice around community engagement, I challenged what I knew, what I was certain of, and, in turn, created new possibilities.

Cartoons that make fun of organization charts abound on the internet. One of my favorites represents a regular, pyramid-like organigram complemented with colored lines representing a multitude of connections between people across grades and functions—like attending the same school, affairs, secret resentments, drug sales, threesomes, knowing about corruption, religious affiliation, owing favors, and so on.[23] The comedy stems from the nature of some of these links as well as from the unexpected paths crisscrossing this group. But the underlying message is a serious one: you never know about an organization and how work *really* happens by looking at its superficial structure.

To get things done, you can never rely solely on the chain of command. Doing so would miss a large part of the dynamics that influence outcomes. Systems thinker Barry Oshry explains that, for the most part, we fail to see the archetypal patterns of relating that *really* influence perceptions and actions in organizations. We attribute to others failings that, in fact, result from dances of power occurring as part of systemic relationships.[24] From an operational perspective, the chain of command is crippled by bottlenecks caused by a glut of managerial tasks that are focused on running the system rather than changing it.

Relationships that aren't hierarchical play important roles when it comes to finding new solutions to problems, to innovating, to mobilizing resources widely or differently. This is critical with respect to creating buy-in around an idea or a project, no matter where you stand in the hierarchy and as vital for buy-in from upper management (for approval, resources, and sponsorship) as for top-down and lateral buy-in (for support, contribution, and participation). An effective engagement plan requires identification of and interaction with not just individual stakeholders but the different networks with a possible stake in the idea or project.

Some networks—especially the most informal ones, founded upon friendship, the appeal of similarity, or shared experience—are hard to identify. You should never assume that you know where the informal networks can be found or how they will behave. When several co-workers and I built support for our diversity movement, we were happily surprised to encounter a couple of supporters among those we'd assumed were heralds of the old boys' club. I recall our disappointment, too, when we did not receive the support we had expected from informal networks involving women and young executives.

Other networks are accessible to any curious mind. They can be organized communities or loose networks gathering people around topics of interest. They can be found via organizational network analysis or through recommendation or observation. Internal social platforms, for those organizations equipped with them, are a most valuable source of information and a huge time saver. From the public conversations that happen there, it can be understood who interacts with whom about what. These networks are precious because they do or enable what the organization chart is very bad at. Internal networks keep the organization together, by bridging between people and across silos. They give access to more diverse ideas, by connecting perspectives and enabling variety. They tend to equalize relationships, in contrast to the domination-and-submission dynamics that pervade in-person interactions in the workplace. They disseminate information quickly and increase the number of potential relays of engagement. Connecting an idea or a project to existing networks clearly boosts their chances of success.

In spite of this, some professionals still ignore networks and stick solely and stubbornly to the chain of command, with formal organizational structure serving to block rather than enable. By way of example, after a handful of my colleagues first started experimenting with Yammer in 2009, usage grew slowly and organically, becoming more widespread in 2011–12 following our employee-driven diversity initiative, which relied on the platform. The purchase of Yammer by Microsoft in 2012 signaled its increasing popularity, prompting senior executives at our company to ask the communications and IT departments to explore the viability of company-wide deployment. Little progress was made, despite an upsurge in employee interactions on Yammer and the successful adoption of the platform by one of our main competitors. The official working group's recommendations were constantly blocked or overturned, and, while the input of external consultants was sought, no effort was made to engage with the internal user groups who were already making use of the platform. Ultimately, in 2014, the company's executives decided to discontinue use of Yammer.

In this particular case, the saga continued. Protests and appeals by community managers to the newly appointed CEO secured a temporary respite. But a fresh review by the IT department once again excluded the input of colleagues who were successfully making use of the platform, narrowly and myopically following a chain-of-command process. In fact, it was not until 2020, when the company's hand was forced by the ultimate digital transformation catalyst—the COVID-19 pandemic— that it formally adopted Yammer and deployed it to all employees, eleven years after the initial experimentation. An ongoing "error of omission"—as Russell Ackoff terms those acts where people don't do what they should have done[25]—was finally brought to an end.

There is a wealth of evidence that when informal alliances do occur, everybody wins. Indeed, we need to think of our organizations less in terms of roles and reporting lines and more in terms of multiple and interacting networks: networks of conversations, knowledge, and energy.[26] Part of our work is to identify these networks and to engage with those that fit with our ideas and projects. If networks are seemingly scarce, then it might be useful to generate or invigorate them by connecting people together. Communicating in networks creates ideas, information, and meaning.

Viewing the organization as a network enables us to look beyond labels that usually frame contributions. It is tempting to assume that work roles are defined by job titles, but we shouldn't take them at face value. Anthropologist Gregory Bateson argued that "we are always in relation to something. We live in a world that is only made of relationships." Bateson urged us not to be fooled by the separation suggested by the labels we use. Labels are only a matter of convenience. In *An Ecology of Mind*, the film Nora Bateson made about her father, Gregory observes, "A role is a half-arsed relationship. It's one end of a relationship. You cannot study only one end of a relationship and make any sense. What you will make is disaster."[27]

This perspective opens a world of possibilities. Suddenly, a person's contribution is not defined or constrained by their role or hierarchical position. A quality assurance professional can contribute to the communications network, bringing their experience, their worldview, and their connections to the work; an accountant can be involved in the quality improvement network; a community manager can contribute to the selection of an enterprise social platform; and so on. When we allow the system to connect to more of itself, bridging between people across the whole system, combining expert knowledge with field experience, we de-segment it, creating mutual recognition and trust, bringing richness and complexity to the work.

Work Is a Social Act

Networks amount to so much more than the context in which work happens or a means for improving or speeding up that work. Today, in a world made increasingly complex by data, variables, and the diversity of consumer demands, networks *are* the work. Labor is about inviting, forming, and nurturing relationships. Work is no longer a role or a task; work is interaction.[28] Before his premature passing in early 2020, Esko Kilpi wrote inspired and thoughtful articles about knowledge work, which he described as "creative work we do in interaction"—a definition that applies equally well to the manufacturing work I have witnessed.[29] No work today is done in isolation, devoid of knowledge flows and relationships. Kilpi explained that the inputs and outputs of work are now "problem definitions and exploration for solutions," in a world where most problems are connected and systemic and, therefore, can be neither fully solved nor answered through standard operating procedures. This is why interactions are not just important for the work, they *are* the work: people get together and share information, exchange ideas, make sense of the problem and what should be done. They invent, adjust, assess. Work is "complex patterns of communicative interaction between interdependent individuals." It is fundamentally "a social act."[30]

For some jobs, including therapy, teaching, coaching, and primary care, connection is of the essence.[31] Leadership, too, has relationships at its core. It is through connection with others that leaders are able to catalyze change. Allison Pugh speaks of *connective labor*, defined as "the relational work between practitioner and recipient, where workers serve as a human witness of the other in their efforts to produce a particular end such as learning or healing."[32] As with so much else, including social relations in general, this connective labor has been dramatically impacted by the coronavirus pandemic. In order to avoid the risk of infection, vast amounts of relational work have been mediated where possible by technology, with an increase in remote teaching, remote consulting, and teletherapy.

These online interactions have been helpful for some but draining for others. As Pugh observes, "without bodily co-presence there is none of the sustaining resonance that feeds the clinician."[33] The same could be said of leaders, coaches, and consultants. The depth and the rich messiness of human interaction has been reduced to flatter, functional, less connective exchanges. We've experienced Zoom fatigue, even as the trend toward automation of relationship-based work has been accelerated, as evidenced by fully online education services, virtual preschools, and automated healthcare.[34] While automation has some advantages, it diminishes the catalytic nature of connective labor. This is because a computer can never be a *witness*. It can be a surveillance device, but it cannot *see* a person like another human does. It is seeing and being seen that confers *dignity*, "an ongoing demonstration of another person's worth," according to Pugh.[35] That is the power of human interaction.

In this sense, *collaborative work* should be a tautology. Many people's experience of work, however, tells a different story: the opportunity for quality interactions with other people does not exist. The structural design and performance management of our organizations promotes task specialization and competition. As Kilpi, drawing on the insights of systems theory, notes, our "enterprises are not organized to facilitate the management of interactions, only the actions of parts taken separately."[36] A focus on the parts illuminates my employer's lengthy delay in committing to a social networking platform: the vital connections that could enable internal interaction, creativity, and productivity remained invisible to the decision-makers.

While the COVID-19 pandemic has accelerated awareness of the importance of supporting infrastructure, it is less clear whether perceptions about the nature of work have been similarly affected. Hubert Guillaud, writing about the limits of video interactions, with so many now "stuck in Zoom," suggests that "the crisis revealed enterprises to themselves, without necessarily changing them."[37] Typically, the organizational approach to collaboration involves committees, working groups, and task forces. It is heavy on governance, limited in participants, and often characterized by tokenistic functional representation. This is more diplomacy than co-creation.

The raw material of collaborative work is the exchange of information, not the information itself. More than once I have witnessed the failure of expensive database projects led by people who believed in data as valuable in itself. These projects were founded on the belief that the accumulation of huge amounts of fresh data would illuminate more about the business's customers, markets, and influencers and would guide our own actions and responses. Inevitably, there was a disjuncture between reality and aspiration. People had neither the time nor the incentive to populate these databases, which were rarely consulted. What is more, raw data lacks the richness of context, and by the time it is uploaded to a database it is often already obsolete. From what I have seen, the discipline of knowledge management remains divided between those who favor information-as-stock, advocating the use of databases, and those who understand that knowledge is in the network, in human relationships, generated through interactions between people.[38]

When we view work in terms of interrelations, it changes not only how we think of knowledge but also our understanding of what skills to value. We now need many more relational skills, not just functional expertise. The competent workers of today are those who are able to interact with many people and ideas, demonstrating mastery of several disciplines, including social tools, blending and hybridizing knowledge, skills, and experience. They are what Kenneth Mikkelsen and Richard Martin refer to as "neo-generalists."[39] As Kilpi argues, we need to shift our focus from generic competencies to agency, contextual presence, and empathy. At the same time, we need to stop thinking of leadership as a position, character, or skill, and understand it as something that is relational, temporal, and "an emergent property of responsive interaction in the whole network."[40] Leadership is contextual, and the neo-generalist worker should be able to lead or follow as the situation demands, sharing knowledge, facilitating, connecting, inspiring, and enabling. In "Networked Leadership," Kilpi elaborates:

> The leader is someone people trust to be at the forefront in the area, which is temporally meaningful for them. People recognize as the leader someone who inspires and enables them in the present. People, the followers, decide whom to follow, why, when and for how long.[41]

From this perspective, we understand that the excellence of our work depends on the quality of the relationships we are involved in. Our work benefits from the density and the diversity of our networks, and also from the quality and meaningfulness of interactions. Some of this quality is influenced by the system—including its communication infrastructure and its culture, which can enable or constrain collaboration—while some of it depends on what the other parties bring. For the most part, though, it is down to us. Each of us is equally responsible for the relationships we are involved in. If they prove to be dysfunctional, then we need to question our own role in making them so.

Wirearchy

In October 1999, Jon Husband coined the term *wirearchy*, defining it as "a dynamic two-way flow of power and authority based on knowledge, trust, credibility and a focus on results, enabled by interconnected people, information and technology."[42] Husband's concept was inspired by the potential and opportunity offered by the emergence and development of digital networks, opening the way to social transition. This stood in stark contrast to his years of experience immersed in and observing the industrial processes and ideology that still informed how contemporary organizations, including banks and management consultancies, were run. Wirearchy reflected the changing reality of work with networks at its core, challenging the coercive paradigms, status, and control of knowledge exerted by traditional hierarchies.

The concept soon became a frequent point of reference in communities interested in organizational change, especially those that wished to unravel the "generic codifications of Taylorism," including job evaluation methods, competency models, remuneration practices, rules, and operating procedures. Wirearchy suggested that the fundamental dynamics supporting the interactions of networked people, technology, and information could and would change.[43] At a time when information and knowledge had begun to flow constantly and from every direction in an organization, this new organizing principle would not *replace* hierarchy but *evolve* it, providing a much-needed alternative to our usual vertical structures of power and influence. Wirearchy would provide what hyperlinked professionals required in order to do good work together and meet customers' fast-changing and varied demands. It would encourage a different mindset at all levels of the organization, offering unprecedented possibilities for collective value creation.

Wirearchy is intended to stimulate reflection, as well as tinkering, experimentation, and discovery.[44] How is this principle already at play in our organizations? How can it be supported and expanded? What does it mean for individuals and groups, for leadership and management at work?[45] Wirearchy implies that businesses let go, at least partly, of certain things that have served them well in the past such as their focus on parts, on individual potential, on secrecy, on analysis, and on the elimination of uncertainty. The work instead relates to facilitating connections, nurturing collective talent, encouraging transparency, developing ongoing sense-making capabilities, and engaging with uncertainty. It is an evolution from command-and-control to what Husband terms *champion-and-channel*, that is, "the championing of ideas and innovation, and the channeling of time, energy, authority, and resources to testing those ideas and the possibilities for innovation they carry."[46]

No one pretends this is easy. In a 2015 essay collection facilitated by Husband, *Wirearchy: Sketches for the Future of Work*, Thierry de Baillon acknowledges how difficult the necessary change will be for most organizations: "Decades of centralization in search for efficiency, years of capitalistic formatting in search of profit, have ossified their structure into blind hierarchies and one-way chains of power."[47] However, for those who dislike parent–child relationships at work, wirearchy represents a tangible hope that an adult-to-adult model is not only possible but preferable, and should become the default operating mode, enabling us to create value going forward. "In an interconnected world," Husband notes, "we will all need to take responsibility for why and what it is that we do, and we will perforce do this in a context of co-creation with other people."[48]

Networks for Equality

If networks now reflect the fundamental pattern of our lives, can they contribute to harmonious, domination-free interactions between humans? By nature, they are neither vertical nor horizontal but diverse and entangled, fluid and seemingly always in motion. There appears to be no "up" or "down" in a network. But can we consider the networked society and the connected company as solutions against social and economic damages induced by inequality?

Had this text been written earlier in my journey into engagement leadership, the answer would have been an unequivocal yes. What I perceived through the various experiments I was part of was an equalization of opportunities, a release of the hierarchical constraints on access to information, a democratization of speech. As the internet opened up a wealth of opportunities, this optimism was largely shared. Today, some of the idealism and naïvety is gone. The internet accelerated high-carbon globalization, caused billionaire-owned monopolies, and made generalized surveillance possible. As shown in Jeff Orlowski's 2020 film *The Social Dilemma*, social networks enabled the spread of hate and disinformation, the manipulation of elections, the corrosion of common ground and democracy. In 1999, *The Cluetrain Manifesto*—a set of ninety-five theses about the transformations induced by the internet—sparked a great deal of interest, exposing the authors' optimistic vision of the birth of a "powerful global conversation" and its subversion of hierarchies. A 2016 review of the manifesto notes that "reading it now is like waking with a hangover and looking at all of the empty bottles, each of which seemed like a great idea at the time."[49]

Yet networks can do so much for equality. In what sense, and with what caution? In the previous chapter, we explored equality through the lenses of power differences and diversity. Let's now take a look at how networks affect frictions, imbalance, diversity, and power differences.

Networks, Power, and Information

Power differences and power plays plague traditional organizations. They silence certain voices, amplify others, distort collective sense-making, and, sometimes, result in very poor business decisions. I have witnessed a handful of such disasters, causing the loss of millions of dollars—as well as untold nonfinancial costs—which could have been avoided if people had been able to challenge the hierarchy. It is little wonder that this archaic system of leadership and organization is subject to frequent criticism.

For many years, numerous voices have been heard arguing against the hierarchical operating model and suggesting that it should be replaced by models that are flat, decentralized, podular, teal, agile, communal, and so on. Often, value-creation networks are seen as solutions for hierarchy-induced problems. They replace asymmetrical relationships with symmetrical ones, and they reduce the importance of artifacts that affect the ability to enter into relationships, such as titles, positional status, and assigned levels of power. However, the question remains, are they any better when it comes to power?

Unfortunately, as Kilpi explained in a 2017 video, academic research into symmetrical relationships remains insufficient, and for all the knowledge we have of asymmetry, we still lack a clear understanding of how democratic relations at work truly function.[50] Symmetrical systems tend to obscure the visibility of power, which can be detrimental to accountability and fairness. It is an illusion to believe that issues linked to power disappear in a network, since power itself doesn't go away. Just as energy in a closed system is constant, so is power. It becomes less evident, though, and more difficult to apprehend. Who decides about what? Why? Are decisions equally enforced? Can they be appealed? Hierarchical power in the hands of line managers may turn into clique power in a network in the hands of friends, founders, or insiders. It may lead to bias and preferentialism. What happens in a network in case of disagreements? Confusion, paralysis, and conflicts can arise, especially when no one is "right" but everyone has a different perspective on both context and solution. Mob rule and the negation of minorities can happen. Consultant Julie Diamond, who writes about how flat organizations become toxic, argues that "dispersed power, flat structures, or power in the hands of many" does not necessarily equate to the "better use of power."[51] Indeed, the problem doesn't lie with hierarchy but with what it can give birth to in terms of power dynamics. We need to recognize that such problems are also possible in flatter, more democratic organizational models.

<u>POWER-WITH</u>

At the turn of the twentieth century, leadership pioneer and social organizer Mary Parker Follett advanced our understanding of conflict resolution, democracy, and power. While F. W. Taylor's scientific management gained ground across businesses, Follett's theory highlighted the importance of the human elements in management: human volition, relations, and perceptions. As Meredith Newman and Mary Guy establish in a paper published in *Administrative Theory & Praxis* in 1998, "Follett's web" stands in sharp contrast to the ideas fostered by "Taylor's triangle"—the triad formed by Taylor, engineer and consultant Henry Gantt (the creator of the Gantt chart), and efficiency expert Frank Bunker Gilbreth.[52]

Central to Follett's theory is "the web of human relationships," and it is through these relationships that people discover both meaning and identity. Reality is to be found "in the relating, in the activity-between."[53] Within this relational web, conflict is inevitable but can also be a source of creative growth. To this end, Follett makes a distinction between *power-over*, which must be eliminated, and *power-with*, "a jointly developed power, a co-active, not a coercive power."[54] Power-over is morally unacceptable and inefficient; power-with boosts morale and often results in a win-win situation: "Coercive power is the curse of the universe, coactive power, the enrichment and advancement of every human soul."[55] It is by contributing to power-with that networks help advance equality.

They do so by enabling information and knowledge to flow freely and rapidly from one node to another, from one individual to another, or to many others. In a hierarchy, information is "cascaded" down—when it is not withheld. Each level digests it, makes sense of it, makes decisions based upon it, and determines what, when, and how it should be made available to the next level. This process is slow and gradually filters out the richness of the original information, diminishing its usefulness at best, distorting or rendering it meaningless at worst. Over the years, I have grown accustomed to the ritual corporate-strategy cascade exercise. Having initially created excitement among senior leaders (and exhausted the internal comms department), it dies out after one or two levels of cascade, ending up as a set of nonengaging generalities in a PowerPoint document. Senior executives would be shocked if they realized how little other people in the organization know about what they do, what they try to achieve, and what influences their course of action. The reverse holds true, but at least people further down the hierarchy are fully aware that those higher up have no clue about what the front line is doing.

In a network, there is no information hierarchy. This is a huge advantage for organizations. Indeed, everyone is an expert of their own context. Information that may not be useful to the CEO may be important for the shop-floor worker and vice versa. It should be up to them to decide. "No one knows what information an individual will choose to notice," note Margaret Wheatley and Myron Rogers. "When we shrink people's access to information, we shrink their capacity."[56] Enabling generalized and rapid access to rich information is the right thing to do. This way, people make sense of information that isn't filtered by other people with different perspectives from their own. This leads to more informed and rapid action, which is contextually relevant. Knowledge is held in the network, flowing to those who need it regardless of job title, role, or status. Digital networks where anyone can share, read, comment, and notify other people are important enablers of power-with.

Power-with does not compete with hierarchy; it evolves it. In "Network Leadership," Kilpi observed that hierarchies will always exist but that "hierarchies in network architectures are dynamic, contextual heterarchies. In fact, this is the only way that there can be leaders in democratic systems."[57] Even in "teal" organizations—the ultimate organizational paradigm for self-management and employee autonomy, according to Frédéric Laloux—hierarchy isn't abandoned. Instead, Laloux suggests, "what is dismantled is the static form of hierarchy that is in the buttress of the org chart." Husband elaborates that "necessary adaptations to new conditions would likely involve temporary, transient but more intelligent hierarchy." This is where people pay greater attention to "understanding and using feedback loops and double loop learning."[58]

In organizational systems that have become rigid by a century of Taylorist efficiency, where we have become complicit in the power games, our ability to reflect on our mental models and to learn is vital.

Some conditions favor learning and power-with while limiting toxic network effects. These include holding regular public discussions about norms and decision-making, establishing and enforcing mechanisms to identify and quickly address power issues, ensuring the transparency and openness of networks, and normalizing self-organized teamwork. It is also worthwhile to encourage vigilance of network dynamics, since power-with can easily morph into power-over.

Networks, Diversity, and Integration

In systems that are fully focused on efficiency, diversity is an inconvenience. It is a source of slowness, misunderstanding, and errors. It requires alignment and the coordination of resources. While, in the past, global variations could be streamlined through standardized production, today traditional organizations are beset with friction. This is in sharp contrast to the superfluidity of markets. As we saw in Chapter 6, firms handle their own diversity in two main ways: either they mask it behind a veil of uniformity or, while sanctifying the *attributes* of diversity, they organize and segment it. As Deleuze and Guattari observed in *A Thousand Plateaus*, "whenever a multiplicity is taken up in a structure, its growth is offset by a reduction in its laws of combination."[59]

It is no surprise, then, that the network appears valuable to diversity. In a network, ideas and knowledge flow from person to person regardless of the structure they belong to or their ethnicity, gender, sexual preference, faith, or disability. With the prevalence of social media, it has become so much easier to connect with people beyond one's own close circle of acquaintance. People with little opportunity to participate in traditional communication flows have gained increased access to other like-minded people, as well as greater visibility. Through networks, I have encountered new thoughts, new friends, new opportunities. Facebook's original mission statement included the following aspiration: "To give people the power to share and make the world more open and connected." Twitter describes its mission as "to give everyone the power to create and share ideas and information instantly without barriers." This worked quite well for some time, connecting billions of people in unexpected ways, powering the diversity of the world. Until it started to malfunction.

The huge number of people making use of these platforms, together with the revenue that could be generated through targeted advertising, prompted social media platform owners to develop algorithms that filter the content we see. This informs what information we see on our feeds, the recommendations we receive, suggestions regarding who we should connect with, and the visibility to other people of what we post. For a while, it was possible to trick the algorithms, but that's becoming increasingly difficult. In 2017, Facebook updated its corporate mission to reflect its increased focus on communities. Networks, which had been powerful tools for diversity, became instruments of division.

Social media has generated a vast array of echo chambers, reinforcing beliefs, othering divergent perspectives, and fostering animosity.[60] These platforms have begun to thrive on anger and moral outrage— emotions that can generate high levels of engagement. Sadly, anger has proven to be more contagious than love.[61] In "Angry by Design," a 2020 article published by *Humanities & Social Sciences Communications*, Luke Munn shows how Facebook's feed "privileges incendiary content, setting up a stimulus–response loop that promotes outrage expression."[62] Meanwhile, YouTube's recommendation system leads users toward extreme content. To Munn, the explosion of hate speech online can be explained in large part by hate-inducing design. In his book *L'ère de l'individu tyran* (The era of the tyrant individual), Eric Sadin ties these "mind-burning technologies" to the disintegration of social bonds. Networks stir the "implicit denial of others," which sustains the "fury of all against all."[63] As a woman who came to the world of networks via people connecting for diversity and gender equality, it is sobering to see the extent of harassment that women are exposed to on social media. The Center for Humane Technology maintains a long and distressing Ledger of Harm, the contents of which dramatically undermine the rosy claims of the social platforms.[64] Hopefully, the design flaws supported by the business model and the monopolistic situation of these organizations are temporary. Changes in market dynamics and the need for public oversight cannot be ignored.

INTEGRATION

Integration has been described by Barry Oshry as a togetherness process.[65] Among the archetypal forces that constrain and enable organizations, it is integration that pushes the system to become more connected. Where parts interact, they come together as interdependent components of a larger whole, supporting each other in the common work they do. Integration is in tension with individuation, just as collaboration is with independence. Integration differs from homogenization, which drives commonality and sameness across the system. For Follet, integration was the best possible response to the diversity dilemma. Differences are sources of friction but, rather than conceal diversity or let it play a purely symbolic role, why not aim for creative resolution that adds value to the whole system? In *The New State*, published in 1918, she states,

> The ignoring of differences is the most fatal mistake in politics or industry or international life: every difference that is swept up into a bigger conception feeds and enriches society; every difference which is ignored feeds on society and eventually corrupts it.[66]

Earlier in the book Follet observes,

> Unity, not uniformity, must be our aim. We attain unity only through variety. Differences must be integrated, not annihilated, not absorbed.

Her community work experience prompted Follett to write on conflict resolution. Neither domination and submission (in which one party's ideas are lost) nor compromise (in which all parties let go of some of their ideas) is optimal. Instead, organizations should strive for the integration of divergent interests into something new and whole. Participants need to openly confront their ideas, come to see and understand each other's viewpoints, and develop creative solutions that are equally satisfying to all in the pursuit of a common goal. This is very different from concession or conciliation. The cooperative process elevates the group through inventiveness and creativity. As Follett notes, "We are seeking an integrative unity as the foundation of business development."[67]

It is by contributing to integration that networks help advance diversity. They do so by enabling the visibility and accessibility of people and their ideas to a wide variety of others. Networks, in both their communication infrastructure and their relationship patterns, help more people speak up, allowing for more perspectives to be voiced and heard. They facilitate and trigger variety in connections, increasing the possibility of exposure to other ideas. Integration requires differences to be brought into the open, and this is precisely what open networks enable. Follett appreciated that some differences are irreconcilable, but the "inter-penetrating of understanding"[68] that sensitizes us to an appreciation of other values and evolves the quality of our own thinking should be cultivated by organizations in order to be successful.

High-quality interactions between people are not limited to networks, yet networks support and reinforce them. Internal social platforms—when senior leadership understands their potential and uses them—and voluntary initiatives considerably boost the development of transverse networks, connecting people across functions, sites, layers, and cultures. My own experience of networks started in reaction to the cultural uniformity of my employer. People from all parts of the company, from a variety of different backgrounds and contexts, came together to share insights and develop ideas together. I had previously spotted this diversity during townhall events—a crowd of strangers, a silent audience—but this was the first time I had seen it in action. We had fully connected, developing innovative ideas through equitable relationships, creating value for our organization.

OUR WORLD IS networks, and our work is relations. Networks as pattern, tool, and mindset offer tremendous opportunities for organizations and for their people to thrive. By enabling power-with and creative integration, networks are an essential aspect of engagement leadership. They give life to one of the three basic principles of engagement: equality.

But how do we network an organization in practice? How do we create more relationships? How do we make information flow more easily? How do we open up and diversify, enabling more effective collaboration? The practice of equality is the topic of the next chapter, and I will illustrate it with examples drawn from real-life experiences.

8

Creating Equality
at Work

Positive social change results mostly from connecting more deeply to the people around you than rising above them, from coordinated rather than solo action.

REBECCA SOLNIT, "WHEN THE HERO IS THE PROBLEM"

AT THE GLOBAL Peter Drucker Forum in Vienna in November 2019, a panel discussion focused on "rethinking the organization" from an ecosystem perspective. The topic naturally brought up the impact of hierarchy and the obstacles created by power differences. One panelist asked, "Does the least powerful person in the room feel free to talk?"[1] This was and remains a valid question, despite the coronavirus crisis exploding our understanding of what now constitutes a "room" where discussion and debate take place. What concerns me, though, is that while the least powerful voices should certainly be heard, we need to ensure that they are "in the room" in the first place. Too often, the people who matter—those at the customer interface; those with the most relevant knowledge, experience, and expertise; those most directly affected by the decisions made—are not invited to join in the conversation at all. In fact, those who tend to be "in the room" rarely have a deep or personal investment in the topics under consideration.

There is no doubt that discussing how to make a strategy work is interesting and useful. However, far more important is determining the content of the strategy itself. This needs to factor in what is relevant, what is sustainable, and what is compatible with the environment in which we work. It needs to contain objectives that are meaningful to different stakeholder groups, including the employees themselves, and these objectives need to be oriented toward the fulfillment of mission and purpose rather than only the accumulation of profits. Such a conversation needs to be inclusive, touching all parts of the organization. Done well, it can foster agility, engagement, and capability throughout the organization.

Were this to happen, we wouldn't be very far from a familiar political model, established in ancient Greece about 2,500 years ago: democracy. Can work ever be envisioned as a democracy of equals? The democratic model has inspired numerous organizational thinkers and enlightened managers, who see it as a way to evolve corporations toward more dialogue, equality, and consent. This has led to proposals that, as we shall see, are worthy of our interest. In addition, however, we should also consider the potential of networks as an intentional design feature. How can networks enable work that is stripped of domination-and-submission relationships? What form of leadership can uplift both people and business, and what would that look like in practice?

Work as a Democracy of Equals?

In January 2021, the establishment of the Alphabet Workers Union (AWU), a trade union for employees of Google's parent company, was announced, commanding the attention of the media given the rarity of unions in the U.S. technology industry.[2] AWU was the product of a decade of activism concerning a range of issues that had affected Google/Alphabet and signaled the will of several hundred workers to rebalance power relationships in the company.[3] As explained on the AWU website,

> We've seen a downward trend in the effectiveness of "working within the system" at Alphabet, and believe we need something better. Our union can still work "within the system," but now our engagements with management will be on more equal footing, and we will be heard more clearly and consistently. Think of it as guaranteeing that we, the employees of Alphabet, have a real seat at the table that will actually be listened to.[4]

Workers' unions, particularly in countries that value their contribution to social dialogue, bring into the corporate world *representation*, which is an essential principle of democracy. Democratizing the organization is not a new idea. We know that equality in the workplace is an enabler of good, humane work. Nevertheless, questions remain regarding the effectiveness of enterprise democracy to erase the unhealthy imbalance of power in work relationships.

Organizations: Political but Not Democratic

The organizations in which we work are more than business entities. In many respects, they are political entities as well, greatly affecting our communal affairs.[5] As with any human community, organizations hold tensions between different views and interests, which they manage, inhibit, or mediate through norms and processes. As economic forces that extract natural resources and generate flows of goods, funds, and people across the planet, organizations have a huge impact on the world we live in. Some of them even shape how we think, how we connect, and how we vote.

The work experience itself can be described in political terms. People in democratic societies expect equality as citizens but often experience inequality as workers. For many, the paradox becomes unbearable, leading to disengagement and resentment. "When passing through the door of our workplaces we step back into a constitutional monarchy much like those of the 1700s," Stowe Boyd writes in "Today's Business Organization Is an Oligarchy, and That Needs to Change."[6]

Organizational operating models influence how people relate to the world and engage in society. "Mouvement du management et paysage politique" (Managerial evolution and political landscape), a 1993–94 study led by Patrick Guiol, Jacques Le Goff, and Philippe Portier, reveals that the degree to which a company embraces democratic principles impacts greatly on its workers' political choices, tolerance, satisfaction in social relations, and leisure activities.[7] With the same level of education, workers in participatory companies that favor consultation and profit-sharing have a more open relationship with the world, both intellectually and socially, than those in nonparticipatory companies, which are driven by an authoritarian conception of hierarchy and of contractual subordination.

The managerial-political culture affects workers' health as well, as shown in subsequent studies, such as Guiol's and Jorge Muñoz's "Management, participation et santé des salariés" (Management, participation, and workers' health), published in 2007.[8] The authors reveal the "pathogenic character" of nonparticipatory organizations, in which the incidence of workplace accidents and occupational disease tends to be significantly higher than in participatory organizations. Elsewhere, Guiol notes a strong disparity between men and women in how they are affected by this pathogenicity. Men suffer more under managerial authoritarianism, revealing "a greater male vulnerability to imposed power, a probable consequence of an injunction to virility confronted with a denial of recognition."[9]

Though organizations are political, they hardly present the basic criteria that define democracies, notably, voting equality ("one person, one vote") and the consent of the managed and governed. Obviously, corporate responsibilities and decisions are not subject to employees' choice, and hierarchical subordination prevails. An organization pursues an aim, while a democracy is characterized by its means of action, including the popular vote and the separation of powers. Over time, companies prove not to be unconditional, stable communities. They recruit people whose skills they need and let those people go when they don't need them anymore. Unlike the political sphere, which deals with all aspects of public life, businesses are focused on producing specific types of goods and services.

Another essential political characteristic is missing in business, according to some observers: the protection granted to constituents.[10] Only when organizations protect their employees from market turbulence and financial pressure is enterprise democracy really possible. But under the dogma of shareholder value creation, which has permeated the governance, strategy, and processes of listed companies since the 1980s, employees are viewed simply as adjustment variables. Labor is considered a raw material. On balance sheets, work is counted not under strategic assets but under expenses.[11] Currently, the value generated by the company for the shareholder is the fundamental criterion for judging its performance, resulting in increased dividends and massive share buybacks even in the midst of one of the worst global economic crises, which was accompanied by mass layoffs.[12]

Guiol underlines, in a 2018 article, the extreme imbalance of power between capital contributors and work contributors:

> Without having to provide the slightest guarantee of competency, the shareholder benefits from an access to power, while the employee signs a work contract that is a subordination contract. In exchange for their employment, they must relinquish all ownership of their work and any right to have a say in it.[13]

Today's typical shareholder, moreover, is a pension fund that has no active interest in what the businesses they invest in do or how they operate. They are seeking short-term gain before switching to other, more profitable opportunities. Whether the businesses are equitable or democratic is of no interest to them.

The essential dissimilarity between organizations and democracies, though, has not deterred a certain amount of convergence. It may be a concern when democracies are run like corporations, but the corporate move toward greater democracy, even if somewhat unsteady and uncertain at present, is rich in possibilities.

The Slow, Arduous Journey of Enterprise Democracy

In their introduction to a 2018 issue of *Esprit* magazine dedicated to democratizing organizations, Thibaud Brière and Thibault Le Texier explain that "enterprise democracy" first appeared in the nineteenth century under the influence of utopian socialism.[14] Henri de Saint-Simon and Charles Fourier called for human emancipation through democratically run organizations. Pierre-Joseph Proudhon and the early anarchist movement went further, demanding the abolition of property (to be replaced by mutual exchange) and total equality. Enterprise democracy took hold in several countries during the twentieth century—in Germany in the early 1920s, in France just after the Second World War—but its progress was halted by the Cold War. Company leaders were reluctant to share control with employees, possibly fearful of the influence of communist ideals, while leftist parties and workers' unions didn't want to compromise with owners.

Today, most organizations borrow some elements from democracy, through employee representation, spaces for free discussion, or self-management. Some business leaders have grown to understand the benefits that result from a democratic approach, even if the original intent often was to regulate the subordination relationship and negotiate counterparties to it. However, increasing employee participation alone falls short of making organizations truly democratic. As Brière and Le Texier observe, "Most efforts focus on working conditions, not on work organization or capital–labor relations, and these benefits are generally reserved for managers and knowledge workers."[15]

In fact, the case against enterprise democracy is supported by some solid arguments, explaining why progress remains slow and uneven. Democracy can seem ponderous and ill adapted both to employees and to those employers who balk at sharing control over assets and strategic decisions. Subject to populism and demagoguery, as we see too often in the political arena, there is some mistrust of the democratic system, which is considered less neutral and less stable than process-based bureaucracy. Where there is a lack of social dialogue and the relationship between employers and staff tends toward the adversarial, democracy can be perceived to be burdensome. To function properly, it must be accompanied by a significant educational and communication effort, which not everyone is ready to make.

For some, enterprise democracy is nothing more than a pipe dream.[16] Often, its pursuit is an initiative started or imposed by a leader at the top of the organization. When they depart, the democratic system leaves with them. One of the iconic "liberated companies" in France, biscuit-maker Poult (which had been run democratically since 2007), was returned rapidly to traditional managerial methods by the investment fund that purchased it in 2015, prompting its CEO, a democratization activist, to leave the organization.[17] In some cases, so-called enterprise democracy only hides power plays and sectarian aberrations. An example of this, as exposed by a recent press investigation, is the "democratic" Hervé Group, which combined dubious psychological control of its three thousand employees with the guru-like status it had created for its founder.[18]

Proponents of a full rebalancing of power between owners and workers argue that, until democratization efforts challenge corporate ownership, they will fail. The practice of allocating stock options and shares to employees tends to encourage a capitalist rather than a democratic mindset. Anyway, as long as employees do not have a blocking minority of the shares, the notion of employee shareholding could be pure delusion. Today, argue Brière and Le Texier,

> enterprise democracy generally resembles a *liberal* democracy, which limits the powers of the sovereign and gives each individual a sphere of autonomy, but not a *popular* democracy, which assumes that the people can choose their leaders and get rid of them.[19]

There appears to be an urgent need for enterprise democracy. It could help ease the discrepancy between social equality and professional inequality. A more vigorous and widespread enterprise democracy would serve not only workers but organizations and society in general, too. It is encouraging that this has become an area subject to scrutiny by business theorists and leaders, raising the prospect of inspirational and tangible change in the medium to long term.

One school of thought revolves around the extension of the corporate purpose and the redefinition of a company's very nature: a company should not exist to serve its shareholders alone but should be concerned with a broader set of interests represented by a greater variety of *stakeholders*. The acknowledgment of stakeholders and the role they play in shaping corporate identity and purpose gained popularity in the 1980s with the publication of Edward Freeman's *Strategic Management: A Stakeholder Approach*. Freeman described stakeholders as "any group or individual that is affected by or can affect the achievement of an organization's objectives."[20] Sadly, though, such insight did not result in organizations opening themselves up to the participation of third parties.

In 2012, having researched stakeholder marketing, I developed a business case for the creation of a stakeholder engagement position, which I hoped would deliver on the enormous co-creative potential for the launch of a new vaccine.[21] My hope was that we could involve others in the wider ecosystem as partners, including customers. Although my proposal was accepted, I soon realized that old-world views prevailed, with stakeholders thought of as "targets" to be conquered, appeased, and convinced. To my disappointment, they were segmented and addressed in silos, in extractive, transactional terms.

In *Refonder l'entreprise* (Recasting the enterprise), Blanche Segrestin and Armand Hatchuel advocate "characterizing the company not as a group of interests, but as a project of collective creation."[22] What distinguishes this from mere stakeholder acknowledgment is that it grants rights, control, and power to those stakeholders. *Entreprises à mission*—mission-driven companies, social purpose corporations, benefit corporations—take into account objectives related to the social communities that host them and the scientific and environmental field in which they operate.[23] They look beyond the interests of shareholders, opening themselves up to the scrutiny of other stakeholders, too.

Food company Danone is among several organizations to have adopted such status in 2019, aligning its social and environmental objectives with the United Nations' Sustainable Development Goals and setting up an "independent Mission Committee" that reviews its roadmap and progress.[24] Amid the disruption caused by the coronavirus pandemic, however, this strategy has been challenged by shareholders; Danone's senior executive initially stood firm, arguing that their approach was better both for the company and for collective interests in the long term. However, in March 2021, the CEO who had led this strategy was ousted by the shareholders.[25]

Another school of thought suggests reducing the relative power of capital. For example, this could be achieved by decoupling ownership from leadership. In this way, share ownership would not provide automatic entitlement to power. The legitimacy of managers would depend not on the ownership of capital or the means of production but on their ability to set up and support the creative collective, enabling additional capacity. This would help management focus on its integrative and facilitative function, adding genuine socioeconomic value. According to Segrestin, "the role of management is to organize collective sense-making in order to make shared decisions possible."[26] To further rebalance power, to legitimize the standards imposed on the workplace and reconcile the work experience with democratic equality expectations, sociology professor Isabelle Ferreras suggests the adoption of economic bicameralism. This is the symmetrical representation of employees (labor contributors) and shareholders (capital contributors), similar to bicameralism in the political realm. In the United Kingdom, the House of Lords shares power with the House of Commons. Implementing a similar governance arrangement in the workplace (where we spend one-third of our lives) would enable "collective self-determination as to the norms that govern our life together."[27]

Considering the extension of current political realities in the work-place provides many other avenues to explore when looking to create enterprise democracy.

Experiments conducted to make democratic representation better reflect constituent diversity could also help close the gap in the work-place. Part of the current frustration with elected representatives is that they tend to be political professionals—a caste nurtured in an environment of high sociocultural capital and distanced from the realities of the broader population. Rather than *replacing* this suboptimal representation with direct democracy, some argue that it should be *complemented* with jury-like citizen participation. In France, the Citizens' Convention on Climate offers an example of such participatory and deliberative democracy, albeit with a contested outcome that many French citizens have found unsatisfactory.[28]

Political science professor Hélène Landemore makes the case in her 2020 book *Open Democracy* for complementing electoral representation with other forms of representation that are open to ordinary citizens. This would involve randomly selected individuals "representing and being represented in turn," as happens with grand juries.[29] Professor of medical ethics Emmanuel Hirsch called for a similar democratic contribution to the management of the coronavirus pandemic.[30] In France, for example, a citizen collective of thirty-five people randomly selected by the government to represent their fellow citizens has been formed to contribute to the coronavirus vaccination program.[31]

For some time, Taiwan has gone even further in social participation, with an ingenious and profound mobilization of citizens in the country's governance.[32] This has produced particularly remarkable effects in the local response to the coronavirus pandemic. Because citizen juries are typically based on sortition, they seldom control their agenda and have a limited impact on their communities. In Taiwan, however, multiple crowdsourcing mechanisms, platforms, and opportunities (including the yearly Presidential Hackathon) are open to anyone and have enabled millions of people to reach a "rough consensus" on contentious issues and steer their collective destiny. According to Digital

Minister Audrey Tang, "Participation only works if there is a real effect on power."[33]

Citizen participation is a political concept that I find particularly applicable and useful to the corporate world. The good news is that it is feasible and relatively straightforward. There has to be, though, an authentic willingness to co-create with colleagues, and no hint of the savior syndrome we encountered in Chapter 4. Each time I work with an organization, I strive to bring people from the back seat to the driver's seat. I can't steer alone, and neither can the senior executives who seek my services—especially when the work to be done involves some level of change affecting a large number of people. We need more perspectives. So I assemble volunteer teams, mirroring as much as possible the diversity of their organization. Ideally, contributors are drawn from various hierarchical levels, yet they work as equals during the entire engagement. I design interventions with them. They are neither audience, focus group, nor token representatives. They shape and act together, with my assistance. For this to be effective, the interventions must take place at the beginning of the initiatives, when collective meaning-making can happen. Too often, employees are involved when projects approach their implementation phase, and it is too late for authorship and ownership.

Quite systematically, this experience of intervention opens them up, for the first time in their organization, to a whole new way of work: the network operation. This is a design principle, inspired by both human and digital networks, that, alongside democratization of the workplace, offers the possibility of diminishing—if not eradicating—the inequality of organizational relationships.

The Network as Organizational Design Principle

From 2014 to 2018, I led Innovation & Engagement for Global Quality for Sanofi Pasteur, a pharmaceutical group that had experienced nagging manufacturing quality issues for fifteen years. A vast array of operational improvement and change management approaches had been tested previously, drawing on most management fads of the day, but always with the same results: short-lived improvement followed by the emergence of new issues. What these approaches had in common was a hierarchical view of the world, with intelligence considered to be concentrated at the top. We were stuck in "the dance of blind reflex," to quote Barry Oshry.[34] This is evidenced by a pattern of dysfunctional relationships in which those at the top of a system suck up responsibility, taking it away from other people. Employees further down the hierarchy are considered empty vessels who need to be filled with knowledge and instructions by those at the top. With each inevitable failure, this dominant worldview was never questioned. Instead, fingers were pointed at the negligence or incompetence of employees. If we were going to enjoy any success on this occasion, it was these long-established behaviors that needed to change.

It became a priority to shift our interactions from imbalance to partnership, from silos to connection, from top-down and bottom-up to networked. The concept of wirearchy provided us with a direction. Helen Bevan's remarkable work with change movements on behalf the NHS in the UK showed what was possible at scale.[35] Meanwhile, our experience with digital community engagement in this same pharmaceutical organization brought with credibility, allies, and ideas regarding what would and would not work. In addition, as part of our broad framework, we relied on living systems theory, on the company's enterprise social network, and on the change leadership approach developed by John Kotter.

Connecting the System to More of Itself

The living systems theory, to which Myron Rogers and John Atkinson introduced us, suggests that a system is made healthier when it is kept permanently connected to more of itself.[36] It is a dynamic process that enables the system to benefit from a more intense and more open circulation of information. Why so? Because that intense, open circulation of information enables learning, growth, and adaptive change. We act upon the information we have. However, we screen it through our identity, through our understanding of who we are, and tend to disregard information that does not conform to that understanding while being biased toward that which confirms it. For Rogers, this is "death in a living system."[37]

Because traditional organizations are segmented and lack diversity, we spend a considerable amount of time and energy collecting information that tells us nothing new. Internal communication exposes us to filtered information while we interact mostly with people whose world-views are close to our own, such as colleagues in the same department, of similar hierarchical rank, function, culture, age, or background. There is little opportunity to challenge our experience, to explore beyond what's possible, to make discoveries, and to inject these back into the system. Over time, the result is a loss of both resilience and flexibility. "When we shrink people's access to information, we shrink their capacity," observe Rogers and Margaret Wheatley in *A Simpler Way*. "With information free to move, possibilities can sprout up anywhere in the system."[38]

Informal networks exist even in the most structured companies. This is how people get work done despite organizational obstacles. Constantly, however, these informal networks are ignored and disregarded, even when they prove to be the primary source of resistance during organizational restructures, process redesigns, and technology rollouts. So much money and time could be saved if only those leading change sought to engage with these networks. In a system that is connected to more of itself, everyone has access to all information (confidentiality being the exception rather than the norm); there is no hierarchy to information ("most important" is an opinion, not a fact); people act on the information they possess; and no one can tell in advance what information is useful to whom, because everyone is an expert on their own context. As network specialist Valdis Krebs highlights, so-called influencers matter less to the system than do those who keep it connected: "It is not the centrality of a few that matters, it is the weaving of many that is key to a successful community or organization."[39] We need to value those who *stick together* rather than those who *stick out*.

Volunteer groups offer a great opportunity to connect the system to more of itself, bringing diversity and opening up new pathways for information.[40] The point is to create multidirectional networked flows of information that encompass people from any level in the organization. For maximum impact, these groups should definitely not be limited to "side issues" but should be actively involved in core strategy and challenges. There is a need, too, to break free of expert culture, involving nonexperts in these groups so that, as Esko Kilpi argued, we can "shift our focus from competencies to agency."[41]

Creating relationships in a knowledge-work system *is* the work. Creating authorship generates engagement, relevance, and commitment to success. The grassroots diversity movement I became involved with in 2010 created a new network of lasting relationships between people in the same organization who otherwise had no professional reason to connect with one another. At Sanofi, our quality improvement work was driven by what John Kotter refers to as a "Guiding Coalition," one of the eight accelerators at the core of the change approach that bears his name. Diversity, in terms of skills, ranks, and functions, ensures that

> the Guiding Coalition can gather and process information as no hierarchy ever could. All members of the Coalition are equal; no internal hierarchy slows down the transfer of information. The coalition can see inside and outside the enterprise, knows the details and the big picture, and uses all this information to make good enterprise-wide decisions about which strategic initiatives to launch and how best to do so.[42]

In our case, over the four-year period there were four successive groups of twenty-five people, all of whom were selected on the strength of their applications (which had been anonymized and sent to juries composed in equal parts of volunteer peers and executives). We were able to gather volunteers from across the company, representing different functions, grades, countries, tenures, genders, and ages. The number of applications grew each year. This global volunteer group was mirrored by smaller groups at site level, focusing on local issues.

Similarly, an airline I worked with in 2019 to run a major digital change program, with the help of thirty-five volunteer employees, has now launched its third coalition. This network has accelerated the implementation of their project in a way that they'd thought impossible, creating a strategic advantage at the time the COVID pandemic hit. The airline decided to make it a recurrent feature of how they work together. I also have been involved in projects with smaller volunteer teams of fewer than ten people. On each occasion, regardless of team size, new connections have been created and new perspectives exchanged. Increased dialogue has resulted in increased trust, which, ultimately, has led to the co-creation of some amazing solutions—all because the system was connected to a little bit more of itself, with the speed and scale of results escalating when these same groups were supported by digital technologies.

Social Networking Tools and the Network Mindset

Social networking technologies have been available for more than a decade, yet organizations are still ill equipped or awkwardly shy in their usage of these powerful tools—so much so that some people talk about a passing fad that has turned into a fiasco.[43] Poor adoption by employees is attributed to the lack of support when these tools are installed. Then there are the absence of a compelling business case, insufficient digital literacy, the disturbing resemblance to private social networking, the perceived uselessness of chat functions, the confusion caused by overlapping or competing tools, and uncertainty about what can be said or shared. These are all valid reasons for the slow adoption of social networking, and they indicate a regrettable loss of opportunity given the power of these tools. Collaboration has not failed us, argues social business expert Luis Suarez; we have failed it.[44] But this is not irremediable.

The pandemic crisis has been an eye-opener for many about the need for user-friendly digital collaboration infrastructure that enables work to be done. Even when the dominant tools—videoconferencing, instant messaging, document repositories—cover only a fraction of the needs and limit the awareness of what it is possible to achieve. We could, for once, follow the example of forward-thinking public authorities such as those in Taiwan. With vTaiwan (an online–offline consultation process on matters pertaining to the digital economy), JOIN (a civic engagement platform on a broad range of issues), and pol.is (an opinion analysis and visualization tool), Taiwan has shown the real potential of digital democracy at scale while avoiding the pitfalls of polarization or disinformation.[45]

Social tools have been indispensable elements of my engagement practice for more than ten years. Used well, they provide amazing capabilities to connect the system to more of itself and also to multiply and transform. It was social technologies, not email, meetings, or calls, that enabled colleagues to get together across geographies and advance the diversity agenda at Sanofi in the early 2010s. Without Yammer, we would never have achieved this. Of course, the brand matters less than the features. The tool is useful if it enables public and private communities, asynchronous exchanges, language translation, visual communication, easy and mobile access, search, and integration with other tools used by the company. Many additional features have been developed by vendors over the years but, in my opinion, these remain the essential ones. Naturally, the tool is to be used not as a loudspeaker for more top-down communication—a frequent mistake—but for networked engagement.

Our quality improvement project used the social platform as a communication backbone.[46] That backbone democratized and liberated knowledge. Prior to that, the siloed company structure put pressure on managers to exchange information with their peers. With Yammer, everyone had the opportunity to share their experiences more openly, creating a rich resource of individual insights gathered from all areas of the company. The Quality Mindset group started from scratch at the end 2014. Within a year, it had become the largest online community in Sanofi. It helped facilitate more collaboration between manufacturing plants and more learning between people who had never had any reason to interact. They shared initiatives, questions, ideas, best practices, kudos, and smiles. In one case, an analytic lab technician shared how they had managed to transform a sixty-minute task into a five-minute task, enabling colleagues to do likewise. In another, it was on Yammer that the senior quality executive learned about the solution to a problem they didn't even know existed. The network created a novel dialogue across hierarchies and spread a global corporate sensibility for personal responsibility and change. Not only did it generate tangible business value, it made the company more cohesive, bringing people closer together even when they did not share the same physical space.

Social and digital networking enables people to communicate with one another quickly and directly, removing the need for information channeling and multiplying the possibilities for knowledge to circulate. It provides people with access to information and colleagues—additional resources that can create capacity and reduce the sense of powerlessness. Information flows become richer and more diverse, less dependent on relative power. Access to unfiltered information makes leaders more aware of what is really happening in their organization. It has a transformative effect on the nature of relationships within the system, evolving collective identity so that it becomes associated less with *territory* and more with the *network*. This enhances the capacity to welcome diverse input. As a result, culture becomes reflective of more voices, capable of synchronizing with the complexity of the world, ready to transform disruptions into opportunities.

Culture—more than education, technology, or operations—is the main reason why the corporate adoption of social networking tools remains so disappointing. The cultural change that they entail seems out of reach for some organizations, unwanted by the leaders of others. The network culture is one of transparency instead of secrecy, trust instead of control, influence instead of authority. It reduces power distances and the advantage of social grouping. It brings traditional, status-driven leaders down from their pedestals, making visible a different kind of leadership exemplified by those who add value to the community, those who are helpful, interesting, interested, and generous. This requires a learning mindset and humility. The network is a partner not an executor, and potential mishaps are public. In short, the network mindset is not one that everyone finds comfortable, yet the benefits are immense, especially if networks are reflected in and supported by the organization's governance.

Network Governance: The Dual Operating System

A year after we'd started campaigning for diversity at Sanofi, we met the news that the CEO was enthusiastically sponsoring a company-wide diversity initiative. By then, our grassroots network had grown so big and become so active that it had been noticed by the organization and had contributed to tangible change. Before disbanding the network, we crowdsourced ideas and submitted sixty-three proposals to the newly formed official working group. It was a great feeling to hand over our activist work to the people in charge, those with access to power and resources, those in a position to make our ideas become a reality. Of our proposals, ten were retained by the working group. These were the easiest to implement and were expected to have the highest impact. In turn, these proposals were submitted to the Executive Committee, which retained four of them. Quite a reduction, but better than nothing. The four validated proposals were handed over to Human Resources for implementation. Then we waited and waited and hardly anything happened. We had vastly underestimated the effects of inertia, lack of buy-in, and the phenomenon of the organizational immune system.[47]

The network alone can't do it all. It is self-deluding, especially in large, established organizations, to expect that all will go well when efforts are made to replace old structures with networks, circles, or some other non-pyramidal shape. Even more so when these attempts at change come from the edges of the company—emerging from an innovation department or some other "sandbox"—or are imposed from the outside by a consultancy or a start-up affiliated to the parent company. The weight, the habits, and the needs of large organizations make the likely success of such attempts close to impossible. All the same, a fruitful partnership can be established between the hierarchical structure and the network. A network very closely tied to the pyramid can be entrusted with agility, speed, innovation, creativity, and transversal issues, and thereby improve the effectiveness of the organization as a whole. It is possible to enjoy the best of both worlds. Such a system works even in large, constrained, risk-averse, multicultural organizations as described by John Kotter in "Accelerate!," an article published by the *Harvard Business Review* in 2012 and later developed into a book.[48]

Kotter noticed that organizations in the early stages of their existence tend to operate as networks. Start-ups are characterized by the fluidity of roles and responsibilities. What's important is to get the job done, not who does what. Innovation is welcome from everywhere. People work together unencumbered by too many rules or a strict hierarchy. They react to changes quickly. As organizations grow, however, they require more coordination, more management. Policies, procedures, processes, and role definitions are developed, implemented, and overseen. This helps enormously with reliability and scale, but it also generates all sorts of issues—learned helplessness, territorial thinking, risk aversion—which slow these organizations down. The use of task forces, workstreams, and consultants to regain agility doesn't change anything structurally and can even complicate things further without creating more agency in the system.

What really helps is a way for the organization to leverage the positive effects of structure, while regaining some of its early network-induced agility: a dual operating system. Picture a pyramid on the one side (the traditional organization) and a network on the other side (the additional, volunteer-based system), constantly exchanging information and activity, coordinated by a set of processes, steered by their people, who belong to both sides, not just one. The network "complements rather than overburdens the traditional hierarchy, thus freeing the latter to do what it's optimized to do," Kotter explains. "This is not an 'either or' idea. It's 'both and.' I'm proposing two systems that operate in concert."[49]

While the pyramid does the structural work that requires planning, regularity, and reliability, the network addresses all sorts of initiatives, over variable periods of time, that require speed, creativity, and engagement. It is a dynamic structure, focused on results, that is meant to change as often as needed. It is activated by people's passion for certain topics and willingness to contribute. Very importantly, *everyone* is in a position to contribute: volunteering is neither reserved for nor forbidden to frontline workers. Senior leaders involved in a dual structure cannot stand by and watch what others are doing; otherwise they would undermine its credibility. The dual model requires partnership in volunteering from people across the organization, up and down its ranks. It calls for constant legitimization by the top, so that it is not perceived as a foreign body and rejected by the organization's immune system. As a result, "the network liberates information from silos and hierarchical layers and enables it to flow with far greater freedom and accelerated speed."[50] When such a *human* network is complemented by a *digital* network, the outcomes can be mind-blowing.

The volunteer network I supported at a client organization, which was equipped with Microsoft Teams, managed to generate awareness, interest, and adoption of digital tools within its organization. It was a key enabler for faster-than-expected deployment of new technology across its global sales team, providing the company with a considerable strategic advantage. At Sanofi, the pressing quality issues we had been dealing with finally cleared up when we networked the organization and invited contribution from anyone and everyone. The Quality Mindset digital community on Yammer involved thousands of contributors, becoming a hub where information was exchanged, leaders asked for input, colleagues shared creative solutions and kudos, and change spread from peer to peer. This required very intentional design, which Kotter and his team helped us understand. Of particular importance was the Guiding Coalition, a diverse group of volunteers who guided the change for a year before handing over to a new team.

The dual operating system approach is sometimes criticized for not going far enough, for not being as advanced as some radical organizational innovations. But such criticism often ignores the fact that large, established companies that run sophisticated operations—flying air-planes, making vaccines—cannot afford to upend their whole structure and plunge into risky organizational experiments. They can, however, build on a system they are used to while accelerating its performance by making it smarter and more humane.

Peer Leadership in Action

There are practical effects and new operating principles that emerge when networks of equals sit alongside traditional structures. The harnessing of collective intelligence can have a dramatic impact on organizations and how work is done. Nevertheless, there remains under the dual approach an ongoing tension between diversity and coherence, and it is necessary to establish a clear path to collective learning.

Since early in the twentieth century, individual intelligence—iden-tified as the capacity for learning and reasoning—has been assessed through IQ tests, measuring deviations against a standard score. In 2010, Anita Williams Woolley, Christopher Chabris, Alex Pentland, Nada Hashmi, and Thomas Malone showed the existence of a general *collective* intelligence factor, linked not so much to the individual IQ of group members as to "the average social sensitivity of group mem-bers, the equality in distribution of conversational turn-taking, and the proportion of females in the group."[51] The more capacity there is to decipher others' mindset through nonverbal clues, the more equality there is in participation. The more women there are in a group, the cleverer it is. Evoking Daniel Goleman's 1995 research on emotional intelligence in his book *Super Collectif* (Super collective), Émile Servan-Schreiber explains that "the quality of the relationship between brains is more important than the power of the brains themselves."[52] But what makes larger groups smart?

James Surowiecki attributed the *wisdom of crowds* to five combined factors:

· *Diversity*: Individual knowledge born from each person's singular experience.

· *Independence of thought*: The need to avoid herding. For example, by col-lecting opinions separately before a collective brainstorming exercise.

- *Decentralization*: People closest to the problem are the most likely to know how to solve it, and their knowledge should be accessible to the rest of the organization.

- *Coordination*: People are inherently good at organizing themselves.

- *Aggregation*: the method used to aggregate individual knowledge should be unbiased.[53]

The problem in organizations, because they are ineffective at using these five factors, is that they fail to mobilize the latent knowledge in their teams or among their clients, suppliers, and other stakeholders often enough. "If only we knew what we know," Carla O'Dell and C. Jackson Grayson wrote in 1998, echoing the legendary lament of Hewlett-Packard executive Lew Platt.[54] Platt was later appointed CEO and championed the development of knowledge management, but even that, after initial promise, proved to be another management fad, reinforcing territorialism, segmentation, bureaucracy, and control.

When we designed the Break Dengue initiative in 2012, it was precisely the wisdom of the crowd that we were seeking. Back then, the only preventive against dengue was behavioral: disposing of stagnant water around homes and offices, wearing long clothing, and raising awareness among family members, neighbors, and pupils. As we have seen with COVID-19, behavioral changes can be difficult to sustain over time. Often, only a few new behaviors become habitual, while others fall by the wayside. With dengue, it was clear that even when an effective vaccine became available, it would present only part of the solution; behavioral adaptation would still be vital.

While scientific experts held some of the knowledge necessary to community protection, they did not hold all of it. Citizens fighting the disease on a daily basis had to be engaged as co-solvers of the problem, not merely as consumers. We designed a collaborative system aimed at connecting these dengue activists around the world so that they could exchange and build on each other's successes. It was quite a revolution for a commercial company more accustomed to pushing messages at audiences. Not only did it generate social value, but it enabled better protection of individuals and communities, reduced healthcare expenses, and increased stakeholder goodwill toward the community activists. It also helped identify both opinion leaders and weak signals, providing a space for digital engagement and the development of collaborative skills. The value generated by this collective intelligence was huge but not easily measurable. Assessing value requires interpretation—it's not about counting the number of users or mentions. To be credible with decision-makers, however, engagement and collective intelligence programs need to be backed by robust measurement.

The lessons we learned from this experience informed the objective set of indicators we used to monitor progress when addressing the company's manufacturing quality issues through large-scale engagement and deep cultural change between 2014 and 2018. It is never easy to monitor culture change, not least because indicators of positive change become targets to achieve, and this generates a distortion in behaviors.[55] It is tempting to address culture as an "initiative," monitored for its own sake. However, the reality is that culture is what connects and supports *all* initiatives. Also, culture and attitudes *seem* to relate more to interpretation than to hard data. Yet there is so much we can objectively observe. For our quality issues, success, in our mind, was a combination of engagement and performance, so we picked indicators that measured each dimension. To avoid adding to the burden of measurement, we leveraged indicators from different initiatives affected and enabled by culture—safety, quality systems performance, engagement, shop-floor presence, risk management—focusing on the measurement of elements critical to the success of our quality objectives. The set of indicators was co-designed with employees and evolved on a yearly basis along with the direction taken by the movement. The design deliberately prevented comparison between manufacturing sites. Instead, it measured their level of collaboration.

"Wins" played an important role in the setup. Among Kotter's eight accelerators for change, formerly known as "the 8 steps," one consists of generating short-term wins.[56] "Wins are the molecules of results," Kotter argues. "They must be recognized, collected and communicated—early and often—to track progress and energize volunteers to persist." In *Accelerate*, Kotter explains that wins and their celebration "play a crucial role in building and sustaining a dual system. They give credibility to the new structure."[57] They show that the network is delivering results, attracting more support, and lowering resistance. But what is a win exactly? For us, a win was anything that "makes today better than yesterday, or tomorrow better than today." An action done together differently was what we aspired to, but any improvement, big or small, mattered.

Action was what was important, not just ideas or abstract theory. This was about launching a dynamic of ownership, where anyone had the power to make things better. It began slowly, feeling awkward for some people. "I'm just doing my job!" or "I don't like to brag" were common objections. Gradually, momentum grew. Volunteers went on the hunt for successes in every production building, on every line. They inspired colleagues. The hashtag #itsawin became popular on the social network. Wins started to build up—small ones, big ones, huge ones. One operator enabled by volunteers saved his manufacturing site US$160,000 per year. Another site had two teams devise a simpler collaboration process that saved them a thousand labor hours per year. Elsewhere, volunteers invented ways to make a very serious topic (data integrity) feel fun and engaging, hugely benefiting compliance. Processes were streamlined and simplified. Sustainability, safety, productivity, traceability, and professional training underwent all sorts of improvements, in totally unprecedented ways. There was a flurry of wins that were supported, promoted, and celebrated by the peer network. Over time, our focus shifted from encouraging wins to encouraging their replication and their integration into regular corporate processes.

With what result? Gains were so multifaceted that they were hard to aggregate into a single number. However, in less than two years, 100 percent of our quality indicators turned green, while the pressing issues that were a legacy of fifteen years of top-down work—where "top" thinks and "down" executes—were finally resolved. Accidents were reduced by half, human errors by a third. Timeliness in solving issues skyrocketed on all sites. With quality up, write-offs went down, and more vaccines were made available to customers, to the satisfaction of health authorities worldwide. In 2018, one manufacturing site alone generated a total of 503 wins and a cost saving of US$16 million. Within four years, we estimated that the gains were in the ballpark of US$300 million.

Equality in Diversity

Arguably, crowds of equals are not always that smart. What about the "collective stupidity" that autocrats' electoral successes or the popularity of conspiracy theories seem to evidence? This is a false paradox. Collective stupidity is about conformism, which is prevalent in the corporate world, not about the crowd effect.

An antidote to conformism is cognitive diversity. This can be a "strategic asset," as Scott Page noted in his 2007 book *The Difference*.[58] It is at the heart of the dual operating system, embodied in a change principle that Kotter names Select Few + Diverse Many: "You need more eyes to see, more brains to think, and more hands and feet to act. More people need to be able to make change happen—not just carry out someone else's directives." Thanks to a clever integration system, the method avoids chaos, duplication of effort, and waste. Kotter is adamant about the equal status of the peer network and the regular hierarchy: "The strategy network meshes with the hierarchy as an equal. It is not a super task force that reports to some level in the hierarchy."[59]

From my own experience, I have learned that it does require work to have this well understood by both managers and volunteers. Expecting to be asked for permission and asking for permission are integral to the "dance of blind reflex," the organizational phenomenon described by Barry Oshry.[60] But when the idea takes root, when power imbalance is removed and there is partnership between diverse parts of the system, the energy unleashed is phenomenal. The whole organization clearly benefits from a much richer sense-making capacity.

Nevertheless, Fritjof Capra introduces an important caveat regarding the realization of diversity:

> Diversity is a strategic advantage for a community if, and only if, there is a vibrant network of relationships, if there is a free flow of information through all the links of the network. Then diversity is a tremendous strategic advantage. However, if there is fragmentation, if there are subgroups in the network or individuals who are not really part of the network, then diversity can generate prejudice, it can generate friction, it can generate violence.[61]

Indeed, cognitive diversity requires certain conditions to flourish. One can be genuinely passionate about diversity, deeply convinced of its added value, actively seeking to increase it, and yet miss essential elements that would make diversity truly beneficial, unintentionally putting the system at risk. A well-connected system that enables the free flow of information from anywhere to everywhere is critical. Without hearing and learning from all its constituents, a system cannot adjust and adapt effectively.

We must reduce the power associated with filters and gatekeepers. We cannot depend on information flows between point A and point B being regulated by a single person. This creates distortion. Filters are bottlenecks that slow an organization down and limit its collective intelligence. The days when a CEO delegated information-sharing to the hierarchical chain of command or to the communications department need to be put behind us. Today, the CEO must be involved directly and permanently, and not just as a source of information or decisions but as a node in the network, as a connector, as an enabler of more connections that may not include them. It is essential to create a multitude of possibilities so that, without exception, everybody can access the information they require when they need it from those they trust.

Cognitive diversity breeds positive outcomes when a permanent effort is made toward inclusion in the system. Otherwise, diversity can be an impediment, the possible source of suspicion and distrust. Taiwan, once again a rich source of examples in this regard, made inclusiveness a cornerstone of its citizen engagement strategy.[62] Digital Minister Audrey Tang explains how she and her team continue to seek out *the least connected* places and communities, whether in Indigenous settlements, on islands, or in rural areas.[63] There, they create "connective spaces," using cultural translators, reverse mentors, and technology, replacing traditional top-down townhalls with videoconferences where ministers and municipalities leaders *listen* to what is happening in the field. They connect the system to more of itself. This way, they create more information flows, richer sense-making, and higher trust in interdependencies.

Now, when we understand the benefits of diversity and wish to encourage it while producing specific collective results, what do we do? There is an obvious tension between unity and diversity. "Mission statements, or purpose/value are all fine and we can unite around platitudes but that isn't enough," argues Dave Snowden, the creator of the Cynefin model.[64] He believes that actual solutions differ according to the problems' complexity level. For problems that take place in ordered contexts, alignment is worthwhile. But in complex environments, we deal with adaptive challenges and nonlinear interconnectedness, for which alignment is a capacity-limiting factor, a hindrance.[65] Cynefin expert Sonja Blignaut explains that, instead, there is a need to "embrace messy coherence," or what she refers to as "coherent heterogeneity."[66] Coherence, not alignment, is the answer. But how do we render the differences capable of coherence?

One way is to forget about consensus, as Mary Parker Follett suggested more than a hundred years ago. In a complex world, there is no such thing as right or wrong, no such things as direct causality or undisputed values. As such, consensus is an impossibility. Controversies over the management of the pandemic illustrate this perfectly, with experts defending radically opposed ideas, each backed by strong data and sound arguments. Taiwan's Digital Minister Tang argues for *rough consensus*. Often, there is no need to achieve full consensus or agreement on all of the details of a certain decision. To do so might even prove to be counterproductive. If finely nuanced consensus is the goal, then "those with the most time win. They spend more time responding, therefore dwarfing the opinions of those with less time."[67] They add noise rather than signal. Decision-building efforts, then, have to depend on rough consensus and common understanding. *Good enough* is the way to go.

In the same vein, a collective can create a very broad goal and then leave people free to develop whatever they feel is right to move closer to it, all the time actively supporting each other's experiments. That is what happened with our quality improvement project. Rather than limiting people to specified ways of doing, which would necessarily have been informed by constrained viewpoints, we invited in coherent heterogeneity. The result was a level of creativity and implementation that far exceeded our most optimistic expectations.

Agreeing on what is *not* desired, rather than establishing a common objective, can be one means of creating coherence while allowing for a diversity of approaches. As Snowden observes, when dealing with the complex, disagreement and friction are inevitable but should not be avoided:

> The issue is not to get everyone into a single agreed place, it's not about common understanding, sympathy, shared goals or any other such pious impracticability. It is about getting a level of conflict that allows the maximum number of options to be explored without the conflict becoming destructive.[68]

As we strive for coherence, though, we must pay attention and ensure that a harmful pattern does not evolve. Indeed, there is always the possibility that coherence turns into its pathological form, cohesion. This can happen gradually and naturally, under the influence of unconscious tendencies that make us want to clarify and label who we are as a group, who is in and who stands outside. At this point, in consultant Bonnitta Roy's words, "the collective loses its capacity to authentically participate, and instead falls into paranoia, stasis, and group think that are key indicators of group cohesion."[69]

Learning Together in Context

Through his work with the British coal industry around 1945, engineer Reg Revans noticed that the coal mines with fewer accidents and better productivity than others were those that involved miners in their governance. It was on the basis of this discovery that he developed the action learning approach to problem solving.[70] Several opportunities to work with this method convinced me of its utility, prompting me to participate in a course with the World Institute for Action Learning as a way to find out more about stimulating responsibility, sharing ownership, and nurturing collective intelligence and trust.[71]

According to Revans, learning requires more than the "programmed knowledge" that is derived from textbooks, lectures, case studies, and organizational memory. *Questioning* and *reflection* are essential too, especially among a diverse group composed of practitioners rather than experts.[72] For organizations to stay relevant and improve their operations, the velocity of learning should be at least equal to the velocity of change, which is a tough challenge. Action learning is a process whereby participants examine their own and others' actions and experiences in *action learning sets* of five or so people. A learning set always focuses on a real problem. It is a leaderless, diverse assembly of equals. The participants learn from each other and, through questions, collectively make sense of the problem before them. Through this sense-making, they arrive at solutions that are contextually relevant while also increasing mutual trust and the capacity of the system to learn.

Despite the advocacy of systems scientist Peter Senge and others for the learning organization, there is a healthy degree of skepticism among those who inhabit the corporate world regarding a traditional organization's capacity to learn.[73] In fact, over the years, organizations seem to have excelled at sweeping failures under the carpet instead of learning from them. In "The Myth of the Learning Organisation," consultant John Atkinson writes about the dashed hopes of many organizations that, in good faith and with lots of energy, tried to improve their capacity for collective learning. "The practices got subsumed into the bureaucracy," he observes, "and turned back into parodies of what they were meant to be."[74] To be fair, it is almost impossible to extricate oneself from a capitalist system that favors short-term certainties over learning and experiments. But Atkinson notes that organizations do learn at all times because the situations they face, the contexts in which they operate, are always changing. This requires constant ingenuity, a need to overcome organizational obstacles, bureaucracy, and nonstandard requests. In order to get the job done, every day people are inventing new methods and practices that have not been tried before. The challenge, then, is not to *become* a learning organization but to learn *something new*, something, in Atkinson's words, that "goes against the internal dialogue, formed and reinforced over all those years and decades." If we cannot disturb the organizational identity filter, then nothing changes.

> If you really want a Learning Organisation you must build the capacity to change the internal dialogue. It is dialogue that has created who we are and only a change in our dialogue will change that . . . the route is to change the relationships within and between networks, across silos and across the organisational boundary . . . This is a qualitative change in how people are in relationship with each other, how they decide what matters, how they respond to new information and new people.[75]

Oshry doesn't say otherwise when he recommends changing the pattern of relationships, and to expect resistance when doing so. This is what happens when you trigger a grassroots community or develop the use of a social network within a hierarchical organization. It is not easy, but it is incredibly valuable.

Learning happens reciprocally, in context, and is vital to any living system. This reality may be obfuscated by the word *system* and the mechanistic metaphors associated with it. Mechanistic thinking is not bad in itself, and has been behind many productive innovations. But, as an exclusive lens, it has become toxic to humans and to the planet. As Nora Bateson argues, thinking in terms of parts, wholes, and control prevents an understanding of interdependencies, in particular in terms of learning.[76] Bateson has coined the term *symmathesy*—from *sym* ("together") and *mathesi* ("to learn")—to describe the contextual, mutual learning through interaction that takes place in living entities at all scales. This process is enhanced when informed by quantitative, decontextualized data and by what she refers to as *warm data*—that is, information on the interrelationships and interdependencies between elements within complex systems. A real learning organization is one that fosters "learning together in context, at all scales,"[77] making sense of the world using both cold and warm data. It is one where leaders understand the interrelational processes between and among systems, contributing to mutual learning, not as chief mechanics but as co-learners. As Margaret Wheatley and Myron Rogers say in *A Simpler Way*,

> Life accepts only partners, not bosses. We cannot stand outside a system as an objective, distant director. Our disconnection—our alleged objectivity—is an illusion. If we aren't part of the system, we have no potency. Systems do not accept direction, only provocation.[78]

INEQUALITIES IN STATUS and access to information, domination relationships, and obedience have become obstacles to the performance of organizations. While the workplace is not supposed to be democratic, democracy is nevertheless a valid source of inspiration for our organizations, rebalancing the power relations of all stakeholders and increasing worker participation. But we can go further in the operational and cultural transformation by relying on networks. As tools and principles of interaction, they evolve mindsets and behaviors. A new type of leadership is then required. This is *peer leadership*—an asset for collective performance, organizational learning, and equality in diversity.

However, the risk of fragmentation and scattering is real. A network will not stay in place over time and produce added value simply because of its network nature. What holds it together? What makes the members of an emancipatory and egalitarian networked structure pool their efforts, and not flail around in all directions? What can replace the traditional controls and norms that have become less acceptable and less productive? I believe the answer lies in activist communities, from which the enterprise can learn enormously.

PART IV

Fraternity

We fought for good, stood side by side,
Our friendship never died.
On stranger waves, the lows and highs,
Our vision touched the sky...

I put my trust in you
I put my trust in you
I put my trust in you

JOY DIVISION, "A MEANS TO AN END"

The secular trinity of French republicanism associates Liberty and Equality with Fraternity.[1] This motto is not a direct product of the 1789 Revolution, and may even have religious origins.[2] François Fénelon, an archbishop, theologian, and poet, is generally credited for combining the three terms for the first time in the late 1600s. *Liberty, equality*, and *fraternity* were not considered revolutionary charges at the time. But they would become so in the heated rhetoric of statesman Maximilien Robespierre, founder of the Reign of Terror, and in French citizens' claims against a cruel, coercive, and inequitable old order. The motto disappeared amid the post-revolutionary upheavals but returned in 1848 as a principle of the Republic. From 1880 onward, it was added to the pediment of France's public buildings.

There have always been debates about the compatibility and the order of the three terms. "A kind of terminal efflorescence" of the republican motto according to Mona Ozouf, *fraternity* seems to have posed particular intellectual challenges.[3] It appears to be a duty, while *liberty* and *equality* are rights. *Fraternity* bears a collective dimension, while the first two can be considered individual attributes. With its Christian and communal connotations, *fraternity* has triggered some resistance from proponents of the secular state. Meanwhile, certain rational minds have tilted its meaning toward *solidarity*.[4] Its association with virility and affiliation has annoyed the philosopher Jacques Derrida and still bothers those longing for a more inclusive term.[5] Yet *fraternity* is both brotherhood and sisterhood, open to anyone along the gender spectrum. It suggests emotional closeness, whatever the blood ties. For lack of a better alternative, I will continue to use the word in the remainder of this book while fully acknowledging its limitations and setting aside its application as a social organization for male college students, focusing instead on *fraternity* as an experience of friendship and support.

In previous chapters, we saw how the pursuit of liberty and equality in the workplace generates engagement and, as a result, value. Emancipation—as an intention, an identity, a choice that starts with oneself—creates capacity for the system to withstand greater levels of liberty at all levels. Networks alleviate relationships of domination and submission by enhancing access to diversity and information, thereby increasing collective intelligence. To these powerful values, fraternity adds a dimension of willful togetherness. It signals a healthy collective that collaborates seamlessly—both internally and with its external stakeholders. This is because its constituents trust one another to deliver against their mission in the best possible way, contributing to ecosystems of shared value.[6] Is this ideal within reach? Can fraternity even exist in the context of work? I believe so, especially when it stems from joint purposeful activism. Activism opens up vast possibilities to accelerate and improve collective action, to the benefit of organizations and their customers, employees, owners, and partners. For this, a new skill is required: *community leadership*.

9

Can There Be Fraternity at Work?

WHILE THE QUESTION deserves an in-depth exploration, I am tempted to answer right away with a resounding *Yes!* This is because I have experienced the benefits of fraternity in my work. With many of my past and present colleagues, I feel a special bond that is neither of the friendly and private kind (we don't regularly see each other outside of work) nor purely professional (our bonds exceed mere efficient collaboration and are tinged with emotion). To me, the word that most accurately describes this relationship is *fraternity*. Each time I experience it, work feels more uplifting and delivers improved outcomes. This is why I am so interested in better understanding the concept. Depending on circumstances and, above all, on leaders' intentions and behaviors, this fraternal relationship is more or less possible in the workplace. However, commonplace approaches that either deny the importance of fraternity or force-feed an organization with an appearance of it are doomed to fail.

A Challenge in the Workplace

The origins of fraternity in the professional environment, expressed in structures and behaviors, are immemorial. Roman workers were organized into colleges or communities, such as a community of goldsmiths in operation around the sixth century BCE.[1] During the feudal period of the Middle Ages in Europe, a whole system of solidarity emerged, including companionship, guilds, and the first mutual-aid funds. Fraternities, whose main purpose was charity and mutual support at a time when there was no public social protection, gave rise to freemasonry (as early as 1599 in Scotland) and later on to unions. However, fraternity in the workplace never has been straightforward.

Most of us long for a pleasant work experience with a supportive team and friendly colleagues. Nevertheless, in many ways, friendship is actively discouraged in the workplace. While fraternity carries a positive connotation, *fraternization* is frowned upon in the world of work. To *fraternize*, according to *Merriam-Webster*, is to "associate or form a friendship with someone, *especially when one is not supposed to* [emphasis mine]." It is a cause for dismissal. Relationships between co-workers, including romantic relations between managers and subordinates, can lead to complacency, cronyism, quality issues, security breaches, even fraud. A corporate culture that lacks rigor with respect to fraternizing may cover up abuse and harassment, destroying lives, and bringing down complacent leaders when everything comes out into the open.[2] Such situations often compromise the reputation and the integrity of organizations. Favoritism becomes toxic, detrimental to engagement and performance across a company. Compliance training, codes of ethics, processes, and controls are all intended to prevent such cultures taking hold.

If not fraternization, then fraternity in the form of "friendship" might develop between people who work together on a daily basis. It might even help performance. Research shows that workers are happier in their jobs when they have friendships with co-workers. Gallup found that close work friendships boost employee satisfaction by 50 percent and that people with a best friend at work were seven times more likely to engage fully in their work.[3] In *a Harvard Business Review* article titled "We All Need Friends at Work," Christine Riordan reminds us that camaraderie at work favors group loyalty, dedication, and mutual support for both personal and professional situations, though she also notes that downsides, like "professional jealousy, groupthink, negative cliques, split loyalties, loss of work time to socializing, and broken friendships"[4] can occur. Nevertheless, the positive impact of a supportive social network based on mutual sympathy and camaraderie is often, in organizations with weak leadership and processes, what keeps the human collective functional.

Some organizations still like to proclaim that they're "a family," even though management literature has long suggested that this is a bad idea.[5] LinkedIn co-founder Reid Hoffman even describes this familial framing of the relationship between employers and employees as "the biggest lie."[6] It is not certain that many people believe the lie anyway, especially not the millions who have been laid off at the slightest hint of an economic downturn, or who have had their roles transferred with fewer benefits to subcontractors, or who have been replaced by low-paid overseas workers or by robots, finding themselves pushed toward a fragile employment and economic status. Yet, for a young graduate starting their first job, for someone making the jump from a big corporation to a start-up, for an entrepreneur assembling a new team, the notion of team as family is an almost irresistible mirage.[7]

However, for Scottish Enlightenment philosopher and economist Adam Smith and his contemporaries, it was the notion of relationships of "authentic indifference"—relationships that enable anyone to do business with anyone else without worrying about alliances or enmities—that were hailed among the most positive characteristics of commercial society.[8] But do we have to show indifference to one another in order to work happily together?

Even for those who decide to adopt a detached, indifferent attitude (a job is just a job), it is difficult to escape human passions at work, triggered by conflicts of interests and values, by competition and territoriality. Some of these things are even exacerbated by the very way organizations work, the unintended effects of various habits and processes.

In an article published by the *Academy of Management Review*, Graham Brown, Thomas Lawrence, and Sandra Robinson explain that territoriality in organizations—"an individual's behavioral expression of his or her feelings of ownership toward a physical or social object"—is a deeply engrained organizational behavior.[9] It is an inherent, inevitable, and prevalent aspect of organizational life. Territoriality signals our attention to the parts rather than the whole and is a legacy of the industrial era, which has served us well in the past. Physical markers of territory faded somewhat as flexible-working practices and hot-desking became the norm as a consequence of real-estate cost optimization. The requirement to work remotely during the coronavirus crisis may have erased them altogether. Even so, symbolic territoriality is still alive and kicking: "We make claims on and defend our control of a variety of organizational objects, spaces, roles, and relationships."[10] As both a consultant and a business executive, I have had to pay close attention throughout my career to the perceived ownership of the territories I am stepping into. People typically react as guardians of a space, rather than as nodes open to more connections.

Territoriality can have positive effects on the performance and well-being of organizations and their members, which is why we can't get rid of it easily. It creates a sense of belonging, which can keep people together, enhancing their performance individually and collectively. It also can simplify social interactions and increase efficiency in the distribution of organizational resources, sometimes reducing conflicts by bringing clarity to a situation.

Clarity is the holy grail for many managers. Considerable resources are spent every day on clarification meetings, governance fine-tuning, and Responsible, Accountable, Consulted, Informed (RACI) exercises.[11] I was once loosely involved in a responsibility assignment matrix exercise for a large project, which required several weeks of hard work by my colleagues. Its outcome was a thick, heavy, PowerPoint–generated booklet that attempted to describe all possible interactions and decisions, involving multiple tables and colored dots highlighting who had responsibility and accountability and who needed to be consulted or informed in all circumstances. Apart from the fact that we never quite understood the distinction between responsibility and accountability or between consultation and information, this exercise ultimately proved to be useless. It was intended to remove ambiguity, yet urgency and context continued to dictate future interactions, bypassing the rigidity and tedium of the framework that had been designed. Worse, for several weeks it diverted our energy from work that would have been more useful. It created an illusion of clarity and control that was detrimental to the quality of our collaboration. This type of exercise remains popular in many companies, supported by a consulting industry that often mistakes symptoms for causes and feeds clients the belief that a mechanical solution—a process, a tool—is what is required. Obviously, a RACI matrix challenges fewer behaviors than does a collaborative approach of mobilization and co-creation. Unfortunately, it is also far less effective.

Consultant Yves Morieux explains that "the holy trinity of efficiency: clarity, measurement, accountability" is actually detrimental to collective performance.[12] Clarity creates boundaries and undermines shared responsibility. Accountability opens the door to blame and undermines shared responsibility. Measurement distorts attention and behaviors, undermining shared responsibility as well. Morieux makes a counterintuitive case for the achievement of effective internal cooperation:

> Remove the interfaces, the middle offices—all these complicated coordination structures. Don't look for clarity; go for fuzziness. Fuzziness overlaps. Remove most of the quantitative metrics to assess performance. Speed the "what." Look at cooperation, the "how."

This *how* shouldn't be mistaken for the *individual how* as evaluated through a manager's lens. It is the *systemic how* we should pay attention to: How much does the system enable people to deliver against the organization's goal? Yet we also should never lose sight of Edwards Deming's caveat that "a bad system will beat a good person every time."[13]

A good system is made bad, and a bad system is made worse, by territoriality. Communicating and maintaining proprietary claims takes effort, which is detrimental to the broader mission and related tasks. Territoriality presents a major barrier to risk-taking, to innovation, to information-sharing. Fear of infringing on another's territory keeps people within organizational boundaries, reducing any chance of the organization exploring new, complex, and disruptive opportunities. However, because of its immediate and apparent effects on belonging, control, and clarity, a territorial mindset is often cultivated by managers, by internal marketing, and by processes. The effects can be toxic and divisive. For example, as we saw in Chapter 3, traditional performance management and compensation systems inevitably promote competition. Long after research revealed that incentive plans cannot work because they are based on the wrong psychological assumptions, undermining collective performance despite temporary shows of compliance, there is still a huge industry founded upon the fiction of their utility.[14]

Because we don't understand the capability of the system, we are causing people to compete against one another in the organization, creating winners and losers.[15] More often than not, everybody loses. In 2020, the venerable Institut Pasteur allowed two internal teams to compete with each other in the race to develop a COVID-19 vaccine. As a result, neither team succeeded, and the Institute withdrew from the race altogether.[16] This spectacular fiasco is repeated every day, on a much smaller scale, in organizations that concentrate decision-making and resource distribution in a few hands. Occupying positions of power becomes a goal in itself, with candidates outnumbering positions, and work becoming a struggle for survival.

Fraternity at work has a better chance of developing if people feel they are somehow in the same boat, treated with equal respect, with no obvious "second-class" workers. Yet it seems there always are some. Widespread recourse to subcontractors means that a significant pro-portion of staff participate in collective performance without really belonging to the collective. Some subcontractors show up every day on the factory floor and in offices, interacting, contributing, sharing lunch breaks. Many companies, however, are wary of the legal complications and costs associated with the potential recharacterization of subcon-tracting as an employment contract. This wariness can lead to radical and excessive segmentation of the relationship between employees and subcontractors. The latter do not appear on organization charts and are often excluded from low-key social events, which can seem short-sighted, a missed opportunity to build rapport and team spirit. I recall one occasion, for example, where contractors were excluded from an employee picnic, which struck me as petty and potentially damaging at the time. Such an attitude creates a kind of "shadow class" of workers on the same worksite. It gives the bizarre impression that work cama-raderie is only worthy of certain people, distinguished by employee badges and lanyard colors. Variable-geometry fraternity taints all other relationships with a hint of hypocrisy. Conversely, one of the most pow-erful initiatives I saw emerge from volunteers at an industrial site was an employee buddy system for subcontractors. It was an initiative that respected the differences in work arrangements and legal statuses but found ways to connect workers in fraternity.

The Many Faces of Fraternity

Conceptually, fraternity reflects both the familiar reality of the human experience and an unattainable, multifaceted ideal. For philosopher Jean-François Petit, the origin of fraternity (as reflected in ancient

Greek and Hebraic thought) was the foundation of living together and was not restricted to blood ties—what fellow philosopher Emmanuel Levinas describes in *Totality and Infinity* as "the original experience of human fraternity."[17] Today, our modern societies have witnessed an increase in individualism and egocentricity, the valorization of competition and appearances. Yet, at the same time, incantations in favor of fraternity are increasing. Could fraternity repair social relations damaged by indifference and rivalry? Or is fraternity nothing more than an ideological illusion obscuring more tangible opportunities to alleviate human interactions?

The concept holds multiple tensions. Fraternity is both a personal quality (as in *being fraternal*) and a collective project. Fraternity seems to belong to the realm of universalist aspirations, yet also applies to closed communities, old boys' clubs, and sectarian groups. Many workplace groupings also demonstrate solidarity in a way that simultaneously binds and excludes. Petit sees in fraternity "an undeniable anthropological reality, where the search for personal dignity, the desire for recognition, and the acceptance of a fundamental equality between humans are manifested."[18] It is often approached by way of comparison with related concepts, in order to distinguish its contours through similarity or divergence. With collective work in mind, how does fraternity relate to notions such as compassion, solidarity, respect, trust, or friendship?

"Being More Intensely Present for Each Other"

"I have your back, and you have mine"—fraternity evokes common struggles, a togetherness in action. It is not passive, as compassion might be, but empowering and active.[19] It seems to convey a greater emotional density than solidarity, which is something to be organized. Historian Jacques Le Goff reminds us of the role of Pasteurism (the science born out of Louis Pasteur's discoveries and the acknowledgment that infectious diseases are due to microbes) in exposing "negative solidarity," which can also be understood as interdependence.[20] As we now know all too well in these COVID times, our health depends on the health of others, with vaccination seen as an individual act of self-protection, as well as a contribution to collective herd immunity.

Truly seeing the other may be the distinguishing marker of fraternity.[21] Interactions at work are often shaped by what each person stands for, from a professional perspective. We interact with a colleague, a manager, a senior leader, a team member—someone whose identity seems defined by their function, their role, or hierarchical position and its distance from or proximity to our own. The relationship can be either enriched or impoverished through mutual sympathy, distrust, or animosity. But when there is evidence of fraternity, my experience is that we start to see the person in a different way, independent of their role and independent of personal preferences. The other is humanized, with similarities allowing for connection, bringing us closer together, and differences either keeping us apart or offering us the opportunity for mutual benefit. We experience, as Barry Oshry writes in *Encounters with the Other*, "our commonality with the other but also our difference *as that difference really is*—free of whatever myths, distortions, fantasies, fears, and projections arise as a consequence of our separateness."[22] I have seen it happen in every mobilization I have contributed to.

During the early stages of the movement for quality transformation at Sanofi, I encountered Sarah, a shop-floor operator and volunteer. Our group of twenty-five people of different ranks and functions had come together to help change the way the organization worked so that it could provide vaccines to anyone who wanted them. As we brainstormed, Sarah suddenly burst into tears. We all stopped talking. "What's the matter, Sarah? Is anything making you sad?" I asked. "No," she answered, sniffing. "I am very happy. I'm fine. You see, I have worked at this company for twenty-five years, and this is the first time I have been asked for my opinion."[23] The group let that sink in for a moment. I felt Sarah's realization extend to all of us. We saw each other more intensely, and we felt seen in return.

While we experienced compassion for Sarah's tears, we also developed *fraternity*. We realized that we were in this together, working hard, with purpose, despite the constraints of internal politics, for something authentic and important; we were mutually dependent for the success of our endeavor. Solidarity, the outcome of "social relations of symmetrical esteem," is one of the three forms of recognition—together with love and rights—that philosopher Axel Honneth describes in a theory of recognition.[24] For Honneth, recognition is a fundamental aspect of human interaction and is central to individual and group identity. It is at the heart of social progress. This phenomenon of recognition permeates society as well as the modern workplace. Recognition forms the basis of healthy and effective approaches to engagement.[25] When aiming for impact and sustained performance, we should not overlook the workforce, instrumentalize our colleagues, or stretch people until they burn out. To engage others and ourselves is of a different nature to the implementation of a contractual relationship. Organizations must learn to create the conditions for fraternity, allowing people to be "seen" by their peers, by the hierarchy, recognized and acknowledged, losing their anonymity. Employees need to be respected in their full humanity, their diversity, and their free will. As Esko Kilpi argued, the workplace "needs people who are more fully present, people with responsibility and ownership." Work "is about human beings being more intensely present for each other."[26]

Trustworthiness and the Emergence of Trust

Thinking about fraternity necessarily leads to the notion of trust. A fraternal relationship between individuals leaves little to no room for mistrust. But what is trust anyway? Some say it is a judgment call in the absence of data. I may lack information about a colleague because we've never worked together before or because the situation is new, and so I choose either to trust them or not.

In a much-cited paper on organizational trust published in 1995 in *The Academy of Management Review*, Rogers Mayer, James Davis, and David Schoorman define trust as

> the willingness of a party to be vulnerable to the actions of another party based on the expectation that the other will perform a particular action important to the trustor, irrespective of the ability to monitor or control that other party.[27]

They describe an integrative model of trust whereby trust is tested in a risk-taking situation, an outcome is observed, and this leads the trustor to update their assessment of the trustee. Trust, in this sense, involves a feedback loop. "We trust based on an assessment of the other party's trustworthiness," Graham Dietz argues in a *Journal of Trust Research* paper.[28]

In the model outlined by Mayer, Davis, and Schoorman, there are three components:

- *Ability*: "That group of skills, competencies, and characteristics that enable a party to have influence within some specific domain."

- *Benevolence*: "The extent to which a trustee is believed to want to do good for the trustor."

- *Integrity*: "The trustor's perception that the trustee adheres to a set of principles that the trustor finds acceptable." [29]

Trust is the currency of work well done and of good business. It is dynamic, rather than static. When the dynamic of trust is absent, collaboration is limited, friction slows down the system, and dysfunctional behaviors hamper quality. Analyzing the rise, fall, and struggle for recovery of General Motors in *Rude Awakening*, a 1989 book that still feels relevant today, Maryann Keller writes that "GM's mistrust of its workers ultimately prevented it from making great cars." [30]

I once consulted for a company fraught with mistrust. The engineering department didn't trust R&D, Sales and Marketing didn't trust Engineering, employees based in distant sites didn't trust colleagues based in the company's headquarters, few trusted the finance department, even fewer trusted the leadership team, the CEO didn't trust his Executive Committee, and this mistrust inevitably was reciprocated. In addition, the company was fragmented into informal "clans" made up of people who had worked in the same or similar industries, all of them quick to criticize members of the other groups. Shareholders, moreover, who were the source of both capital and technologies that had been in competition with one another in the past, could not totally overcome the differences in their respective identities and expectations. The whole reality was quite different from the glamorous image projected externally—at least to neophytes like me. Given my insider experience of corporate systems, though, I was only mildly surprised by what I encountered when working with them.

Another debilitating example of distrust can help explain the absence of French research and industry in the race for the development and production of a COVID-19 vaccine. [31] Analysts all agreed that this was the result of strategic errors and the accumulation of internal struggles, small grudges, and petty personal wars within organizations. In effect, France had failed to mobilize its many talents and whatever service they could provide to the global effort to manage the pandemic because of distrust.

Conversely, with trust, everything moves at a faster pace and more effortlessly.[32] Collaboration that is founded on trust saves time and money, reducing the need for oversight and mediation structures. Trust is a powerful enabler, one organizations require for innovation, compliance, quality, risk management, and more. Research findings published in 2018 by MIT *Sloan Management Review* identified trust as essential to future leadership in the digital economy "because we feel safer taking risks, innovating and speaking our minds when doing so in trust-based environments."[33] While there is a general appreciation of the benefits of trust and a desire for it, too often this perspective is skewed by self-centeredness. Here, the desire is for *others* to trust *me*, which can simply mask an aversion to being challenged.[34] Those who exercise tight control often will demand that others place their trust in them without necessarily reciprocating that trust. In such a scenario, trust is expected rather than earned or freely given, the latter being *the* key component of a trust relationship.

In 2015, Robert Phillips, formerly a senior executive at the public relations firm Edelman, published *Trust Me, PR Is Dead*, in which he sought to challenge companies that were still trying to build trust through public relations, messaging, and smokescreens.[35] He argued that this was an obsolete, inefficient approach. The same faults can be found in top-down internal communications intended to establish employee trust in their leaders. It simply does not work, as I witnessed at Sanofi when a trust-in-leadership campaign led by the HR and Communications teams failed to deliver its objective. Trust is an outcome, not a message. Trust can't be mandated. In fact, few people seem to ask, "How can I earn your trust?" Meanwhile, few feel confident, comfortable, or brave enough to express what they do not trust. As John Wenger notes, in building a case for a new manifesto of trust it is not enough for leaders simply to state that people can trust them. True leaders, he argues, "know that trust follows trustworthy behavior."[36] It is a privilege to either receive trust or show trust in another.

Mistrust, however, tends not to be overtly expressed in organizations but lies below the surface, showing up in behaviors that can be mistaken for operational deficiencies when really they're cultural manifestations of this lack of trust. The abundance of group emails, with people copying multiple others for self-protection, is an example of that. An abnormal rate of quality issues is another. When such problems are approached from the point of view of process or technology alone, only the symptoms are addressed, not their causes. Yet if mistrust persists, so do the problems.

A former colleague used to liken trust to a coconut palm. It grows at a slow pace but, as with the sudden break between tree and falling coconut, it can break in an instant. Wenger humanizes the concept:

> My trust in you will build over time, when you are repeatedly and consistently authentic and trustWORTHY. We will not necessarily gain trust in each other simply because we have played some simplistic "trust games" during our one and only staff training day.[37]

Trust is emergent, not manufactured. Rebels at Work cofounder Carmen Medina, however, argues that trust is a muscle and, as such, can be nurtured and trained.[38] The leap of faith it takes to trust people and the acceptance of the inherent risk that goes with it can be developed into a valuable habit. "Trust is an investment in your team and an engagement with them as individuals," she states. Repeated acts of trust and learning feedback loops create a context that is favorable to new ideas and to the people who bring them up, a virtuous circle that strengthens trust by using it.

"A Person Is a Person through Other People"[39]

When I settled in Vietnam in 1993 and started to learn the language, a whole series of discoveries surprised me. The six tones of the Vietnamese language, for example, bring a whole new musicality to speech, requiring new ways to convey emotions or to sing. One thing that I struggled with was the many different ways to say *I* and *you*. In Vietnamese, there is no universal, relationship-independent, self-centric *I*. Instead there are many, each with a specific, reciprocal *You*. In fact, one of the most difficult things to master in Vietnamese is a simple greeting—"hello"—which is so straightforward in many other languages. In this case, it is necessary to reflect your relationship with your interlocutor, capturing familiarity, age difference, gender, family ties, and so on. At first, this peculiarity horrified me, contradicting the newfound independence of a twenty-three-year-old finding her way overseas. I wanted to rebel against what I perceived to be an alienating social interdependence that kept people in a permanent filial relationship, entangled in hierarchical and age-bound norms. Soon, though, I came to appreciate this fundamental cultural difference and how it challenged my assumptions and worldview. After all, wasn't the concept of an independent, separate self a fiction? Weren't we all related to and interdependent on one another? The Vietnamese language offered an insight into the social nature of humankind.

The notion of human entanglement and interdependency—of human fraternity—is also reflected by the Southern African concept of *ubuntu*, often translated as "I am, because you are," and by the Zulu phrase *Umuntu ngumuntu ngabantu*, which means "a person is a person through other people."[40] For John Volmink, the chairman of the Ubuntu Global Network, *ubuntu* is a moral philosophy based on the idea that we humans are complete only when in relationship with each other. I can be a person only through other people. It doesn't cancel our individuality but suggests that we relate, build bridges, and search for meaning through our encounters with others, preserving and enhancing each other's individuality.[41]

Such a worldview contrasts with the philosophical and behavioral traditions of Western culture that have been shaped by patterns of oppositionality and duality—either/or rather than both/and. Everywhere we look we encounter right versus wrong, us versus them, competing ideas that foment polarization rather than recognition of the bridges that connect them. This is particularly blatant in politics but also prevalent in the workplace, with managers failing to see eye to eye with technicians, manufacturing with sales, local offices with headquarters, and so on.

This binary outlook, AnaLouise Keating explains in a *Tikkun* magazine article, not only justifies the status quo but prevents change because it stops us from searching for nuanced commonalities and creative solutions with those who do not share our views; oppositionality "traps us in the very systems we're trying to change."[42] Change agents should take note that arguing for and arguing against an idea are, in fact, two sides of the same coin. Oppositionality limits our potential for creating genuine transformation. Despite this, could it serve as a springboard for engagement? Admittedly, a common engagement strategy consists in rallying a collective against a common enemy. Such an approach can work for a while, but it contains within it the poisonous seeds of division, which inevitably damage group values and solidarity. Instead, Keating recommends "relational approaches to transformation that borrow from but do not become restricted to oppositional thought and action." In a partial move away from binary patterns, *post-oppositionality* "transforms either/or thinking into the acceptance of multiplicity, contradiction, and paradox, energized by a search for complex commonalities spacious enough to contain differences."[43]

A role model for post-oppositionality was Chicana activist and queer feminist Gloria Anzaldúa, with whom Keating collaborated for many years prior to the former's death in 2004. Through her work, Anzaldúa called for a "politics of interconnectivity," bridging between multiple perspectives and identities.[44] In an article on Anzaldúa and her "art of solidarity," Brian Stout suggests that she used bridging as "a way of transcending binaries, opening up new possibilities, and connecting not just across differences but precisely because of them."[45] This could be what fraternity is really about, and why it is so important to collective success in the workplace.

Fraternity Delusions

Fraternity appeals to emotions that the world of work does not necessarily look favorably on. Whether seen as a waste of time, a potential distraction from work, or a doorway to chaos, emotions are often restricted or suppressed. More generally, leadership sensitivity is rarely in evidence among the traditional leaders who perform the vast majority of executive roles in large companies. Even where they recognize that, beyond strategy and competence, leadership is *also* about emotions, their associated behaviors often remain clumsy, proving counterproductive to the large-scale engagement and mobilization of people. To treat fraternity as an unnecessary endeavor or as a customary posture is to limit the potential and the performance of an organization.

The Myth of the Purely Rational Worker

Stephanie is a former colleague and a friend. She leads Internal Communications at a multinational company. She is talented, experienced, and emotionally intelligent. In a recent conversation, she explained how she had tried to persuade her CEO to pay attention to culture, to communicate with employees about values, behaviors, and emotional triggers.

"He's always refused," she told me. "He only wants me to communicate facts, data, and information. Eventually, I gave up. I now push content to employees."[46] I felt sorry for her, agreeing that this was such a waste of her talent, and such a missed opportunity for the CEO and the company. Stephanie added ruefully, "In a sense, it makes my job easier, because I don't need to engage employees." And in this scenario, neither does the CEO. But what is behind such an attitude? Is it shyness? Fear? Or the illusion that everything, including emotions, can and should be controlled? The almost exclusively rational approach to work ties in with the view of decision-making as an analytical process, a trade-off between possible alternatives and individual preferences. Popular with the neoclassical economists, this view has since been widely questioned by advocates of decision-making paradigms like game theory, bounded rationality, and garbage-can models, as well as by those researching our numerous cognitive biases.[47] Nevertheless, the approach remains popular among those managers who view workers as abstracted holders of knowledge, practitioners of skills, and consumers of facts.

Almost 2,500 years ago, Plato identified three modes of persuasion or strategies of rhetoric that, when used together by a writer or a speaker, appeal to their audience.

- *Logos* is the intellectual agenda, the logical appeal based on facts and figures that support the argument.

- *Ethos* is the behavioral agenda, the ability to convince the audience based on the speaker's authority or credibility.

- *Pathos* is the emotional agenda, appealing to the audience's emotions and feelings.[48]

Consultant Didier Marlier refers to them as "the three agendas of leadership."[49] The second half of the twentieth century and the first years of the current century epitomized, for leaders, the era of "content leadership," which is based on knowledge, itself a source of power. According to Marlier, the most senior jobs during this period were granted to those people who were considered intelligent but who tended to be distant and lacking in empathy. Today, though, the world has changed, and our leaders now need to operate by shaping context rather than by leading content. They need to master a much more engaging style of leadership, one that does not rely on logos or ethos alone but on all three dimensions together. The combination of a great strategy, efficient processes, accurate information, and knowledgeable leaders does not guarantee success because it does not mobilize people.

Sadly, despite compelling evidence, many established organizational leaders remain unconvinced of the value and effectiveness of an alternative approach and have yet to change their ways. A few years ago, at the organization where I worked, the results of an annual employee engagement survey were highly negative. The human resources department, which had commissioned the survey, offered one explanation: workers don't *understand* that they are serving an important mission, and therefore they do not feel engaged. It was a purely rational explanation, conforming to the logical agenda. As a result, the solution they came up with was also rational: a communication campaign, using simple visuals, was deployed throughout the organization to *explain* to employees the principles of our industry. Of course, this campaign had absolutely no effect on engagement, but something had been done, enabling the HR and communications departments to move on to their next tasks. This error of analysis and distressing waste of organizational time and money are all too common among modern businesses.

John Kotter has studied change and what makes it possible for several decades now. He has explained over and over that change requires the active involvement of many. Unless an organization has mobilized at least half of its people to actively support and contribute to whatever change is required, it has failed to create enough meaningful dialogue or to generate the necessary energy to make change happen. It is impossible to mobilize that many people through pushed content alone. In *The Heart of Change*, Kotter and Cohen observe that "both thinking and feeling are essential, and both are found in successful organizations, but the heart of change is in the emotions."[50]

Management professor Sigal Barsade, who studies the impact of organizations' "emotional culture" on business outcomes, finds regrettable the perception of emotions as "noise."[51] This perception ignores an important source of employee motivation, with a direct impact on performance, productivity, and profitability. Formal data gathering, analysis, report writing, and presentations help establish understanding; they do not engage people or change anything. In order to draw on emotions, it is necessary to go beyond simplistic approaches and play on a wider palette than the happy–excited–upbeat register. Feel-good internal marketing—out of laziness or a lack of imagination—tends to appeal to pride and nothing more, again missing the mark in terms of engagement. Those exposed daily to problems of collaboration, production, and management feel manipulated when exposed to this disjuncture between senior executive messaging and their lived experience. Rather than mobilizing, miscommunication foments cynicism and reinforces territoriality.

In the pharmaceutical industry, it has become a hackneyed convention to invite a patient to talk to staff about their illness and how it has affected their lives. It is always a moving moment, but so what? What does it change about the way people work together? Nothing. What's really important for engagement, improvement, and performance is the opportunity to see things differently, in a way that elicits a visceral response, which motivates useful action.

On an assignment with a multinational company, I worked with a team of about thirty volunteers from all over the world whose challenge was the successful implementation of a new work process, linked to an innovative IT tool. A genuine partnership was established between these volunteers, the project team in charge of deploying the tool, and the management team. A small group devoted time to creating a knowledge base, responses to frequently asked questions, and a chatbot for their colleagues. This was the "head" part of engagement. Others on the team focused their efforts on the "heart," in a humorous, accessible way that affected project meetings as well as some of their communication materials, including mock newscasts involving eager volunteers from among their colleagues. A video contest focused on data security also produced material that was so funny and relevant that it was subsequently incorporated into training programs for new employees, as well as mandatory courses on data security. Laughing together provided an extraordinary boost for productive work. This was a rare example where the "head" stopped ignoring the "heart," leveraging it meaningfully.

In his "Working Class Manifesto" Kilpi wrote, "We need an approach to work that appreciates whole human beings, their passions and voluntary participation."[52] If so, then why does this fiction of the purely rational worker continue to be entertained and serve as the basis for the majority of our work interactions? In part, it is a legacy of industrial management practices and a consequence of the engineering approach to work. But the distinction between *work* and *life*, as if they were mutually exclusive realities, may have played a role too. These categories, claim Marcus Buckingham and Ashley Goodall in an article on the myth of the work–life balance, "imply that work is bad, and life is good; we lose ourselves in work but find ourselves in life; we survive work, but live life."[53] From this perspective, work is a place where we cannot be our full selves; only in life can we truly be. But we need work to earn a living, and so the challenge appears to be balancing "the heaviness of work with the lightness of life," our rational self with our emotional self, our attention, intellect, and competencies with our creativity, friendliness, and sense of humor.

In her 1977 study *Work and Family in the United States*, Harvard professor Rosabeth Moss Kanter exposed what she called the "myth of separate worlds."[54] This work, among others, pushed some companies to become more attentive to employees' personal organization and to provide slightly more family-friendly working conditions. However, these benefits have not extended to the entire workforce. Far from it, as witness the many stories about sweatshops and assembly lines producing goods for major corporations in so-called third-world nations, as well as the experiences of Amazon warehouse employees around the world.

In fact, globalization, the cost and scarcity of childcare, continuous connection enabled by digital technologies, and travel restrictions during the recent pandemic have made the boundaries between home and workplace more porous than ever, shattering what journalist Daniel Howden referred to as the "dishonest myth" of work–life separation.[55] If we were to depict work and life as a Venn diagram, then work would be a small circle within life's bigger circle, which further challenges this notion that we cannot be our full selves in the workplace. However, the capitalism of "humans as a service," of on-demand work, of razor-thin margins, has little to do with the whole personality of its workers, regardless of where they are located.[56]

Teambuilding and the Happiness Imperative

I first encountered intentional teambuilding, often under the guise of outdoor activities, when I joined a large company. Prior to that, the term was unknown to me. In a small group of people, the sense of being in and belonging to a team emerged organically from working together on a daily basis, knowing each other, celebrating birthdays and collective successes. Nevertheless, psychologist William McDougall is usually credited for laying out the foundations of teambuilding in his 1920 book *The Group Mind*, while organizational theorist Elton Mayo is believed to have conducted the first practical experiments dealing with employee behavior between 1924 and 1932 at the Western Electric Company's Hawthorne Works in Illinois, USA.[57]

Thanks to intentional teambuilding, I did my fair share of raft-building, treasure hunts, escape games, obstacle courses, personality tests, and cooking classes. The organizers tried hard and, most of the time, these activities were quite enjoyable. They often felt like a welcome break in the middle of ultra-conventional seminars. Sometimes, though, they felt like a chore. On occasion, truth be told, I would deliberately avoid teambuilding activities, finding the necessary level of pretense and faked enthusiasm beyond me. I'm not alone. Author Dan Lyons, for example, recalls his short-lived involvement with a startup. He recounts the tragicomic experience of Halloween, with all the employees dressed up as Smurfs, witches, or pirates trying hard to show everyone how much fun they were having as they nurtured a cultish corporate culture and frowned upon the oddballs who didn't try to fit in.[58] Today, physical distancing has replaced many teambuilding activities, perhaps only temporarily, with online games and virtual boards. There is a lot of creativity in this field, which is a good thing. It has helped many teams and individuals manage COVID-imposed separation by maintaining playful bonds. All the same, it remains a disputed question whether teambuilding has any real, positive, and lasting effect on collaboration and performance.[59]

Besides, not every group is a "team" and requires "building." According to Jon Katzenbach and Douglas Smith in *The Wisdom of Teams*, "a team is a small number of people with complementary skills who are committed to a common purpose, performance goals, and approach for which they hold themselves mutually accountable."[60] For groups of individual contributors, or people regrouped as a department because of similar tasks but with few interdependencies, teambuilding may be a misleading intervention, focusing attention on teamwork rather than on issues and potential for improvement.

For those willing to invest time and energy into teambuilding, unafraid of the "touchy-feely" or the forced-fun approach, the outcome is often disappointing. For consultant Jim Morgan, "standard team-building does not work, and given how adults learn, could not work. The teambuilding industry is built on the quicksand of mass delusion among purveyors and buyers." [61] The theory of adult education, initiated in Germany in the nineteenth century and developed by Malcolm Knowles, among others, posits several conditions for the acceptability and effectiveness of training. [62] Few if any of them are met by stereotypical teambuilding activities. Morgan notes that a drum circle is only going to be relevant to the work of a troupe of drummers, while a scavenger hunt won't provide clues about how to address difficult situations at work, which are too far removed from the game. Abstract knowledge derived from collective exercises is not easily translated into practical workplace solutions. Even seemingly useful knowledge and information that participants bring back from teambuilding sessions—such as stages of group development models or personality-type matrixes—are oversimplistic and, sometimes, profoundly misleading tools. [63] At times teambuilding can meet the need for "quick fixes" and "happiness," but it is no catalyst to effective and lasting change.

The quest for happiness leads us to another organizational rabbit hole. A quick search on LinkedIn provides me with about 1,330,000 results for "Chief Happiness Officer," one of the latest additions to executive teams around the world. [64] Of course, there is nothing wrong with being concerned about workers' happiness, but making it a quantifiable goal with a senior leader responsible for its accomplishment does raise questions. This objective is often a matter of shortcuts, of superficial solutions that do not address the very causes of misery in an organization. Research suggests that the pursuit and experience of happiness might even lead to negative outcomes. In their 2011 study on "the dark side of happiness," June Gruber, Iris Mauss, and Maya Tamir show that people who strive for happiness may end up worse off than when they started. [65]

So why does this seem to have become a contemporary obsession, even in our workplaces? William Davies, author of *The Happiness Industry*, suggests that the pursuit of happiness is one of the latest tricks found by capitalism to defend itself against apathy, ennui, and chronic health problems—that is, the indicators of *disengagement*. [66] Threatened by workplace disaffection and clinical disorder, the system has required managers and HR professionals to resort to new interventions in relation to the minds, bodies, and behaviors of their workforce. "The term most commonly used to describe the goal of these new interventions is 'well-being,' which encompasses the happiness and health experienced by employees," Davies explains.[67]

A former colleague of mine, for whom I have a great deal of affection, was an active proponent of mindfulness, which she found to be an excellent way to withstand stress, overwork, and the risks of burnout. She promoted mindfulness to her teams and other colleagues. The result, from my point of view, is that while all these people were meditating, they were not changing the structural conditions of their work. As they sought to rise above the travails of a failing organization, servicing their own happiness, they effectively left the heavy work—involving judgment, organization, and transformation—to others.

"Happiness has become a useful strategy to justify implicit organizational hierarchies of control and submission to corporate culture," argue Eva Illouz and Edgar Cabanas.[68] In their 2019 book *Manufacturing Happy Citizens*, they investigate how the new disciplines of "happiness economics" and "positive psychology" work as mechanisms of social control and internalization:

> Where workplaces promise more empowerment and emancipation from corporate control, a closer look at organizational realities shows that promoting "happiness at work" has been particularly effective in doing precisely the opposite. Workplace happiness has, indeed, come in handy to push responsibility downward, hence making employees more accountable for their own successes and failures, as well as for those of the company. Workplace happiness has also proved convenient to get more commitment and performance from workers, often for relatively fewer rewards; to sideline the importance of objective working conditions when it comes to job satisfaction, including salaries; or to encourage employees to act autonomously at the same time that they are obliged to comply with a company's expectations, to identify with organizational values, and to show acquiescence and conformity to corporate norms. Most important, workplace happiness has proved useful to make work contradictions and self-exploitation more tolerable and even acceptable for employees.[69]

For these reasons, I believe that the pursuit of employee happiness and well-being, while laudable and entirely necessary, is not enough.

Indeed, it does not provide a solid foundation for performance through sustained collaboration, deep change, and engagement.

FRATERNITY AT WORK gets people to be more intensely present for each other; it favors trustworthiness and the emergence of trust, enabling people to bridge with one another in their diversity. It is an essential element of collective performance. Yet it doesn't flourish naturally in the traditional workplace, which favors segmentation rather than integration of the whole. Fraternity is rooted in the emotional realm, which many professionals are reluctant to embrace. Either they choose to ignore this field altogether, relying on the fiction of purely rational workers, or they approach it from the surface, with tricks that are supposed to make people happier. But there is a much deeper and more relevant way to establish fraternity, with directly visible results on collective performance. I have tested its validity on several occasions, in very different contexts and organizations. This way is inspired by the history, dynamics, and tools of social movements. I call it *corporate activism*.

10

Corporate Activism: Fraternity at Work

I N 2012, HELEN BEVAN was responsible for transformation at the NHS Institute for Innovation and Improvement in England. I had first connected with her on Twitter that year, and, subsequently, several times in person, sharing our experiences of the respective change movements we were involved in. Her core belief that we need to strategize change from a social movement perspective was exactly in line with what I considered the very essence of successful change.

At the time I met Bevan, the Arab Spring and Occupy were in full flow. The synergies and differences between Helen's and my own initiatives and those occurring in the sociopolitical arena were highly informative. There was something exciting about being there at the inception of a new source of energy and witnessing the enormous potential and impact this force for change had, whether applied in the health sector or in business. Over time, my own involvement in the Break Dengue activist movement, then in the quality change projects at Sanofi, moved me closer to Bevan's domain of health and care improvement, and I found myself inspired and influenced by her in my own approach.[1] Bevan's deep understanding of transformational movements rests on decades of research and practice, the insights from which she continues to share widely, helping me and many others. What Bevan knows all too well is that the feeling of fraternity that is so necessary for good collective work, but so difficult to achieve in traditional organizations, emerges naturally in a movement.

Hannah Arendt noted that fraternity grows on the soil of "outsider-dom."[2] In *Men in Dark Times* she observed, "fraternity has its natural place among the repressed and persecuted, the exploited and humiliated."[3] Little wonder, then, that I discovered this form of solidarity in a movement that challenged a lack of cognitive diversity and unequal access to decision-making power in our workplace. We felt excluded. However, fraternity has the potential to connect more than just outsiders. Stimulated by an activist approach, it is a powerful glue for both large and small collectives. In a movement, divisions fade away. Hierarchical, functional, and cultural differences do not disappear but have less importance. What matters is the shared identity of the activist. Opinions become action, the static becomes dynamic, and divergent objectives are brought together in service of a shared purpose. It is neither organizational membership nor communication nor teambuilding that create a sense of fraternity but collective action in service of a cause. In effect, a fraternity is a community of intent and impact.

I understand that the terms *activism* and *movement* may offend organizational and managerial thinkers owing to their association with disorder or chaos. Nevertheless, a little conceptual provocation can be useful, while we should remember that this is about so much more than words and taxonomical games. The techniques and tools of activism are a treasure trove of human and economic performance. To ignore their benefits is to condemn our organizations to move forward more slowly, less efficiently, and more haphazardly, ignoring most of their engagement potential. It also means resigning ourselves to a sub-optimal, limiting, and even harmful experience of work. If done right, another way is possible.

Activism and Social Movements: Inspirations for the Workplace

Our largest problems won't be solved by heroes. They'll be solved, if they are, by movements, coalitions, civil society.

REBECCA SOLNIT, "WHEN THE HERO IS THE PROBLEM"

Activism has made a relatively recent entry into the English language. It was first recorded in the political sense of "advocating energetic action" in the early twentieth century and is contemporaneous with the terms *activist* ("one who advocates a doctrine of direct action") and *militant* ("one seeking change by use or advocacy of direct action").[4] While activist movements have a long history, the number of movements and the intensity of those movements seem to have multiplied in the aftermath of the 2008 financial crisis. This intensification may be real, or it may be a change in perception given our increasing access to information; either way, a key driver of many of these movements is the crisis of representation in post-democratic societies, where democracy is emptied of its true meaning under the influence of corporations, experts, economic elites, lobbyists, and business interests.[5] In such cases, it appears that the only way to influence decisions and regain power to act is through the collective movement.

The great social movements of previous centuries, concerning the abolition of slavery, women's suffrage, labor conditions, and civil rights, have all left their mark. Today, the impact of movements concerned with inequality, discrimination, and injustice fill our social media feeds, news channels, and other media outlets, and will have involved the active contributions of at least some of the readers of this book. If activism is more prevalent in the sociopolitical field, I believe it is no less legitimate in organizations. A practice of activism adapted to the workplace already has been applied successfully by a small number of forward-thinking change agents. Their examples deserve to be better known and understood. We need to explore how such activism is beneficial for organizations, for the people who work in them, and for the society in which we live. But what exactly is a social movement? What consequences do movements have on society and on individuals? What can we learn from them for mobilization and engagement at work?

What Is a Movement?

There are probably as many definitions of what a social movement is as there are researchers who study them. The definition included in the University of Minnesota textbook *Sociology* is helpful: a social movement is "an organized effort by a large number of people to bring about or impede social, political, economic, or cultural change."[6] The author adds that "social movements often work *outside* the system by engaging in various kinds of protest, including demonstrations, picket lines, sit-ins, and sometimes outright violence." In a workplace context, then, the organized effort by many and the bringing about of change are to be aspired to, whereas protest and working outside the system are likely to be frowned upon.

Movements organized around protest are hardly a recent phenomenon, as evidenced by the slave revolts in the Roman Empire during the first century BCE.[7] Political scientist Charles Tilly argues that a mass movement in eighteenth-century London in support of the controversial public figure John Wilkes was "the first ever sustained social movement: it involved public meetings, demonstrations, the distribution of pamphlets on an unprecedented scale and the mass petition march."[8] It was, however, the sociologist Lorenz von Stein who introduced the term *social movement* into scholarly discussions, in his 1848 book *Socialist and Communist Movements since the Third French Republic*.[9] This broad category encompasses phenomena as diverse as reform, revolutionary, reactionary, self-help, and religious movements.

What instigates a social movement has been debated for decades, although it is generally accepted that shared discontent with existing conditions is not enough to trigger one. In a 2005 review of social movements literature, Paul Bates, Helen Bevan, and Glenn Robert identified three successive schools of thoughts.[10] Between the 1940s and early 1960s, research into collective behavior focused on emotions and nonrational behavior, finding them central to the formation of social movements. During the 1970s and 1980s, resourcing and political process theories focused on the mobilization of resources by rational, calculative, and opportunistic actors, finding that the recruitment of some activists was essential to the transformation of the larger number of sympathizers into active participants themselves. In the 1990s, new research, Bevan and her colleagues show, focused on "interactive social processes within which people talk, argue, debate, build relationships and, through these interactions develop collective identity and purposes." These various theories complement rather than exclude each other. In fact, it is when all these conditions are present that social movements are most effective. However, the emotional component appears to have had renewed prominence in recent years. In *Networks of Outrage and Hope*, a book on social movements in the internet age, Manuel Castells explains that "social movements are most often triggered by emotions derived from some meaningful event that help the protesters to overcome fear and challenge the powers that be in spite of the danger inherent to their action."[11] Such courage, it should be noted, is also necessary in the workplace. Social movements are mobilized by dual emotional triggers: *outrage* (something is not right) and *hope* (change is possible).

Key Actors of Modern Societies

The "fundamental" social movements, those which transform society, have been studied in detail by Alain Touraine.[12] A sociologist of action, Touraine analyzed the May '68 student movement in France, the Solidarity trade-union movement in communist Poland, the workers' movement, and the feminist movement. He emphasized the centrality of social movements in the dynamics of modern societies. Social movements, Touraine found, are struggles around the major orientations of collective life—what he refers to as "the historicity of society."[13] Because it carried the capacity for social transformation, the labor movement was the key movement of industrial society. Sociologist Michel Wieviorka, who worked with Touraine, observes, "the social movement—the key actor in a society—is a figure which is associated with projects of emancipation, liberation, the challenging of forms of domination, the refusal of the actor to be directed, exploited, manipulated, subjected or alienated."[14]

It is worth noting that the study and practice of activism is concerned with more than protests over rights or dignity. By changing mindsets, activism can save lives. One example is given by Steven Johnson in *Extra Life*, a book in which he explains how, between 1920 and 2020, we have managed to double the average human life span.[15] This progress cannot be attributed to scientific breakthroughs alone. Indeed, the widespread appreciation of vaccines, germ theory, and antibiotics owes much to the hard work of activists. In the United States, for instance, it took fifty years of activism and mobilization before the benefits of milk pasteurization were accepted, thereby reducing the infant mortality rate.

New Mobilizations

In our modern, internet-fueled age, new social movements (NSMs) are the norm when it comes to activist movements. These student, regional, feminist, and other movements took root before the internet appeared and displaced the working-class movements of the twentieth century as the dominant force for change in our lives. Since 2011, though, a number of these movements, while different in their goals, have had a common digital dimension. As researcher Manuel Castells states, they are "interwoven inextricably with the creation of autonomous communication networks supported by the Internet and wireless communication"; Castells finds that it is viable to speak of modern NSMs as "networked social movements."[16] Although they are in very different contexts, these movements do indeed share an autonomous communicative capacity that is made possible by the ubiquity of smartphones, social media, and communication networks. Among them are the 2011 Arab Spring and Occupy movements; the 2013 French movement against same-sex marriage La Manif Pour Tous; the Black Lives Matter movement; the 2014 pan-European far-right political movement Pegida; the 2015 women's rights movement in Argentina #NiUnaMenos (Not One Less); the 2018 Yellow Vests movement in France; the U.S. National School Walkout in support of gun reform; the School Strike for Climate begun in 2018; the Querdenker ("Lateral Thinking") COVID protest begun in 2020 in Germany; and the QAnon movement in the U.S., which spread conspiracy theory around the world under the Donald Trump presidency and inspired a number of those who stormed the U.S. Capitol on January 6, 2021.

Castells observes, "It is this connection between the public cyberspace, bypassing the controlled mainstream media, and the public urban space, whose occupation challenges institutional authority, that is at the core of the new social movements." That is why many autocrats consider social media their enemy. In fact, some national governments go to great lengths to block or censor digital communications, trying to take away the power they grant to activists. In my own case, it was the ability of Yammer to bypass the organization's traditional gatekeepers and engage directly with hundreds of contributors that was its greatest appeal, enabling us to build momentum with our workplace movement.

We have since learned from the Facebook–Cambridge Analytica scandal, from the tremendous traction gained by Trump through his use of Twitter throughout his presidency, from 8chan's enablement of QAnon, and from the boost given by Facebook to antivax theories and a variety of despots that romanticizing social networks is dangerous.[17] We've learned that freedom of digital speech can result in oppression and that social movements can have antisocial outcomes.[18]

Nevertheless, in many respects, networked social movements remain inspirational models of action—for their dynamics and their reach, as well as for their ability to evolve social perspectives and mindsets, starting with those of the activists themselves.

Being an Activist

Through several experiences as an activist in an organization, I discovered a passion for joint action and the excitement of building something together to make an impact. My activist co-workers and I felt deeply excited about the possibility of shaking up conventions in an innovative and constructive way, without anyone imposing this on us. The desire to do something came from within. We focused intensely on the mission we set out to accomplish, precisely because it was more than a mission; it was a cause. Sometimes, we were disappointed. The results were not always what we expected, especially for a purely grassroots movement. We were often left wondering what impact we had accomplished or bemoaning the fact that we appeared to have achieved so little.[19] The fact is, the first and most profound impact was on ourselves. People who take part in social movements are often transformed by their participation. This is what happened to us, and this is what I see in all the activists I support. The discovery of a new power to act transforms people's identity in a lasting way. They never return to their previous state entirely, because they have acquired a new awareness of their possible role in the transformation, a new sense of agency. This is what political scientist Marco Giugni calls the biographical effect of social movements: "People who have been involved in social movement activities, even at a lower level of commitment, carry the consequences of that involvement throughout their life."[20]

Ultimately, according to Jacques Lagroye and colleagues in *Sociologie politique* (Political sociology), activism can be understood as "a form of active participation, not salaried, not oriented primarily toward obtaining material profits, and generally presented as exemplary since its intensity testifies to the importance and value that can be attributed to the activities of the organization."[21] Often, the cause in which we are engaged is not necessarily dissociated from our professional activity. An engaged doctor or an activist filmmaker can practice their profession in a militant way.[22] Commentators note that young people are particularly sensitive to all new forms of mobilization. An article from early 2021 explains that the global pandemic increased the desire to feel useful, whether that is through school support, feminist collages, or help for migrants.[23] Unlike the traditional political approach, youth are inventing new forms of engagement. What if it were possible to operate in the same way at work?

Motivation, Blind Ideology, and Personal Engagement

Activists' motivations have always been a point for debate. While activists express a desire to change things, there remains the question of whether their change agency is simply intended to replace one form of domination with another. Pure selflessness has been questioned by observers who highlight how activists enjoy recognition, a sense of moral superiority, and emotional arousal, among other things. To liberate oneself—before attempting to help with collective emancipation—a good dose of introspection and humility is necessary. This is incredibly difficult to achieve for even the most ardent activist.

Terrorists, who use violence to advance their cause, are highly engaged, militant people. While their ideologies and the methods they use may be radically divergent from those of nonviolent social activists, both groups rely on the engagement of others. Studies of radical engagement and disengagement show that they are not a matter of predisposition or education, but relational, co-constructed processes that unfold in incremental steps, each of which modifies the person's identity.[24] These processes are exacerbated by factors specific to violent ideologies, in particular the strength and exclusivity of secondary socialization—learning what is considered "appropriate" behavior by other group members. It is difficult, though, to ignore the continuum between the logics of ordinary engagement and those of radical engagement. It is important to keep this in mind because an activist group that falls into the cult of its own cause, into blind ideology, loses its capacity to convince many outside its own orbit and to effect lasting change.

Storytelling is a tool almost all activists and change agents rely on, regardless of their ideological leanings or the arenas in which they operate. Storytelling, here, is often a means of persuasion, whether of the self or of others. Public figures, companies, and leaders are frequently invited to tell their story, to craft the narrative in which they place their action. This is something, as psychoanalyst Fethi Benslama explains in *Le saut épique* (The epic leap), that radicalized terrorists do too.[25] There is an element of narcissism about radical engagement and the stories people tell themselves and others about their perception of injustice, frustration, or shame. The individual becomes the hero of their own legend, self-authoring, self-mythologizing.[26] In an "epic leap" the narrative becomes action, and the heroic character can gloriously accomplish their destiny, even if that means sacrificing their happiness, their life, or the lives of others. This is one reason why a terrorist mentality is so difficult to counteract. It is a self-built "subjective propeller" that takes root in personal identity *becoming* the person.

Philosopher Paul-Ludwig Landsberg, in his work on personal engagement, recommended that we guard against all fanaticism about the cause we defend, remaining aware of its imperfection: "The value of an engagement consists in a great part in the productive coexistence between the imperfection of the cause and the definitive character of the engagement." Engagement is a total act that involves intelligence and will. It is also an act of freedom, by a person aware of their own responsibility. Neither a purely intellectual operation nor a product of blind indoctrination, engagement is "a personal movement that contains an act of knowledge."[27] Landsberg's thinking on engagement was painfully prescient. In April 1944, seven years after he published his ideas in the French journal *Esprit,* he died near Berlin in a concentration camp to which he had been deported for his Jewish heritage and his anti-Nazi views.

Activism at Work, for Work

To link social movements to the corporate world may appear incongruous. These two environments seem, like water and oil, immiscible. However, there is no shortage of possibilities for bringing them together. Activism allows us to overcome structural deficiencies in organizations in terms of engagement, collaboration, and innovation. In a social movement, according to Castells, "enthusiastic networked individuals, having overcome fear, are transformed into a conscious, collective actor."[28] Why would companies ignore this powerful transformative potential?

It was not theory but being on the ground, participating directly in several movements, that taught me about these movements' nature and benefits. I saw firsthand how much activism generates energy, builds commonality, evolves mindsets, and develops agency. I witnessed and personally benefited from an invaluable boost in creativity, the improvement of workplace relationships, and a dramatic increase in digital skills.[29] Experiencing different interactions between "the system" and its challengers made me learn about effective organizational change. I sensed that participating as peers in corporate life could foreshadow the participation of all as peers in social life, which might be the basis for a just and peaceful society.[30] For all these reasons, I believe that activism and corporate leadership can be combined, for the benefit of all.

THE DIFFERENT FACES OF CORPORATE ACTIVISM

Corporate activism as I practice it is a new leadership strategy that places the methods, tools, and practices of social movements in service of the organization's purpose. This is about creating the conditions that encourage an activist mindset and way of work, maximizing the opportunity provided by the available human potential to boost innovation and business performance, to retain organizational relevance, and to contribute positively to society. It is about crafting an intentional and deliberate work culture while keeping in mind that movements cannot be manufactured, engineered, directed, or controlled.[31] Corporate activism is fraternity through common action, extending its positive impact to everyone involved, including the customers. It may be among the most powerful drivers for collaboration, excellence, innovation, and change.

It is important to distinguish the corporate activism I practice from two other phenomena that are sometimes also labeled "corporate activism" but that are very different in nature—and in consequences.

Corporate societal activism is the mobilization of companies around social or moral issues that are not necessarily directly associated with the activities of the organization.[32] It is related to corporate social responsibility but is more dynamic and responsive. Societal activism by corporations certainly responds to the personal convictions of executives, but also—and perhaps even more so—to business imperatives in consumer-driven markets.[33] This activism, however benevolent it might be, does not, unfortunately, permeate the way an organization's employees work together.

Employee societal activism is the mobilization of employees, independent of their employer, around societal issues, related or not to their organization's activity. In some cases, this activism challenges directly their organization's course of action. In a *Harvard Business Review* article titled "The Wrong Way to Respond to Employee Activism," Megan Reitz and John Higgins explain that

> employees are increasingly aware of social inequalities and climate change and how their companies are contributing to these ills, with millennials seemingly unwilling to turn a blind eye to their employer's complicity. Climate strikes, calls for unionization, and support for Black Lives Matter and the #MeToo movement are becoming part of the reality in organizations.[34]

Given the power of corporations in shaping the decisions that affect society, employee social activism might even be the *only* way to keep these companies in check. But here as well, it is unconnected to the way people interact and work together within organizations.

To sum up the differences, it could be said that corporate societal activism is driven by leaders—with or without employees' participation—and that employee societal activism is driven by employees—quite often against the will of executives. Neither, however, leverages the activist mindset to improve work and satisfy customers. In contrast, the corporate activism I practice is co-driven by executives and employees and transforms work for the better, which, ideally, positively impacts society in multifaceted ways.

FROM STILLNESS TO MOTION

> I am blown away by the passion and energy that the movement gives!!! This energy is so positive for people who are around me and who participate in this initiative to work differently. I keep talking with my colleagues about the importance and influence that everyone can bring to his or her work. Each idea, however small it appears at first sight, can have super-positive consequences: for our job, in our workplace, for the company, and for our customers too. To bring ideas to life, wherever they come from, unleashes people's passion. I feel very lucky to contribute to this.
>
> **ANGÉLIQUE, CORPORATE ACTIVIST**[35]

Reading Angélique's words today, it is hard to believe that she once was an introverted, compliant colleague, bound by the oppressive rules, norms, statistics, and standard operating procedures of a quality assurance department—before, that is, corporate activism transformed her personally and professionally, multiplying her positive impact not only in her own field of expertise but beyond, where her array of talents could benefit others across the organization.

Addressing a conference in 2014, Michele Zanini suggested that organizations move "from top-down to activist-out" in initiating and enacting change.[36] Instead of selling change to employees, we should invite them to contribute. Rather than managing change, we should rely on self-organizing communities and experimentation. This can be difficult in established organizations, both large and small, with their established habits as well as their operational and environmental constraints. Nevertheless, it is a remarkably effective approach, because the movement dynamic allows things to happen that traditional ways of working do not.

One of the initial benefits of corporate activism is the sense of momentum that it achieves. Organizations are often mired in slow and protracted processes that, at times, can render their stakeholders almost immobile. For reasons of compliance *and* internal policy, coordination *and* control, consensus-building *and* escalation, prudence *and* disinterest—not all of which are problematic, of course—everything can appear to take too long and to be too complicated. There is a need for discussion, analysis, data collection, the application of frameworks, and the crafting of presentations. There is activity for the sake of activity, without any visible progression. As a result, the analogy of the office worker as the hamster in the wheel seems apt. People work a lot, but the organization does not move forward one inch. Instead, it is subject to paralysis by analysis.

In the workshops I lead, I am often struck by workers' inability to come up with small, concrete actions. During an exercise that involves creating the first step of an action plan to move forward an issue they care about, participants are often helpless and waste their time either dissecting the concept or talking about the constraints that prevent them from acting. This is striking. The dominant corporate culture has robbed people of their confidence in their ability to act. The "playful tinkering" advocated by Myron Rogers and Margaret Wheatley is not even considered, buried under years of education and professional practice that have overdeveloped the focus on rational analytics.[37]

Corporate activists are more successful at weathering helplessness, indifference, and frustration. They believe they can act upon circumstances, and they step in. I have seen so many examples that it is difficult to single out one over another. On Raphaël's first day with his new company, his manager had forgotten about him and he was left to wait at the guardhouse for three hours. He became committed to ensuring better reception for newcomers, arguing that a friendlier, warmer welcome would contribute to better relations on the site and, by extension, to better collective performance. This was not at all part of his job description. Nevertheless, with the support of other activists, he set up a voluntary buddy initiative that mobilized hundreds of other colleagues and created a welcoming mood on the site. Part of their work consisted of convincing the HR department of the value of what they were doing, overcoming the territoriality and dismissiveness so common in traditionally structured organizations.

Priya, an improvement activist at another site, noted the long delay between the arrival of new employees at her site and the time when, fully equipped, vaccinated, trained, and certified, they could start working on the line. As with all matters that do not "belong" to anyone but depend on multiple actors—including HR, IT, Occupational Health, Training, Site Management, and Safety—there was hardly any integration. Every department intervened sequentially, one after the other, which resulted in an average lead time of forty-four days. Here too, outside of her professional field, Priya decided to identify each stakeholder, put them in dialogue with one another, and engage them with her passion and energy. Some of them had never met and were ignorant of their interrelated impact on the induction process. Thanks to this new collaboration, the lead time was reduced to twenty-eight days. Another activist, Yogender, then took over and further reduced it to four days! The company had gained forty days of productive work per new hire thanks to the intervention of volunteers.

Many professionals are aware of the issues that cripple their workplace. While some simply cope, ignoring the problems and focusing on their work, corporate activists take action to influence the system for the better. They strive for impact, focus their energy on it, make choices. Many managers justify their lack of interest by bemoaning the time it involves and arguing that their teams have none to spare. However, when you are on *the inside* of activism, as was the case with our workplace diversity movement, you do not count the hours. You don't *have time* on your hands, but somehow you *make the time* for the changes that are required. We found that our usual work was done just as well, even faster, than in the past. But we spared the time for our movement. We dedicated evenings, some Sundays too, with joy, because we had become the drivers of an intentional action that belonged to us all. Away from the idea of balancing personal life with professional activity, we felt more alive at work, energized by passion, thus eliminating the need for work–life balance; life was life and work was seamless in it as a truly energetic part of living. This is what many leaders don't understand as they try to keep employees out of the strategic decision-making process and confine them to execution. Doing this prevents the sense of authorship that so mobilizes activists. Keeping employees in the back seat—or even worse, in the child seat—is an outdated approach that harms the company's interests and actively disengages workers. Instead, employees should be invited into the driver's seat. Time spent in service of a movement is a judicious investment that leads to improvement and engagement and that proves to be far more effective than spending huge budgets on external consultants.

It is easy to blame burnout epidemics on overwork. But employees subject to burnout suffer in the first place from a toxic work culture, a lack of control over their work life, poor management, inefficient processes, and meaningless work. When they choose to join a movement because the cause resonates with their values and who they are, they supply discretionary work effort. However, if the company's leaders refrain from contributing to the movement, or even sabotage it, as I have seen, intense frustration sets in and personal breakdowns happen.[38] Here, again, responsibility lies not with "the workload" but with "how we work together." Some managers fear activism as a distraction, when, in fact, it can make people more efficient. Badly needed leadership skills are developed across the organizational hierarchy. Failure to harness this energy is a regrettable waste, whereas using it in the service of corporate objectives makes total business sense. Regrettably, in large, established, regulated organizations this is not an easy shift to make, as it requires a deep transformation of leadership behaviors.

EFFICIENT OUTREACH, IMPACTFUL ENGAGEMENT

Corporate activism solves another problem often found in organizations: the need for significant infrastructure to disseminate information. Many organizations have communications departments, intranets, newsletters, townhalls, team meetings, emails to all, posters, internal videos, executive blogs, and so much more. This is a heavy load and is rarely as efficient as the communications professionals hope for, caught up as it is in traditional, territorial, top-down cultures.[39] Broadcasting is costly. Employees maintained in a consumerist mode demand ever more information, which they have no time to read.

By contrast, activism spreads organically, from peer to peer. Because of its viral potential, this raises alarms among those who wish to exercise control. Activist messaging can spread without the heavy, costly communication infrastructure associated with top-down cascade thanks to the trustworthiness of peer-to-peer interaction and the authentic passion that activists are able to display in their conversations with others. When enabled by digital networks, these conversations can rapidly extend activists' reach and become more diverse and more valuable to the participants. In an ideal scenario, members of internal communications teams would be activists themselves, participating in the movement from the inside. Regardless, a partnership between activists and Communications is the minimum required.

In the case of our quality-focused movement, we initially refrained from a communication campaign. Anything that looked like what had occurred previously would have undermined the credibility of our activism and limited its viral expansion. Later, when activists felt the need for some communication support, they went to their local communications colleagues and worked together to develop whatever was needed. This partnership changed interactions. The co-construction process fomented trust-based relationships; a totally different outcome than would have happened with a cascade approach.

Activism is, by essence, role-modeling. Volunteers stand for a cause, commit their time, take uncharted pathways, expose themselves to the judgment or apathy of others, step out from behind their professional façades, and engage wholly. It is much more comfortable to sit behind a computer and prepare PowerPoint presentations, but this is not the activist way. Activists show their colleagues that their commitment is real, and that it is possible to act from wherever a person is in the organization. This role-modeling is much more appealing to others. Collectively, it is more constructive than any leader's exhortation. It also makes commitment more sustainable than happens with the typical company initiative. Here, it is not "just" work; it is passion in action.

Paul Ricœur felt that "peer-to-peer" (or "near-to-near") transformation was an alternative to "delusions of greatness." The desire to want to do everything on a large scale can be illusory and dangerous. "The perceived 'greatness' of our project stems from our radical impatience to see it carried out. The more justified we believe the change to be, the more inclined we are to impose it by force," as Pierre-Olivier Monteil paraphrases Ricœur in "Driving Change... with Paul Ricœur."[40] Ricœur himself advocated horizontal, experiment-based change, in which people are given the possibility to explore alternative scenarios, using their own imagination. This sense of *possibility*, rather than the *necessity* of carrying out a given project, is a must-have for engagement in any transformation process.

Throughout my time in the corporate world, I've seen unfold from the top down many global initiatives that have changed the strategic focus or the industrial footprint or the product portfolio of the organization—often at a high human cost. I've never seen any that deeply and sustainably engaged people. The only successes I've witnessed have come from corporate activists, and these people were not necessarily found at the top of their organization. What they had in common was the pursuit not of an operational or financial goal, but of a purpose that made those goals achievable.

Enacting a *Truly* Shared Purpose

It is commonplace today to say that an organization is defined by its raison d'être. Purpose statements have flourished over the past thirty years or so, on company websites, on the walls of corporate headquarters, on the covers of annual reports. There is a whole library of management literature dedicated to purpose, which sustains a thriving business sector. The very wording of corporate purpose statements is subject to fads, just as in fashion. Too often, corporate purpose statements are empty shells, describing only an intangible and timeless identity that has no connection with the lived reality of the organization's employees. I worked in one organization whose purpose was so noble that it seemed to absolve leaders from seeking genuine engagement with employees. I worked for a client who declined to explore its purpose because, to them, their product self-evidently served the world—despite the controversy that surrounded it. A former senior executive from the healthcare industry once told me, "In all honesty, we actually don't care about purpose. We're just in it for the money."

At a "Positive Enterprises" conference a few years ago on, I listened to an impassioned speaker melodramatically praise her purpose-driven company. It fought, she claimed, against the evils of modern civilization—junk food and obesity—raising people's hopes for a better life in America. What her organization did was manufacture, market, and sell juicer machines. When I observed the audience around me, I saw a mixture of fascination with the show and puzzlement about the message. Such an inflated perception of the company's impact couldn't help but raise doubts about the authenticity of its purpose.

In a *Financial Times* article, "The Boardroom's Futile Pursuit of Purpose," Stefan Stern notes, "Companies may make grandiose claims about their purpose: Philip Morris's desire to 'make history' and 'change the world' with a 'smoke-free' (but not tobacco-free) future, Facebook's aim to 'build community' and 'bring the world closer together,' Airbnb's 'belonging,' and so on."[41] Why? Maybe because everyone else is doing it and because it speaks to a generation of consumers and workers.

"Multinational corporations are luring millennial workers with empty promises and self-serving slogans," writes Maria Hengeveld in *The Nation*.[42] In fact, "purpose-washing" is said to be the greenwashing of the 2020s. Gentle mockery, though, can quickly give way to more acute criticism, especially when a virtue-signaling, customer-pleasing purpose comes at the expense of disasters further down the supply chain, or when purpose is clearly contradicted by actions.[43] Julie Battilana and Tiziana Casciaro note in the *Harvard Business Review* that the very signatories of a Business Roundtable 2019 statement on purpose (signed by 181 CEOs from the largest companies in the United States and suggesting that instead of supporting shareholder primacy, the purpose of a corporation is to support and deliver value to all stakeholders, including customers, employees, suppliers, the communities in which they work, and shareholders)[44] have, throughout the COVID-19 crisis, laid off more employees, donated less to relief efforts, offered less customer discount, and spent more on share buybacks and dividends than those who did not sign the statement.[45] For Hengeveld, McKinsey & Company, which has been involved in a number of scandals in recent years, epitomizes "the essence of the purpose project at work—namely, to deflect attention from the fact that corporations are driven by a compulsion to place profit before anything else, and to do 'the right thing' only when it benefits the bottom line."[46] In this sense, then, the purpose paradigm is nothing but a scam.

Purpose has also become synonymous with a corporation's soul. In *Strategy, Leadership and the Soul*, Jennifer Sertl attributes the idea of purpose to "soul: the intrinsic corporate identity that underlies all it does."[47] Widely credited for turning around Microsoft since he became its CEO in 2014, Satya Nadella echoed this in a 2018 interview with Simon London:

> One of the key things, I feel, is that just like individuals, companies have an identity. I talk about it even as a soul. It's that collective purpose that a company represents. In Microsoft, we talk about our mission as being empowering every person and every organization on the planet to achieve more. Every one of those words, for me, telegraphs that soul.[48]

This somewhat ethereal conception of purpose is all well and good, but it does pose some problems. By oversimplifying intentions, the expression of such purpose loses nuance and practicality. It is too impermanent to spur activism. It requires a strategic and operational infrastructure—vision statement, mission statement, value map, behavior matrix, HR and managerial intervention—all of which tend to be top-down, limiting, and enclosing, without removing ambiguity of interpretation or the possibility of unintended consequences.[49] In short, this infrastructure reinforces a culture of obedience and conformity.

Purpose. It's a complicated thing. To invite people into a particular organizational journey, to have them stay and contribute, there needs to be a purpose, one that resonates with them and what they care about.[50] According to Dan Pontefract in *The Purpose Effect*, there is a "sweet spot" that materializes when personal purpose, role purpose, and organizational purpose are defined, aligned, and acted upon.[51]

Various commentators, from Peter Drucker to Simon Sinek, have attempted to condense these varied notions of purpose, using them to explain why an organization exists and why it does what it does. But for all that, purpose—*not* the one lauded on websites and in annual reports—is an essential element of corporate activism. For an activist mindset to take root and flourish in an organization, a certain type of purpose is required: one that triggers action and that is identified and defined collectively. It must be neither too close nor too distant from the organization's business goals, and it should be situated in time and attached to a specific window of opportunity.

Activist Purpose

Compelling, activism-friendly purpose acknowledges that some situations must change, that something should and can be made better. It is underpinned by humanistic values. Since it is co-created, it is understood by all. I remember widespread perplexity when one of my former employers came up with a purpose statement that proved to be so remote from the actual work of the company and the employees who did that work that it made no impact whatsoever on engagement and mobilization. Activist purpose is linked to what the organization does to create goods, provide services, or generate revenue, but it is broader than that. It is co-created and as such, holds the potential for hope and for collective action right now.

A STEP (OR TWO OR THREE) BACK FROM BUSINESS

The first rule when establishing collective purpose at work is to step back from the product you are trying to sell, but to do so subtly, refraining from opportunism, while maintaining a relevant connection between purpose and the organization's activity. This is not as obvious as it sounds. For example, identifying the purpose of the dengue activist community in 2012 took several iterations, many days of work, and a lot of persuasion. It started with a legitimate desire to promote the company's product: a new vaccine. But no movement is ever created around a product. So we had to step back—doubly so. A movement in support of our vaccine was too close to home, while a more generic movement in support of a vaccination against dengue still felt too self-serving. No authentic activist would contribute. We required even more distance, eventually uniting around the fight against the dengue disease without specific reference to vaccination. Now, *this* was a purpose that could potentially connect and attract activists: generous, helpful people who would go beyond the organization's interests.

The additional benefit of stepping back was that it gave broader perspective to the work. It created a bigger space for interactions. Other players, from very different walks of life, could meet us there. This was something that would have been unlikely had we been focused only on our organization's product. Of course, this extension was not without risk, which we had to tolerate. What would happen if one of our competitors, developing an alternative product to ours, called us and asked to join the movement? If we were sincere in our sense of purpose, we would have no choice but to welcome them and collaborate. Before launching the project, I made sure that our executives were aware of and had agreed to the risks involved.

An extended field creates more possibilities to join forces. It not only increases diversity of thought, which is great for new ideas, but it also uncenters your own organization, helping to loosen the grip of territoriality and bureaucracy. The commitment to different stakeholders by virtue of joint purpose helps regulate the inertial forces that stem from an organization's tendency to consider itself as its own raison d'être.

AN OPPORTUNITY TO ACT NOW

> We are now faced with the fact that tomorrow is today. We are confronted with the fierce urgency of now. In this unfolding conundrum of life and history there is such a thing as being too late. Procrastination is still the thief of time. Life often leaves us standing bare, naked and dejected with a lost opportunity.
>
> REV. MARTIN LUTHER KING JR., "BEYOND VIETNAM: A TIME TO BREAK SILENCE"

For a movement to take place, people need to feel the urgency, grasping the opportunity to act *now*. Not tomorrow, not later when we have more time, but *now*. Urgency is an action motivator that overcomes inertia, which itself is an action inhibitor. In the workplace, John Kotter explains in *A Sense of Urgency*, it is alert, fast-moving action for change that is focused on the important issues.[52] It is opposed to complacency on one side (everything is going well, why change?) and to false urgency on the other (frenetic and frantic activity, the pileup of incomplete initiatives and projects, lots of meetings, shift of focus, worry and burnout).

Organizations tend to be complacent when they're successful but find themselves in a state of false urgency when they're under stress. Focused, energetic, constructive energy is by far the most desirable state, but it generally doesn't happen on its own and it is fragile.

The opportunity to act now—which Kotter calls "The Big Opportunity"—is "a window into a winning future that is realistic, emotionally compelling and memorable."[53] This window is likely to close if we don't act. If that happens, the negative consequences include the perpetuation of an unequitable situation and the inability to meet client expectations. A Big Opportunity statement reads like and serves as a manifesto. It has a more limited lifespan than the organization's core purpose, but it has a specific intention and responds to a particular situation or context. It is bound to evolve, to be modified more often than the core purpose. Importantly, it is text-rich, several lines long rather than a single phrase. In its density it addresses multiple elements, nuances, outrages and hopes, reasons and emotions. Each of these provides a potential entry point for activists.

This is precisely what allows different perspectives to be connected "in diversity," which is one of the conditions for the growth of a movement. The opportunity brings together and aligns the two components of the dual operating system discussed in Chapter 8: the pyramid and the network. It is one of the connective features that ensures the two parties work together rather than splinter or compete. This opportunity is the activist purpose of an organizational movement. But beware: it only works if it comes as the product of a collective sense-making effort.

The Power of "We"

On a sunny day in the spring of 2019, on the outskirts of Frankfurt, about thirty employees of a major airline were meeting for the first time, along with some of the organization's senior leaders. They came from all over the world and had volunteered to contribute to a new kind of initiative, a movement for change, involving the digital transformation of their company. Nearly a hundred employees had volunteered, and a jury of employees had selected these thirty from among the anonymized applications, based on their expressed motivation and their diversity, including in roles, experience, tenure, and digital abilities.

My work had begun earlier, in engaging the leadership team to support the movement and the new ways of working that would follow. We were now entering a critical new phase that would entail the transformation of this employee group into an embryonic activist movement. But a movement for what? It was down to the group itself to decide, with the assistance of coaches. The manifesto they came up with at the end of their first gathering was powerful. It had passion; it had soul; it was generous and inspiring; it recognized what had to change; it offered hope; it invited action. Beyond their text, though, was the power of human connection, of getting to know one another, to do something together, and to develop trusting relationships. They had talked about real, deep issues and how those issues impacted them personally, had reflected on how to be most helpful to their colleagues, had embraced an unprecedented partnership with their management team, and had taken ownership, stepping up into leadership.

In his blog post "The Power of We," John Wenger recalls a piece of work with three senior leaders of a cemetery.[54] He asked about their purpose. They struggled a bit with an answer, then one of them tried: "To provide good customer service?" Wenger half-jokingly suggested they then all go work in the local hardware shop instead, which prompted them to reflect on why they did what they did and why they felt it mattered. The three leaders eventually came up with a more purposeful outlook on their role: to assist families going through a bereavement.

> From here, the conversation flowed. They spoke with each other as if they were on the same team, rather than trying to manage what used to look like competing demands and interests. Also, they began to see a clearer way to delineating the kinds of behaviors and attitudes they wanted to see in their workplace. If everything was about achieving that higher purpose, they could see how to enlist everyone into achieving it. They have found their "We."[55]

Activism moves mountains, because in the very first place this collective discovery of a cause is a strongly engaging process. It involves emotions and values. The emotional connection established between activists as they find their *we* extends to the organization that shares and supports this purpose. Never will a key performance indicator, a new strategic initiative, a process improvement, even good customer service trigger engagement and mobilization as strongly as a collectively established purpose does. It is only the latter that makes an activist mindset possible.

Shared purpose is one of the three elements usually found in effective teams, according to Marshall Ganz. The other two are interdependent roles and explicit norms. Ganz has had a long activist career, having begun in his early twenties and contributed to a number of high-profile movements, including the civil rights movement, the Californian farm workers' movement of the 1960s and 1970s, federal political campaigns, and grassroots progressive campaigns. From his field experience with millions of co-activists, Ganz has built and made available a whole body of knowledge that is now foundational to the science of organizing.[56]

Organizing is turning mobilization into real, sustainable change. It comprises five key practices: building relationships, telling stories, structuring teams, strategizing, and acting. Relationship-building, and combining strong ties and weak ties, is critical and comes even before the definition of the problem to solve. Collective capacity, as Ganz and Liz McKenna explain in "The Practice of Social Movement Leadership," is "built from the trust, learning, and solidarity growing out of the formation of affiliative horizontal relationships that enable the development of shared interests, the construction of shared resources, and the commitment to use them."[57] While building these relationships, telling stories is essential to organizing to communicate our values and to motivate people to take action.[58] The Public Narrative framework developed by Ganz brings three stories together into one: a Story of Self ("why you were called to what you have been called to"), a Story of Us (a collective story that illustrates the "shared purposes, goals, vision" of a community or organization), and a Story of Now ("the challenge this community now faces, the choices it must make, and the hope to which 'we' can aspire").[59] At Camp Obama ahead of the 2008 presidential campaign, campaign workers were trained to share these three stories with the potential voters they approached. Ganz taught the importance of relationships, rather than campaign platforms.

There is much more to learn from this rich, original, and on-the-ground thinking. One thing is clear: creating collective capacity *is* a leadership practice, the primary one, and its scope extends way beyond social justice. The handbook *Organizing: People, Power, Change* was adapted from Ganz's work and from the resources of the Leading

Change Network and the New Organizing Institute. It states that "leadership is accepting responsibility for enabling others to achieve purpose in the face of uncertainty."[60] The same phrase could apply to leadership in the workplace, if only corporate leaders were willing to learn from the world of social mobilization.

Activism That Heals

Multiple dividing lines and differences affect our society: identities, political divisions, economic disparities, access to power, access to healthcare, and so on. At work, these sociopolitical differences are generally concealed.[61] However, there is a very real, workplace-specific, and overlooked divide: the one that separates frontline employees from those in middle to upper management. Issues are dealt with in successive layers of hierarchy. We either don't talk to each other, or do so only at the interface between two layers. In my first dozen years in a large industrial company, I never interacted with a frontline colleague. I had only seen some on occasional plant tours. One of them, whom I met later through our corporate activist movement, explained:

> Do you have any idea what you feel working on the shop floor? Doing the same thing over and over, day after day. You go home, come back to do it again. You feel you work *for* the company but are not *part* of the company. Especially if you work on the second or third shifts, from mid-afternoon to the early morning of the next day. Everything happens on day shifts: every major event or big meeting.[62]

I had no idea. I had never thought about it.

For the quality improvement project that started in 2014, we wanted to unleash people's collective intelligence through purpose. But how to achieve that? It is easy to have a conversation about purpose with leaders sitting in the upper part of the hierarchal pyramid. But how to overcome the sense of disengagement of those responsible for operational activity, communicating with and involving those on the shop floor?[63] How to secure their active participation in the creation of whatever was needed to deliver better-quality vaccines?

In my experience, frontline workers are rarely receptive to top-down engagement messages. What they want to see is real change. In a compliance-heavy industry, they have been trained to follow procedures, not to be creative. They have little trust in leaders or experts. That's why we needed to evolve the way we worked, interacted, and collaborated. As Michele Zanini confirms in an April 2021 blog post, "Unless we change our organizational DNA, purpose-filled work will be remain largely confined to the managerial elite."[64]

We opted for a movement approach, which took effort, experimentation, rethinking of habitual leadership behaviors, unusual tools, and the completely novel. We focused on simplification, on *unlearning* whatever steered us toward overcomplication, perfectionism, territorialism, and excessive caution, while maintaining rigor and compliance in our work. When we came across existing initiatives that served the same purpose, we did not try to replace or contain them, but encouraged and promoted them.[65] We saw that diversity and varied ownership of approaches were far more valuable than uniformity of practice or communication.

Volunteer activists role-modeled, encouraged, and propagated. Among them were shop-floor workers. With them, I delivered workshops and led discussions involving our night-shift colleagues. These were held between 11 p.m. and 1 a.m., in the presence of some of our leaders, and remain among the most exciting memories of my career. For once, we involved most employees in the transformation effort. We showed up where they were, we listened to what they had to say, and we sought solutions together.

Luis Maldonado is one of those frontline activists who helped change mindsets. He had joined the company's Pennsylvania manufacturing facility six years earlier as a production technician for flu vaccines. He worked on the second shift, usually between 4 p.m. and 4 a.m. After his anonymous application was accepted, in June 2015, Luis joined the first global coalition of volunteers in charge of steering the movement. His work was so phenomenal that the rest of the volunteers nominated him, without his knowledge, for the 2016 "Unsung Hero" Employee Engagement Award, which he won. I cannot describe how proud we all felt. Luis kindly gave me permission to quote from his award acceptance speech:

> As global members we made changes throughout, to engage the entire company:
>
> We now have all functions and meetings to include all shifts at all levels.

We implemented a program to engage employees in sharing wins.

We are now exchanging different ideas on all sites.

Communities of practice, working together as a group in various sites.

We have weekly meetings with other sites at the same time through Skype and teleconferencing. THAT IS AWESOME!

We communicate and share on social media, Yammer.

What I see now is employees working together, different departments, buildings, and sites collaborating with each other.

Working for a common goal, changing the way we work to have vaccines available for those who want them.

It shows that when employees are engaged and feel a part of the company, it will move the organization forward.

ENGAGE YOUR EMPLOYEES AND THEY WILL TAKE YOUR COMPANY TO ANOTHER LEVEL.[66]

A true fraternity was born thanks to this movement, a bond that persists despite the years, the changes of jobs and places of residence, the political differences, and the ideological confrontations that have become a fact of life in the United States and elsewhere.[67]

Contributing to a cause shared by others is naturally a great way to connect. Since this cause brings individuals together, it is a focal point that helps them overcome at least some of their differences. Yet they are not required to withhold their diversity. Activism is voluntary, and no one has the authority to require that volunteers put aside what makes them who they are. As Barry Oshry states in *The Importance of Seeing Difference*,

> the goal of connecting with our Other in voluntary, ongoing, and mutually meaningful projects is not only to experience our commonality with the other but also our difference as that difference really is—free of whatever myths, distortions, fantasies, fears, and projections arise as a consequence of our separateness.[68]

Corporate activism was one way to solve a performance problem that had been going on for years. But it is not an end in itself. It was the tool that allowed the emergence of a new reality in our company. Corporate activism was what made the system look at itself differently. Employees saw themselves as a community of people who cared about each other.[69] It was unprecedented. It changed everything.

11

Creating Fraternity
at Work

Togetherness is not community because community implies a set of common
values, and this is a work in progress in the movement...Thus, community
is a goal to achieve, but togetherness is a starting point and the source of
empowerment.

MANUEL CASTELLS, NETWORKS OF OUTRAGE AND HOPE

W E DREAMED OF an annual Global Collaboration Day. It would be celebrated throughout the organization by those who wanted to participate. There would be a global segment, with a speech from the CEO. A presentation by the IT department would focus on the company's collaborative technology roadmap. One or two practical examples would showcase how communities build value. These would be followed by an appreciation of the volunteers and the community facilitators, as well as promotion of the various communities that existed in the organization. There would also be a local segment, governed by time zone and national language, during which employees would learn about internally and externally focused local communities and have an opportunity to thank local volunteers who had done so much to change the work culture for the better. The event would be relayed on our internal social network, with a hashtagged conversation, a livestream when possible, and links to resources. Community volunteers, by helping prepare this event, would serve as role models for collaborative working, digital networking skills, mutual aid, and, importantly, fraternity at work.

For two years, a small group of volunteers, each involved in various internal communities, tried to convince the company to support them in this project. But it never worked out. We repeatedly failed to generate enough interest among the senior executives, despite constant external exhortations about the value of community, agility, silo-breaking, and digital transformation. I remain convinced that the initiative didn't fly because the original idea didn't come from the top. Despite two powerful executives agreeing to sponsor us, the initiative had no place on the strategic plan or in the corporate structure. Without the full backing and ownership of an operational, communications, IT, or HR function, the idea remained the property of a loose collective of volunteers from across the organization, drawing on their experiences in the field. As such, it could command neither the full attention of senior executives nor the financial and temporal resource it was theirs to grant.

In the following pages, we will consider how communities of intent and impact, born in the world of work, serve organizations and wider society, identifying the leadership approach that makes them possible.

Communities of Intent and Impact

Lebanon has long organized its public life around the finely tuned balance between its inhabitants' identity and religious affiliation. However, on October 17, 2019, a wave of protests against a corrupt and incompetent political class challenged this approach, first in Beirut then throughout the country. In a radio interview, economics professor Ishac Diwan described the unprecedented phenomenon that happened on the streets: "People listened to each other talk. In this suffering, people recognized themselves as individuals and not as confessional group members."[1] Diwan depicted a community epiphany, a sudden realization of togetherness, giving life to a new identity. From this may arise solutions to the multifaceted problems that have afflicted this nation for so long.

It is an overwhelming sensation to recognize "comrades in intent" among strangers. These are brothers and sisters in purpose, all contributing to a group that no longer owes its existence to circumstances but to human will. It is this sense of fraternity that the Yellow Vests who occupied French roundabouts for weeks on end remember most vividly. This same feeling can arise in the workplace, without rebellion or violence, if we place communities of intent and impact at the heart of work. Agnès, for example, sums up what participation in our quality improvement movement gave her: "It brought me new connections, indestructible bonds. To have believed in the same thing at the same time, I didn't think it was possible. I have fabulous memories."[2]

It is in the fulfillment—in activist community—of an intention that also serves the interests of the organization that workers find the meaning that engages them. Trust that emerges from working together toward a collective aim builds community, which itself generates increased levels of trust. It's a phenomenon I stumbled on almost by chance when I helped trigger a workplace movement back in 2010. While the concept of community is prevalent in Anglo-American cultures, even embedded in some countries' founding narratives, in France it has tended to be treated with suspicion, suggestive of segmentation and communitarianism. How, then, may we establish common understanding of this idea? The field is too vast to address in detail, but some thinkers offer valuable pointers. It will be helpful, though, to look at a certain type of professional community: peer learning collectives.

What Is Community?

Sociologist Norbert Elias noted in his 1974 essay "Towards a Theory of Communities" that community refers to such multiple realities that a definition of the term can only be "a generalizing abstraction built so high in the air" that it becomes almost useless to comprehension and action.[3] He highlighted the "nostalgic" and "romantic undertones" of the word, arguing that since Ferdinand Tönnies's research on the effects of modernization on relationships, "the use of the term community has remained to some extent associated with the hope and the wish of reviving once more the closer, warmer, more harmonious type of bonds between people vaguely attributed to past ages."

Exploring the intersection of community and politics, Elizabeth Frazer explained in *The Problems of Communitarian Politics* that community may be approached as a value—similar to notions such as fraternity—or as a set of characteristics.[4] The two are sometimes closely linked. Mark Smith, in *The Encyclopedia of Pedagogy and Informal*

Education, lists some of these characteristics, suggesting that community can arise from a shared geography, a shared attribute, or a shared interest.[5]

The handbook *Organizing: People, Power, Change*, adapted from the works of Marshall Ganz, suggests that the job of a community organizer is "to transform a community—a group of people who share common values or interests—into a constituency—a community of people who are standing together to realize a common purpose. The difference between community and constituency lies in the commitment to take action to further common goals."[6] A sense of shared identity may arise from such community, further reinforcing it. Social anthropologist Anthony Cohen moves the topic of community further away from structural terms, elaborating on the symbolic construction of community.[7] He argues that "communities of meaning" are cultural and experiential phenomena, delineated by symbolic boundaries, generating a sense of belonging for their members.

In previous chapters, I referred to Mary Parker Follett's ideas on conflict resolution, democracy, and power. Follett also had some very modern ideas about community. In a 1919 article for *The Philosophical Review*, she claimed that community is a creative process of integration.[8] Community happens "when all 'wishes' unite in a working whole," in the interweaving of everything. For Follett, this notion was necessary for the sound development of industry and for the expansion of "productive interrelatings" in the workplace. What, then, has happened since Follet's time to make the idea of community problematic in the world of work?

Perhaps we have been lured by a misleading shortcut, assuming that by default an organization is a community. It is not, or at least, not as self-evidently as corporate propaganda might want us to believe. The shared experience of relating to a given employer does not by itself create a community of purpose and action, no matter what the employer has to say on the matter. An organization is first and foremost an aggregation of people contributing to a particular endeavor. It holds the possibility of togetherness and community, which may be either nurtured or disregarded. Large organizations are often home to divergent or even opposing attitudes toward the nurturing of community, with some managers strong advocates and others discouraging such an approach.

Coupled with hollow or incantatory corporate communication, this phenomenon contributes to the perception of a misaligned—sometimes hypocritical—organization, feeding employee disengagement.

It is not realistic or advisable to hope that a unique community can span the whole of a company. Even a small organization holds several formal or informal communities within it. It is in its interest to cultivate, support, and connect them, enabling them to nurture each other. A single, exclusive community lacks the engagement power of communities that are multiple and open and, as such, are closer to the concerns of those who populate the community. Multiple, smaller communities increase diversity, agility, and mobilization capacity. It is not in the interest of the corporate activist to aim for a monopoly on engagement, to squeeze out everything that is not in "their" community. This would only reproduce the hegemonic functioning of obsolete structures, undermining their cause. The right approach is to recognize, value, and connect existing communities.

What matters more than integration is the richness of cross-boundary connections that all these communities enable and their activist potential. Some workplace communities form around a shared personal interest (such as, say, photography or running), others form around a common identity, while still others coalesce around a common professional practice. In absolute terms, all these communities are interesting because they associate people in a different way than is suggested by a company's organizational chart. They connect the system to more of itself. But the ones with the greatest potential for engagement work are those communities that are open to all. These are learning communities—allowing in one way or another for the growth of their members and the improvement of the system—driven by motives that serve the general interest.

While they share fundamental principles of action, communities come in all shapes and sizes. Some are extremely short-lived. Temporary or flash communities can be formed to solve a problem or to tackle an opportunity.[9] With social technology, it has never been so easy. In June 2020, a Donald Trump campaign rally in Tulsa, Oklahoma, took place in an almost empty hall, projecting an image of defeat.[10] The U.S. President had been conned by a flash community.[11] Hundreds of teenage TikTok users and K-pop fans on Twitter had arranged to reserve tickets with no intention of attending the event. TikTok has proved to be the digital service par excellence for flash communities, thanks to the way its algorithm works.[12] It helps create nameless communities, brought together by a common decision to like a post, with no other ambition than creativity and play.

Sometimes, though, the flash community that assembles behind a viral hashtag on Twitter or Instagram gives rise to a lasting movement, such as #BlackLivesMatter or #MeToo. Not every community has to be planned or set in stone or to exist for a long time. The way communities gather can be entirely fluid. Sustainability is often an intention expressed by aspiring community builders, but the objective of permanence creates constraint and bureaucratization, which are harmful to engagement. This is why a community approach should favor collectives of varying duration, some lasting and others not.[13] Above all, it must cultivate the openness, transparency, and activist spirit that allow people to connect according to how they perceive challenges and opportunities.

Learning in a Community of Practice

According to Étienne Wenger-Trayner, communities of practice (CoPs) are "groups of people who share a concern or a passion for something they do and learn how to do it better as they interact regularly."[14] This distinguishes them from formal working groups, project teams, and informal networks. Wenger-Trayner describes a phenomenon that he has been studying for many years, initially under the guidance of social anthropologist Jean Lave. Lave researched knowledge acquisition, not only in its individual and academic form, but as a collective, relational practice, taking place in context. In 1991, Lave and Wenger-Trayner published *Situated Learning*, a landmark publication that brought to light the phenomenon of communities of practice.[15] The type of learning involved here is quite different from the concepts and theories codified by experts and absorbed in the classroom or in front of an e-learning screen. Étienne and Beverly Wenger-Trayner explain that three elements converge and must be developed to form a community of practice:

· A shared domain of interest, a joint enterprise (What do we care about?)

· A community or group of people who interact, communicate, and support each other with mutual respect and trust (Who are we together?)

- A shared practice that community members develop and improve through peer learning (What do we do?)[16]

When project managers, or nurses, or quality control professionals get together to share experiences and reflect on common challenges, they learn and create knowledge for others. Davide Nicolini, Harry Scarbrough, and Julia Gracheva, writing in a 2016 study of communities of practice and situated learning in healthcare, observe that they do so in a way that is "associated with engagement, belonging, inclusiveness and developing identities."[17] It is unsurprising, therefore, that this approach produces effects that are more lasting and transformative than pushed, decontextualized education. As it is confronted by accelerated scientific and technological change, as well as increased dependence on professional expertise, the health sector understandably has developed a keen interest in communities of practice. CoPs can be indispensable where performance relating to, say, patient safety or the quality of pharmaceutical production requires evolution in human behavior or change across systemic boundaries.

In a brochure published by the Health Innovation Network of South London, Myron Rogers, Katherine Joel, and Melissa Ream explain that "learning is social" and that CoPs, fueled by passion, require little oversight.[18] Traditional improvement efforts tend to be driven from the top and are concerned with the management of micro metrics. By contrast, the authors argue that communities of practice are self-organizing, self-managed, collaborative networks, circumventing the bureaucracy and segmentation that is a feature of many organizations, both large and small.

While working with a large company, I witnessed the launch of several extremely standardized communities of practice, the scope and membership of which were decided by senior management, subject to rigorous operating processes, each led by a CoP leader appointed by the hierarchy. Few if any of these groups produced the expected results. They were communities of practice in name only, not in spirit. Passion was absent, as was voluntary participation, and they were constrained by the control of senior executives. To avoid this trap, Health Innovation Network states that CoPs

> are self-organising and self-governing groups of people who share a passion for the domain of what they do and strive to be better

practitioners. They pursue a shared learning agenda and they create value for their members and stakeholders through developing and spreading new knowledge, practices, capabilities and organisational capacity. They create knowledge networks across professional and hierarchical boundaries, and access the intelligence that is everywhere in the system.[19]

Not only do individual contributors benefit from enriched learning and higher motivation to apply what they learn, but the value extends to the whole organization.[20] CoPs make a valuable contribution to organizational speed and agility, to the resolution of unstructured problems (notably those caused by fragmentation, distrust, and lack of cooperation), to knowledge-sharing beyond traditional structural boundaries, and to the development and maintenance of long-term organizational memory. Because they cross boundaries yet gather people who share commonalities of action, CoPs create local, situation-specific, and system-wide improvements. Rogers points out how advantageous this is because "real change takes place in real work. Change is embodied; it's what we do. It is situated, not in a laboratory."[21]

Learning is not necessarily the original goal of communities of practice. Sometimes they focus on mutual support or address issues that matter for a certain group of professionals. This is the case, for example, of PEPS-SOS, a grassroots community of several thousand members of the French police force, led by a handful of police activists, who have come together to prevent suicides among their colleagues.[22] Whatever the purpose, learning does take place through all the interactions that community members have. Over time, a CoP acquires a shared repertoire of routines, as well as tacit rules of conduct and knowledge. As community members become more competent, they also become more involved in the main processes of their community, moving from what Lave and Wenger-Trayner describe as "legitimate peripheral participation" to "full participation."[23]

This agency-generating empowerment process, tied to people's altruistic and professional motivations, has been at work in every community of practice I have been involved with. Far from the mere absorption of skills designed by others, learning is continuously created through social practices and grows through an increased participation in the community. As noted by a RAND Europe 2018 report on healthcare-based CoPs, the art of the practice "is in creating social settings within which this sort of 'situated learning' can be nourished and supported."[24]

Notably, it was this attention to social contexts within a broader quality community at Sanofi, rather than exclusive focus on knowledge about quality, that allowed us to raise the general level of proficiency and, eventually, the quality performance of the organization. A straightforward approach to competence-building, focused on knowledge transfer from those who know to those who do not, is far too simplistic to be effective. It ignores such critical elements as context, desire, and social dynamics. Instead, an indirect approach should be favored, cultivating togetherness in such a way that a learning community is formed.

Community-Enabled Human Collectives

Communities of intent and impact in the workplace go beyond the transactional in achieving greater effectiveness. They are transformational in their approach to collective performance, helping reduce the destructive effects of industrial management.[25] Communication science professor Romain Huët, a longtime volunteer for a suicide-prevention hotline, has made potential suicides the subject of his professional research practice. A significant proportion of those he has listened to over the years, whom he calls "the unfortunates" and "the exhausted," name work as the source of their suicidal feelings. In *De si violentes fatigues* (Such violent fatigue), Huët relates their mental exhaustion and the social impact of toxic work.[26]

Those broken by work report power relations, contempt, harassment, the cult of performance and of humiliation, and hierarchical domination, against all of which they are expected to remain passive. They are unable to perform intentional actions, which affects their self-confidence. Work requires "an always guarded attention, infinite care, a rigorous will, while the distinctive contribution of the worker is invisible." It is very hard to take pride in one's work when the production processes are broken down into so many isolated acts that distinctive contributions are almost invisible. The unfortunates and the exhausted, "devoting their lives to something inessential, are bruised by the feeling of their uselessness." They resent the type of socialization that seems adequate to the modern world of work, "a form of superficial and neutral bonding, when it is not a matter of belittling or even daily humiliation."[27] For them, work is neither a source of satisfaction nor a means of integration into the world. Instead, it causes pain, dashed hopes, a sense of oppression, and a feeling of insignificance.

Communities of intent and impact allow for a work experience more in line with the expectations and potential of workers and citizens of the twenty-first century, while also delivering greater economic value. In his "Working Class Manifesto," Esko Kilpi observed, "The new structures of work and new designs for value creation are about communities continuously organizing themselves around shared information, shared interests and shared practices."[28] This approach extends its many benefits beyond the workplace to society as a whole.

Building Social Resilience

The base of social capital—the networks of relationships among people who live and work in a particular society—can be better developed and sustained if there exist horizontal relationships among those in the community. These relationships operate in reciprocal exchanges that generate trust. From trust comes a stronger, sustainable social collective. In fact, based on his analysis of living systems, Fritjof Capra argues that sustainability is a property of community.[29] Nature sustains life by nurturing communities in the form of ecosystems of plants and other organisms. Our illusion of perpetual growth on a finite planet, however, has become problematic. It is the source of multiple systemic disorders, but community does offer the hope of an alternative.

Unlike extractive business models which create winners and losers, lively communities are the source of generative value for all stakeholders. "Community structures create abundant, organic and regenerative growth," the Community Roundtable explains.[30] Integrating and aligning multiple stakeholders, community enables collective meaning-making and a shared understanding of needs and solutions. Participants' returns are higher than each of their separate investments, fueling these generative dynamics. As a result, there is more loyalty, generosity, advocacy, and reinvestment in these communities. The more useful they are, the more engaging they become.

Our societies are shaped by this phenomenon. An example is provided by Robert Putnam, who in 1992, with his colleagues Robert Leonardi and Raffaella Nanetti, studied the governance of contemporary Italy.

In *Making Democracy Work*, they showed that the variations in institutional performance of the regional governments established twenty years before could be explained by age-old specific civic traditions in each region.[31] Historically, horizontal governing power structures and vibrant civic engagement in the Center-North of Italy laid the foundations for strong social capital and wealth. Vertical power structures—based on a feudal and autocratic system—in the South eroded these foundations and did not allow for similar growth. Democracy is path-dependent; the patterns of association and cooperation that create dense, horizontal personal ties facilitate good governance and prosperity over time.

Fostering community dynamics also promotes resilience. The phenomenon of resilience has been analyzed for a long time and from many angles but is often understood as an individual's ability to recover from a traumatic setback. The COVID-19 crisis has brought the notion of collective resilience to the attention of many. How exactly do communities contribute to this?

A useful perspective is provided by research focused on disaster recovery. "Disasters and Community Resilience," a 2017 Academy of Management Journal article by Hayagreeva Rao and Heinrich Greve, provides insights that are particularly valuable.[32] The authors study the impact of the 1918 flu pandemic on the formation in Norway of general grocery retail cooperatives—nonprofit community organizations intended to provide mutual aid and pool community risk. While subsequent disasters such as climate shocks have resulted in the formation of more retail cooperatives, the pandemic had a negative effect on cooperation, weakening collective action and impairing the ability of Norwegian communities to build new community organizations for the next two to three decades. According to Rao and Greve, two principal variables explain whether a collective can rapidly bounce back after a disaster. First is the framing of the disaster and how it is understood. Second is the preexisting civic capacity that Putnam and his colleagues examined in Italy. A disaster framed as natural, such as a hurricane, an earthquake, or a tsunami, tends to reinforce bonds, through a sense of shared fate. A disaster attributed to other members of the collective—contagious people, in the case of a pandemic—tends to weaken cooperation and undermine the overall community. This effect is either amplified or balanced by the civic capacity already existing in the community.

The capacity to create diverse patterns of association is key to hedge against unexpected events. Overlapping volunteer networks help collectives respond more effectively to disasters, not only because the system is more connected to itself, but also because the diversity of organizational forms generates a diversity of routines and competencies. To develop resilience, Aaron Wildavsky explains in *Searching for Safety*, we should develop our ability to investigate, learn, and act, even when we have no foreknowledge of what we will be responding to.[33] One way to achieve this, Rao and Greve note, is by increasing the diversity of volunteer networks in a community, as this augments the ability to acquire, process, and learn from information, matching volunteers to the relevant social problems. Network diversity, they argue, "allows people in a community to meet each other in a variety of venues, which lowers the cost of mobilizing volunteers."[34]

What applies to society is also perfectly valid at the organizational level. What better time to hear this message and act than now? The organizations that COVID-19 didn't wipe out are faced both with disaster and with opportunities that go beyond the economic. They will need all their stakeholders' intelligence and desire to navigate what comes next. In a 2020 podcast interview with Paul Michelman of the MIT Sloan Management Review, organizational resilience expert Morela Hernandez explains that "the community's response—and more than that, the active involvement of community members as it's related to an organizational crisis—is directly related to the organization's ability to recover and thrive postcrisis."[35]

It's an ideal that contrasts starkly with the competition and selfishness we have become accustomed to. It raises questions about how good we are at sharing, mutualizing assets, and serving common interests that are all necessary to the practice of community. After all, there is a reason why the tragedy of the commons—individual neglect of the wellbeing of society for personal gain—attracts so much commentary on how to fix such scenarios from both a top-down governance perspective and the collaborative management side.[36] In 1968, ecologist Garrett Hardin argued that free will could not be trusted to regulate the use of common resources as humans are just too selfish.[37] Their rational self-interest leads to resource depletion, as can be seen with the diminishment of fish stocks and forests because of human activity. Among many critics who have sought either to challenge or debunk Hardin's thesis was Nobel laureate and political economist Elinor Ostrom, who contended that the so-called tragedy was based on unrealistic assumptions. When humans manage common resources, she suggested, there is always dialogue, social relations, and community.[38] What causes depletion instead is an ideology of profit maximization. In her 2009 Nobel Prize lecture Ostrom observed,

> Humans have a more complex motivational structure and more capability to solve social dilemmas than posited in earlier rational-choice theory. Designing institutions to force (or nudge) entirely self-interested individuals to achieve better outcomes has been the major goal posited by policy analysts for governments to accomplish for much of the past half century. Extensive empirical research leads me to argue that instead, a core goal of public policy should be to facilitate the development of institutions that bring out the best in humans. We need to ask how diverse polycentric institutions help or hinder the innovativeness, learning, adapting, trustworthiness, levels of cooperation of participants, and the achievement of more effective, equitable, and sustainable outcomes at multiple scales.[39]

Were we to substitute, say, corporate for public, business executive for government, and organization for institution, we would find ourselves with an overview explaining the value and sustainability of an engagement approach in the workplace.

In light of our current global crisis, it will certainly be difficult to win back business from customers with diminished incomes, to deal with rising commodity prices, to manage inflation, and to rebuild robust supply chains. But this is nothing compared to how difficult it will be to recover if we don't acknowledge and work to communally fix our fractured work collectives.[40] In lockdown, new silos emerged, inequalities grew, anxiety skyrocketed, and employees experienced detachment from the wider organization and from norms that previously seemed unchangeable. Now more than ever is the time to foster social capital in organizations through communities of intent and impact.

Community Is the "Present" of Work

The future of work is an appealing notion and has inspired numerous books and conferences, as well as sustained interest from all those in large organizations who despair of the immutability of working practices and conservative management. For too long, I was one of them. Change agents, corporate rebels, and gig-mindsetters around the world are eager for the future to begin now, bringing with it communities of intent, networked collaboration, humanized exchanges, and meaningful activity.[41] Some believe that responses to the COVID-19 pandemic have accelerated the future's arrival through the implementation of distributed working practices and the widespread adoption of digital tools. However, the fundamentals have not yet come fully alive in most organizations. Distributed work is still called "remote work," as people continue to conflate work with a physical location. Meetings follow one rapidly after another on Zoom or Teams, unnecessarily consuming online time just as they did in the physical office. Asynchronous work remains the exception rather than the rule, while so-called collaboration is still subjected to a hierarchical system of control and performance management methods and tools. In this sense, the "future of work" remains aspirational, although a few anomalous organizations are already enjoying the benefits it can deliver. For the rest, it is necessary to focus on the present and do what they can to shift the status quo.

To this end, in 2009, Rachel Happe and Jim Storer founded The Community Roundtable (CR) to help advance the business of community.[42] They have since provided community managers and corporate executives with precious coaching, peer support, benchmark, recognition, research, and more. Their annual State of Community Management report, drawing from hundreds of community programs across various industries, contains a wealth of insights and stories on the impact of corporate communities from both an internal and external perspective. The 2020 edition explains that communities unlock human potential, and that they are unrivaled in this respect:

> Communities rapidly pair needs and expertise, allowing individuals to learn incrementally and iteratively. Communities remove bottlenecks inherent in hierarchies in making tacit knowledge and conversations transparent and accessible. This broad access to knowledge empowers and distributes leadership, allowing more individuals to seize and

respond to opportunities. Executives shift their focus from making decisions to optimizing organizational culture and maximizing currently constrained human potential.[43]

Communities improve efficiency and speed across an organization's ecosystem. They accelerate innovation, generate organizational change that increases fluidity and relevance, help individual members feel seen and heard, and support people in their work. Is it possible to calculate the return on investment (ROI) of a community? Absolutely, according to The CR. It can be achieved by comparing the cost of the community with the outputs it delivers in terms of successful searches and answered questions. This is certainly a reductive formula, for the benefits of a community far exceed the value of the knowledge that is exchanged within it, but it has the merit of simplicity and "speaks" the language of the professionals who control access to resources.

External communities, involving prospects and customers, generate massive returns—with an average ROI of 6,130 percent—and are now better integrated into regular marketing and stakeholder engagement strategies.[44] To date, however, internal communities have attracted much less managerial support. They tend to be underresourced and less integrated into an organization's workflows. Nevertheless, they still have an impressive ROI of 1,967 percent. Communities are the engine of innovation and offer a compelling model for a more fluid organization. They create the possibility to develop skills that are highly valuable, including people engagement, content curation, hybrid work (both online and in the physical workplace), experimentation, curiosity, and inclusion.

Joining forces with many others who are different from us increases our impact through the interconnection of everyone's networks. The field of possibilities opens widely. It was a community-enabling effort that made a 2013 Sanofi experiment relevant for a quarter of a million people around the world. They were connected in action against a disease (dengue) that affects them all. Rather than adding channels to push corporate content toward more people, we designed an approach that made it possible for a community of activists to co-create solutions together.[45] It had ripple effects in the most unexpected fields, including police forces in the UK.[46]

In 2012, a national working group was established to examine ways to increase well-being across the two hundred thousand employees of English and Welsh police forces. Suicides, posttraumatic stress disorder, and depression are much more numerous among the police than the general population, yet the police culture makes it difficult for people to voice their mental health concerns. Change is hampered by stigma around getting help, by shame, and by fear of career setbacks if people are seen as less "strong" than they should be. The working-group leaders realized that imposing solutions from the top would have, at best, a marginal impact. Break Dengue was among the inspirations that led them to develop an open activist community instead. The program Oscar Kilo was established in 2017 to address police well-being, and its framework was subsequently extended to other emergency services staff.[47] It connects people across ranks, professions, and territories through various digital platforms, events, and in-person conversations, and it reaches the front lines on the street via "well-being vans."[48] Most importantly, Oscar Kilo enables people to talk to and support one another rather than leaving them to rely on a central source of knowledge and assistance.

Communities empower people, broadly and deeply, beyond the immediate proximity of their network of colleagues. Members feel seen and heard by their peers. This validation lowers their vulnerability, increases their agency, and makes people more likely to share their work in progress, opening it up to contribution by other people, creating wider ownership as well as greater relevance. Community building, where community is open and voluntary, enriches and supports organizational cooperation. Management professor Stéphanie Dameron identifies two distinct but interrelated forms of cooperative relationship in the workplace.[49] The first, complementary cooperation, is based on calculative rationality, combining calculation and opportunism, and seeks to harness strategic resources. The second, community-based cooperation, is based on identity rationality, or the need to belong, and seeks to generate group affiliation. The two forms of cooperation intermingle and generate each other. Both are required.

On several occasions, I encountered professionals who were deeply uncomfortable with community engagement. "We shouldn't need this," a colleague once told me. In his view, well-thought-out processes and effective hierarchy should suffice. Another was convinced that what his company needed the most was more rationality and less affect. He too showed unlimited confidence in the efficacy of processes to organize interactions and value creation. This is a tragic and unfortunately widespread blindness, for the world of business has become more relational than ever.[50] "Businesses are no longer the sole creator of a brand; it is co-created by consumers through shared experiences," explains Brian Solis in his 2010 book *Engage!*[51] Across his many blog posts, Esko Kilpi elaborated that work and leadership should be understood in terms of "interaction" rather than as "job," "position," or "organizational activity."[52] Connections that arise within communities, born from a shared sense of belonging, acknowledgment of emotions, and co-creation, are what really engage consumers and employees, thereby creating value. Digital communities, moreover, reduce the time it takes to build trust, creating intentional webs of relationships and collaborative behaviors.

Belonging may be defined as the experience of being accepted and included by those around us. A study conducted in 2018 by leadership consultants BetterUp attempted to calculate, from surveys and experiments with thousands of U.S. full-time employees, the value of belonging in the workplace. It is considerable. When someone feels a strong sense of belonging as an employee, they are 50 percent less likely to leave than those with a low sense of belonging, their performance is 56 percent higher, and they have 75 percent fewer days off sick. In addition, they are 167 percent more likely to recommend their organization as a great place to work. When individuals are excluded, though, they are less willing to work on behalf of the team that has excluded them, even when their reduced productivity hurts their own financial interests. Exclusion, then, can lead to team- and self-sabotage. So, what is the value of belonging? "For a 10,000-person company," the study finds, "if all workers felt a high degree of belonging, this would correlate with an annual gain of over $52,000,000 from boosts in productivity."[53]

Even if highly valuable, though, a fraternal community can only endure when the sense of community is genuine. This cannot be mandated from above. Nevertheless, we can create favorable conditions for fraternity. Such an endeavor, such responsibility, is the real leadership work of today.

Fraternity-Inducing Leadership

The team effort—the perfectly synchronized flow of muscle, oar, boat and
water; the single, whole, unified, and beautiful symphony that a crew in motion
becomes—is all that matters. Not the individual, not the self.

DANIEL JAMES BROWN, *THE BOYS IN THE BOAT*

I began rowing shortly after I turned thirty. I had never been exposed
to the sport before. All I knew about rowing related to an awfully trite
metaphor for teamwork. Summer was on its way in a city I'd just made
my home. The boats floating on the Saône looked beautiful. A co-worker
convinced me to give it a try, and I soon found myself joining the members of the Cercle de l'Aviron de Lyon.[54] I didn't have the right shoes or
clothes, and I felt awkward and ignorant. But the welcome I received
from Maurice, Rocco, and the others was simple, good-natured, and
warm. I took my place in a yolette, a coxed boat of four, and made my
first clumsy strokes. It felt like absolute bliss—something that has lasted
for close to twenty years now. I gradually improved my technique, contributing to the crew effort and enjoying it. Our community, which
could trace its history back to a club founded by a group of friends in
the nineteenth century, continues to fill me with joy because of its social
diversity, volunteer spirit, and intergenerational solidarity. The Sunday
lunchtime drinks are fun, too. We take pleasure in exercising outdoors,
in gliding on the water, in watching nature and the seasons change, in
spotting wildlife, in returning home with sore muscles, satisfied. We are
all different, yet are united by the love of rowing.

Rowing in silence for hours, for so many years, has given me ample
opportunity to reflect on work, and on leadership and engagement.
After all, in this sport, team spirit is essential. However trite it may once
have seemed to me, the metaphor is right, albeit somewhat superficial
given that there is so much more to rowing that could inform our understanding of the workplace and how to improve it.[55]

First, there is the very particular collective dynamic of rowing, which
brings into play more than the simple search for synchronicity among
the crew. The dynamic is egalitarian, fluid, fed by a common desire. In a
boat, there is no hierarchy, no status. There are just different roles—cox,
stroke, four—which in amateur rowing are taken in turn. Even if someone likes to set the pace, they can't be the stroke for too long because it's

exhausting. Each person is there for their own reasons, but together the crew aspires to the perfect stroke, an elusive goal that is rarely achieved and that, when it is achieved, is experienced for only a few seconds. The quest is addictive.

Second is sensory openness, the mobilization of many senses as the rower seeks to understand and adapt to all kinds of situations. Most of the coordination work is based on nonverbal communication. To synchronize, it is necessary to watch the blades at the front of the boat; to listen to all sounds coming from cox, boat, oars, and water; and to feel how the boat is gliding by paying attention to body sensations, particularly in the stomach and pelvis area. A classic exercise involves everyone rowing with their eyes closed. Listening happens by feeling the team and the boat. The openness of perceptions has a direct influence on the quality of the row.

Third is continuous and humbling self-development. We must work on ourselves before we can hope to change others. With teamwork, there is also a need for individual capacity and personal accountability. Rowing takes enormous concentration and exercise, combining multiple parameters with each stroke: body and head posture, hand height, balance, thrust from legs and arms, slide control, the dynamics and trajectory of the oars in and out of the water, rhythm, breathing, contraction of the abdominal muscles... It's a never-ending learning process. There is always something to improve, even for champions. We need to go deep to coordinate everything simultaneously yet remain open to "feeling" the team.

A collective quest, sensory openness, self-betterment. What if these were guideposts for a better kind of work? What if they pointed the way to the type of leadership we need today, capable of creating fraternity in the workplace? In Chapter 2, we considered what failed leadership could tell us about leadership, with an emphasis on individual experience, decisiveness, self-confidence, and superiority. Often, though, what is required is collective experience, emotional fluency, and people willing to question themselves and make space for others.

Leadership as a Collective Experience

Leadership follows a curious mathematical rule: the more you share it, the bigger it grows. Throughout my corporate career, I never felt more like a leader than when I shared decision-making power with many other people. Maybe this was simply a case of returning decision-making to its true nature. In a 2019 *Entreprises et histoire* (Enterprises and history) article on the topic, sociologist Patrick Castel and historian Marie-Emmanuelle Chessel point out a paradox: the managerial narrative represents the decision as a switch, enabling us to move from situation A to situation B.[56] The decision is made by a solitary individual or a small group, generally one located at the top of a system. In fact, numerous field and historical research studies reveal a very different reality. A decision is hardly a switch but rather a process—collective and distributed—the boundaries of which are difficult to identify because each decision is part of a longer process and is embedded in other decisions. Our bias for causality and our need to identify who is responsible after the fact both influence the stories we tell ourselves about decision-making and the way we are trained to make decisions.

Perhaps all we need to do is recognize the collective, distributed dimension of leadership, using other words to describe it? Henry Mintzberg suggested in a 2006 article for the *Financial Times* that "community-ship is the answer."[57] Researcher and writer June Holley talks about network weaving, claiming, in an interview with Ryan Mohr,

> The thing about network weaving as a kind of leadership is that everyone is a network weaver and can be a better network weaver. It's not like leadership is something that just a few people display. It's something that all of us can manifest. It really takes all of us working on a network to make it more effective.[58]

To connect people or ideas together, to cultivate quality relationships, to open the network to new perspectives, to be a bridge, is leadership. Peter Block speaks of leadership as convening. Every gathering, regardless of its topic, should be an opportunity to create engagement, a possibility for people to become owners of their collective future. Leadership is about "intention, convening, valuing relatedness, and presenting choices."[59] It is about creating civic capacity in the organization.

"It's hard to find good leaders these days," lamented a board director with whom I recently had a conversation. That's because we still view leadership as a personality characteristic or a style. We are still searching for "great" leaders, who will set a vision, enlist others' support of it, and hold people accountable through measurements and reward. Not only is this a misunderstanding of the leadership task today, but it also entertains the detrimental belief that only special people can rise to this level, that they alone are worthy of special training and the attention of the HR department. Rather than something scarce which is reserved for an elite, it is better to view leadership as an ability available to all. The first option constrains the system and reduces its possible impact, while the second raises the competence of the whole system, creating more capacity for change. Rather than focusing on the "heroic" individual and the problems they solve, the second option focuses on the social fabric, on people's interrelationships and purpose. Naturally, the point is not to neglect the problems, but it is necessary, first, to nurture the human collective that will deal with them, engaging people in a way that creates accountability and commitment, modeling the desired future.

We can't be leaders if we have "followers" who depend on us for solutions. This is not leadership but depletion, the result of hubris, manipulation, and ignorance. We can only be leaders if we actively contribute to conditions that make everyone else a leader too, regardless of their position in the hierarchy, academic background, gender, age, affinities, preferences, or any other variable. In *Organizing*, the handbook based on the work of Marshall Ganz, the definition of organizing is synonymous with leadership: "Organizing is not about solving a community's problems or advocating on its behalf. It is about enabling the people with the problem to mobilize their own resources to solve it (and keep it solved)."[60] Enabling, not delegating or commanding.

Intentional relationships are the foundation of purposeful collective actions. They involve constant attention and work. Through intentional relationships, commitment to work together to achieve common purpose is developed, which is a phenomenal source of power. The "new power" described by Henry Timms and Jeremy Heimans is made by many and is open, participatory, and peer-driven.[61] It is fundamentally different from the transactional "old power"—more like the passage of electrical current than the exchange of currency. Systems leadership encompasses this new approach.[62] "Systems leadership is not an individual pursuit," John Hagel and Gemma Mortensen explain in a 2018 white paper on the work of the World Economic Forum's Global Future Council on Platforms and Systems. "It is a rejection of old notions of top-down hierarchical leadership and is in its very essence a collaborative, collective pursuit."[63] Systems leadership is about weaving together an intentional system of people and resources that brings about change in the system as a whole. To this end, platforms—including the technology, governance, and protocols that help people connect at scale for impact—are essential. But, as with everything digital, they are of little value if leadership behaviors remain stuck in the twentieth century. Kilpi eloquently described the necessary shift in a 2016 piece on network leadership:

> Leadership used to be based on asymmetric power relations, but networks work differently. Network relations are typically more symmetric. There is less dependency between people. In symmetric systems, leadership needs to be handed to the community itself without any single individual being in control, or trying to be in control. The solution is simple in theory but very hard in practice. It is about active participation and responsiveness. Leadership is communication. The leaders, people worth following, raise bottom up. There is always going to be hierarchies, but hierarchies in network architectures are dynamic, contextual heterarchies. In fact, this is the only way that there can be leaders in democratic systems.[64]

Leadership as Emotional Fluency

How do you know there is a sense of community in an organization? Mintzberg says it's easy: "You feel the energy in the place, the commitment of its people, their collective interest in what they do."[65] It is a matter of feeling what happens, not of surveys, indicators, or data analytics.[66] It is about energy, not structure and processes. With all due respect to engineering minds, collaboration has nothing to do with cogs and wheels. For those who still rely on this image to describe the proper functioning of a team, it is time to discard it. It leads us to think of the work collective in a misguided way, as an inert set of spare parts that can be observed without affect, arranged, repaired, oiled. At its head is the leader, the chief mechanic, the organizational engine expert. Such a vision ignores what is neither manageable nor predictable, the human element that covers individualities, emotions, journeys, prejudices. Dysfunctionality and toxicity become evident when this human dimension is ignored.

Fraternity is a human bond that is not arranged but nurtured. The engine metaphor should be replaced by a gardening one. The effective leader is equipped not with a wrench, but with a watering can. In *Team of Teams,* former U.S. Army General Stanley McChrystal explains why the garden has replaced chess as his preferred metaphor. In the modern war, "the movement-by-movement control that seemed natural to military operations proved less effective than nurturing the organization."[67] Pernille Hippe Brun, drawing in *On the Move* on lessons from a range of Nordic leaders, sees nurturing as a distinctive leadership trait and a reason for their success in businesses around the world.[68] Leading is gardening. It means making sure the soil is fertile, that it is nourished by light, water, and constant care so that grass and trees and flowers can flourish. "You cannot make a plant grow by commanding it to do so," Hippe Brun reminds us. You certainly cannot expect it to attain the exact size, color, or fragrance you planned. Leadership-as-gardening means accepting a fair level of surprise. Surprise is not chaos when the whole system is kept together by a shared intent and an ongoing, collective, meaning-making dynamic resulting from what McChrystal describes as "a constant flow of shared consciousness." In these conditions, surprise is an asset. It is a sign that innovation is not the preserve of the managerial elite. It is an expression of creative diversity, a proof of the system's vitality.

The shift from engineering to gardening brings into play an array of skills and abilities not commonly used in traditional leadership. In addition to reasoning, analysis, knowledge mobilization, and competitive strategy, the leader-gardener must call upon new senses. Just as rowers perceive their crewmates' rhythm by ear and through subtle vibrations in their bodies, these leaders are attentive to nonverbal perceptions, helping them to understand and to interact. In Jen Frahm's book *Change. Leader,* Jillian Reilly suggests that they grasp "the mind-body connections and are attuned to [their] physical state and the feedback it provides."[69] Because our bodies are deep sources of wisdom and help us make sense of the unknown and how we move through it, "truly resourceful and capable leaders work to align the cognitive and somatic." Alongside emotional intelligence, which is widely recognized as a critical resource for professional success, Reilly argues that somatic intelligence is of equal relevance.[70] In an uncertain world, the capacity to decipher physical signals, to translate into conscious knowledge the wisdom and experiences that our bodies hold and express through feeling and movement, is a precious skill. It supplements cognition and logic, providing another source of data.

Leader-gardeners understand the impact that a word, a gesture, a look, or the lack thereof may have on other people. They are aware that we all tend to overestimate our emotional intelligence (especially those of us who lack it the most) and our ability to decipher the intentions of others (especially when our own are often obscure to us).[71] As such, they favor curiosity in their exchanges. They avoid as much as possible relationships of power and domination, despite sometimes having been shaped by them. In a blog post on leadership and humiliation, Eugenio Molini observes,

> All leaders (when I say all I mean all) I have worked with, have been humiliated many times on their way to become what they are now. Many that aspired to leadership have succumbed along the way. Many of those that have made it, lead as they have learned: by more or less subtly humiliating peers and subordinates. Some have learned that they have to treat people well if they are to be productive. Too few have learned that humility . . . is the only sustainable antidote against humiliation.[72]

Leader-gardeners leave behind assertiveness, pride, and sleek corporate communication in favor of sharing dilemmas, questions, and uncertainties. They make space for other viewpoints and elicit connection through play, curiosity, creation, empathy, and art.[73] Naturally, they do not do this in a heroic way, standing out with exceptional skills. Instead, they invite their colleagues to practice their emotional fluency with them.

In 2014, *Administrative Science Quarterly* published a longitudinal study by Sigal Barsade and Olivia O'Neill that examined the internal culture and employee and client outcomes in a long-term care setting.[74] The authors identify a culture characterized by feelings of affection, compassion, caring, and tenderness for others, demonstrating that this is possible when there is a will to make it so. Multiple data points allow Barsade and O'Neill to assert that this type of culture "positively relates to employees' satisfaction and teamwork and negatively relates to their absenteeism and emotional exhaustion." They also show a positive association with clients' outcomes. The authors name this a culture of companionate love. Having experienced it, I know it is incredibly powerful. It is "an act of care and love" to make to connections, John

Atktinson and David Nabarro suggest in a post on systems leadership, when connection is driven by curiosity and generosity.[75] Making the time to connect, tending to the quality of our relationships, is important and a source of joy. Caring and love enable us to sense a system, to "get the feel" of what happens within it.

Obviously, there is no need for companionate love when one still believes in the power of structures and processes, in leadership as a rare talent, in an individualistic approach to career progression, or when the collective is seen as a mere resource instead of a passionate community. This is a choice. But it is a choice that limits the capacity for individual impact and hinders the performance of the organization. Through their openness to the realm of the sensitive, leader-gardeners allow the organization to capture a greater diversity of input, making it more intelligent and better able to address the complex situations of today's world. Emotional fluency helps change the nature of conversations, the way the system looks at itself, the identity through which it makes sense of novelty. Because this path harnesses its living nature rather than opposing or constraining it, it is the only effective way to truly change the system.[76] It goes far beyond what any reorganization, strategic plan, or cascaded methodology can achieve. The grace of authentic encounters that a common endeavor enables also changes the people involved with longer-lasting effects than can be accomplished through training, reward, or punishment.

Leadership as Self-Effacing Work

The leader has always been presented as the one who stands out from the others, who is special in one way or another, hierarchically or symbolically positioned above a group. As such, leaders are made visible, receive recognition, and are valued. But what if true leadership consisted of blending in with the group? Of disappearing?

The challenge of leadership calls for an in-depth look at the space we hold for ourselves and for others in a work collective, at the way we make an impact, and at how this impact could be more transformational. We need to get better at noticing what we have retained of obsolete leadership, of old methodologies and established customs that serve neither organizations nor their people. For example, anything that fuels narcissism must be met with caution, unless it is a tactical device to advance transformation. Ego is a healthy driver for action but, because it is so easily instrumentalized in our capitalist culture, it can rapidly become toxic. To act selflessly signals real change.

In *The Boys in the Boat*, Daniel James Brown notes that when part of a crew, "rowers must subsume their often fierce sense of independence and self-reliance." At the same time, they must "hold true to their individuality, their unique capabilities as oarsmen or oarswomen or, for that matter, as human beings."[77] No rowing coach would wish to simply duplicate their most capable rower, for the best crews are an integration of diverse and complementary abilities and personalities, not a group of clones. This perhaps touches on one of the dilemmas of leadership: bringing our own unique contribution while allowing the collective to work as one. We need to be fully present, not just passing through, while working to become dispensable. Indeed, our absence must not affect the collective's cohesion or performance.

This could be misunderstood as extensive delegation, but that doesn't fundamentally change power and interaction patterns, it just makes them a little more livable. In fact, the transformational leader and the change agent should aim to make themselves redundant. "In delivering change, you have to ensure the capabilities and self-sufficiency of your colleagues to continue the work without you," Richard Martin, one of the editors of this book, wrote in an exchange we had on the topic. "This is why the heroic leader approach is usually the wrong one. The change leader must be self-effacing, fading into the background over time. They may be the catalyst that started things off, but they should no longer be needed by the end."[78] Eugenio Moliní reports the satisfaction of a client who, at the end of a workshop, was pleased that the consultant's presence had been almost invisible.[79] The session had been consciously designed that way so that the team took ownership of the work. As Dag Hammarskjöld, Secretary General of the United Nations in the 1950s, once said, "You will know Life and be acknowledged by it according to your degree of transparency, your capacity, that is, to vanish as an end, and remain purely as a means."[80]

Designing to disappear takes a lot of work. It is much more difficult than holding all the available space, exerting domination, sucking up responsibility. This is a common misunderstanding among people who are told to let go. If they believe that they can no longer intervene, they question their own utility, wondering how they will spend their days. They worry about what they should do if they see that a group heading for failure. I have often encountered these apprehensions among managers I have worked with as colleagues and clients. Kilpi noticed it too:

> As managers contemplate widening the circle of involvement, they sometimes believe that it means to have less ability to provide input based on their knowledge and experience. Paradoxically, engaging more people requires more from managers than the current management paradigm.[81]

Indeed, it is not at all a question of letting go, but of evolving our forms of intervention. More indirect, less directive and controlling, focused on favorable conditions and nurturing relationships. It is about supporting individuals in such a way that this support soon becomes unnecessary; about producing coherence in a diverse system; about facilitating the emergence of novelty. It requires identifying who needs to be heard, wherever they sit in the organizational structure, and inviting them in ways that render their participation meaningful. It requires making intentional and sometimes difficult choices that the opposing forces of busyness, obedience, complexity, and fear will seek to thwart. Its foundations lie in constant introspection, endless learning, and courageous experimentation. This is an immense task that calls for the use of a wider range of skills and for more, not less, involvement.

When this is done well, when engagement leadership enables a collective to function as a fraternal community, then working together generates a much broader and deeper positive impact than what traditional models allow. The group better respects human abilities and needs. It is more efficient, more innovative, more agile, and all stakeholders benefit from it. Instead of disengagement and burnout, this approach opens up the possibility of flow, in the sense intended by psychologist Mihály Csíkszentmihályi.[82] Flow is a unique experience, simultaneously individual and communal, elusive and addictive, like the search for the perfect rowing stroke, and has been evident in all the communities of intention and impact that I have come across. These are characterized by effortless, high-quality, creative work, and a self-organized arrangement of everyone's contribution.

Who wouldn't want to work like this? Engagement leadership makes it possible.

Envoi

I T IS A singular journey that has led me to reflect on the issues of leadership, collective work, and their impact on society. You may not share all my thoughts. But there are at least two things on which I hope we will agree. The first is that the world of work should be more respectful of people. It should be conducive to human creative potential—an enabler of solidarity and positive impact. If that were the case, the world would be a better place for all of us. The second is that change does not happen by itself. It requires, at the outset, an assumption of individual responsibility, an act of courage, a constructive rebellion.

The workplace should not simply be the physical or digital location where we work. It can also be a community of intention and impact, purposefully designed and nurtured to leverage the diversity of thoughts. All stakeholders, not just employees, can be continuously involved, powered by social tools and united by common cause. The workplace can adapt and thrive thanks to ceaseless collective sense-making. This should not be the preserve of the few. The quality of our workplace relationships matter. We need people who care for one another and collaborate across levels and functions. Is this a realistic hope? I believe so, for I have seen it happen. The challenge is to normalize it and scale this way of working across organizations. No longer should it be considered an anomaly.

Often when presented with this opportunity in organizations, people with the least amount of power understand immediately why and how it can make things better. With agency, they can demonstrate their creativity, their commitment, and their desire to take part. Those who do already have power, though, high up in the hierarchy, treat this with a degree of suspicion and distrust. They remain oblivious to the need for emancipation, doubting what the people they lead can achieve. Their focus tends to be more on what they will lose—control, order, superiority—than on what the organization will gain. Mutual influence and understanding are necessary. To evolve new systems, everyone needs to contribute. In fact, change is about questioning and learning about how today's complex systems work. This enriches all our leadership capabilities. We must redirect our attention, adapting our behaviors, evolving patterns of relationships—all of which make it possible to collaborate differently, leveraging the new opportunities that emerge.

To address the immense challenges that confront us, now and in the future, our fragmented societies need to restore constructive and inclusive human connections. We need to value those links of mutual knowledge that do not lock people into an identity or status. The workplace is a pertinent space for this effort. This is where billions of human beings spend their days, every week of the year, for their livelihood. This is where a collective endeavor that is more than "a job" can be built, together, whatever the size of the enterprise. This is an endeavor that welcomes the contribution of all, with no regard for academic qualifications, gender, cultural fit, or any other form of differentiation. It draws power from diversity, bringing together the multiple perspectives of people willing to contribute to something greater than themselves, forming community. This is where real value gets created. "I have said that community creates," Mary Parker Follett explained in "Community Is a Process." "It creates personality, power, freedom. It also creates purpose, continuously creates purpose."[1]

Genuine engagement does not arise from communication alone. It is not a synonym for individual happiness or satisfaction. Importantly, it cannot be activated from outside—emotional manipulation must not be used to achieve an end. Engagement results from acting together. It is about setting ourselves in motion *because we want to*. It is about bringing values and purpose to life. Above all, engagement is a practice. It is not enough to read about it. We need to resist the comfort of privileged self-segregation, of emotion-neutralizing abstractions, of cozy boardrooms. Instead, we need to enter the arena of operational work, engage in mobilization efforts, exchange as equals with as many different people as possible, especially those interacting with the customers, those on the shop floor, those in the warehouse. It is our responsibility to connect the system to more of itself, to create new pathways and new conversations, to serve as bridges, connectors, enablers. "Caminante, no hay puentes, se hace puentes al andar," Gloria Anzaldúa wrote in *Borderlands/La Frontera*: "Traveler, there are no bridges, you make bridges as you go."[2]

A movement toward more liberty, equality, and fraternity at work starts, as we have seen, with an individual distancing themselves from a dominant model—one inherited from the past, which has become restrictive and counterproductive—with others eventually electing to do the same. At the beginning, there is personal risk-taking and a sense of both refusal and encouragement, even if this sense only takes the form of a voice in the change agent's head telling them "no," partly in disgust at what is, partly in disbelief at what might be, partly in recognition of the rules and norms that constrain them. In *The Rebel*, an examination of the development of revolutionary thought, Albert Camus wrote, "I rebel, therefore we exist."[3] That phrase could sum up the essence of this book.

The refusal of a soul-destroying order is accompanied by a proposal for new modes of organization. A boundary is crossed. What was previously acceptable becomes unacceptable, an oppression that must be replaced by a relationship of equal dignity. In finding our voice, we become aware of a universal value to which we can aspire, as can all our fellow human beings: a common ground for all of us. Rebellion pulls us away from our singular circumstances, bringing us into the collective experience. In effect, rebellion is the fundamental reality of our lives, because it *creates* the human community. From a small gesture of personal emancipation (liberty) there follows the purposeful connection of many (equality). From that point, there is a progression to activist communities leading change, doing our best work together (fraternity). We can free ourselves from the violence of division and resentment. We can free ourselves from apathy and the sense of impotence that keep the current patterns in place. But that is only a beginning. The work of change is a never-ending process.

The way we get to the future is the future we get, says Myron Rogers. How do we—as individuals, collectives, organizations—head into the future?

Are we going in a way that truly encourages action, risk-taking, autonomy and accountability? Or are we punishing change agents for their audacity? What are we doing to create capacity for change in the system, and why? How do we invite others to join in, generating shared ownership?

Are we fully leveraging networks to transform relationships and collective knowledge? In what ways are we personally involved in digital networks? How do we contribute to the persistence of unequal interactions or, on the contrary, to the diversification of perspectives that are heard and valued?

How do we foster the development of social capital in the organization? With whom do we join forces, and for what purposes? What are we activists for? What do we support? What do we aspire to? What do we want to change? What impact do we have, and how do we know? What communities are we involved in?

What are we doing in practice to augment liberty, equality, and fraternity in our systems? How do our organizations become, with our contribution, more innovative, more fulfilling, more alive?

When leadership demonstrates its capacity to change, when it builds bridges and encourages change by anyone from anywhere, when it nurtures the solidarity of the human community at work, then it is truly transformative, living up to its revolutionary potential. We know it's possible. Success requires that we make choices in a spirit of humility, courage, and curiosity, with both generosity and love. The results are incredible.

Acknowledgments

I WOULD LIKE TO express my deepest gratitude to all those who have crossed my path, in person or through digital means, at work or in other activities, around the globe. They have opened my horizons and allowed this reflection to exist: friends, teachers, colleagues, guides, clients, mentors, inspirations. To name them all would be to risk forgetting some. But the decisive conversations, the helping hand, the shared indignation, the fun times, the common action—I remember them all.

Precious encounters have marked my journey as a corporate activist. In addition to the failed leaders and petty bureaucrats who fueled my desire for change, I've been fortunate to meet Corinne Hardy, Nicholas Brooke, Angus Thomson, Susan Scrupski and the Change Agents Worldwide community, Jon Husband, Lois Kelly, Ayelet Baron, Rachel Happe, Jane McConnell, Whitney Johnson, Bjoern Negelmann and the Enterprise 2.0 community, Big Opportunity volunteers, Helen Bevan and her team, Pat Cormier, Russell Raath, John Kotter, Nancy Dearman and the Kotter team, Zsuzsanna Devecseri, Monique Verrier, Myron Rogers, John Atkinson, Fatiha Hajjat, Fabienne Cassagne, Jillian Reilly, Dan Pontefract, Vlatka Ariaana Hlupic, Megan Reitz, John Higgins, Jen Frahm, Sigi Lautenbacher, and many more.

For the reflection to become a book, it took Ana Neves's invitation to speak at the Social Now Lisbon conference, Richard Martin's talent on the first draft of my manuscript and the Figure 1 team on the second draft, and of course the wise counsel of all those I consulted during the process.

My heartfelt thanks to my husband, Leo, and my children, Gustave and Violette, for being there and for their patience, support, and understanding while I wrote this book. I love you.

Endnotes

PART I. LEADERSHIP MATTERS

1 Martin Chemers, *An Integrative Theory of Leadership* (Psychology Press, 1997).

1. What Got Us Here Won't Get Us There

1 Michel Cartier, in collaboration with Jon Husband, *21ème siècle: L'émergence de l'information* (vers. 3, Jan. 2020), www.21siecle.quebec; in English: *The 21st Century: The Emergence of Information*, www.21century.world. See also *Un nouveau Nouveau Monde*, nouveaumonde2.com; "Michel Cartier," *Wikipedia*, fr.wikipedia.org/wiki/Michel_Cartier_(prospectiviste).

2 "List of countries by population in 1907," *Wikipedia*, en.wikipedia.org/wiki/List_of_countries_by_population_in_1907; World Bank data retrieved from www.google.com/publicdata/explore?ds=d5bncp pjof8f9_&ctype=L&strail=falsE&bcs=D&Nselm=H&Met_y=sp_pop_totL&scale_y=liN&Ind_y=falsE&R dim=worlD&idim=world:EartH&Ifdim=worlD&Tstart=-297651600000&tend=1532642400000&h l=eN&Dl=eN&Ind=false; "World population density (people/km2)," Worldometer, www.worldometers. info/world-population/#density; Greta Keenan, "A brief history of vaccines and how they changed the world," World Economic Forum (Apr. 9, 2020), www.weforum.org/agenda/2020/04/how-vaccines-changed-the-world/; Max Roser, Esteban Ortiz-Ospina, and Hannah Ritchie, "Life expectancy," Our World in Data (2013), ourworldindata.org/life-expectancy; "Life expectancy at birth, total (years)," The World Bank, data.worldbank.org/indicator/SP.DYN.LE00.IN.

3 "L'essentiel sur... les immigrés et les étrangers," Institut National de la Statistique et des Études Économiques (INSEE) (July 1, 2021), www.insee.fr/fr/statistiques/3633212; "The age gap in religion around the world," Pew Research Center (June 13, 2018), www.pewforum.org/2018/06/13/young-adults-around-the-world-are-less-religious-by-several-measures/.

4 Pascal Coppens, "How China uses technology to deal with the corona virus—and what we can learn from that," Nexxworks (Mar. 12, 2020), nexxworks.com/blog/how-china-uses-technology-to-deal-with-the-corona-virus-and-what-we-can-learn-from-that.

5 Jamie Susskind, *Future Politics: Living Together in a World Transformed by Tech* (Oxford University Press, 2018).

6 Cartier, *The 21st Century* and "Nous vivons une réorganisation sociétale," (Sept. 2013), nouveaumonde2.com, author's translation.

7 Graeme MacKay, in *The Hamilton Spectator* (Mar. 11, 2020) and mackaycartoons.net/2020/03/18/wednesday-march-11-2020/ (Mar. 18, 2020).

8 *Tackling the Mental Health Impact of the COVID-19 Crisis: An Integrated, Whole-of-Society Response* (Organisation for Economic Co-operation and Development, May 12, 2021), www.oecd.org/coronavirus/policy-responses/.

9 Marta Cooper and Jill Petzinger, "There's a German word people use in times of despair, and it's as apt today as it was in the 19th century," *Quartz* (Oct. 18, 2016, updated Aug. 15, 2018), qz.com/811186/weltschmerz-theres-a-german-word-people-use-in-times-of-despair-and-its-as-apt-today-as-it-was-in-the-19th-century/.

10 Yann Quercia, "Sondage: 21% des Français adhèrent à au moins cinq théories du complot," Public Sénat (Feb. 6, 2019), www.publicsenat.fr/article/societe/sondage-21-des-francais-adherent-a-au-moins-cinq-theories-du-complot-137727; "Belief in conspiracy theories in the United States in 2019," Statista (Jan. 22, 2019), www.statista.com/statistics/959315/belief-in-conspiracy-theories-in-the-us/.

11 "Baromètre 202 de la haine en ligne," Netino (2020), netino.fr; Jamais Cascio, "Facing the age of chaos" (Apr. 29, 2020), medium.com/@cascio/facing-the-age-of-chaos-b00687b1f51d.

12 Michael Haralambos and Michael Holborn, *Sociology: Themes and Perspectives* (Collins Educational, 2000).

13 Peter Vander Auwera, "Innotribe Sibos 2014—Building Bridges," *Petervan's Blog* (June 20, 2014), petervan.wordpress.com/2014/08/08/innotribe-sibos-2014-the-build-up/.

14 "Divorces," Institut National d'Études Démographiques (June 2021), www.ined.fr/fr/tout-savoir-population/chiffres/france/mariages-divorces-pacs/divorces/; "Naissances hors mariage: Données annuelles de 1994 à 2020," INSEE (Mar. 29, 2021), www.insee.fr/fr/statistiques/2381394; "236300 mariages célébrés en France en 2015, dont 33800 mariages mixtes," *INSEE Première*, no. 1638 (Mar. 2017), www.ined.fr/fr/tout-savoir-population/memos-demo/faq/mariages-mixtes-france/; "Dueling realities: Amid multiple crises, Trump and Biden supporters see different priorities and futures for the nation," PRRI (Oct. 19, 2020), www.prri.org/research/amid-multiple-crises-trump-and-biden-supporters-see-different-realities-and-futures-for-the-nation/; Gretchen Livingston and Anna Brown, "Intermarriage in the U.S. 50 years after Loving v. Virginia," Pew Research Center (May 18, 2017), www.pewresearch.org/social-trends/2017/05/18/intermarriage-in-the-u-s-50-years-after-loving-v-virginia/; "Timeline of same-sex marriage," *Wikipedia* (retrieved Aug. 25, 2021), en.wikipedia.org/wiki/Timeline_of_same-sex_marriage; Sydney Calkin, "One year on, it's clear that the new Irish abortion services have serious limitations," *The Conversation* (Jan. 15, 2020), theconversation.com/one-year-on-its-clear-that-the-new-irish-abortion-services-have-serious-limitations-129491.

15 Amanda Barroso and Anna Brown, "Gender pay gap in U.S. held steady in 2020," Pew Research Center (May 25, 2021), www.pewresearch.org/fact-tank/2021/05/25/gender-pay-gap-facts/; *Breadwinners Survey* (Ameritrade, Mar. 2020), retrieved from s2.q4cdn.com/437609071/files/doc_news/research/2020/breadwinners-survey.pdf; *Breadwinner Moms* (Pew Research Center, May 29, 2013), retrieved from www.pewsocialtrends.org/wp-content/uploads/sites/3/2013/05/Breadwinner_moms_final.pdf.

16 Vanessa Springora, *Le Consentement* (Grasset, 2020).

17 Bradley Campbell and Jason Manning, *The Rise of Victimhood Culture: Microaggressions, Safe Spaces, and the New Culture Wars* (Palgrave Macmillan, 2018).

18 Francis Fukuyama, *Identity: The Demand for Dignity and the Politics of Resentment* (Farrar, Straus and Giroux, 2018).

19 Alain Eraly, *Une démocratie sans autorité?* (Erès, 2019).

20 Fukuyama, *Identity*.

21 Alec Tyson, "Republicans remain far less likely than Democrats to view COVID-19 as a major threat to public health," Pew Research Center (July 22, 2020), www.pewresearch.org/fact-tank/2020/07/22/republicans-remain-far-less-likely-than-democrats-to-view-covid-19-as-a-major-threat-to-public-health/.

22 Helen Lewis, "How capitalism drives cancel culture," *The Atlantic* (July 14, 2020).

23 Eraly, *Une démocratie sans autorité?*, author's translation.

24 Tonia Ries, "The inversion of influence," Edelman Research (Jan. 18, 2016), www.edelman.com/post/inversion-of-influence.

25 *2019 Edelman Trust Barometer Global Report* (Edelman, Feb. 2020), www.edelman.com/trust/2019-trust-barometer.

26 Katherine Schaeffer, "A look at the Americans who believe there is some truth to the conspiracy theory that COVID-19 was planned," Pew Research Center (July 24, 2020), www.pewresearch.org/fact-tank/2020/07/24/a-look-at-the-americans-who-believe-there-is-some-truth-to-the-conspiracy-theory-that-covid-19-was-planned/.

27 Eraly, *Une démocratie sans autorité?*, author's translation.

28 Moisés Naím, *The End of Power: From Boardrooms to Battlefields and Churches to States, Why Being in Charge Isn't What It Used to Be* (Basic Books, 2013).

29 Nick O'Donovan, "From knowledge economy to automation anxiety: A growth regime in crisis?," *New Political Economy* 25 (2020), 248–66.

30 Craig Roth, "2019: When we exceeded 1 billion knowledge workers," Gartner (Dec. 11, 2019), blogs. gartner.com/craig-roth/2019/12/11/2019-exceeded-1-billion-knowledge-workers/.

31 Thomas Davenport, *Thinking for a Living: How to Get Better Performances and Results from Knowledge Workers* (Harvard Business Review Press, 2005).

32 Jennifer Schenker, "The platform economy," The Innovator (Jan. 19, 2019), innovator.news/ the-platform-economy-3c09439b56.

33 Jennifer Schenker, "Interview of the week: Simon Torrance," The Innovator (Nov. 11, 2018), innovator. news/the-platform-economy-3c09439b56.

34 Rita Gunther McGrath, "The new disrupters," *MIT Sloan Management Review* 61, no. 3 (2020), 28–33.

35 Dave Gray with Thomas Vander Wal, *The Connected Company* (O'Reilly Media, 2012).

36 James Allen, Frederick F. Reichheld, Barney Hamilton, and Rob Markey, *Closing the Delivery Gap* (Bain, 2005), www.bain.com/insights/closing-the-delivery-gap/; Annette Franz, "The #CX perception gap," *CX Journey* (Mar. 14, 2018), cx-journey.com/2018/03/the-cx-perception-gap.html.

37 "Customer service stats for 2020," CustomerThermometer, www.customerthermometer.com/ customer-service/customer-service-and-satisfaction-statistics-for-2020/; "Consumer activism: A growing threat to corporate reputation," Commetric (Nov. 29, 2019), commetric.com/2019/11/29/ consumer-activism-a-growing-threat-to-corporate-reputation/; Lawrence Glickman, "The American tradition of consumer politics," *The American Historian* (May 2017).

38 "Women in the workforce: United States (quick take)," Catalyst (Jan. 30, 2020), www.catalyst.org/ research/women-in-the-workforce-united-states/; Pippa Stevens, "Companies are making bold promises about greater diversity, but there's a long way to go," CNBC (June 15, 2020), www.cnbc. com/2020/06/11/companies-are-making-bold-promises-about-greater-diversity-theres-a-long-way-to-go.html.

39 Kerri Anne Renzulli, "Here are the 15 jobs disappearing the fastest in the US," CNBC (Apr. 28, 2019), www.cnbc.com/2019/04/26/the-15-us-jobs-disappearing-the-fastest.html.

40 ManpowerGroup, "Global talent shortages hit record highs: ManpowerGroup reveals how to close the skills gap with new research on what workers want," Cision PR Newswire (Jan. 17, 2020), www. prnewswire.com/news-releases/global-talent-shortages-hit-record-highs-manpowergroup-reveals-how-to-close-the-skills-gap-with-new-research-on-what-workers-want-300988748.html.

41 I. Mitic, "Gig economy statistics: The new normal in the workplace," Fortunly (Aug. 16, 2021), fortunly. com/statistics/gig-economy-statistics#gref.

42 David Fahrenthold, "Sinkhole of bureaucracy: Deep underground, federal employees process paperwork by hand in a long-outdated, inefficient system," *Washington Post* (Mar. 22, 2014).

43 Gary Hamel and Michele Zanini, "Busting bureaucracy" (n.d.; accessed Nov. 6, 2020), www.garyhamel.com/blog/busting-bureaucracy.

44 Anders Vinthers and Céline Schillinger, "Deming, finally!," We Need Social blog (June 2017), weneedsocial.com/blog/2017/6/13/deming-finally.

2. The Persistent Fallacy and Failure of Leadership

1 John Steinbeck, *Cannery Row* (Penguin, 1945).

2 Matthew Karnitschnig, "The incompetence pandemic," *Politico* (Mar. 16, 2020), www.politico.com/ news/2020/03/16/coronavirus-pandemic-leadership-131540.

3 Christine Crudo Blackburn and Leslie Ruyle, "How leadership in various countries has affected COVID-19 response effectiveness," *The Conversation* (May 27, 2020), theconversation.com/ how-leadership-in-various-countries-has-affected-covid-19-response-effectiveness-138692.

4 Donna Ladkin, "What Donald Trump's response to COVID-19 teaches us: It's time for our romance with leaders to end," *Leadership* 16 (2020), 273-78.

5 Bobby Allyn, "Top reason for CEO departures among largest companies is now misconduct, study finds," NPR (May 20, 2019), text.npr.org/725108825.

6 John G. Stumpf, "How Wells Fargo's CEO built the team at the world's most valuable bank," *Fortune* (July 23, 2015).

7 Carlos Ghosn, Global Leadership Series speech, INSEAD (Sept. 24, 2002).

8 "Carlos Ghosn's network of influence made it 'easy to flee' Japan, say prosecutors," *The Guardian* (Jan. 5, 2020).

9 Abigail Disney, "Let me be very clear...," Twitter (Apr. 21, 2019), twitter.com/abigaildisney/status/1119985336308912128; Adam Gabbatt, "Disney heir on CEO's $66m pay: 'No one on the freaking planet is worth that,'" *The Guardian* (Apr. 27, 2019).

10 Jeff Cox, "CEOs see pay grow 1,000% in the last 40 years, now make 278 times the average worker," CNBC (Aug. 16, 2019), www.cnbc.com/2019/08/16/ceos-see-pay-grow-1000percent-and-now-make-278-times-the-average-worker.html; Lawrence Mishel and Jori Kandra, "CEO compensation surged 14% in 2019 to $21.3 million: CEOs now earn 320 times as much as a typical worker," Economic Policy Institute (Aug. 18, 2020), www.epi.org/publication/ceo-compensation-surged-14-in-2019-to-21-3-million-ceos-now-earn-320-times-as-much-as-a-typical-worker/.

11 Lauren Hirsch, "Patriotic millionaires' letter to Davos calls for 'higher and fairer' taxes on the global elite," CNBC (Jan. 22, 2020), www.cnbc.com/2020/01/22/davos-2020-patriotic-millionaires-letter-calls-for-higher-taxes-on-global-elite.html.

12 Tom Rees and Ben Wright, "Millionaires accused of hypocrisy over Davos demands for higher tax," *The Telegraph* (Jan. 23, 2020).

13 Nicola Bartlett, "Brexiteer James Dyson accused of 'staggering hypocrisy' after moving HQ to Singapore," *Mirror* (Jan. 22, 2019); Jack Peat, "These are the Brexiteers looking to secure their EU rights ahead of the UK's departure from the bloc," *The London Economic* (June 22, 2020), www.thelondoneconomic.com/politics/these-are-the-brexiteers-looking-to-secure-their-eu-rights-ahead-of-the-uks-departure-from-the-bloc-192220/.

14 Thomas Gryta and Ted Mann, "GE powered the American century—then it burned out," *Wall Street Journal* (Dec. 14, 2018).

15 Anne Quito, "Jack Dorsey admits Twitter's 'like' button should never have existed," Quartz (Apr. 16, 2019), qz.com/work/1597035/ted2019-jack-dorsey-rethinks-twitters-like-feature/.

16 Steven Salzberg, "Nobel laureate joins anti-vaccination crowd at Autism One," Forbes (May 27, 2012).

17 Antoine Bristielle, "Didier Raoult, symptôme du malaise démocratique," *Le Monde* (June 25, 2020).

18 Françoise Salvadori, "La longue histoire des résistances à la vaccination," Planet Vie (Apr. 1, 2020), planet-vie.ens.fr/thematiques/sante/prevention/la-longue-histoire-des-resistances-a-la-vaccination.

19 Jonathan Quick and Heidi Larson, "The vaccine-autism myth started 20 years ago. Here's why it still endures today," *Time* (Feb. 28, 2018); Donald McNeil, Jr., "Measles cases in Europe quadrupled in 2017," *New York Times* (Feb. 23, 2018).

20 C.E. Kearns, L.A. Schmidt, and S.A. Glantz, "Sugar industry and coronary heart disease research: A historical analysis of internal industry documents," *JAMA Internal Medicine* 176 (2016), 1680–85; Alessandra Potenza, "Inside the fight over the sugar conspiracy," *The Verge* (Feb. 23, 2018), www.theverge.com/2018/2/23/17039780/sugar-industry-conspiracy-heart-disease-research-mark-hegsted-harvard.

21 Amy Wang, "Gwyneth Paltrow's Goop touted the 'benefits' of putting a jade egg in your vagina. Now it must pay," *Washington Post* (Sept. 5, 2018); Charlotte Gush, "Woman suffers serious burns from Goop-approved vaginal steaming," Dazed Digital (Aug. 8, 2019), www.dazeddigital.com/beauty/body/article/45550/1/woman-suffers-burns-goop-approved-vaginal-steaming-gwyneth-paltrow.

22 Valeriya Safronova, "Catherine Deneuve and others denounce the #MeToo movement," *New York Times* (Jan. 9, 2018).

23 Akhenaton (@AkhenatonIAM), "Non à la #vaccinationobligatoire...," Twitter (July 17, 2021), twitter.com/AkhenatonIAM/status/1416344748944674823.

24 Katie Rogers, "White women helped elect Donald Trump," *New York Times* (Nov. 9, 2016).

25 Ladkin, "What Donald Trump's response to COVID-19 teaches us."

26 Peter Block, *Community: The Structure of Belonging* (Berrett-Koehler, 2009).

27 James Meindl, Sanford Ehrlich, and Janet Dukerich, "The romance of leadership," *Administrative Science Quarterly* 30 (1985), 78–102.

28 Ladkin, "What Donald Trump's response to COVID-19 teaches us."

29 Abraham Zaleznik, "Managers and leaders: Are they different?," *Harvard Business Review Magazine* (May–June 1977).

30 John Kotter, "What leaders really do," *Harvard Business Review Magazine* (May–June 1990).

31 Brigid Carroll, Jackie Ford, and Scott Taylor, *Leadership: Contemporary Critical Perspectives*, 2nd ed. (Sage, 2019).

32 Scott Barry Kaufman, "The myth of the alpha male," *Greater Good Magazine*, Greater Good Science Center, University of California–Berkeley (Dec. 10, 2015), greatergood.berkeley.edu/article/item/the_myth_of_the_alpha_male.

33 Tomas Chamorro-Premuzic, "Why do so many incompetent men become leaders?," *Harvard Business Review* (Aug. 22, 2013), hbr.org/2013/08/why-do-so-many-incompetent-men.

34 Ernesto Reuben, Pedro Rey-Biel, Paola Sapienza, and Luigi Zingales, "The emergence of male leadership in competitive environments," *Journal of Economic Behavior & Organization* 83 (2012), 111–17.

35 Amanda Shipman and Michael D. Mumford, "When confidence is detrimental: Influence of overconfidence on leadership effectiveness," *Leadership Quarterly* 22 (2011), 649–65.

36 "Narcissistic people most likely to emerge as leaders," Ohio State University *Newswise* (Oct. 7, 2008), www.newswise.com/articles/narcissistic-people-most-likely-to-emerge-as-leaders.

37 Rebecca Solnit, "When the hero is the problem: On Robert Mueller, Greta Thunberg, and finding strength in numbers," *Literary Hub* (Apr. 2, 2019), lithub.com/rebecca-solnit-when-the-hero-is-the-problem/.

38 Marc-Olivier Bherer, "Olivier Assayas: 'Les films de super-héros sont fondés sur la passivité du spectateur,'" *Le Monde* (Dec. 27, 2019).

39 Rachel Happe, "Elizabeth Warren and the grass ceiling of networked leadership" (Mar. 5, 2020), rhappe.medium.com/elizabeth-warren-and-the-grass-ceiling-of-networked-leadership-8bf4f531f267.

40 Gallup, *State of the Global Workplace* (Gallup, 2019).

41 Gallup, *State of the Global Workplace*.

42 Gallup, *State of the Global Workplace*.

43 Tom Popomaronis, "Warren Buffett: This is the 'most surprising' lesson I didn't learn in business school," CNBC (Oct. 16, 2019), www.cnbc.com/2019/10/16/billionaire-warren-buffett-most-surprising-business-lesson-he-didnt-learn-in-business-school.html.

44 Jim Hartner, "Dismal employee engagement is a sign of global mismanagement," Gallup (2017), www.gallup.com/workplace/231668/dismal-employee-engagement-sign-global-mismanagement.aspx.

45 Gallup, *State of the Global Workplace*.

46 Steve Crabtree, "Untapped human capital is the next great global resource," Gallup Workplace (n.d.), www.gallup.com/workplace/231764/untapped-human-capital-next-great-global-resource.aspx.

47 Hartner, "Dismal employee engagement."

48 "Britain's Healthiest Workplace: The latest findings," Vitality (2019), www.vitality.co.uk/business/healthiest-workplace/findings/; the full study is linked to at the bottom of the summary.

49 "Mental health in the workplace," World Health Organization Department of Mental Health and Substance Use (May 2019), www.who.int/teams/mental-health-and-substance-use/promotion-prevention/mental-health-in-the-workplace.

50 "Burn-out an 'occupational phenomenon': International Classification of Diseases," World Health Organization (May 28, 2019), www.who.int/news/item/28-05-2019-burn-out-an-occupational-phenomenon-international-classification-of-diseases.

51 Ben Wigert and Sangeeta Agrawal, "Employee burnout, Part 1: The 5 main causes," Gallup (July 12, 2018), www.gallup.com/workplace/237059/employee-burnout-part-main-causes.aspx.

52 Le Monde, with AFP, "France Télécom et ses trois anciens dirigeants reconnus coupables de harcèlement moral institutionnel," *Le Monde* (Dec. 20, 2019).

53 Le Monde, "France Télécom et ses trois anciens," author's translation.
54 Jeffrey Pfeffer, *Dying for a Paycheck: How Modern Management Harms Employee Health and Company Performance—and What We Can Do about It* (Harper Business, 2018).
55 "Global democracy has another bad year," *The Economist* (Jan. 22, 2020).
56 The Economist Intelligence Unit, *Democracy Index 2019* (The Economist, 2019).
57 Sarah Marsh, "'I never thought Trump would win': Meet the Americans who chose not to vote," *The Guardian* (Nov. 18, 2016).
58 Aziz Huq and Tom Ginsburg, "How to lose a constitutional democracy," *Vox* (Feb. 21, 2017), www.vox.com/the-big-idea/2017/2/21/14664568/lose-constitutional-democracy-autocracy-trump-authoritarian.
59 Steven Levitsky and Daniel Ziblatt, *How Democracies Die* (Crown, 2018).
60 Oscar Agestam, *The Patterns of Democratic Backsliding: A Systematic Comparison of Hungary, Turkey, and Venezuela* (Södertörns högskola, Institutionen för Samhällsvetenskap, 2018).
61 Nancy Bermeo, "On democratic backsliding," *Journal of Democracy* 27 (2016), 5–19.
62 Fondation Camp des Milles, *Indice d'analyse et d'alerte républicaine et démocratique (AARD): Édition 2021.* (Fondation Camp des Milles, 2021), www.campdesmilles.org/pourlademocratie.
63 Antoine Flandrin, "La Fondation du Camp des Milles redoute la montée des extrêmes," *Le Monde* (May 6, 2019), author's translation.
64 Nicola Gennaioli and Guido Tabellini, "Identity, beliefs, and political conflict," Vox EU CEPR (2019), voxeu.org/article/identity-beliefs-and-political-conflict.
65 *Three Steps from Racism to Genocide: A Process Which Can Be Resisted*, Camp des Milles Foundation (n.d.), www.campdesmilles.org/mur-interactif/index2.php.
66 Chantal Mouffe, "The controversy over left-wing populism," *Le Monde Diplomatique* (May 2020), mondediplo.com/2020/05/14populism.
67 Peter Sloterdijk, *Réflexes primitifs: Considérations psychopolitiques sur les inquiétudes européennes* (Payot, 2019).
68 "In four years, President Trump made 30,573 false or misleading claims" (interactive feature), *Washington Post*, Fact Checker (updated Jan. 20, 2021), www.washingtonpost.com/graphics/politics/trump-claims-database/.
69 Catherine Fieschi, *Populocracy: The Tyranny of Authenticity and the Rise of Populism* (Agenda Publishing, 2019).
70 "Pierre Rosanvallon: 'Le populisme est le symptôme de tous les dysfonctionnements de notre société contemporaine,'" *La première*, RTBF (Jan. 11, 2021), www.rtbf.be/.
71 Katie Camero, "What is 'cancel culture'? J.K. Rowling controversy leaves writers, scholars debating," *Miami Herald* (July 8, 2020); Laure Murat, "La 'cancel culture,' dernier recours d'une population sans autre voix que l'internet," *Le Monde* (Aug. 1, 2020), author's translation.
72 Céline Schillinger, "Can we have a voice in the corporate world?," We Need Social blog (Jan. 13, 2017), weneedsocial.com/blog/2017/1/13/can-we-have-a-voice-in-the-corporate-world.

PART II. LIBERTY

3. Can There Be Liberty at Work?

1 Christophe Dejours and Pascale Molinie, "Le travail comme énigme," in *Sociologie du Travail*, no. 94 (1994), 35–44.
2 Dejours and Molinie, "Le travail comme énigme," author's translation.
3 Philippe D'Iribarne, "Visions de la Liberté et cultures de travail," in Pierre Musso and Alain Supiot (Eds.), *Qu'est-ce qu'un régime de travail réellement humain?* (Hermann, 2018), author's translation.
4 Frédéric Petitbon, Julie Bastianutti, and Marguerite Descamps, *Managers—Libérez, délivrez... surveillez?* (Cherche Midi, 2018), author's translation.
5 Zia ur-Rehman, Declan Walsh, and Salman Masood, "More than 300 killed in Pakistani factory fires," *New York Times* (Sept. 12, 2012).

6   Simon Carraud, "French telco Orange found guilty over workers' suicides in landmark ruling," Reuters (Dec. 20, 2019), www.reuters.com/article/us-france-justice-orange-sentences-idUSKBN1Y012D.

7   Will Evans, "Ruthless quotas at Amazon are maiming employees," *The Atlantic* (Nov. 25, 2019); Mark Brown, Michael Buehler, and Edmundo Werna, "More than 2 million people die at work each year. Here's how to prevent it," Future of Construction (Mar. 23, 2017), www.futureofconstruction.org/blog/more-than-2-million-people-die-at-work-each-year-heres-how-to-prevent-it/; "Worker fatalities," Occupational Safety and Health Administration, U.S. Department of Labor (retrieved Nov. 6, 2020).

8   Adam Yamaguchi, "Surviving an unlivable wage," *CBSN Originals*, CBS News (Mar. 26, 2020), www.cbsnews.com/video/surviving-an-unlivable-wage/.

9   Vivian Ho and Mario Koran, "Laborers and domestic workers stay behind as thousands flee California wildfires," *The Guardian* (Oct. 30, 2019).

10 Loach, Ken (Dir.), *Sorry We Missed You* (Sixteen Films et al., 2019); Killian Fox, "'It's a form of modern slavery': MPs on Ken Loach's film about the human cost of the zero-hours economy," *The Guardian* (Oct. 6, 2019).

11 Dominic Rushe, "Boeing's 'culture of concealment' led to fatal 737 Max crashes, report finds," *The Guardian* (Mar. 6, 2020).

12 VitalSmarts, "Corporate culture chasm: Employees view their culture much more negatively than management," Cision PR Newswire (July 19, 2016).

13 Megan Reitz and John Higgins, *Being Silenced and Silencing Others: Developing the Capacity to Speak Truth to Power* (Ashridge Executive Education, Hult University, 2017), ww.iedp.com/media/3469/being-silenced-and-silencing-others.pdf.

14 Hakima Bounemoura, "Lanceur d'alerte: 'Ma vie est foutue, je suis devenu un paria,' raconte Karim Ben Ali," *20 Minutes* (Jan. 13, 2020), www.20minutes.fr/high-tech/2659951-20200113-video-lanceur-alerte-vie-foutue-devenu-paria-raconte-karim-ben-ali.

15 "Li Wenliang: Coronavirus death of Wuhan doctor sparks anger," *BBC News* (Feb. 7, 2020), www.bbc.com/news/world-asia-china-51409801.

16 Erwan Cario and Marius Chapuis, "Harcèlement sexuel à Ubisoft: 'On savait,'" *Libération* (July 10, 2020); Megan Farokhmanesh, "Ubisoft's toxic culture problems allegedly span more than a decade of abuse," *The Verge* (July 20, 2021), www.theverge.com/2020/7/21/21332534/ubisoft-serge-hascoet-harassment-sexism-racism-metoo.

17 Gary Hamel and Michele Zanini, *Humanocracy: Creating Organizations as Amazing as the People inside Them* (Harvard Business Review Press, 2020).

18 Gwynn Guilford, "GM's decline truly began with its quest to turn people into machines," *Quartz* (Dec. 30, 2018), qz.com/1510405/gms-layoffs-can-be-traced-to-its-quest-to-turn-people-into-machines/.

19 Elad Sherf, Subrahmaniam Tangirala, and Vijaya Venkataramani, "Why managers do not seek voice from employees: The importance of managers' personal control and long-term orientation," *Organization Science* 30 (2019), 447–66.

20 Angélique Del Rey, *La tyrannie de l'évaluation* (La Découverte, 2013), author's translation.

21 W. Edwards Deming, *Out of the Crisis* (MIT Press, 1982); John Hunter, "Dr. Deming called for the elimination of the annual performance appraisal," The Deming Institute (Oct. 29, 2012), deming.org/dr-deming-called-for-the-elimination-of-the-annual-performance-appraisal/.

22 Anders Vinthers and Céline Schillinger, "Deming, finally!," We Need Social blog (June 2017), weneedsocial.com/blog/2017/6/13/deming-finally.

23 Max Nisen, "How Millennials forced GE to scrap performance reviews," *The Atlantic* (Aug. 18, 2015).

24 Project Implicit's Implicit Association Test can still be taken at implicit.harvard.edu/implicit/takeatest.html.

25 Daniel Hamermesh, *Beauty Pays: Why Attractive People Are More Successful* (Princeton University Press, 2013).

26 Arianne Cohen, *The Tall Book: A Celebration of Life from on High* (Bloomsbury USA, 2009).

27 Katie Langin, "Racial and gender biases plague postdoc hiring," *Science* (June 3, 2019).

28 Marcus Buckingham, "Good data or bad data: The idiosyncratic rater effect" (Feb. 2018), www.marcusbuckingham.com/good-data-bad-data-idiosyncratic-rater-effect/.

29 Marcus Buckingham and Ashley Goodall, "The feedback fallacy," *Harvard Business Review Magazine* (Mar.–Apr. 2019).

30 Alexandra Mateescu and Aiha Nguyen, *Explainer: Algorithmic Management in the Workplace* (Data & Society, 2019), datasociety.net/wp-content/uploads/2019/02/DS_Algorithmic_Management_ Explainer.pdf.

31 "2020 UK GCSE and A-Level grading controversy," *Wikipedia* (accessed Sept. 8, 2021), en.wikipedia. org/wiki/2020_UK_GCSE_and_A-Level_grading_controversy.

32 Alex Rosenblat, Karen E.C. Levy, Solon Barocas, and Tim Hwang, "Discriminating tastes: Uber's customer ratings as vehicles for workplace discrimination," *Policy & Internet* 9 (2017), 256–79.

33 Joy Buolamwini, "Gender shades: Intersectional phenotypic and demographic evaluation of face datasets and gender classifiers," master's thesis, MIT, 2017; The Movement for Algorithmic Justice can be found online at www.ajl.org.

34 Margaret Wheatley and Myron Rogers, *A Simpler Way* (Berrett-Koehler, 1996).

35 "The principles of scientific management," *Wikipedia* (accessed Sept. 8, 2021), en.wikipedia.org/wiki/ The_Principles_of_Scientific_Management.

36 Louis Brandeis, *Business—A Profession* (Small, Maynard, 1914).

37 John Kotter, *Accelerate: Building Strategic Agility for a Faster-Moving World* (Harvard Business Review Press, 2014).

38 John Atkinson, "Myron's maxims," *Heart of the Art* (Jan. 17, 2016), www.heartoftheart.org/?p=1196.

39 Pierre-Olivier Monteil, *Éthique et philosophie du management* (Erès, 2016).

40 Mats Alvesson and André Spicer, "(Un)Conditional surrender? Why do professionals willingly comply with 'managerialism'?," *Journal of Organizational Change Management* 29 (2016), 29–45.

41 Mats Alvesson and André Spicer, *The Stupidity Paradox: The Power and Pitfalls of Functional Stupidity at Work* (Profile, 2016).

42 Monteil, *Éthique et philosophie du management*, author's translation.

43 Daniel Pink, *Drive: The Surprising Truth about What Motivates Us* (Riverhead, 2009).

44 Edward Deci and Richard M. Ryan, *Intrinsic Motivation and Self-Determination in Human Behavior* (Springer, 1985).

45 Matthew Crawford, *Shop Class as Soulcraft: An Inquiry into the Value of Work* (Penguin, 2009).

46 Cecil Dijoux, "Matthew Crawford: L'attention ou le nœud de la condition des travailleurs de la connaissance," *#hypertextual* (Apr. 30, 2017), thehypertextual.com/2017/04/30/ matthew-crawford-lattention-ou-le-noeud-de-la-condition-des-travailleurs-de-la-connaissance/.

47 David Graeber, *Bullshit Jobs: A Theory* (Simon & Schuster, 2018).

48 David Graeber, interview, "Bullshit jobs and the yoke of managerial feudalism," *The Economist* (June 19, 2018).

49 Alain Supiot, *La gouvernance par les nombres* (Fayard, 2015).

4. It Starts with Oneself: On Becoming a Change Agent

1 Peter Vander Auwera, "Corporate Rebels manifesto," *Petervan's Blog* (Sept. 4, 2012), petervan. wordpress.com/2012/09/04/corporate-rebels-manifesto/.

2 Jennifer Schenker, "Celine Schillinger: The woman that transformed Sanofi," *Informilo* (Sept. 2014).

3 Michel Volle, "De la main d'oeuvre au cerveau d'oeuvre," in Pierre Musso and Alain Supiot (Eds.), *Qu'est-ce qu'un régime de travail réellement humain?* (Hermann, 2018).

4 Jon Husband, "Understanding semantic straitjackets: How today's management science stifles creativity, innovation and responsiveness and what to do about it," LinkedIn (Oct. 13, 2015), www. linkedin.com/pulse/understanding-semantic-straitjackets-how-todays-science-jon-husband/.

5 Dave Gray, *Liminal Thinking: Create the Change You Want by Changing the Way You Think* (Two Waves, 2016).

6 John Wenger, "Counter-acting the Stockholm Syndrome," *Quantum Shifting* (Oct. 23, 2013), quantumshifting.wordpress.com/2013/10/23/counter-acting-the-stockholm-syndrome/.

7   Joseph M. Carver, "Love and Stockholm Syndrome: The mystery of loving an abuser" (2003), drjoecarver.makeswebsites.com/clients/49355/File/love_and_stockholm_syndrome.html.
8   Paul H. Ray and Sherry Ruth Anderson, *The Cultural Creatives: How 50 Million People Are Changing the World* (Three Rivers, 2001).
9   Helen Bevan, "Rocking the boat and staying in it: Being an NHS change agent," NHS Horizons Team, NHS Change Day 2014 (Mar. 3, 2014), www.nwpgmd.nhs.uk/sites/default/files/Dr%20Helen%20Bevan.pdf.
10 Lois Kelly and Carmen Medina, *Rebels at Work: A Handbook for Leading Change from Within* (O'Reilly Media, 2015).
11 Caroline Mackenzie, "*Agency*: Un mot, un engagement," *Rives méditerranéennes* 41 (2012), 35–37.
12 Caroline Mackenzie, "L'agency sur le terrain: L'expérience militante," *Rives méditerranéennes*, 41 (2012), 137–44.
13 "LMS Market by component (solution and services), delivery mode (distance learning, instructor-led training and blended learning), deployment type, user type (academic and corporate), and region—global forecast to 2025," Markets and Markets (June 2020), www.marketsandmarkets.com/Market-Reports/learning-management-systems-market-1266.html.
14 Carol S. Dweck, *Mindset: The New Psychology of Success* (Random House, 2006).
15 Shelley Taylor and Jonathon Brown, "Illusion and well-being: A social psychological perspective on mental health," *Psychological Bulletin* 103 (1988), 193–210.
16 "Illusory superiority," *Wikipedia* (accessed Sept. 8, 2021), en.wikipedia.org/wiki/Illusory_superiority; "The illusion of control–you are your worst enemy," Interaction Design Foundation (2016), www.interaction-design.org/literature/article/the-illusion-of-control-you-are-your-worst-enemy.
17 "Karpman drama triangle," *Wikipedia* (accessed Sept. 8, 2021), en.wikipedia.org/wiki/Karpman_drama_triangle.
18 Lois Kelly, "Oh those joyfully rebellious role models" (Oct, 24, 2019), medium.com/@LoisKelly/oh-those-joyfully-rebellious-role-models-76fcec9b80b0.
19 John Atkinson, "How the organisation subverts its subversives," *Heart of the Art* (Mar. 29, 2018), www.heartoftheart.org/?p=6233.
20 John Hagel, "Never under-estimate the immune system," *Edge Perspectives with John Hagel* (Dec. 2017), edgeperspectives.typepad.com/edge_perspectives/2017/12/never-under-estimate-the-immune-system.html.
21 Freya Lucas, "Tall poppies quick to be cut down, leading to low workplace morale, study finds," *The Sector* (June 3, 2019), thesector.com.au/2019/06/03/tall-poppies-quick-to-be-cut-down-leading-to-low-workplace-morale-study-finds/.
22 Céline Schillinger, "Regain freedom at work," We Need Social blog (June 19, 2015), weneedsocial.com/blog/2015/6/28/regain-freedom-at-work.
23 Boris Groysberg, "How star women build portable skills," *Harvard Business Review Magazine* (Feb. 2008).

5. Creating Collective Liberty at Work

1   Ewan McGaughey, "Democracy in America at work: The history of labor's vote in corporate governance," *Seattle University Law Review* 42 (2019), 697–753; Simon Jäger, Shakked Noy, and Benjamin Schoefer, "What does codetermination do?," Harvard Law School Forum on Economic Governance (June 2021), corpgov.law.harvard.edu/2021/06/29/what-does-codetermination-do/.
2   Joseph Raelin, "Emancipatory discourse and liberation," *Management Learning* 39 (2008), 519–40.
3   Paulo Freire, *Pedagogy of the Oppressed* (1970; Bloomsbury Academic, 2000).
4   Anne-Emmanuèle Calvès, "Empowerment: The history of a key concept in contemporary development discourse," *Revue tiers monde*, no. 200 (2009), 735–49.
5   "What is empowerment?" HR Zone (n.d.), www.hrzone.com/hr-glossary/what-is-empowerment.
6   Catherine Neveu, "Un projet d'émancipation à l'épreuve de sa mise en pratiques," *Revue du MAUSS*, no. 48 (2016), 173–86.
7   John Wenger, "Why you can't empower someone" (Apr. 2014), medium.com/@johnqshift/why-you-cant-empower-someone-1053ddbb765c.

8 Sandrine Coquet, as posted on Yammer, Women Inspiring Sanofi Pasteur group (May 2012).

9 Catherine Boyd, "Empowered teams need enabling leadership," Post*Shift (Apr. 19, 2018), postshift.com/empowered-teams-need-enabling-leadership/.

10 Joanne Ciulla, *Ethics, the Heart of Leadership* (Praeger, 1998), especially "Leadership and the problem of bogus empowerment."

11 Didier Marlier, "How can I fly like an eagle when I am surrounded by turkeys?," Enablers (Dec. 12, 2014), enablersnetwork.com/2014/how-can-i-fly-like-an-eagle-when-i-am-surrounded-by-turkeys/.

12 Francisco Miraval, "To liberate people and organizations, first liberate them from YOUR ideas," Flux (Mar. 22, 2017), medium.com/thingsflux/to-liberate-people-and-organizations-first-liberate-them-from-your-ideas-238c9735034a.

13 Peter Block, *Stewardship: Choosing Service over Self-Interest* (Berrett-Koehler, 1993).

14 Patrick Gilbert, Ann-Charlotte Teglborg, and Nathalie Raulet-Croset, "The liberated firm, a radical innovation or a mere avatar of participatory management?," *Gérer & Comprendre*, no. 3 (2018), 1–10.

15 Aimee Groth, "Zappos is going holacratic: No job titles, no managers, no hierarchy," *Quartz* (Dec. 30, 2013), qz.com/161210/zappos-is-going-holacratic-no-job-titles-no-managers-no-hierarchy/; see also www.holacracy.org/.

16 Ted Rau, "Holacracy and sociocracy," Sociocracy for All (accessed Sept. 8, 2021), www.sociocracyforall.org/holacracy-and-sociocracy/.

17 Aimee Groth, "Zappos has quietly backed away from holacracy," *Quartz* (Jan. 29, 2020), qz.com/work/1776841/zappos-has-quietly-backed-away-from-holacracy/.

18 Gary Hamel and Michele Zanini, "The end of bureaucracy," *Harvard Business Review* (Nov.–Dec. 2018).

19 Margaret Wheatley and Myron Rogers, "Self-organization: The irresistible future of organizing," *Strategy & Leadership* (July–Aug. 1996), 18–24.

20 Carla Correa, "A timeline of the NXIVM sex cult case," *New York Times* (Sept. 8, 2021).

21 Cliff Berg, "Why self-organizing teams don't work," LinkedIn (May 27, 2019), www.linkedin.com/pulse/why-self-organizing-teams-dont-work-cliff-berg/.

22 Simon Mont, "Autopsy of a failed holacracy: Lessons in justice, equity, and self-management," *Nonprofit Quarterly* (Winter 2017).

23 Carmen Medina, "Holacracy and the desire to control," LinkedIn (June 2015), www.linkedin.com/pulse/holacracy-desire-control-carmen-medina/.

24 Pim de Morree, "Bursting the bubble: Teal ain't real," Corporate Rebels (Dec. 20, 2017), corporate-rebels.com/teal-aint-real/.

25 Paul Jansen, "Lessons from going Dutch—The challenges of implementing Buurtzorg in the UK," Corporate Rebels (Sept. 2020), corporate-rebels.com/lessons-buurtzorg-uk/.

26 Jo Freeman, "The tyranny of structurelessness" (1971–73), www.jofreeman.com/joreen/tyranny.htm.

27 Henri Lipmanowicz and Keith McCandless, *The Surprising Power of Liberating Structures* (Liberating Structures Press, 2016).

28 See www.liberatingstructures.com.

29 "History," The World Café (accessed Sept. 9, 2021), www.theworldcafe.com/about-us/history/.

30 John Atkinson, Emma Loftus, and John Jarvis, *The Art of Change Making* (The Leadership Centre, 2015).

31 Myron Rogers in conversation with the author, "Leadership, Agency & Culture" (July 10, 2020), www.youtube.com/watch?v=Ary15KFUXJU.

32 Rogers in conversation with the author.

33 Margaret Wheatley, *Who Do We Choose to Be? Facing Reality, Claiming Leadership, Restoring Sanity* (Berrett-Koehle, 2017).

34 Wheatley, *Who Do We Choose to Be?*

35 Yuval Noah Harari, "The myth of freedom," *The Guardian* (Sept. 18, 2018).

36 Dan Ariely, *Predictably Irrational: The Hidden Forces That Shape Our Decisions* (HarperCollins Canada, 2018); Richard Thaler and Cass R. Sunstein, *Nudge: Improving Decisions about Health, Wealth, and Happiness* (Penguin, 2008).

37 Jacques Ellul, *La technique, ou, L'enjeu du siècle* (Economica, 1954).

38 Peter Block, *Community: The Structure of Belonging* (Berrett-Koehler, 2009).

39 Céline Schillinger, "Volunteer power," We Need Social blog (Mar. 2015), weneedsocial.com/blog/2015/3/24/volunteer-power.

40 "4 change principles," Kotter (n.d.; accessed Sept. 9, 2021), www.kotterinc.com/4-change-principles/.

41 Pierre-Olivier Monteil, *Éthique et philosophie du management* (Erès, 2016).

42 Céline Schillinger, "One human at a time: Some lessons learnt—so far—from an epic change journey," We Need Social blog (Feb. 9, 2018), weneedsocial.com/blog/2018/2/7/one-human-at-a-time.

43 John Atkinson, "Myron's maxims," *Heart of the Art* (Jan. 17, 2016), www.heartoftheart.org/?p=1196.

44 Mickey Connolly, "The heart of transformation," *Conversant* (Feb. 17, 2015), www.conversant.com/the-heart-of-transformation/#.WcvtRf6Wypp.

45 Amaury Grimand, with Johan Glaisner and Anouk Grevin, "Un travail à soi—Repères pour un management de l'appropriation du travail," *@GRH*, no. 23 (2017), 95–119.

46 Christophe Dejours and Jean Philippe Deranty, "The centrality of work," *Critical Horizons* 11 (2015), 167–80.

47 Christophe Dejours, *Travail vivant: Emancipation et travail* (Payot, 2013), author's translations.

48 Anders Vinthers and Céline Schillinger, "Deming, finally!," We Need Social blog (June 2017), weneedsocial.com/blog/2017/6/13/deming-finally.

49 Ayelet Baron, *Our Journey to Corporate Sanity* (Param Media, 2016).

50 Margaret Wheatley and Myron Rogers, *A Simpler Way* (Berrett-Koehler, 1996).

51 John Kotter, *Accelerate: Building Strategic Agility for a Faster-Moving World* (Harvard Business Review Press, 2014).

52 Wheatley and Rogers, *A Simpler Way*.

PART III. EQUALITY

1 Billy Bragg, *The Three Dimensions of Freedom* (Faber & Faber, 2019).

2 Isaiah Berlin, Henry Hardy, and Roger Hausheer, *The Proper Study of Mankind: An Anthology of Essays* (Chatto & Windus, 1997).

3 "Justice as fairness: John Rawls and his theory of justice," *Bill of Rights in Action* (Constitutional Rights Foundation) 23, no. 3 (2007); Alain Boyer, *Apologie de John Rawls* (puf, 2018); John Rawls, *Justice as Fairness: A Restatement* (Harvard University Press, 2001).

4 See, for example, the constitution of Massachusetts (1779) and the Universal Declaration of Human Rights (1948).

5 Alexis de Tocqueville, *Democracy in America*, translated by Gerald Bevan (1834; Penguin Classics, 2003).

6 Karl Marx, *Grundrisse: Foundations of the Critique of Political Economy (Rough Draft)*, translated by Martin Nicolaus (writ. 1857–58; Penguin, 1973).

6. Can There Be Equality at Work?

1 Ben Smith, "Newsrooms are in revolt. The bosses are in their country houses," *New York Times* (June 14, 2020).

2 Alessia Contu, "Decaf resistance: On misbehavior, cynicism, and desire in liberal workplaces," *Management Communication Quarterly* 21 (2008), 364–79.

3 As shared by the author on Twitter (June 12, 2019), twitter.com/CelineSchill/status/1138717896543297536.

4 Simon Terry, Twitter (June 13, 2019), twitter.com/simongterry/status/1138959348955140096.

5 Fritjof Capra, *The Hidden Connections: Integrating the Biological, Cognitive, and Social Dimensions of Life into a Science of Substainability* (Doubleday, 2002).

6 "Different levels: An interview with Fritjof Capra," *International Journal of Communication* 1 (2007).

7 Joseph Raelin, "Hierarchy's subordination of democracy and how to outrank it," *Management Learning* 51 (2020), 620–33.

8 Cass. Soc. 13 Nov. 1996, no. 94-13187, translated at *Employees vs. Independent Contractors*, L&E Global (2021), knowledge.leglobal.org/eic/country/france/legal-framework-differentiating-employees-independent-contractors-7/.

9   Jacques Uso, "Subordination and relationship of subordination: A dangerous amalgam," *Office et Culture*, no. 49 (Sept. 2018).

10 Asher Adelman, "Zogby poll: As Independence Day nears, Workplace Democracy Association survey finds one in four working Americans describe their employer as a 'dictatorship,'" Workplace Democracy Association (June 23, 2008), workplacedemocracy.wordpress.com/ workplace-democracy-survey/.

11 Elizabeth Anderson, *Private Government: How Employers Rule Our Lives (and Why We Don't Talk about It)* (Princeton University Press, 2017).

12 *No Relief: Denial of Bathroom Breaks in the Poultry Industry* (Oxfam America, 2016); Simon Head, "Worse than Wal-Mart: Amazon's sick brutality and secret history of ruthlessly intimidating workers," *Salon* (Feb. 23, 2014), www.salon.com/2014/02/23/ worse_than_wal_mart_amazons_sick_brutality_and_secret_history_of_ruthlessly_intimidating_workers/.

13 Reuters, "Apple defeats class action lawsuit over bag searches," *Fortune* (Nov. 8, 2015).

14 Anderson, *Private Government*.

15 Esko Kilpi, "Redefining work" (Dec. 2015), medium.com/@EskoKilpi/redefining-work-447bff8a6547.

16 Kilpi, "Redefining work."

17 Joseph Stiglitz, *The Price of Inequality: How Today's Divided Society Endangers Our Future* (Norton, 2012).

18 David Goodhart, *Head, Hand, Heart: Why Intelligence Is Over-Rewarded, Manual Workers Matter, and Caregivers Deserve More Respect* (Free Press, 2020).

19 Esko Kilpi, "We need to shift our focus from competencies to agency" (Nov, 4, 2018), medium.com/@ EskoKilpi/we-need-to-shift-our-focus-from-competencies-to-agency-42a68dc0ef7d.

20 Bernard Lahire (Ed.), *Enfances de classe: De l'inégalité parmi les enfants* (Seuil, 2019).

21 Daniel Markovits, *The Meritocracy Trap: How America's Foundational Myth Feeds Inequality, Dismantles the Middle Class, and Devours the Elite* (Penguin, 2019).

22 Roge Karma, "'The Meritocracy Trap,' explained," *Vox* (Oct. 24, 2019), www.vox.com/ policy-and-politics/2019/10/24/20919030/meritocracy-book-daniel-markovits-inequality-rich.

23 Eric Berne, *Games People Play: The Psychology of Human Relationships* (Penguin, 1964).

24 Dave Pollard, "Hierarchy is the enemy of learning," *How to Save the World* (Aug. 29, 2018), howtosavetheworld.ca/2018/08/29/hierarchy-is-the-enemy-of-learning/.

25 Robert Greenleaf, *The Servant as Leader* (Center for Applied Studies, 1970).

26 Raelin, "Hierarchy's subordination of democracy."

27 Bernard Bass, *Leadership and Performance beyond Expectations* (Free Press, 1985).

28 Pierluigi Digennaro, "Subordination or subjection? A study about the dividing line between subordinate work and self-employment in six European legal systems," *Labour Law Issues* 6, no. 1 (2020), labourlaw.unibo.it/article/view/11254.

29 Felicia Rosioru, "The changing concept of subordination," in György Kiss (Ed.), *Recent Developments in Labour Law* (Akadémiai Kiadó, 2013).

30 Trebor Scholz, *Digital Labor: The Internet as Playground and Factory* (Routledge, 2011); Dominique Cardon and Antonio Casilli, *Qu'est-ce que le Digital Labor?* (INA, 2015), especially Casilli, "Digital labor: Travail, technologies et conflictualités," author's translation; Antonio Casilli, Paola Tubaro, Clément Le Ludec, Marion Coville, Maxime Besenval, Touhfat Mouhtare, and Elinor Wahal, *Le micro-travail en France: Derrière l'automatisation, de nouvelles précarités au travail?* (DiPLab, 2019), hal. archives-ouvertes.fr/hal-02139528.

31 National Telecommunications and Information Administration, *Falling through the Net: A Survey of the "Have Nots" in Rural and Urban America* (U.S. Department of Commerce, 1995); Laura Robinson, Jeremy Schulz, et al., "Digital inequalities 2.0: Legacy inequalities in the information age" and "Digital inequalities 3.0: Emergent inequalities in the information age," *First Monday* (June 9, 2020), firstmonday.org/ojs/index.php/fm/article/view/10842/9561 and firstmonday.org/ojs/index.php/fm/ article/view/10844/9562.

32 Don Anair, Jeremy Martin, Maria Cecilia Pinto de Moura, and Joshua Goldman, *Ride-Hailing's Climate Risks: Steering a Growing Industry Toward a Clean Transportation Future* (Union of Concerned Scientists, Feb. 25, 2020), www.ucsusa.org/resources/ride-hailing-climate-risks.

33 Ruling by the Labour Chamber of the Court of Cassation: Arrêt n°374 du 4 mars 2020 (19-13.316)— Cour de cassation—Chambre sociale ECLI:FR:CCAS:2020:S000374 (English translation).

34 Kate Conger, "Uber and Lyft drivers in California will remain contractors," *New York Times* (Nov. 4, 2020).

35 Laurie Macfarlane, "Six charts that reveal America's deep divides," *Open Democracy* (Nov. 3, 2020), www.opendemocracy.net/en/oureconomy/six-charts-that-reveal-americas-deep-divides/.

36 Grayson Perry, "The rise and fall of Default Man," *New Statesman* (Oct. 8, 2014).

37 Dan Lyons, *Disrupted: My Misadventure in the Start-Up Bubble* (Hachette, 2016).

38 Guillaume Erner, "Le Macronisme a-t-il toujours été de droite? Avec Frédéric Rouvillois et Marie Tanguy," *L'invité(e) des Matins*, France Culture (Sept. 21, 2020), www.franceculture.fr/emissions/linvitee-des-matins/le-macronisme-a-t-il-toujours-ete-de-droite-avec-frederic-rouvillois-et-marie-tanguy; Marie Tanguy, *Confusions* (JC Lattès, 2020), author's translation.

39 Ben Fuchs, Megan Reitz, and John Higgins, "Do you have 'advantage blindness'?," *Harvard Business Review* (Apr. 10, 2018), hbr.org/2018/04/do-you-have-advantage-blindness.

40 Megan Reitz and John Higgins, "Mastering the art of speaking up: Why labels matter," HR Zone (Mar. 4, 2020), www.hrzone.com/lead/culture/mastering-the-art-of-speaking-up-why-labels-matter.

41 Owen Jones, "Google's sexist memo has provided the alt-right with a new martyr," *The Guardian* (Aug. 8, 2017).

42 Cynthia Fleury, *Ci gît l'amer: Guérir du ressentiment* (Gallimard, 2020).

43 Anand Giridharadas, *Winners Take All: The Elite Charade of Changing the World* (Knopf, 2018).

44 Dylan Matthews, "Meet the folk hero of Davos: The writer who told the rich to stop dodging taxes," *Vox* (Jan. 30, 2019), www.vox.com/future-perfect/2019/1/30/18203911/davos-rutger-bregman-historian-taxes-philanthropy; Joseph Stiglitz, "Meet the 'change agents' who are enabling inequality," *New York Times* (Aug. 20, 2018).

45 David Larcker and Brian Tayan, *Diversity in the C-Suite: The Dismal State of Diversity among Fortune 100 Senior Executives* (Rock Center for Corporate Governance, Stanford University, 2020).

46 Caroline Fourest, *Génération offensée: De la police de la culture à la police de la pensée* (Grasset, 2020) and "Why the American press keeps getting terror in France wrong," *Tablet* (Nov. 10, 2020), www.tabletmag.com/sections/news/articles/caroline-fourest-liberalism-france.

47 Eddy L. Harris, *Paris en noir et black*, translated by Jean Guiloineau (Liana Levi, 2009).

48 Adèle Van Reeth, with Matthew Crawford, "La révolution peut-elle être menée par l'élite?," *Les Chemins de la Philosophie*, France Culture (Oct. 29, 2020), www.franceculture.fr/emissions/les-chemins-de-la-philosophie/trump-dans-loeil-des-philosophes-44-la-revolution-peut-elle-etre-menee-par-lelite.

49 Christopher Lasch, *The Revolt of the Elites and the Betrayal of Democracy* (Norton, 1995). For François Furet, see Goodreads, www.goodreads.com/author/show/35399.Fran_ois_Furet, and *Wikipedia*, en.wikipedia.org/wiki/Fran%C3%A7ois_Furet#Bibliography.

50 Mona Chollet, *Réinventer l'amour: Comment le patriarcat sabote les relations hétérosexuelles* (La Découverte, 2021).

51 United Nations Development Programme, *Tackling Social Norms: A Game Changer for Gender Inequalities*, 2020 Human Development Perspectives (UNDP, 2020).

52 Nathalie Hense and Ilya Green, *Marre du rose* (LP) (Albin Michel Jeunesse, 2009).

53 Édith Maruéjouls-Benoit, *Mixité, égalité et genre dans les espaces du loisir des jeunes: Pertinence d'un paradigme féministe* (Université Michel de Montaigne–Bordeaux III, 2014), and in Marion Germa, "La ville comme espace genré: Entretien avec Édith Maruéjouls," *Observatoire du Design Urbain* (2014), obs-urbain.fr/ville-espace-genre-entretien-edith-maruejouls/; Robyn Beaman, Kevin Wheldall, and Coral Kemp, "Differential teacher attention to boys and girls in the classroom," *Educational Review* 58 (2007), 339–66; Pascal Huguet and Isabelle Régner, "Stereotype threat among schoolgirls in quasi-ordinary classroom circumstances," *Journal of Educational Psychology* 99 (2007), 545–60.

54 *What Was the Global Cost of Talent in 2017?* (Universum, 2018), https://universumglobal.com/blog/global-cost-talent-2017/.

55 Camille Rainville, "Be a lady they said," *Writings of a Furious Woman* (Dec. 2017), writingsofafuriouswoman.wordpress.com/2017/12/09/be-a-lady-they-said/; Paul McLean (Dir.), Camille Rainville (Writ.), *Be a Lady They Said* (2020), vimeo.com/393253445.

56 Paola Cecchi-Dimeglio, "How gender bias corrupts performance reviews, and what to do about it," *Harvard Business Review* (Apr. 12, 2017), hbr.org/2017/04/how-gender-bias-corrupts-performance-reviews-and-what-to-do-about-it; Malin Malmstrom, Jeaneth Johansson, and Joakim Wincent, "We recorded VCs' conversations and analyzed how differently they talk about female entrepreneurs," *Harvard Business Review* (May 17, 2017), hbr.org/2017/05/we-recorded-vcs-conversations-and-analyzed-how-differently-they-talk-about-female-entrepreneurs.

57 Ezra Klein, "The tragedy of Hillary Clinton," *Vox* (Aug. 20, 2020), www.vox.com/2020/8/20/21376834/hillary-clinton-dnc-democratic-convention-speech-2020-joe-biden-sexism; Jay Newton-Small, "Hillary Clinton speaks, male pundits hear her 'shouting,'" *Time* (May 16, 2016); Deborah Tannen, "The self-fulfilling prophecy of disliking Hillary Clinton," *Time* (Mar. 15, 2016).

58 Clifford Nass, Youngme Moon, and Nancy Green, "Are machines gender neutral? Gender stereotypic responses to computers with voices," *Journal of Applied Social Psychology* 27 (1997), 835–928.

59 UNESCO and EQUALS Skill Coalition, *I'd Blush If I Could: Closing Gender Divides in Digital Skills through Education* (UNESCO, 2019).

60 Rebecca Solnit, *The Mother of All Questions: Further Reports from the Feminist Revolutions* (Haymarket, 2017).

61 Christopher Karpowitz and Tali Mendelberg, *The Silent Sex: Gender, Deliberation, and Institutions* (Princeton University Press, 2014); Karpowitz, Mendelberg, and Lee Shaker, "Gender inequality in deliberative participation," *American Political Science Review* 106 (2012), 533–47.

62 Lucy Vernasco, "Seven studies that prove mansplaining exists," Bitchmedia (July 14, 2014), www.bitchmedia.org/post/seven-studies-proving-mansplaining-exists.

63 Carol Kinsey Goman, "10 body language traps for women in the workplace," Troymedia (July 8, 2019), https://troymedia.com/career-human-resource-information/body-language-traps-women-work/#.YanHutDMJPZ.

64 Brittany Karford Rogers, "When women don't speak," *BYU Magazine* (Spring 2020).

65 Olga Stoddard, Chris Karpowitz, and Jessica Preece, *Strength in Numbers: A Field Experiment in Gender, Influence, and Group Dynamics*, IZA Institute of Labor Economics Discussion Paper no. 13741 (Sept. 2020), papers.ssrn.com/sol3/papers.cfm?abstract_id=3704122; Katherine Goldstein, "I was a Sheryl Sandberg superfan. Then her 'Lean In' advice failed me," *Vox* (Dec. 6, 2018), www.vox.com/first-person/2018/12/6/18128838/michelle-obama-lean-in-sheryl-sandberg.

66 Emily Stewart, "Why struggling companies promote women: The glass cliff, explained," *Vox* (Oct. 31, 2018), www.vox.com/2018/10/31/17960156/what-is-the-glass-cliff-women-ceos.

67 "Even in lockdown, mothers bear the brunt of child care," *The Economist* (May 27, 2020); "How the pandemic is affecting working mothers," Knowledge@Wharton (Sept. 29, 2020), knowledge.wharton.upenn.edu/article/how-the-pandemic-is-affecting-working-mothers/.

68 Avivah Wittenberg-Cox, "If you can't find a spouse who supports your career, stay single," *Harvard Business Review* (Oct. 24, 2017), hbr.org/2017/10/if-you-cant-find-a-spouse-who-supports-your-career-stay-single.

69 "Violence against women," Organisation for Economic Co-operation and Development (accessed 2020), data.oecd.org/inequality/violence-against-women.htm.

70 UNDP, *Tackling Social Norms*.

71 Liz Ford, "Not one single country set to achieve gender equality by 2030," *The Guardian* (June 3, 2019).

7. The Network Opportunity

1 Change Agents Worldwide can be found online at changeagentsworldwide.com.

2 Céline Schillinger, "Forget social networks, think social impact," TEDx Bedminster and We Need Social (Oct. 2, 2014), weneedsocial.com/blog/2014/10/2/forget-social-networks-think-social-impact.

3 Anne McCrossan, *Emergent Code: Chronicles of the Digital Human* (accessed Sept. 21, 2021), emergentcodechronicles.com; Chris Woodford, "The internet," Explain That Stuff! (July 6, 2021), www.explainthatstuff.com/internet.html; Valérie Schafer and Alexandre Serres, *Histories of the Internet and the Web* (Living Books About History, 2016), www.livingbooksabouthistory.ch/en/book/histories-of-the-internet-and-the-web.

4 Vannevar Bush, "As we may think," *The Atlantic* (July 1945).

5 For details, see "Project Xanadu," *Wikipedia* (accessed Sept. 21, 2021), en.wikipedia.org/wiki/Project_Xanadu.

6 Marshall McLuhan, *Understanding Media: The Extensions of Man* (MIT Press, 1964).

7 Becky Robinson, "Women invented the internet, too" (May 13, 2019), medium.com/@rshrobinson/women-invented-the-internet-too-4d3a2fef14ff.

8 Rick Levine, Christopher Lock, Doc Searls, and David Weinberger, *The Cluetrain Manifesto: The End of Business as Usual* (Perseus, 2000).

9 Claire Richard, interview with Valérie Schafer, "'Il n'y a pas une histoire d'internet, mais des généalogies, de réseaux, de communautés...,'" Orange Digital Society Forum (Aug. 27, 2019), digital-society-forum.orange.com/fr/les-actus/1241-34il-n39y-a-pas-une-histoire-d39internet-mais-des-genealogies-de-reseaux-de-communautes34.

10 Claire Evans, *Broad Band: The Untold Story of the Women Who Made the Internet* (Portfolio, 2018).

11 Mikko Kivelä, Alexandre Arenas, Marc Barthelemy, James P. Gleeson, Yamir Moreno, and Mason A. Porter, "Multilayer networks," *Journal of Complex Networks* 2 (2014), 203–71.

12 Duncan Watts, *Six Degrees: The New Science of Networks* (Vintage Digital, 2014); Sergey Edunov, Smriti Bhagat, Moira Burke, Carlos Diuk, and Ismail Onur Filiz, "Three and a half degrees of separation," Facebook Research (Feb. 4, 2016), research.fb.com/blog/2016/02/three-and-a-half-degrees-of-separation/; Kivelä et al., "Multilayer networks"; Watts, *Six Degrees*.

13 John Urry, "Mobile sociology," British Journal of Sociology 61, s1 (2010), 347–66.

14 Francis Pisani, "Networks as a unifying pattern of life involving different processes at different levels: An interview with Fritjof Capra," *International Journal of Communication* 1 (2007).

15 Mark Granovetter, "The strength of weak ties," *American Journal of Sociology* 78 (1973), 1360–80, and "Economic action and social structure: The problem of embeddedness," *American Journal of Sociology* 91 (1985), 481–510.

16 Manuel Castells, *The Rise of the Network Society*, Vol. I: *The Information Age: Economy, Society and Culture* (Wiley-Blackwell, 1996), and Castells and Gustavo Cardoso, *The Network Society: From Knowledge to Policy* (Johns Hopkins Center for Transatlantic Relations, 2005).

17 Pierre Dansereau, "Ecosystem," *The Canadian Encyclopedia* (2006; updated 2015), www.thecanadianencyclopedia.ca/en/article/ecosystem.

18 Suzanne Simard, David A. Perry, Melanie D. Jones, David D. Myrold, Daniel M. Durall, and Randy Molina, "Net transfer of carbon between ectomycorrhizal tree species in the field," *Nature* 388 (1997), 579–82.

19 David George Haskell, "Life is the network, not the self," *Cosmos & Culture*, NPR (Apr. 4, 2017), www.npr.org/sections/13.7/2017/04/04/522011396/the-key-to-life-is-the-network?t=1607029924059, and *The Songs of Trees: Stories from Nature's Great Connectors* (Viking, 2017).

20 Pisani, "Networks as a unifying pattern of life."

21 Gilles Deleuze and Felix Guattari, *A Thousand Plateaus: Capitalism and Schizophrenia*, translated by Brian Massumi (University of Minnesota Press, 1987).

22 Dave Snowden, "Diversity & coherence," Cognitive Edge (Nov. 21, 2020), www.cognitive-edge.com/diversity-coherence/.

23 Reuven Gorsht, "What a 'Real' org chart may look like," Twitter (Sept. 4, 2014), twitter.com/reuvengorsht/status/507507686918062080.

24 Barry Oshry, "From system blindness to system sight," PwC, London, UK (June 2015), www.youtube.com/watch?v=VYpO-pK7IFA, *Seeing Systems: Unlocking the Mysteries of Organizational Life* (Berrett-Koehler, 1995), and *The Terrible Dance of Power* (Power + Systems 2007), www.powerandsystems.com/files/downloads/The Terrible Dance of Power.pdf.

25 Russell Ackoff, interviewed by Phyllis Haynes (Haynes Media Works, Jan. 12, 2010), www.youtube.com/watch?v=Mzs5V5-0VsA, and *Differences That Make a Difference: An Annotated Glossary of Distinctions Important in Management* (Triarchy, 2010).

26 Steve Zaffron and Gregory Unruh, "Your organization is a network of conversations," *MIT Sloan Management Review* (July 10, 2018), sloanreview.mit.edu/article/your-organization-is-a-network-of-conversations/.

27 Nora Bateson (Dir.), *An Ecology of Mind: A Daughter's Portrait of Gregory Bateson* (Impact Media Group, 2011), vimeo.com/ondemand/bateson.

28 Esko Kilpi, "Work is interaction" (Mar. 17, 2015), medium.com/@EskoKilpi/work-as-interaction-bfecdd8ea1a1.

29 Esko Kilpi, "A working class manifesto" (Apr. 30, 2017), medium.com/@EskoKilpi/a-working-class-manifesto-d53a01b867ff.

30 Kilpi, "Work is interaction."

31 Scott Jaschik, "'Relationship-Rich Education': Authors discuss their new book on the importance of the human connection in higher education," *Inside Higher Ed* (Nov. 3, 2020), www.insidehighered.com/news/2020/11/03/authors-discuss-their-new-book-relationships-higher-education.

32 Alison Pugh, "The meaning makers: connective labor, automation and the stratification of human contact," Berggruen Institute Sociology Speaker Series (Feb. 26, 2020), www.berggruen.org/events/the-meaning-makers-connective-labor-automation-and-the-stratification-of-human-contact/; Pugh can be found at allisonpugh.weebly.com.

33 Alison Pugh, Twitter (Sept. 12, 2020), twitter.com/allison_pugh/status/1304806966896852996.

34 Jena Lee, "A neuropsychological exploration of Zoom fatigue," *Psychiatric Times* (Nov. 17, 2020), www.psychiatrictimes.com/view/psychological-exploration-zoom-fatigue.

35 Allison Pugh, "Automated health care offers freedom from shame, but is it what patients need?," *The New Yorker* (May 22, 2018). See also, from Pugh, "An inequality of being seen," *Noēma* (June 16, 2020), and "The social meanings of dignity at work," *The Hedgehog Review* (Fall 2012).

36 Kilpi, "Redefining work."

37 Hubert Guillaud, "Coincés dans Zoom (3/4): Miroir des cultures managériales," Internetactu (Dec. 8, 2020), www.internetactu.net/2020/12/08/coinces-dans-zoom-34-miroir-des-cultures-manageriales/.

38 Esko Kilpi, "Your facts are not my facts" (Nov. 7, 2016), medium.com/@EskoKilpi/your-facts-are-not-my-facts-2cd62aafb70b#.bpn2hjlkk.

39 Kenneth Mikkelsen and Richard Martin, *The Neo-Generalist: Where You Go Is Who You Are* (Lid, 2016).

40 Kilpi, "We need to shift our focus," "A relational view of leadership" (Aug. 18, 2018), medium.com/@EskoKilpi/a-relational-view-to-leadership-7c561c4b0720, and "Networked leadership" (Apr. 10, 2016), medium.com/@EskoKilpi/networks-and-leadership-d8400046eae6.

41 Kilpi, "Networked leadership."

42 Jon Husband, "What is wirearchy?," Wirearchy (Feb. 16, 2013), wirearchy.com/what-is-wirearchy/. See also his keynote at Social Now 2019, "Strongly Connected Organizations" (June 2019), socialnow.org/jon-husband-strongly-connected-organisations/.

43 Jon Husband, "Hierarchy to wirearchy: Designing flows for networks of purposeful people," Wirearchy (Sept. 26, 2016), wirearchy.com/2016/09/26/hierarchy-to-wirearchy-designing-flows-for-networks-of-purposeful-people/.

44 Jon Husband et al., *Wirearchy: Sketches for the Future of Work* (The Wirearchy Commons 2015), wirearchy.com/wirearchy-the-ebook/.

45 Jon Husband, "Your organization is already a wirearchy," Wirearchy (Feb. 4, 2014), wirearchy.com/2014/02/04/your-organization-is-already-a-wirearchy/, and "On leading, managing and co-creating in the connected workplace," Wirearchy (June 23, 2013), wirearchy.com/2013/06/23/on-leading-managing-and-co-creating-in-the-connected-workplace/.

46 Husband, "What is wirearchy?"

47 Husband et al., *Wirearchy.*

48 Husband, "What is wirearchy?"

49 Levine et al., *The Cluetrain Manifesto*; Raphael Dörr, "Book of the week: The Cluetrain Manifesto—The End of Business as Usual," ChangeCom (Apr. 5, 2016), changecom.wordpress.com/2016/04/05/the-cluetrain-manifesto/ .

50 Kilpi, "A relational view of leadership."

51 Julie Diamond, "How flat organizations become toxic," *Start It Up* (Sept. 27, 2019), medium.com/swlh/how-flat-organizations-become-toxic-efb6c0f59a3a.

52 Meredith A. Newman and Mary E. Guy, "Taylor's triangle, Follett's web," *Administrative Theory & Praxis* 20 (1998), 287–97.

53 Mary Parker Follett, *Creative Experience* (1924; Thoemmes Continuum, 2003).
54 Mary Parker Follett, *Mary Parker Follett—Prophet of Management: A Celebration of Writings from the 1920s*, collected by Pauline Graham (Harvard Business School Press, 1995).
55 Follett, *Mary Parker Follett—Prophet of Management*.
56 Margaret Wheatley and Myron Rogers, *A Simpler Way* (Berrett-Koehler, 1996).
57 Kilpi, "Networked leadership."
58 Frédéric Laloux, *Reinventing Organizations: A Guide to Creating Organizations Inspired by the Next Stage of Human Consciousness* (Nelson Parker, 2014); Jon Husband interviewed by Stowe Boyd, Socialogy (Dec. 29, 2014), wirearchy.com/2014/12/29/stowe-boyds-socialogy-interview-december-2014/; Chris Argyris, "Double loop learning in organizations," *Harvard Business Review Magazine* (Sept. 1977).
59 Deleuze and Guattari, *A Thousand Plateaus*.
60 Kazutoshi Sasahara, Wen Chen, Hao Peng, Giovanni Luca Ciampaglia, Alessandro Flammini, and Filippo Menczer, "Social influence and unfollowing accelerate the emergence of echo chambers," *Journal of Computational Social Science* 4 (2020), 381–402.
61 Rui Fan, Ke Xu, and Jichang Zhao, "Higher contagion and weaker ties mean anger spreads faster than joy in social media," Cornell University (2016), arxiv.org/abs/1608.03656.
62 Luke Munn, "Angry by design: Toxic communication and technical architectures," *Humanities & Social Sciences Communications* 7 (2020), www.nature.com/articles/s41599-020-00550-7.
63 Éric Sadin, *L'ère de l'individu tyran* (Grasset, 2020).
64 *Ledger of Harms*, Center for Humane Technology (updated June 2021; accessed Sept. 22, 2021), ledger.humanetech.com.
65 Barry Oshry, "Power and Love: A systems perspective" (2009), newstories.org/wp-content/uploads/2015/01/Power-and-Love.pdf.
66 Mary Parker Follett, *The New State: Group Organization the Solution of Popular Government* (1918; Penn State University Press, 1998).
67 Mary Parker Follett, "Business as an Integrative Entity," in *Dynamic Administration: The Collected Papers of Mary Parker Follett* (Harper, 1940).
68 Follett, *Creative Experience*.

8. Creating Equality at Work

1 As shared by the author on Twitter (Nov. 21, 2019), twitter.com/CelineSchill/status/1197454410298920960.
2 Kate Conger, "Hundreds of Google employees unionize, culminating years of activism," *New York Times* (Jan. 4, 2021).
3 Noam Scheiber and Kate Conger, "The great Google revolt," *New York Times Magazine* (Feb. 18, 2020).
4 "Busting union-busting myths," Alphabet Workers Union (accessed Sept. 23, 2021), alphabetworkersunion.org/power/busting-myths/.
5 Colin MacCabe and Holly Janacek, The Keywords Project, "The politics of 'political'—how the word has changed its meaning," Oxford University Press blog (Nov. 23, 2018), blog.oup.com/2018/11/politics-of-political/.
6 Stowe Boyd, "Today's business organization is an oligarchy, and that needs to change," *Work Futures* (Mar. 10, 2016), medium.com/work-futures/today-s-business-organization-is-an-oligarchy-and-that-needs-to-change-17af726c46d0.
7 Patrick Guiol, "Les enjeux de la participation," *Esprit* (Mar. 2018).
8 Patrick Guiol and Jorge Muñoz, "Management, participation et santé des salariés. Des médecins et des salariés parlent," *Revue internationale de l'économie sociale*, no. 304 (2006), 76–96.
9 Patrick Guiol, Aurélie Hess-Miglioretti, Pascale Mériot, and Jorge Muñoz, "De singulières disparités de consommations sanitaires: hommes et femmes face au pouvoir dans l'entreprise," in Delphine Dulong, Christine Guionnet, and Érik Neveu (Eds.), *Boys don't cry! Les coûts de la domination masculine* (Presses universitaires de Rennes, 2010), author's translation.
10 Thibault Le Texier, "Le management est-il anti-démocratique?," *Esprit* (Mar. 2018).

11 Samuel Jubé, "Pour une image fidèle du travail dans la comptabilité financière," in Pierre Musso and Alain Supiot (Eds.), *Qu'est-ce qu'un régime de travail réellement humain?* (Hermann, 2018).

12 Franck Bouaziz, "Sanofi, toujours plus de dividendes, ou comment injurier l'avenir," *Libération* (Feb. 5, 2021); "US corporate share buybacks resume after pandemic-related hiatus," FitchRatings (Feb. 5, 2021), www.fitchratings.com/research/corporate-finance/us-corporate-share-buybacks-resume-after-pandemic-related-hiatus-05-02-2021.

13 Guiol, "Les enjeux de la participation," author's translation.

14 Thibaud Brière and Thibault Le Texier, "Démocratiser l'entreprise. Introduction," *Esprit* (Mar. 2018), author's translation.

15 Brière and Le Texier, "Démocratiser l'entreprise. Introduction," author's translation.

16 Loïc Le Morlec, "Se libérer des croyances de l'entreprise libérée," RH Info (Dec. 12, 2018), www.rhinfo.adp.com/rhinfo/2018/se-liberer-des-croyances-de-lentreprise-liberee-3/.

17 Florine Galéron, "Plan social chez Poult: l'ex-entreprise libérée face à la chute des ventes de biscuits," *La Tribune* (Occitanie–Toulouse), (Sept. 21, 2021).

18 Sylvain Tronchet, "Le Groupe Hervé: Derrière la façade de l'entreprise 'libérée,' des salariés classés et sous surveillance?," France Inter (Jan. 22, 2021), www.franceinter.fr/le-groupe-herve-derriere-la-facade-de-l-entreprise-liberee-des-salaries-classes-et-sous-surveillance.

19 Brière and Le Texier, "Démocratiser l'entreprise. Introduction," author's translation.

20 Edward Freeman, *Strategic Management: A Stakeholder Approach* (Pitman, 1984).

21 G. Tomas Hult, Jeannette Mena, O.C. Ferrell, and Linda Ferrell, "Stakeholder marketing: A definition and conceptual framework," *Academy of Marketing Science Review* 1 (2011), 44–65.

22 Blanche Segrestin and Armand Hatchuel, *Refonder l'entreprise* (Seuil, 2012), author's translation.

23 "Social purpose corporation," with research from Yoshihiro Fumoto, 501 Commons (accessed Sept. 23, 2021), www.501commons.org/resources/tools-and-best-practices/starting-a-nonprofit/social-purpose-corporation.

24 "Raison d'être Danone: From the 'dual project' to 'entreprise à mission,'" Danone (accessed Sept. 23, 2021), www.danone.com/about-danone/sustainable-value-creation/danone-entreprise-a-mission.html.

25 Leïla Abboud, "Danone board ousts Emmanuel Faber as chief and chairman," *The Financial Times* (Mar. 15, 2021).

26 Blanche Segrestin, "La mission, un nouveau contrat social pour l'entreprise," *Esprit* (Mar. 2018), author's translation.

27 Isabelle Ferreras, *Firms as Political Entities: Saving Democracy through Economic Bicameralism* (Cambridge University Press, 2017).

28 "The Citizens' Convention on Climate, what is it?," Convention Citoyenne pour le Climat (accessed Sept. 23, 2021), www.conventioncitoyennepourleclimat.fr/en/.

29 Nathan Heller, "Politics without politicians," *The New Yorker* (Feb. 19, 2020); Hélène Landemore, *Open Democracy: Reinventing Popular Rule for the Twenty-First Century* (Princeton University Press, 2020).

30 "Appel à une gouvernance démocratique de la crise sanitaire," Éthique et Pandémie (accessed Sept. 23, 2021), ethique-pandemie.com/initiative-nationale/.

31 "Session bilan du collectif citoyen vaccination," Conseil Économique Social et Environnemental (Aug. 15, 2021), www.lecese.fr/actualites/session-bilan-du-collectif-citoyen-vaccination.

32 "Digital democracy—What Europe can learn from Taiwan—Web discussion with Audrey Tang" (Bertelsmann Stiftung, Sept. 2020), www.youtube.com/watch?v=I5uMMKaSbSw.

33 Azeem Azhar, "How Taiwan is using technology to foster democracy (with Digital Minister Audrey Tang)," *Exponential View* podcast, S5E2 (Nov. 2020), hbr.org/podcast/2020/10/how-taiwan-is-using-technology-to-foster-democracy-with-digital-minister-audrey-tang; Nathan Gardels, "The frontiers of digital democracy," *Noēma* (Feb. 4, 2021).

34 Barry Oshry, *Seeing Systems: Unlocking the Mysteries of Organizational Life* (Berrett-Koehler, 1995).

35 More on Helen Bevan in Chapter 10. Helen can be found on Twitter at @HelenBevanTweet.

36 Myron Rogers, "Living systems," Leadership Centre (accessed Sept. 23, 2021), www.leadershipcentre.org.uk/artofchangemaking/theory/living-systems/.

37 Myron Rogers, "Systems leadership workshop," NHS London Leadership Academy, NHS Kent, Surrey and Sussex Leadership Collaborative and the Health Innovation Network (Feb. 2017), www.youtube.com/watch?v=uKSTMNDjAVI.

38 Margaret Wheatley and Myron Rogers, *A Simpler Way* (Berrett-Koehler, 1996).

39 Valdis Krebs, "Thinking about networks-2," Cognitive Edge (Jan. 31, 2021), www.cognitive-edge.com/thinking-about-networks-2/.

40 Céline Schillinger, "Volunteer power," We Need Social blog (March 2015), weneedsocial.com/blog/2015/3/24/volunteer-power.

41 Esko Kilpi, "We need to shift our focus from competencies to agency" (Nov. 4, 2018), medium.com/@EskoKilpi/we-need-to-shift-our-focus-from-competencies-to-agency-42a68dc0ef7d.

42 John Kotter, *Accelerate: Building Strategic Agility for a Faster-Moving World* (Harvard Business Review Press, 2014).

43 Gaëlle Roudaut, "Le réseau social d'entreprise: l'effet de mode qui a fait plouf!," *Le Mag RH* 12 (Feb. 2021), 140.

44 Luis Suarez, "Stop blaming the tools when collaboration fails," *Elsua* (Dec. 7, 2016).

45 vTaiwan: info.vtaiwan.tw; JOIN: www.join.gov.tw; pol.is: pol.is/home.

46 Céline Schillinger, "Sanofi Pasteur unlocks quality excellence and unleashes innovation with Yammer," Microsoft 365 blog (Jan. 25, 2017), www.microsoft.com/en-us/microsoft-365/blog/2017/01/25/sanofi-pasteur-unlocks-quality-excellence-and-unleashes-innovation-with-yammer/.

47 John Hagel, "Never under-estimate the immune system," Edge Perspectives with John Hagel (Dec. 2017), edgeperspectives.typepad.com/edge_perspectives/2017/12/never-under-estimate-the-immune-system.html.

48 John Kotter, "Accelerate!," *Harvard Business Review Magazine* (Nov. 2012), and *Accelerate*.

49 Kotter, "Accelerate!"

50 Kotter, "Accelerate!"

51 Anita Williams Woolley, Christopher F. Chabris, Alex Pentland, Nada Hashmi, and Thomas W. Malone, "Evidence for a collective intelligence factor in the performance of human groups," *Science* 330 (2010), 686–88.

52 Émile Servan-Schreiber, *Super collectif: La nouvelle puissance de nos intelligences* (Fayard, 2018), author's translation; Daniel Goleman, *Emotional Intelligence: Why It Can Matter More Than IQ* (Bantam, 1995).

53 James Surowiecki, *The Wisdom of Crowds* (Anchor, 2004).

54 Carla O'Dell and C. Jackson Grayson, Jr., *If Only We Knew What We Know: The Transfer of Internal Knowledge and Best Practice* (Free Press, 1998).

55 Céline Schillinger, "How to measure culture change without killing it," We Need Social blog (May 13, 2020), weneedsocial.com/blog/2016/3/28/how-to-measure-culture-change-without-killing-it.

56 "The 8-step process for leading change," Kotter (accessed Sept. 23, 2021), www.kotterinc.com/8-steps-process-for-leading-change/.

57 Kotter, *Accelerate*.

58 Scott Page, The Difference: How the Power of Diversity Creates Better Groups, Firms, Schools, and Societies (Princeton University Press, 2007).

59 "4 Change Principles," Kotter (accessed Sept. 12, 2021), www.kotterinc.com/4-change-principles/; Kotter, "Accelerate!"

60 Barry Oshry, *Context, Context, Context: How Our Blindness to Context Cripples Even the Smartest Organizations* (Triarchy, 2018).

61 Fritjof Capra, "Ecology and community," Center for Ecoliteracy (Oct. 25, 2009), www.ecoliteracy.org/article/ecology-and-community.

62 Angela Chen, "Inclusiveness seen as key to Taiwan's success in containing COVID-19," *Microsoft News* (Nov. 19, 2020), news.microsoft.com/apac/2020/11/19/inclusiveness-seen-as-key-to-taiwans-success-in-containing-of-covid-19/.

63 "Digital Democracy—What Europe can learn from Taiwan."

64 Dave Snowden, "Coherent heterogeneity," Cognitive Edge (Aug. 25 and 26, 2019), www.cognitive-edge.com/coherent-heterogeneity-1-of-2/ and www.cognitive-edge.com/coherent-heterogeneity-2-of-2/.

65 Sonja Blignaut, "All that jazz . . . Making coherence coherent," *Agile and Change* (Dec. 20, 2018), agileandchange.com/all-that-jazz-making-coherence-coherent-6f09b8b2e93.

66 Sonja Blignaut, "Why we suck at 'solving wicked problems,'" More Beyond (Dec. 7, 2018), www.morebeyond.co.za/why-we-suck-at-solving-wicked-problems/, and "Creating messy coherence" (Jan. 3, 2021), sonjablignaut.medium.com/creating-messy-coherence-c0ae404e2627.

67 Azhar, "How Taiwan is using technology to foster democracy."

68 Dave Snowden, "Requisite conflict . . .," Cognitive Edge (Jan. 21, 2018), www.cognitive-edge.com/requisite-conflict/.

69 Bonnitta Roy, "How system thinking is killing your creativity," *Our Future at Work* (Mar. 1, 2016), medium.com/open-participatory-organized/how-system-thinking-is-killing-your-creativity-2b127aee0b11#.gissb8m8v.

70 Yury Boshyk and Robert Dilworth (Eds.), *Action Learning: History and Evolution* (Palgrave Macmillan, 2010).

71 The World Institute for Action Learning can be found at wial.org.

72 Joanna Kozubska (Dir.), *Action Learning—Introduction by Reg Revans* (International Foundation for Action Learning, 1984), www.youtube.com/watch?v=2bJ9RXkYPSU.

73 Peter Senge, *The Fifth Discipline: The Art & Practice of the Learning Organization* (Crown Business, 1990).

74 John Atkinson, "The myth of the learning organisation," *Heart of the Art* (Mar. 29, 2018), www.heartoftheart.org/?p=6181

75 Atkinson, "The Myth of the Learning Organisation."

76 Nora Bateson, "*Symmathesy*: A word in progress" (Nov. 3, 2015), norabateson.wordpress.com/2015/11/03/symmathesy-a-word-in-progress/.

77 "Warm Data," The International Bateson Institute (accessed Sept. 23, 2021), batesoninstitute.org/warm-data/; Audrey Lobo-Pulo, "The subtle art of data gathering with Warm Data," *Phoensight* (Nov. 13, 2019), medium.com/phoensight/the-subtle-art-of-data-gathering-with-warm-data-676d7b5385b5.

78 Wheatley and Rogers, *A Simpler Way*.

PART IV. FRATERNITY

1 "Liberty, Equality, Fraternity," French Presidency (accessed Sept. 26, 2021), www.elysee.fr/en/french-presidency/liberty-equality-fraternity.

2 Jean-Louis Quantin, "Aux origines religieuses de la devise républicaine," *Communio* 14 (May–Aug. 1989), 23–33.

3 Mona Ozouf, "Liberté Egalité Fraternité," in Pierre Nora, Ed., *Les lieux de mémoire,* Vol. 3: *Les France* (Gallimard, 1992).

4 "Entretien de Mona Ozouf avec Henri Peyronie et Alain Vergnioux, 20 juin 2002," *Le Télémaque,* no. 28 (2005), 27–48

5 François Nault, "La fraternité: En lisant Derrida, Schmitt et la Bible," *Revue d'éthique et de théologie morale* 4, no. 4 (2007), 29–52.

6 Mark Kramer and Marc W. Pfitzer, "The ecosystem of shared value," *Harvard Business Review Magazine* (Oct. 2016).

9. Can There Be Fraternity at Work?

1 Jean-Pierre Waltzing, *Étude historique sur les corporations professionnelles chez les Romains depuis les origines jusqu'à la chute de l'Empire d'Occident* (1895; Wentworth, 2018).

2 Kristin Swain, "Can you be fired for fraternization?," The Lewis Law Group, P.A. (Feb. 1, 2018), www.lewislawgrouppa.com/can-you-be-fired-for-fraternization; Naresh Khatri and Eric Tsang

"Antecedents and consequences of cronyism in organizations," *Journal of Business Ethics* 43 (2003), 289–303; Chaim Gartenberg, "Ubisoft survey reveals that 25 percent of employees have seen or experienced workplace misconduct," *The Verge* (Oct. 2, 2020), www.theverge. com/2020/10/2/21499334/ubisoft-employees-workplace-misconduct-ceo-yves-guillemot-response.

3   Annamarie Mann and Amy Adkins, "Why we need best friends at work," Gallup Workplace (Jan. 15, 2018), www.gallup.com/workplace/236213/why-need-best-friends-work.aspx.

4   Christine Riordan, "We all need friends at work," *Harvard Business Review* (July 3, 2013), hbr. org/2013/07/we-all-need-friends-at-work.

5   Reid Hoffman, Ben Casnocha, and Chris Yeh, "Your company is not a family," *Harvard Business Review* (June 17, 2014), hbr.org/2014/06/your-company-is-not-a-family.

6   Ezra Klein, "LinkedIn founder Reid Hoffman on the biggest lie employers tell employees," *Vox* (July 23, 2015), www.vox.com/2015/5/22/8639717/reid-hoffman-the-alliance.

7   Emi Nietfeld, "After working at Google, I'll never let myself love a job again," *New York Times* (Apr. 7, 2021).

8   Allan Silver, "Friendship in commercial society: Eighteenth-century social theory and modern sociology," *American Journal of Sociology* 95 (1990), 1474–1504.

9   Graham Brown, Thomas Lawrence, and Sandra Robinson, "Territoriality in organizations," *Academy of Management Review* 30 (2005), 577–94.

10 Brown et al., "Territoriality in organizations."

11 For a general outline, see "Responsibility assignment matrix," *Wikipedia*, en.wikipedia.org/wiki/Responsibility_assignment_matrix.

12 Yves Morieux, "How too many rules at work keep you from getting things done," TED@BCG London (July 2015).

13 "A bad system will beat a good person every time," The Deming Institute (Feb. 26, 2015), deming. org/a-bad-system-will-beat-a-good-person-every-time/.

14 Alfie Kohn, "Why incentive plans cannot work," *Harvard Business Review Magazine* (Sept. 1993).

15 Kelly Allan, "Deming 101: 2015 & beyond," 2014 Annual Deming Institute Fall Conference (Oct. 4, 2015), www.youtube.com/watch?v=JbMmUMXj5As.

16 Émilie Lanez, "Covid19—Vaccin Pasteur, l'histoire secrète d'un fiasco," *Paris Match* (Mar. 30, 2021).

17 Jean-François Petit, "Une utopie pour retisser du lien," *Revue projet*, no. 329 (2012), 4–11; Emmanuel Levinas, *Totality and Infinity: An Essay on Exteriority*, translated by Alphonso Lingis (Duquesne University Press, 1961).

18 Petit, "Une utopie pour retisser du lien," author's translation.

19 Emmanuelle Duez, Eléonore de Perthuis, and Rose Ollivier, "La fraternité, nouveau levier de succès en entreprise?," *Harvard Business Review France* (Dec. 23, 2020), www.hbrfrance.fr/chroniques-experts/2020/12/32751-la-fraternite-nouveau-levier-de-succes-en-entreprise/.

20 Jacques Le Goff, "Le droit à la fraternité n'existe pas," *Revue projet*, no. 329 (2012), 14–21, author's translation.

21 Barry Oshry, "Can we truly see the other?," *The Seeing + Systems Blog* (June 24, 2020), seeingsystems.blogs.com/my_weblog/2020/06/can-we-truly-see-the-other.html.

22 Barry Oshry, *Encounters with the Other: A History and Possibilities* (Triarchy, 2018).

23 Sarah T., in conversation with the author (Aug. 2015).

24 Axel Honneth, *The Struggle for Recognition: The Moral Grammar of Social Conflicts*, translated by Joel Anderson (MIT Press, 1992).

25 Agathe Cagé, *Respect!* (Éditions des Équateurs, 2021).

26 Esko Kilpi, "A working class manifesto" (Apr. 30, 2017), medium.com/@EskoKilpi/a-working-class-manifesto-d53a01b867ff.

27 Roger C. Mayer, James H. Davis, and F. David Schoorman, "An integrative model of organizational trust," *Academy of Management Review* 20 (1995), 709–34.

28 Graham Dietz, "Going back to the source: Why do people trust each other?," *Journal of Trust Research* 1 (2011), 215–22.

29 Mayer et al., "An integrative model of organizational trust."

30 Maryann Keller, *Rude Awakening: The Rise, Fall, and Struggle for Recovery of General Motors* (HarperCollins, 1989); Gwynn Guilford, "GM's decline truly began with its quest to turn people into machines," *Quartz* (Dec. 30, 2018), qz.com/1510405/gms-layoffs-can-be-traced-to-its-quest-to-turn-people-into-machines/.

31 Dominique Nora, "Sanofi: L'histoire secrète d'une déroute industrielle," *L'OBS* (Mar. 25, 2021), www.nouvelobs.com/economie/20210325.OBS41848/sanofi-histoire-secrete-d-une-deroute-industrielle.amp.

32 Paul Lawrence and Robert Porter Lynch, "Leadership and the structure of trust," *The European Business Review* (May 20, 2011), www.europeanbusinessreview.com/leadership-and-the-structure-of-trust/.

33 Douglas Ready, "The enabling power of trust," *MIT Sloan Management Review* (Dec. 5, 2018), sloanreview.mit.edu/article/the-enabling-power-of-trust/.

34 Christine Capra, "Trust in networks is fundamental to social change," Greater Than the Sum (Oct. 12, 2015; rpt. Sep. 26, 2018), networkweaver.com/trust-in-networks-is-fundamental-to-social-change/.

35 Robert Phillips, *Trust Me, PR Is Dead* (Unbound, 2015).

36 John Wenger, "Can I trust you? Time for a manifesto of trust" (June 6, 2014), medium.com/@johnqshift/can i-trust-you-d0880a5261ea.

37 Wenger, "Can I trust you?"

38 Carmen Medina, "Trust is a muscle!!," Rebels at Work blog (Oct. 30, 2018), www.rebelsatwork.com/blog/2018/10/30/trust-is-a-muscle, and "Rebels at Work personal stories: Carmen Medina," Rebels at Work blog (June 12, 2017), www.rebelsatwork.com/stories/2017/6/12/carmen-medina.

39 Abeba Birhane, "Descartes was wrong: 'A person is a person through other persons,'" *Aeon* (Apr. 7, 2017), aeon.co/ideas/descartes-was-wrong-a-person-is-a-person-through-other-persons.

40 Nkem Ifejika, "What does ubuntu really mean?," *The Guardian* (Sept. 29, 2006).

41 "Ubuntu philosophy," Ubuntu Leaders Academy (accessed Sept. 26, 2021), www.academialideresubuntu.org/en/o-ubuntu-en/foundation.

42 AnaLouise Keating, "From status-quo stories to post oppositional transformation" *Tikkun* (Winter 2019).

43 Keating, "From status-quo stories to post oppositional transformation."

44 Scott Neigh, "Review: Transformation Now!" *A Canadian Lefty in Occupied Land* (Sept. 18, 2015), scottneigh.blogspot.com/2015/09/review-transformation-now.html.

45 Brian Stout, "Bridging: The art of solidarity," *Building Belonging* (Oct. 18, 2019), citizenstout.substack.com/p/bridging-the-art-of-solidarity.

46 Stephanie, in a conversation with the author (2021).

47 Dan Ariely, *Predictably Irrational: The Hidden Forces That Shape Our Decisions* (HarperCollins Canada, 2018).

48 Christof Rapp, "Aristotle's rhetoric," *Stanford Encyclopedia of Philosophy* (2002; rev. 2010).

49 Didier Marlier and Chris Parker, Engaging Leadership: Three Agendas for Sustaining Achievement (Palgrave Macmillan, 2009).

50 John Kotter and Dan Cohen, *The Heart of Change: Real-Life Stories of How People Change Their Organizations* (Harvard Business Review Press, 2002).

51 Sigal Barsade, interviewed by Frieda Klotz, "Employee emotions aren't noise—They're data," *MIT Sloan Management Review* (Nov. 2019).

52 Kilpi, "A working class manifesto."

53 Marcus Buckingham and Ashley Goodall, "Work-life balance is a myth. Do this instead," *Time* (June 6, 2019).

54 Rosabeth Moss Kanter, *Work and Family in the United States: A Critical Review and Agenda for Research and Policy* (Russell Sage Foundation, 1977).

55 Daniel Howden, "The dishonest myth of work-life balance," Workable (accessed Sept. 26, 2021), resources.workable.com/stories-and-insights/work-life-balance-myth.

56 Jeremias Prassl, *Humans as a Service: The Promise and Perils of Work in the Gig Economy* (Oxford University Press, 2018).

57 William McDougall, *The Group Mind: A Sketch of the Principles of Collective Psychology with Some Attempt to Apply Them to the Interpretation of National Life and Character* (Kessinger, 1920); Elton Mayo, *Hawthorne and the Western Electric Company: The Social Problems of an Industrial Civilisation* (Routledge, 1933).

58 Dan Lyons, *Disrupted: My Misadventure in the Start-Up Bubble* (Hachette, 2016).

59 Jim Morgan, "The truth about teambuilding: Teambuilding, real and not so much," *The Radical Agilist* (accessed April 4, 2021), zenronin.com/teambuilding-not-real/; Cameron Klein, Deborah DiazGranados, Eduardo Salas, Huy Le, C. Shawn Burke, Rebecca Lyons, and Gerald F. Goodwin, "Does team building work?," *Small Group Research* 40 (2009), 181-222.

60 Jon Katzenbach and Douglas K. Smith, *The Wisdom of Teams: Creating the High-Performance Organization* (Harper Business, 1993).

61 Morgan, "The truth about teambuilding."

62 Malcolm Knowles, Elwood Holton, and Richard Swanson, *The Adult Learner: The Definitive Classic in Adult Education and Human Resource Development* (Butterworth-Heinemann, 2005).

63 Anthony Zurcher, "Debunking the Myers-Briggs personality test," *Echo Chambers* blog, BBC (July 15, 2014).

64 Josh Kovensky, "Chief Happiness Officer is the latest, creepiest job in corporate America," *The New Republic* (July 23, 2014).

65 June Gruber, Iris B. Mauss, and Maya Tamir, "A dark side of happiness? How, when, and why happiness is not always good," *Perspectives on Psychological Science* 6 (2011), 222-33.

66 William Davies, *The Happiness Industry: How the Government and Big Business Sold Us Well-Being* (Verso, 2015).

67 William Davies, "All the happy workers," *The Atlantic* (June 6, 2015).

68 Edgar Cabanas and Eva Illouz, *Manufacturing Happy Citizens: How the Science and Industry of Happiness Control Our Lives* (Wiley, 2019).

69 Edgar Cabanas, Eva Illouz, and David Broder, "Against happiness," *Jacobin* (Aug. 29, 2019), www.jacobinmag.com/2019/08/happiness-self-help-positive-psychology-eva-illouz-edgar-cabanas.

10. Corporate Activism: Fraternity at Work

1 Céline Schillinger, "Quality as a movement for change. Seriously?," We Need Social blog (Oct. 30, 2014), weneedsocial.com/blog/2014/10/29/quality-as-a-movement-for-change-seriously.

2 Maria Popova, "Between the world and us: Hannah Arendt on outsiderdom, the power and privilege of being a pariah, and how we humanize each other," *Brainpickings* (Apr. 12, 2016), www.brainpickings.org/2016/04/12/hannah-arendt-men-in-dark-times/.

3 Hannah Arendt, *Men in Dark Times* (Harvest Books, 1968).

4 Douglas Harper, *Online Etymology Dictionary* (Ohio University), www.etymonline.com.

5 Fabienne Décieux and Oliver Nachtwey, "Occupy: Protest in der Postdemokratie," in *Soziale Kämpfe in der Postdemokratie* (Forschungsjournal Soziale Bewegungen, March 2014).

6 *Sociology: Understanding and Changing the Social World* (University of Minnesota Libraries Publishing, 2016), open.lib.umn.edu/sociology/.

7 Keith R. Bradley, *Slavery and Rebellion in the Roman World, 140 B.C.-70 B.C.* (Indiana University Press, 1989).

8 Charles Tilly, Lesley J. Wood, and Ernesto Castaneda, *Social Movements, 1768-2018* (Routledge, 2019).

9 Lorenz Von Stein, *Die sozialistischen und kommunistischen Bewegungen seit der dritten französischen Revolution* (1848).

10 Helen Bevan, Paul Bate, and Glenn Robert, "Towards a million change agents. A review of the social movements literature: Implications for large scale change in the NHS" (National Health Service, UK, 2005), discovery.ucl.ac.uk/id/eprint/1133/.

11 Manuel Castells, *Networks of Outrage and Hope: Social Movements in the Internet Age* (Polity, 2012).

12 For more on Alain Touraine, see his personal website, alaintouraine.blogspot.com, and "Alain Touraine," *Wikipedia.fr*, fr.wikipedia.org/wiki/Alain_Touraine.

13 Jean-Paul Lebel, "Alain Touraine—Des mouvements sociaux à l'acteur," *Les Grands Dossiers des Sciences Humaines*, no. 30 (2013), 25, author's translation.

14 Michel Wieviorka, "Alain Touraine and the concept of social movement," keynote, ISA World Congress of Sociology (July 2014), wieviorka.hypotheses.org/318.

15 Steven Johnson, *Extra Life: A Short History of Living Longer* (Riverhead Books, 2021).

16 Castells, *Networks of Outrage and Hope.*

17 Julia Carrie Wong, "The Cambridge Analytica scandal changed the world—but it didn't change Facebook," *The Guardian* (Mar. 18, 2019); Michael Shear, Maggie Haberman, Nicholas Confessore, Karen Yourish, Larry Buchanan, and Keith Collins, "How Trump reshaped the presidency in over 11,000 tweets," interactive feature, *New York Times* (Nov. 2, 2019), www.nytimes.com/interactive/2019/11/02/us/politics/trump-twitter-presidency.html; Kevin Dolak, "How the controversial website 8chan became central to the QAnon delusion," Oxygen (Mar. 24, 2021), www.oxygen.com/true-crime-buzz/qanon-mass-delusions-roots-in-the-4chan-and-8chan-websites; Sarah Emerson, "Anti-vax groups thrive on Facebook as nationwide coronavirus vaccinations begin," *OneZero* (Dec. 17, 2020), onezero.medium.com/anti-vax-groups-thrive-on-facebook-as-nationwide-coronavirus-vaccinations-begin-76470a5d392c; Julia Carrie Wong, "How Facebook let fake engagement distort global politics: A whistleblower's account," *The Guardian* (Apr. 12, 2021).

18 Jonathan Coley, Dakota Raynes, and Dhruba Das, "Are social movements truly social? The prosocial and antisocial outcomes of social movements," *Sociology Compass* 14 (2020), e12820, doi.org/10.1111/soc4.12820.

19 Céline Schillinger, "Culture and the real impact of change agents," We Need Social blog (Jan. 1, 2019), weneedsocial.com/blog/2019/1/1/culture-and-the-real-impact-of-change-agents.

20 Marco Giugni, "Political, biographical, and cultural consequences of social movements," *Sociology Compass* 2 (2008), 1582–1600.

21 Jacques Lagroye, Frédéric Sawicki, and Bastien François, *Sociologie politique* (Dalloz, 2012), author's translation.

22 Olivier Fillieule and Bernard Pudal. "Sociologie du militantisme: Problématisations et déplacement des méthodes d'enquête," in Éric Agrikoliansky (Ed.), *Penser les mouvements sociaux: Conflits sociaux et contestations dans les sociétés contemporaines* (La Découverte, 2010).

23 Mattea Battaglia, "'Une envie de se sentir utile': Une nouvelle génération de jeunes engagés," Le Monde (Jan. 26, 2021).

24 Isabelle Sommier, "Engagement radical, désengagement et déradicalisation. Continuum et lignes de fracture," *Lien social et Politiques*, no. 68 (Fall 2012); John Horgan, "From profiles to pathways and roots to routes: Perspectives from psychology on radicalization into terrorism," *Annals of the American Academy of Political and Social Science*, 618, no. 1 (2008), 80–94.

25 Fethi Benslama, *Le saut épique, ou le basculement dans le jihad* (Actes Sud, 2021).

26 Frédéric Manzini, review of *Le Saut épique* by Fethi Benslama, *Philosophie magazine* (Apr. 27, 2021), www.philomag.com/livres/le-saut-epique.

27 Paul-Louis Landsberg, "Réflexions sur l'engagement personnel," *Esprit* (Nov. 1937), author's translations.

28 Castells, *Networks of Outrage and Hope.*

29 Simon Terry, "Yammer for continuous improvement—Adapting to change" (Apr. 15, 2021), simonterry.com/2021/04/15/yammer-for-continuous-improvement-adapting-to-change/.

30 Estelle Ferrarese, "Nancy Fraser and the theory of participatory parity," translated by Nathalie Ferron, Books & Ideas (Sept. 14, 2015), booksandideas.net/Nancy-Fraser-and-the-Theory-of-Participatory-Parity.html.

31 Bevan et al. "Towards a million change agents."

32 Dafna Sheinberg, "8 brands that are taking a clear stance on political issues," PostFunnel (Sept. 21, 2020), postfunnel.com/8-brands-that-are-taking-a-clear-stance-on-political-issues/.

33 Heather Cox Richardson, "April 4, 2021," *Letters from an American* (Apr. 4, 2021), heathercoxrichardson.substack.com.

34 Megan Reitz, John Higgins, and Emma Day-Duro, "The wrong way to respond to employee activism," *Harvard Business Review* (Feb. 2021), hbr.org/2021/02/the-wrong-way-to-respond-to-employee-activism.

35 Angélique Girbal, "Our opportunity to make ideas happen with passion" (testimonial), *I'm In—Global Guiding Coalition* (Dec. 2016).

36 Michele Zanini, "Build change platforms, not change programs," MIX Mashup, New York City (2014), youtu.be/Zal5HcZgoCw.

37 Margaret Wheatley and Myron Rogers, *A Simpler Way* (Berrett-Koehler, 1996).

38 Kate Morgan, "Why we may be measuring burnout all wrong," BBC Worklife (Apr. 29, 2021), www.bbc.com/worklife/article/20210426-why-we-may-be-measuring-burnout-all-wrong; Robyn Morris, "Employee work motivation and discretionary work effort," PhD thesis, Queensland University of Technology, 2009, eprints.qut.edu.au/31725/; Céline Schillinger, "Are there limits to engagement?," We Need Social blog (Mar. 17, 2021), weneedsocial.com/blog/overengagement.

39 Céline Schillinger, "Les légumes à manger en hiver" (Apr. 2021), www.linkedin.com/posts/celineschillinger_collaboration-culture-projetcommun-activity-6789943113570910208-fM2p/.

40 Pierre-Olivier Monteil, "Driving change... with Paul Ricoeur," *Philonomist* (Jan. 31, 2020), www.philonomist.com/en/article/driving-change-paul-ricoeur.

41 Stefan Stern, "The boardroom's futile pursuit of purpose," *Financial Times* (Feb. 22, 2021).

42 Maria Hengeveld, "Big business has a new scam: The 'purpose paradigm,'" *The Nation* (Jan. 4, 2019).

43 Sian Conway, "The problem with purpose-washing," #ethicalHour (Feb. 21, 2020), ethicalhour.co.uk/the-problem-with-purpose-washing/.

44 "Business Roundtable redefines the purpose of a corporation to promote 'an economy that serves all Americans,'" Business Roundtable (Aug. 19, 2019), www.businessroundtable.org/business-roundtable-redefines-the-purpose-of-a-corporation-to-promote-an-economy-that-serves-all-americans.

45 Julie Battilana and Tiziana Casciaro, "Power sharing can change corporations for the better," *Harvard Business Review* (May 13, 2021), hbr.org/2021/05/power-sharing-can-change-corporations-for-the-better.

46 Ian MacDougall, "McKinsey's rules: When consultants work for governments," series, *ProPublica* (2019-20); Hengeveld, "Big business has a new scam."

47 Jennifer Sertl, *Strategy, Leadership and the Soul* (Triarchy, 2010).

48 Satya Nadella, interview with Simon London, "Microsoft's next act," *McKinsey Quarterly* (Apr. 3, 2018).

49 Simon Terry, "Portfolio of purpose" (Apr. 19, 2021), simonterry.com/2021/04/19/portfolio-of-purpose/; Lila MacLellan, "The surprising fragility of a powerful perk: Company culture," *Quartz* (Nov. 27, 2018), qz.com/work/1417538/the-surprising-fragility-of-a-powerful-perk-company-culture/.

50 Seth Godin, "In search of your calling," *Seth's Blog* (July 25, 2015), seths.blog/2015/07/in-search-of-your-calling/.

51 Dan Pontefract, *The Purpose Effect: Building Meaning in Yourself, Your Role, and Your Organization* (Figure 1, 2016).

52 John Kotter, *A Sense of Urgency* (Harvard Business Review Press, 2008).

53 John Kotter, *Accelerate: Building Strategic Agility for a Faster-Moving World* (Harvard Business Review Press, 2014).

54 John Wenger, "The power of we," *Quantum Shifting* (Dec. 2, 2012), quantumshifting.wordpress.com/2012/12/02/the-power-of-we/.

55 Wenger, "The power of we."

56 See Marshall Ganz's faculty page at Harvard University, scholar.harvard.edu/marshallganz, and "Marshall Ganz," *Wikipedia*, en.wikipedia.org/wiki/Marshall_Ganz; Katie Anastas, "Timeline of UFW strikes, boycotts, campaigns 1965-1975," Mapping American Social Movements Project, University of Washington (accessed Sept. 27, 2021), depts.washington.edu/moves/UFW_timeline.shtml; Marshall Ganz, adapted and revised by Shea Sinnott and Peter Gibbs with individuals from Dogwood Initiative, Leadnow, One Cowichan, the David Suzuki Foundation, Stonehouse Institute, and genius, *Organizing: People, Power, Change*, The Commons Social Change Library (2014), commonslibrary.org/organizing-people-power-change/, download at commonslibrary.org/wp-content/uploads/Organizers_Handbook.pdf.

57 Marshall Ganz and Liz McKenna, "The practice of social movement leadership," *Mobilizing Ideas* (June 23, 2017), mobilizingideas.wordpress.com/2017/06/23/the-practice-of-social-movement-leadership/.

58 Marshall Ganz, "The power of story in social movements," *Proceedings of the Annual Meeting of the American Sociological Association, Anaheim, California, Aug. 18-21, 2001*, nrs.harvard.edu/urn-3:HUL. InstRepos:27306251.

59 Marshall Ganz, "Public narrative, collective action, and power," in Sina Odugbemi and Taeku Lee (Eds.), *Accountability through Public Opinion: From Inertia to Public Action* (The World Bank, 2011). See also Ganz's "What is public narrative and how can we use it?," Working Narratives (accessed Sept. 27, 2021), workingnarratives.org/article/public-narrative/.

60 Ganz, Organizing.

61 Trung T. Phan, "How 1 memo lead to an exodus at software firm Basecamp," *The Hustle* (May 3, 2021), thehustle.co/05032021-basecamp-exodus/.

62 Luis Maldonado, acceptance speech, Employee Engagement Unsung Hero Award (June 2016).

63 Michael Bazigos and Emily Caruso, "Why frontline workers are disengaged," *McKinsey Quarterly* (Mar. 2, 2016).

64 Michele Zanini, "If you're serious about purpose at work, you must flatten the hierarchy" (Apr. 6, 2021), www.michelezanini.com/purpose-for-me-but-not-for-thee/.

65 Céline Schillinger, "Leadership on the shop floor," We Need Social blog (Sept. 11, 2017), weneedsocial. com/blog/2017/9/11/leadership-on-the-shop-floor.

66 Maldonado, acceptance speech.

67 Brice Couturier, "L'hystérisation du débat public engendre la polarisation politique," *Le Tour du Monde des Idées*, France Culture (May 10, 2019) www.franceculture.fr/emissions/ le-tour-du-monde-des-idees/le-tour-du-monde-des-idees-du-vendredi-10-mai-2019.

68 Barry Oshry, "The importance of seeing difference," *Power + Systems Blog* (July 7, 2020), seeingsystems.blogs.com/my_weblog/2020/07/the-importance-of-seeing-difference.html.

69 Peter Vander Auwera, "The essence of work, Part 4: Caring," *Petervan's Blog* (Aug. 2015), petervan.wordpress.com/2015/08/30/the-essence-of-work-part-4-caring/

11. Creating Fraternity at Work

1   Guillaume Erner, "De Beyrouth à Santiago: Pourquoi tant de colères?," *L'invité(e)s des matins*, France Culture (Oct. 24, 2019), www.franceculture.fr/emissions/linvite-des-matins/de-beyrouth-a-santiago-pourquoi-tant-de-coleres, author's translation. See also Ishac Diwan, Adeel Malik, and Izak Atiyas, *Crony Capitalism in the Middle East: Business and Politics from Liberalization to the Arab Spring* (Oxford University Press, 2019).

2   Agnès Hardy-Boyer, in a conversation with the author (2019).

3   Norbert Elias, "Towards a theory of communities," in Colin Bell and Howard Newby (Eds.), *The Sociology of Community: A Selection of Readings* (Franck Cass, 1974).

4   Elizabeth Frazer, *The Problems of Communitarian Politics: Unity and Conflict* (Oxford University Press, 1999).

5   Mark Smith, "Community," *The Encyclopedia of Pedagogy and Informal Education* (2001, 2002, 2013), infed.org/mobi/community/.

6   Marshall Ganz, adapted and revised by Shea Sinnott and Peter Gibbs with individuals from Dogwood Initiative, Leadnow, One Cowichan, the David Suzuki Foundation, Stonehouse Institute, and genius, *Organizing: People, Power, Change*, The Commons Social Change Library (2014), commonslibrary. org/organizing-people-power-change/; download at commonslibrary.org/wp-content/uploads/ Organizers_Handbook.pdf.

7   Anthony Cohen, Symbolic Construction of Community (Routledge, 1985).

8   M. P. Follett, "Community is a process," *The Philosophical Review* 28 (1919), 576-88.

9   Esko Kilpi, "Interactive competence and flash communities" (Sept. 2012), eskokilpi.wordpress. com/2012/09/20/interactive-competence/, and "Connecting the dots" (Dec. 13, 2015), medium. com/@EskoKilpi/connecting-the-dots-da8c91cb053a.

10 Tom Lutz, "Brad Parscale faces Trump 'fury' after Tulsa comeback rally flops," *The Guardian* (June 21, 2020).

11 Taylor Lorenz, Kellen Browning, and Sheera Frenkel, "TikTok teens and K-Pop stans say they sank Trump rally," *New York Times* (June 21, 2020).

12 Danny Hawk, "Folk games, flash communities and TikTok," New Rules (Jan. 12, 2021), newrules. website/2021/01/12/danny-hawk-folk-games-flash-communities-and-tiktok/.

13 Esko Kilpi, "Hedging the future of work" (May 17, 2017), medium.com/@EskoKilpi/ hedging-risks-and-the-future-of-work-72a6de2d60c3.

14 Étienne Wenger-Trayner and Beverly Wenger-Trayner, "Introduction to communities of practice: A brief overview of the concept and its uses" (2015), wenger-trayner.com/ introduction-to-communities-of-practice/.

15 Jean Lave and Étienne Wenger, *Situated Learning: Legitimate Peripheral Participation* (Cambridge University Press, 1991).

16 Wenger-Trayner and Wenger-Trayner, "Introduction to communities of practice."

17 Davide Nicolini, Harry Scarbrough, and Julia Gracheva, "Communities of practice and situated learning in health care," in Ewan Ferlie, Kathleen Montgomery, and Anne Reff Pedersen (Eds.), *The Oxford Handbook of Health Care Management* (Oxford University Press, 2016).

18 Myron Rogers, Katherine Joel, and Melissa Ream, *Patient Safety Communities of Practice at HIN: Leading Change across System Boundaries* (Health Innovation Network South London, 2016), healthinnovationnetwork.com/wp-content/uploads/2017/01/HIN_COP_Brochure_v6_LoRes.pdf.

19 Convener application form, Health Innovation Network Patient Safety Collaborative Communities of Practice, Health Innovation Network South London (accessed Sept. 27, 2021), healthinnovationnetwork.com/wp-content/uploads/2017/01/Cultivating_Communities_of_ Practice_-_a_Call_for_Conveners_-_FAQs_v2-1.pdf.

20 E.L. Lesser and J. Storck, "Communities of practice and organizational performance," *IBM Systems Journal* 40 (2001), 831–41.

21 Rogers et al., *Patient Safety Communities of Practice at HIN*.

22 PEPS-SOS can be found at www.peps-sos.fr and twitter.com/Peps_Sos.

23 Lave and Wenger, *Situated Learning*.

24 Bryn Garrod and Tom Ling, "System Change through Situated Learning: Pre-evaluation of the Health Innovation Network's Communities of Practice" (RAND Europe, 2018).

25 Han Byung-Chul, *The Burnout Society*, translated by Erik Butler (Stanford Briefs, 2010).

26 Romain Huët, *De si violentes fatigues: Les devenirs politiques de l'épuisement quotidien* (puf, 2021).

27 Huët, *De si violentes fatigues*, author's translations.

28 Esko Kilpi, "A working class manifesto" (Apr. 30, 2017), medium.com/@ EskoKilpi/a-working-class-manifesto-d53a01b867ff.

29 *Fritjof Capra on Systems Thinking about Community* (Be With Briefs, 2020), www.youtube.com/watch?v=bafZaal7alo.

30 The Community Roundtable, *State of Community Management 2020* (Community Roundtable, 2020), communityroundtable.com/what-we-do/research/the-state-of-community-management/ the-state-of-community-management-2020/.

31 Robert Putnam, Robert Leonardi, and Raffaella Y. Nanetti, *Making Democracy Work: Civic Traditions in Modern Italy* (Princeton University Press, 1992).

32 Hayagreeva Rao and Henrich Greve, "Disasters and community resilience: Spanish flu and the formation of retail cooperatives in Norway," *Academy of Management Journal* 61 (2018), 5–25.

33 Aaron Wildavsky, *Searching for Safety* (Routledge, 1988).

34 Rao and Greve, "Disasters and community resilience."

35 Morela Hernandez, interviewed by Paul Michelman, "Humanity: A leader's secret weapon," podcast, *MIT Sloan Management Review* (June 9, 2020), sloanreview.mit.edu/audio/ humanity-a-leaders-secret-weapon/.

36 Michelle Nijhuis, "The miracle of the commons," *Aeon* (May 4, 2021), aeon.co/essays/ the-tragedy-of-the-commons-is-a-false-and-dangerous-myth.

37 Garrett Hardin, "The tragedy of the commons: The population problem has no technical solution; it requires a fundamental extension in morality," *Science* 162 (1968), 1243–48.

38 Elinor Ostrom and James Walker (Eds.), *Trust and Reciprocity: Interdisciplinary Lessons for Experimental Research* (Russell Sage Foundation, 2005).

39 Elinor Ostrom, "Beyond markets and states: Polycentric governance of complex economic systems," Nobel Prize lecture (2009), www.nobelprize.org/prizes/economic-sciences/2009/ostrom/lecture/.

40 Emma Jacobs, "Are you working in a fractured organisation?," *The Financial Times* (May 31, 2021).

41 Jane McConnell, *The Gig Mindset Advantage: Why a Bold New Breed of Employee Is Your Organization's Secret Weapon in Volatile Times* (Figure 1, 2021).

42 The Community Roundtable can be found at communityroundtable.com.

43 Community Roundtable, *State of Community Management 2020*.

44 Community ROI Calculator, Community Roundtable (accessed Sept. 27, 2021), communityroundtable.com/what-we-do/models-and-frameworks/roi-calculator/.

45 Céline Schillinger, "Forget social networks, think social impact," TEDx Bedminster and We Need Social (Oct. 2, 2014), weneedsocial.com/blog/2014/10/2/forget-social-networks-think-social-impact.

46 Céline Schillinger, "Police! Community engagement and wellbeing at work," We Need Social blog (Aug. 18, 2020), weneedsocial.com/blog/2020/8/17/lessons-from-the-british-police.

47 Oscar Kilo can be found at oscarkilo.org.uk, on LinkedIn at www.linkedin.com/in/oscarkilouk/, and on Twitter at twitter.com/OscarKiloUK.

48 "Wellbeing vans have over 10k visitors," Oscar Kilo (Jan. 29, 2020), oscarkilo.org.uk/wellbeing-vans-have-over-10k-visitors/.

49 Stéphanie Dameron, "La dualité du travail coopératif," *Revue française de gestion*, no. 158 (2005), 105–20.

50 Céline Schillinger, "Three ways social media make you a better leader," *Forbes* (Jan. 24, 2019).

51 Brian Solis, *Engage: The Complete Guide for Brands and Businesses to Build, Cultivate, and Measure Success in the New Web* (Wiley, 2010).

52 Esko Kilpi, "A relational view to management" (Feb. 19, 2012), eskokilpi.wordpress.com/2012/02/19/a-relational-view-to-management/, "Work is interaction" (Mar. 17, 2015), medium.com/@EskoKilpi/work-as-interaction-bfecdd8ea1a1, and "A relational view of leadership" (Aug. 18, 2018), medium.com/@EskoKilpi/a-relational-view-to-leadership-7c561c4b0720.

53 "The value of belonging at work: New frontiers for inclusion," BetterUp, Inc. (June 2018) www.betterup.com/en-us/resources/reports/the-value-of-belonging-at-work-the-business-case-for-investing-in-workplace-inclusion.

54 The Cercle de l'Aviron de Lyon can be found at avironlyon.com, on Twitter at @CercleAvironL, on Facebook at www.facebook.com/CercleAvironLyon, on Instagram at www.instagram.com/cercle_aviron_lyon/, and elsewhere.

55 Céline Schillinger, "Of passion, togetherness and rowing," We Need Social blog (June 9, 2014), weneedsocial.com/blog/2014/5/2/of-passion-togetherness-and-rowing.

56 Patrick Castel and Marie-Emmanuelle Chessel, "La décision toujours en question," *Entreprises et histoire*, no. 97 (2019), 7–22.

57 Henry Mintzberg, "Communityship beyond leadership," LinkedIn (Nov. 19, 2018), www.linkedin.com/pulse/communityship-beyond-leadership-henry-mintzberg/.

58 Ryan Mohr, "Everyone a network weaver (interview with June Holley)," *In Too Deep* (Apr. 24, 2019), blog.kumu.io/everyone-a-network-weaver-interview-with-june-holley-f0fd52b7573b.

59 Peter Block, Community: The Structure of Belonging (Berrett-Koehler, 2009).

60 Ganz, *Organizing*.

61 Jeremy Heimans and Henry Timms, *New Power: How Power Works in Our Hyperconnected World—and How to Make It Work for You* (Anchor, 2018).

62 Céline Schillinger, "Good bye, old world," We Need Social blog (Apr, 11, 2020), weneedsocial.com/blog/2020/4/11/good-bye-old-world.

63 John Hagel and Gemma Mortensen, *Systems Leadership and Platforms: How to Mobilize People to Transform Systems and Build the Platforms to Scale These Efforts*, World Economic Forum White Papers (Oct. 10, 2018), www.weforum.org/whitepapers/systems-leadership-and-platforms-how-to-mobilize-people-to-transform-systems-and-build-the-platforms-to-scale-these-efforts.

64 Esko Kilpi, "Network leadership" (Apr. 10, 2016), medium.com/@EskoKilpi/networks-and-leadership-d8400046eae6.

65 Mintzberg, "Communityship beyond leadership."

66 John Atkinson and David Nabarro, "Systems leadership—Feeling systems," *The Heart of the Art* (2020), www.heartoftheart.org/?p=7604.

67 Stanley McChrystal, with Chris Fussell, Tantum Collins, and David Silverman, *Team of Teams: New Rules of Engagement for a Complex World* (Portfolio, 2015).

68 Pernille Hippe Brun, *On the Move: Lessons for the Future from Nordic Leaders* (People's Press, 2019).

69 Jen Frahm, *Change. Leader: The Changes You Need to Make First* (May 1, 2021), drjenfrahm.com/product/change-leader-3/.

70 Jillian Reilly, "Sense making is such an important skill in these wild times..." (Dec. 2020), www.linkedin.com/posts/jillianreilly_sense-making-is-such-an-important-skill-in-activity-6737675644534046720-fr00/.

71 Oliver Sheldon, David Dunning, and Daniel Ames, "Emotionally unskilled, unaware, and uninterested in learning more: Reactions to feedback about deficits in emotional intelligence," *Journal of Applied Psychology* 99 (2014), 125–37.

72 Eugenio Molini, "Liderazgo, humillación y humildad—Leadership, humility, humiliation" (Apr. 2, 2016), molini.eu/es/leadership-humility-humiliation/.

73 Lois Kelly, "Creative expression is a different kind of holy," *Foghound* (Mar. 27, 2019), foghound.com/blog/creative-expression-is-a-different-kind-of-holy.

74 Sigal Barsade and Olivia O'Neill, "What's love got to do with it? A longitudinal study of the culture of companionate love and employee and client outcomes in a long-term care setting," *Administrative Science Quarterly* 59 (2014), 551–98.

75 Atkinson and Nabarro, "Systems leadership."

76 Céline Schillinger, "Culture and the real impact of change agents," We Need Social blog (Jan. 1, 2019), weneedsocial.com/blog/2019/1/1/culture-and-the-real-impact-of-change-agents.

77 Daniel James Brown, *The Boys in the Boat: Nine Americans and Their Epic Quest for Gold at the 1936 Berlin Olympics* (Viking, 2013).

78 Richard Martin, in conversation with the author (2021). Richard can be found at richardmartinwriter.com.

79 Eugenio Molini, "Design to disappear as an end, remaining a pure means" (Dec. 12, 2015), molini.eu/es/design-to-disappear-as-an-end-remaining-a-pure-means/.

80 As reported by Eugenio Molini in "Design to disappear as an end."

81 Kilpi, "Interactive competence and flash communities."

82 Mihály Csíkszentmihályi, *Flow: The Psychology of Optimal Experience* (Harper Perennial, 1990).

Envoi

1 M.P. Follett, "Community is a process," *The Philosophical Review* 28 (1919), 576–88.

2 Gloria Anzaldúa, *Borderlands/La Frontera: The New Mestiza* (Aunt Lute Books, 1987).

3 Albert Camus, *The Rebel*, translated by Anthony Bower (Vintage, 1951). See also Marilyn Maeso, L'abécédaire d'Albert Camus (Éditions de l'observatoire, 2020), and Adèle Van Reeth, "'L'Homme révolté d'Albert Camus: Comment aimer un monde qui n'est pas aimable?," *es chemins de la philosophie*, France Culture (June 25, 2021), www.franceculture.fr/emissions/les-chemins-de-la-philosophie/lhomme-revolte-dalbert-camus-comment-aimer-un-monde-qui-nest-pas-aimable.

Index